Library LANs

Supplements to
COMPUTERS IN LIBRARIES

Library LANs

Case Studies in
Practice and Application

EDITED BY MARSHALL BREEDING

Meckler

Westport · London

Library of Congress Cataloging-in-Publication Data

Library LANs : case studies in practice and application / edited by
   Marshall Breeding.
        p. cm. -- (Supplements to Computers in libraries ; 39)
     Includes bibliographical references and index.
     ISBN 0-88736-786-0 (acid-free paper) : $
     1. Local area networks (Computer networks)--Library applications-
  -Case studies. 2. Library information networks--Case studies.
  3. Libraries--Automation--Case studies. I. Breeding, Marshall.
  II. Series.
  Z678.93.L63L53   1992
  021.6'5--dc20   91-35665
                                                      CIP

British Library Cataloguing-in-Publication Data is available.

Meckler Publishing, the publishing division of Meckler Corporation,
   11 Ferry Lane West, Westport, CT 06880.
Meckler Ltd., 247-249 Vauxhall Bridge Road,
   London SW1V 1HQ, U.K.

Printed on acid free paper.
Printed and bound in the United States of America.

To
Marsha, Michelle, and Amanda

Contents

List of Figures

Preface

Networked microcomputers represent a logical advancement in automation beyond that of stand-alone systems. Over the years, libraries have grown to depend on computers to automate many functions. As individual computers proliferate throughout the library, there eventually comes a point when the computers need to be linked together in a network in order to get the best use out of them.

Many librarians may perceive computer networks as overly complicated and therefore may be tempted to avoid the process altogether. Although dealing with networks may indeed be one level of complexity beyond that of stand-alone microcomputers, I believe that the task of installing and maintaining local area networks within the library is a manageable task. The majority of the networks described in this book were implemented and are managed by staff within their libraries.

This book aims to provide information about local area networks in libraries through a case studies approach. The case studies in this volume represent successfully implemented LANs in various library settings. Each of the authors demonstrates how their library has gone about the process of selecting, implementing, and maintaining a library microcomputer network. The contributors offer a great deal of practical information regarding the process of installing each of the hardware, software and human components that must cohere together to form a successful network. These articles describe the function that the network was designed to perform, who the main users of the network are, and how well the network has lived up to expectations. Most of the articles also reveal how much funding was required for the project and suggest ways that their network might evolve in the future. The majority of the contributions include diagrams of the network described in the case study to illustrate the components involved and the overall structure.

It is my hope that the articles in this book will help those involved with library microcomputers to discover how local area networks can be useful, and further, to provide a practical guide in selecting and implementing networks. Although these articles are not intended as step-by-step instructions on how the various networks were installed, the reader should, in many cases, be able to find a network in the volume with many similar features to the reader's own environment.

The case studies that follow cover a wide range of networks in the library environment and should give the reader a feel for the many options that the current technology avails. Some of the networks exist solely for the purpose of providing access to databases on CD-ROM. Others serve more administrative functions, allowing library staff microcomputer to share printers, software, and disk storage space and to communicate amongst themselves through electronic mail. The size of the networks in this volume span from ones consisting of as few as three microcomputers, to ones that connect scores of systems. Some of the networks are quite simple, while others demonstrate the complexity encountered in large interconnected networks.

In chapter 1 of this volume, I have written an introduction to the general concepts and terminology related to microcomputer local area networks. This chapter intends to provide the reader with sufficient background information to place the case studies that follow into perspective and to offer relatively nontechnical explanations of some of the terms that are widely used in network literature.

I have organized the remainder of the book into four sections. The case studies in Part I deal with Macintosh LANs, Part II covers networks devoted to CD-ROM applications, Part III includes case studies of relatively small general-purpose networks, and Part IV describes larger, more complex networks.

Part I includes four case studies that deal with Macintosh networks. Henry Harken begins this section with a description of a relatively large Macintosh at the University of Arizona, West, and how it was planned and implemented along with the new campus and library building. The network described consists of over 50 nodes, including network printers, file servers, modems, and a gateway to TCP/IP networks. In chapter 3, James Alloway and Robert Schwarzwalder describe a simple Macintosh network which they implemented to support a Hypercard application that provides reference and instructional information in the reference area of the Engineering/Transportation Library at the University of Michigan. Though they envision further expansion, the network they describe consists of a single AppleShare server and two client Macintosh stations. Robert Skinner continues this section by presenting the various Macintosh networks associated with a newly-constructed Arts library at Southern Methodist University. Skinner writes about some of the design considerations involved in cabling a new building in addition to the discussions about implementing the Macintosh networks themselves. These Macintosh networks support staff microcomputer use, including access to their NOTIS system, a microcomputer laboratory, and will eventually include a public access LAN which will offer an array of information services. Lois Bellamy and John Silver conclude this section with a case study of a more complex Macintosh network at the Health Science Library at the University of Tennessee, Memphis. This network performs a variety of functions within the library and interconnects with many other Macintosh LANs through a campus-wide network. It includes items such as CD-ROM, gateways to TCP/IP networks, shared modems, network printers, and file servers.

One of the most popular reasons for establishing a local area network in a library relates to providing access to CD-ROM products. Part II consists of case studies of networks created specifically for this purpose. In the opening chapter of this section C. Anne Turhollow and Michael Perkins describe the process that led to the decision to implement a CD-ROM network at the San Diego State University Library. The case study then outlines the process of selecting a Meridian Data system and how they used a consultant to provide the initial installation of the network. The University of Hawaii at Manoa employs two different CD-ROM networks: one uses MultiPlatter and the other Artisoft's LANtastic. Martha Chantiny devotes her case study to the selection and implementation of the LANtastic CD-ROM network. She provides much practical information on how to install and configure the LANtastic software to access CD-ROM applications. In Chapter 8, Bonnie Nelson debates the options of either implementing a CD-ROM LAN from component parts or relying on a ready-built turnkey system, and how the John Jay College of Criminal Justice opted for the latter. Her case study proceeds to describe their implementation of a CD-ROM network using SilverPlatter's MultiPlatter product. Harry Kriz, Nikhil Jain, and E. Alan Armstrong provide a second case study using LANtastic to network CD-ROMs. In this network, eight public workstations access sixteen CD-ROM drives. An additional workstation on the network provides access to the network through an interface to the campus digital voice/data network. The article describes the hardware and software they used to support this remote access workstation. David Lewis and Terry Plum describe a do-it-yourself CD-ROM network that the University of Connecticut Library constructed partially from funding received from basketball revenues. Components of this network include Novell NetWare, Token Ring hardware, and CBIS CD-ROM servers. Concluding the CD-ROM network section, Thomas Wilson and Charles Bailey describe the Intelligent Reference Information System project at the University of Houston Libraries. Their network uses Meridian Data CD-ROM servers, Novell NetWare, and Token Ring hardware. Wilson and Bailey discuss the details of selecting and implementing such a system, as well as how they dealt with specific problems that arose in the process.

The third part of this volume contains a collection of case studies about relatively simple general-purpose local area networks. These networks, though fairly small in size, provide a variety of services in the library, unlike the CD-ROM networks of the preceding section that exist for a single function. Dave Bloomberg opens the section with his discussion of a library network built upon Digital Equipment Corporation's PCSA network system. Bloomberg writes this case study more from the network user's point of view rather than that of the implementor. He discusses some of the issues that arise when many of the networking decisions are made by groups outside the library. Mary Ann Chappell, Dan O'Brien, and Sharon Gasser collaborated to produce a case study of a LAN that supports automation in the Acquisitions Department of the Carrier Library at James Madison University. This network exemplifies the use of Novell NetWare ELS, a scaled-down version of Novell's Advanced NetWare product. In chapter 14, James Huesmann describes the selection and implementation of departmental LAN in Serials based on IBM's PC LAN product. Next, Laurie Potter's case study of the networks at the Savitt Medical Library at the University of Nevada School of Medicine describes the abandonment of a 10-NET system in favor of a Novell NetWare Ethernet LAN. To round out this section, Dan Marmion describes how the Edmon Low Library at the Oklahoma State University uses a Token Ring LAN primarily to provide access to a newly-implemented NOTIS library management system.

Part IV contains the larger and more complex networks. The networks in this section represent major implementations of networking technology within the library environment. Ellen Watson and Stephen Patrick begin this section with their discussion of the Bradley Library Information Support System (BLISS). This project exemplifies a cooperative effort between a library and computing services within a university to create an integrated electronic information system. The networks described in this case study employ a number of UNIX-based servers to provide general computing services and information resources both within the library and throughout the campus.

John Rutherford describes a Novell Ethernet at Central Connecticut State University designed both as a CD-ROM network and as one to provide access for microcomputers in a faculty computing center located within the library to network software and print resources. This network uses Novell NetWare, CBIS CD-ROM servers, and a Zenith file server. This case study is a good example of the processes involved in implementing a relatively large multi-purpose network within the library.

T. Scott Plutchak's case study covers a local area network within the medical library at St. Louis University and its relationships to other networks within the broader medical center. This network is the only one in the volume that uses Arcnet network interface cards and cabling.

The University of California, Long Beach uses Novell NetWare as the basis for its interconnected Ethernet and Token Ring networks that offer CD-ROM, file and printer sharing, as well as access to BITNET and Internet resources throughout the library. Maria Sugranes and Jonothon Cone skillfully describe these networks in their case study.

Tim Bucknall, Rikki Mangrum, and Will Owen collaborate to describe the network at the Davis Library at the University of North Carolina at Chapel Hill. This network, primarily designed for a CD-ROM access, also performs file and printer sharing, and provides access to other campus Novell networks and mainframe systems. One of the unique services on this network is a system that patrons use to schedule times that they can use the public CD-ROM stations. This article includes discussion in problems that arose in the process of implementing the network and how they resolved the difficulties.

Barbara Burke's case study describes the Banyan/VINES network implemented in the Colorado State University's Libraries. This network combines CD-ROM access, file and printer sharing, and communications with other networks for all the microcomputers in the library. Burke clearly describes the implementation and functions of this network as well as the characteristics of Banyan/VINES, as its only representative in this volume.

The next group of three case studies describe large 3Com networks in differing library environments. Susan Bateman and Sanjay Chadha together discuss the 3Com 3+Open networks used in the Houston Academy of Medicine, Texas Medical Center Library. The case study describes the migration to this system from a 3Com EtherSeries network to its current configuration. In addition to general office automation services, this network offers a Paradox database application for the management of information services on the network.

Another 3Com network case study follows--however, more complex. Ellen Moy Chu describes the networks implemented at the Division of Computer Research and Technology Library of the National Institutes of Health. This multi-purpose network offers a wide range of services to its users including CD-ROM access, file and printer sharing, electronic mail, and interconnectivity with other networks and mainframe systems.

Michael Ridley and Paul Lavell devote their case study to the 3Com network at the Health Science Library at McMaster University and its interconnections with other networks in the Health Science Centre. This full-featured network also illustrates a large, complex network, and the case study discusses many of the details involved in implementing and managing this type of network.

Drew University has made significant efforts toward providing microcomputers throughout the campus. Each of the students and faculty have access to their own microcomputer system, most of which connect to a campus-wide asynchronous network. Pamela Snelson provides us with a general description of this network and how the library takes advantage of this valuable resource.

It is always helpful when embarking on a project, such as implementing a LAN, to be able to learn from the experiences of individuals who have successfully completed similar projects. Each of these authors have endured the trials imposed upon them through the process of installing or managing a Library LAN. In sharing their experiences in this book, it is my hope that the readers will benefit from their knowledge and insight.

Marshall Breeding
Vanderbilt University

The Contributors

James Alloway, Assistant Librarian, Basic Science and Engineering Library, University of Michigan.

E. Alan Armstrong, Electronic Reference Services Librarian, Reference Department, University Libraries, Virginia Polytechnic Institute and State University.

Charles W. Bailey, Jr., Assistant Director for Systems, University of Houston Libraries, University of Houston.

Susan G. Bateman, Systems Specialist, Houston Academy of Medicine–Texas Medical Center Library.

Lois M. Bellamy, Systems Librarian, Health Science Library, University of Tennessee, Memphis.

Dave Bloomberg, Computer Systems Coordinator, Wimberly Library, Florida Atlantic University.

Marshall Breeding, Library Networks and Microcomputer Analyst, Vanderbilt University.

Tim Bucknall, Coordinator for Electronic Information Services in the Humanities Reference Department at Davis Library, University of North Carolina, Chapel Hill.

Barbara Burke, Microcomputer Services Librarian, University Libraries, Colorado State University.

Sanjay R. Chadha, Systems Analyst, Houston Academy of Medicine–Texas Medical Center Library.

Martha Chantiny, Small/Microcomputer Systems Support Librarian, Sinclair Undergraduate Library, University of Hawaii at Manoa.

Mary Ann Chappell, Loan Services/Automation Librarian, Carrier Library, James Madison University.

Ellen Moy Chu, Division of Computer Research and Technology Library, National Institutes of Health.

Jonothon Cone, Assistant Systems Software Specialist, Automated Systems at the University Library and Learning Resources, California State University, Long Beach.

Sharon Gasser, Acquisitions Librarian, Carrier Library, James Madison University

Henry R. Harken, Electronic Systems Librarian, Fletcher Library, Arizona State University West.

James L. Huesmann, Murphy Library, University of Wisconsin–La Crosse.

Nikhil Jain, Programmer, Automation Services Department, University Libraries, Virginia Polytechnic Institute and State University.

Harry M. Kriz, Automated Systems Research and Development Librarian, University Libraries, Virginia Polytechnic Institute and State University.

Paul Lavell, Computer Systems Specialist, Health Sciences Library, McMaster University.

David W. Lewis, Head of Research and Information Services Department, Homer Babbidge Library, University of Connecticut.

Rikki Mangrum, Microcomputer Services Librarian for Business Administration/Social Sciences Reference in Davis Library, University of North Carolina, Chapel Hill.

Dan Marmion, Head, Library Systems, Edmon Low Library, Oklahoma State University.

Bonnie R. Nelson, Deputy Chief Librarian and Systems Librarian, John Jay College of Criminal Justice.

Dan O'Brien, Campus Network Specialist, Academic Computing Department, James Madison University.

Will Owen, Systems Librarian in the Academic Affairs Library, Davis Library, University of North Carolina, Chapel Hill.

Stephen J. Patrick, Director of Computing Services, Bradley University.

Michael J. Perkins, Coordinator, Electronic Reference Services, San Diego State University.

Terry Plum, Coordinator for Computer Based Services in the Research and Information Services Department, Homer Babbidge Library, University of Connecticut.

T. Scott Plutchak, Director of the Medical Center Library at St. Louis University.

Laurie Potter, Medical Reference Librarian, Savitt Medical Library, University of Nevada School of Medicine.

Michael Ridley, Head of Systems and Technical Services, Health Sciences Library, McMaster University.

John Rutherford, Director of the Faculty Computing Center of the Elihu Burritt Library, Central Connecticut State University.

Robert Schwarzwalder, Information Services Coordinator, Basic Science and Engineering Libraries, University of Michigan.

John T. Silver, Educational Computing Specialist, Health Science Library, University of Tennessee, Memphis.

Robert Skinner, Assistant Director for Fine Arts at Southern Methodist University and Head of the Jake and Nancy Hamon Arts Library, Southern Methodist University.

Pamela Snelson, Coordinator of Access Services, Drew University.

Maria R. Sugranes, Manager for Automated Systems at the University Library and Learning Resources, California State University, Long Beach.

C. Anne Turhollow, Assistant Coordinator, Electronic Reference Services, San Diego State University.

Ellen I. Watson, Director of the Cullom-Davis Library, Bradley University.

Thomas C. Wilson, Head of Systems, University of Houston Libraries, University of Houston

1

Introduction:
Overview and General Concepts

Marshall Breeding
Vanderbilt University

This chapter aims to introduce Local Area Networks (LANs) to library computer users and to provide some background information to acquaint the reader with some of the concepts used in the case studies that comprise the body of this volume. It does not assume any previous technical knowledge of the reader, but only a general familiarity with some type of microcomputer. The intended audience of this material includes library staff who have some degree of responsibility for microcomputers in the library, especially those who anticipate installing a LAN in the near future or those evaluating the need for a LAN.

Computer networking can be a complicated topic, but one does not need to know the subject exhaustively to set up and manage a LAN in a library. It is quite possible for a library staff member with little technical knowledge to purchase a network package and set up a LAN by reading the manuals and documentation. This introductory chapter attempts to present enough of an overview of the concepts of computer networking so the reader can place the networks described in the following articles, or other networks that they work with, into some perspective and see how they compare to other networking options.

My general attitude about LANs in the library environment is that network implementors should do as much as possible to mitigate the degree of complication that a network imposes on computer users. Establishing a LAN will inevitably introduce some degree of increased complexity to using a microcomputer, but it should not cause dramatic complications. Microcomputers have become an important tool for library staff to accomplish their work. A LAN should simply be an extension of that tool and a means for that tool to become more powerful and efficient. If the LAN implementor does his/her job well, the computer users should be pleased with the new things that they can do with the network, once they have recovered from the initial learning curve, and not be disgruntled because they can't figure out the network.

The main purposes of a LAN involve sharing computer resources and facilitating communication among computer users. With a LAN, individual microcomputers have access to more resources than would be available otherwise. LANs allow users of the network to share common databases, spreadsheets, and documents, high-quality printers, as well as to communicate with each other throughout the network through electronic mail.

Not only does a LAN provide better functionality than isolated stand-alone microcomputers, but in many cases can provide more overall computing resources to staff at less cost. For example, once connected to a LAN, a minimally configured floppy disk system can greatly extend its functionality through access to a hard disk and laser printer. In many cases it is more economical to concentrate resources on a LAN server rather than purchase hard disks and printers for each microcomputer in an organization. Especially when purchasing fairly large numbers of microcomputers, libraries can economically provide users with faster processors and better displays if disk storage and printer access can be relegated to the network. The cost of a group of diskless workstations and a file server and laser printer is generally less than a comparable number of fully equipped stand-alone microcomputers.

Components of a LAN

A Local Area Network includes many components. These components take many forms—some software, some hardware, and some human. Each of these components must fit together well in order to cohere into a successful network. These components include workstations, servers, and the network cabling and hardware.

Workstations

Workstations are microcomputers that use network resources. Computers attached to a LAN may provide resources, use resources, or both. When a computer only uses network resources, network terminology deems it as either a workstation or a client.

The minimal configuration for a network workstation includes a central processing unit, keyboard, monitor, and network interface card. It is possible for all disk access and printing capability to be provided only by the network. In most networks, however, it is typical for most workstations to have their own disk storage and printing capability, and to depend on the network for supplementary functions. It is common, for example, for a network workstation to have its own dot-matrix printer to print draft copies and to use a laser printer on the network for the finished copy. Such an arrangement leaves each individual workstation less vulnerable to network failures and relieves the network of the strain that might be imposed through the constant access of programs that could reside on local disk systems.

A microcomputer on a network can function without any disk storage of its own—either in the form of a floppy disk or hard disk—if its network interface card includes a PROM (Programmable Read-Only Memory) chip that allows the system to receive its start-up programs from the network. Such a system without any local disk drive is termed a diskless workstation. Network implementors may choose to implement diskless workstations for both economic and security concerns. The economic reasons seem clear: it is less expensive to set up diskless workstations because the cost of the boot PROM chips are much less than a floppy disk drive. Security concerns may be less obvious. Without disk drives, it is impossible for users to load software onto the network that may not be authorized or that may include undesirable functions. Software tainted with computer viruses and Trojan Horse programs that have received so much attention in recent years fall into this category. Many government and business environments may want to prevent network users from copying and distributing sensitive data, and might use diskless workstations to discourage this activity. In the library environment the opposite usually applies. Libraries generally promote the distribution of information, and would therefore want to provide disk drives so that network users can store and keep retrieved information.

Servers

The computers that provide network resources of some type are called servers. Servers are usually some type of microcomputer to which some special equipment and/or software has been added to perform special functions for the benefit of the network. The types of servers include file servers, print servers, communications servers, fax servers, and database servers.

When a computer system exists for the sole purpose of performing a network function it is called a dedicated server. The term non-dedicated server refers to systems that can function as a workstation at the same time that it performs its network role. When a user's workstation can double as a network server, then the network implementors can avoid the cost of an additional computer system. Such non-dedicated servers, however, may not perform as well as dedicated servers since their computing ability must be split between two tasks. Smaller networks tend to implement non-dedicated servers, while large networks generally require dedicated servers.

File Servers. One main function of a LAN lies in providing users access to supplementary disk storage on a large hard disk located on a central machine on the network. A network file server generally consists of a high-performance microcomputer system with a very large hard disk. Since the file server must service the disk storage needs of many users on the network, the network implementor must carefully consider the performance and capacity of this system.

Network file servers require special software to manage access to disk storage by the network users. This network software must include features to allow access to the server by multiple users at the same time but to restrict access to only authorized users. The server's software should also include capabilities for network administrators to configure, monitor, and manage the resources on the server.

The server's disk storage can store both software and data. All network users can potentially access software loaded on a network file server. Rather than each user having to load individual copies of their software from their local disk drives, each workstation on the network may execute programs from a common copy located on a network file server. Network use of software facilitates standard use of software—everybody uses the same version, and upgrading to a new version only has to be done once.

Although networks allow multiple users to share a single copy of a given piece of software, this does not remove the legal requirements of software licenses. The shared use of network software does not mean that libraries only have to purchase one copy of each application. Software must still be used within the restrictions that the vendors impose. This may mean that the library will need to purchase a copy of the software package for each user on the network, even though the network will function with only one copy of the software. Many vendors, however, will offer a network license for their products that provides the one necessary copy of the software, along with a license for each person on the network to legally use that copy, and usually additional copies of documentation and manuals. Although the cost of a network license of the software generally exceeds the cost of a single copy, such a license will generally be much less than the cost of buying individual copies for each network user.

Network file servers can also store data for all the users of a network. File servers generally provide both private and public disk storage space. Each network user usually owns a private area on the file server that no other network user may access. File servers may also offer public directories which all users can view. Data may also be stored in areas that are accessed by particular authorized groups of users, but not others. The network administrator may authorize some users to create, add to, and modify data files, while other users can only view data.

A complication to storing data on a network lies in the dangers of simultaneous access by multiple users. If two people attempt to update the same piece of data at the same time the data might become corrupted. Network file servers protect data through file and record locking. File locking means that the network software will permit only one user to have update capability to a file at a time. If someone has the file open with update privilege, then anyone else who tries to access the same file will have only viewing privilege. Some network data systems have record locking capability. With record locking, multiple users may simultaneously access a file with update capability, and the system will control updates to individual records.

One of the great advantages to using shared data storage on a central file server relates to data security. Practically all networks have some system established for the regular backup of data. Not only are network file servers generally much more reliable than a hard disk on a standalone microcomputer, but since the data of so many users are at stake, network managers are highly motivated to ensure regular backups. Individual users almost always take a lax attitude toward protecting their own data files. Network administrators must also protect data from the possible dangers imposed by computer viruses and other ill-behaved software.

LAN users access a network file server in just the same way that they access non-networked disks. Any good network system will make access to remote disks space on the network just as easily accessible as the ones attached to the user's own system. With MS-DOS machines, local drives are accessed through logical drive letters such as A: B: or C:. Once attached to a file server, users access their authorized network drives through higher drive letters. For example, one might have a drive G: defined as private disk space on the network file server and H: as a directory of departmental report documents. With the Macintosh and other machines with a graphical interface, network drives appear as icons just as do local disk drives. The network software on the user's workstation in conjunction with the software on the network server takes care of assigning logical drives on the user's system that correspond to the physical disk space on the server. As part of the security system on the network, users may have to enter a password in order to access network drives.

Print Servers or *Network Printers.* Local area networks also facilitate the sharing of printers. Most organizations cannot afford to purchase a laser printer for each microcomputer user. With a network printer on a LAN, all authorized users on the network can print on a common laser printer as if it were attached to their own machine. Networks can usually include high-end laser printers since their cost can be amortized across many users. Laser printers provide fast, quiet, and highly flexible printing functions.

A print server consists of a microcomputer connected to the network, which has one or more printers connected to it. Just as with the file server functions on the network, some type of software is required to control and manage access to the network printers. Many network systems combine the file server and print server functions into a single system.

The print server must manage printing for a lot of people at the same time, controlling all the printing requests that network users send to the printer. In order to manage multiple simultaneous print requests, the print server must receive each request, store it, and send documents to the printer one at a time. The term spooling refers to this process of receiving, storing, and releasing print requests directed to the server. The print server must also contend with requests for special forms. Downloadable fonts pose another complication for network print servers, but most network printing systems will accommodate them.

Just as described for file servers, access to a network printer follows whatever conventions that apply to local printers for your system. For example, MS-DOS systems use LPT1: as the logical designator for a locally attached printer. If connected to a LAN, the user might user LPT2: to access a network printer.

Communications Servers. One other type of network server relates to communications functions. Some LANs may have some common means of communication with other networks or systems. If microcomputer users in your organization need access to mainframe systems or dial-up access to outside computer services, you might want to set up a communications server so that all network users can share a high-speed modem, or a pool of modems.

Modem sharing is one communications function that may be implemented on a LAN. There are products available for most network systems that allow all authorized users to access a high-speed modem. Although the number of users that can simultaneously access network modems is limited to the number of modems and phone lines available, such a scheme may be more economical and convenient than providing individual modems for each user.

Fax Servers. The ability to send and receive material by fax has become a necessity for most organizations. Any microcomputer can send and receive a fax once equipped with a fax board and software. Recently, many products have emerged in the market that make it possible to perform fax transmission and receipt over a network. Through the implementation of such a fax server, all the users of the network can send and receive faxes through the network without having to have their own fax board and phone line. These products often require a dedicated microcomputer to manage incoming and outgoing fax messages for network users.

Database Servers. Database servers not only store data for the network, but also perform most of the work related to retrieving data. In traditional networked database applications, the data may be stored on a network file server, but the workstation must run the software that searches, retrieves, and displays the data. A database server takes over much of the work from client workstations. The software on the workstation formulates a request for data which is then passed to the database server which then performs the search on the database and passes back the results of the search to the workstation. The computations involved in performing the search are done on the server's processor, not on the workstation's. This model of database access allows a more powerful processor of a database server to relieve workstations on the network of some of the work involved in information retrieval. The most common type of database server implementation is known as Structured Query Language, or SQL.

Network Hardware

A network requires several hardware items in order for the individual computers to function as interconnected systems. Each computer must have some type of interface board installed in it to communicate with the network, and this network board must have some type of cable that attaches it to the other machines on the network. Some networks may need other equipment such as repeaters, routers, bridges, and gateways in order for all the systems to communicate.

Network Interface Cards. The network interface card (NIC) connects the system unit of the microcomputer to the cabling system. The current computer network market offers dozens of options to choose from when selecting a NIC. There are types of network interface cards available, including Ethernet, Token Ring, Arcnet, and AppleTalk. Buyers of network equipment will find many models and brands for each of these types. Some network software packages will run on a variety of NIC types, while others have limited options. Some network products may either come packaged with NICs or specify a particular model, while others give the network implementor a wide selection of possibilities. Each category of NIC requires a particular type and configuration of network cabling.

Each class or type of NIC uses a particular network protocol. The network protocol relates to a standard set of rules and conventions used in low-level network communications. One does not need to know a great deal about how low level communications works to install or use a network, but one does need to make sure that the network software supports the network protocol and its corresponding NICs and cabling. The network protocols operate transparently to the user, or even to the network software. The software that implements these protocols usually resides in firmware on the network interface card itself.

Network Cabling. In order for a LAN to work, the microcomputers involved must connect to each other through some sort of cabling system. Network cabling comes in many different types including coaxial, shielded twisted-pair, unshielded twisted-pair, or fiber optic. The cabling system consists not only of the cable itself, but also the various connectors needed to connect the cables to the computers and other network equipment.

Many microcomputer LANs use coaxial cabling. This type of cable consists of a central wire surrounded by a layer of insulation, a layer of shielding, and then by an outer layer of insulation. Coaxial cable comes in many forms, each with varying thickness and electrical characteristics. If your network requires coaxial cabling, make sure that the cable that you buy corresponds to the specifications required by your system.

Fiber optic cable supports faster data communications than any other transmission medium, but comes at a higher price. With this type of cable, pulses of light transmit information rather than an electrical current. Fiber optic cable is a thin cable with one or more thin glass fibers in its core. To be used in computer networks, fiber optics require interfaces to convert the digital signal between its electrical and optical forms.

Twisted-pair cabling, also widely used for LANs, can come with or without shielding, and multiple pairs of wires may be bundled within a single cable. A twisted-pair cable may include a single pair of wires, or as many as 100 pairs. With shielded cable, each pair within a bundle may have a shield, and the whole bundle will have an outer shield. Unshielded twisted-pair cabling in recent years has become popular in computer networks. Because telephone systems use this same type of wiring, and therefore it already exists in most buildings, networks that use unshielded twisted-pair cabling can be established without significant cable installation expense.

Cable installation often requires considerable effort. However, many recently built libraries may have been built with computer networks in mind and will have various types of network cabling integrated into the building structure. If the network that you are implementing consists of a group of computers located in the same room or in adjacent rooms on the same floor, then you might be able to install the cabling yourself. If your network will span multiple floors or across the entire building, you will most likely need to delegate the task to a qualified electrician or cable installer.

Part of the cable installation process must include the testing of the cables and connectors before they are placed into service. For most cable types, installers can use time domain reflectometry (TDR) equipment to verify the cable integrity before and after installation. This equipment will detect the presence of breaks or flaws in the cables.

Network Communications Equipment. Some networks may require special equipment in addition to the NICs and cabling system. Such equipment might include repeaters, network hubs or concentrators, multiuser access units, gateways and routers. You are likely to need such network devices with larger networks, or when interconnecting networks.

A repeater allows networks to span distances greater than the specifications of a particular cable type. If, for example, your network requires a total cable length of 2000 feet and your cabling system allows only 1000 feet, you could divide your network into two cable segments of 1000 feet each and connect the two segments with a repeater. The repeater will amplify and retransmit all the data as it is passed between the two cable segments. Multiport repeaters allow several cable segments to connect together into a central hub. From the network software's point of view, such a network appears as a single unit, while the cables actually exist as individual segments.

Many types of networks require some type of central device to manage network communications. Token Ring networks, for example, require a multistation access unit (MAU). Each computer on the network must be connected to a port on the MAU. When the number of nodes on the network exceeds the ports on a single MAU, multiple MAUs can be chained together. Ethernet networks on unshielded twisted-pair cabling systems also require that each machine connect to a central hub.

While repeaters allow multiple cable segments of the same type to interconnect within a single network, bridges allow separate networks to communicate with each other. A repeater passes all information between the network segments. Information passes across a bridge only when its destination is not on the network in which it originated. Because of this capability, a bridge can help to eliminate unnecessary traffic on each network. Bridges can also connect some different types of networks. A bridge could, for example, connect an Ethernet LAN with a Token Ring LAN, or connect a broadband Ethernet LAN with a baseband Ethernet LAN.

Gateways allow interconnection of entirely dissimilar networks. When the protocols of two LANs differ so much that they cannot be handled by a bridge, then a gateway will handle the translation from one network format to the other. A gateway, for example, could be used to connect a Novell Ethernet LAN to an SNA network, or could connect an AppleTalk network to a TCP/IP Ethernet network.

Network Software

In addition to the hardware components described above, a network also requires several layers of software components. These layers include the software drivers to the NIC, an interface between the computer's operating system and the network, and software that defines and controls access to network resources. Other optional software components of a LAN might include a menuing system, network administration and configuration software, or electronic mail or messaging programs.

When you buy a network operating environment, it will likely include most of the software layers described above. It is not necessarily the case that a network implementor will need to acquire each of these software components separately, but it is fairly important that network administrators understand the purpose and general concepts behind each software element.

Device Drivers. Most systems require a device driver that tells your computer about the particular hardware characteristics of the NIC. This driver may be loaded as part of the computers initialization in the CONFIG.SYS file, or it may be executed as a terminate-and-stay-ready program from the command line. This device driver will pass information to the computer about how the NIC uses interrupts (IRQ), Input/Output (I/O) addresses and memory blocks. Each NIC comes with a certain IRQ and I/O address pre-selected. If your computer uses that IRQ or I/O address for something else, you will need to change the options on the NIC and make corresponding changes in the way that you load the device driver for the NIC.

Suppose, for example, that you have purchased a Novell NE2000 Ethernet board to connect your microcomputer to the network. You read the documentation and learn that it comes set to use IRQ3 and I/O address 300. Your network requires that you load the device driver in your CONFIG.SYS with the entry: DEVICE=C:\NETWORK\NE2000.SYS. You find, however, that the computer system locks up because of this device driver. You then check your computer's documentation and learn that the second serial port uses IRQ3 and your CD-ROM interface board uses I/O address 300. To make the NIC work in your computer you must change jumpers on the board so that it uses alternate settings, probably something like IRQ 5 and I/O address 360. After making the changes on the board and reinstalling it in your system, you would then load the device driver specifying that the NIC now uses non-default settings. The command to load the driver might look something like: DEVICE=C:\NETWORK\NE2000.SYS /IRQ=5 /IOBASE=360. This represents one of the most common software problems that a network implementor will encounter while installing a network.

Network Operating System. Another layer of the network software environment are the various modules of the network operating system itself. What these modules do exactly and how they are loaded into the system vary greatly among all the network products on the market. Networks need software to allow the operating system of the microcomputer to interface with the resources on the network. In general terms, the network operating system extends the normal operating system of the computer so that it can address network resources as if they were part of the local system. The computer system needs to know which logical disk drives and printers are local and which it needs to request through the network. Most network operating environments employ a strategy of redirection so that the system channels requests for non-local drives and printers to the NIC, and the network services the requests.

One of the main concerns that network implementors should study relates to the amount of memory used by the network software. Memory used by network modules takes away from the memory space that other software applications can use. If the network software uses too much memory, users may no longer have enough memory to run some large software applications. This issue frequently arises in networks involving CD-ROM applications since CD-ROM drives require additional software drivers, and since the software to search the products tends to require a lot of memory.

Network Server Software. Network servers require software to enable them to provide and manage resources on the network. Providing resources is naturally more complex than using them. A server needs the same type of device drivers and network operating software required by workstations, but also needs the capability to define network resources, manage access to these resources so that only authorized users access each resource, plus it has to manage many simultaneous requests. The tasks required of network servers are so complex that almost all the high-end network products use an operating system other than MS-DOS as the native environment of the server. MS-DOS, designed as a single tasking, eight bit operating system, simply lacks sufficient sophistication to manage a large network server. Novell's 286 and 386 products use their own non-DOS operating system, Banyan/VINES uses UNIX, and Microsoft LAN Manager uses OS/2—all multitasking operating systems.

It is only the network products designed for smaller implementations that can rely on MS-DOS to manage network servers. Some of these scaled-down systems often allow the same microcomputer to be used both as a server and a workstation. But these products have limited features and performance compared to the ones that employ dedicated, non-DOS servers.

The network software that runs on a server will include management utilities that a network administrator will use to define and control all the resources provided by that server. One function of the network management utility is to define and set privilege levels for each person that will use the network. The network administrator assigns a username and password to all network users. The network operating system will not allow a user to gain access to any resources until that user has entered the correct name and password.

The network management utility also defines the resources on the server. The network administrator will organize the disk space on the server into various directories, give network names to those directories, and will specify who has access to those directories, and whether that access includes the ability to read, write, browse, erase, create, or scan data in that directory.

Most network packages choose to give access by individual users rather than to specific microcomputers on the network. This access strategy allows a user to have the same level of access no matter what system on the network she/he happens to be using. In practice, however, each user generally accesses the network from the same system. In these cases, the network administrator will likely set up most of the workstations to log onto the network, enter the password and assign network drives and printers as part of the computer's automatic start-up procedure. With MS-DOS machines this automatic network sign-on would be done by placing network commands into the AUTOEXEC.BAT file. Once set up this way, each microcomputer user on the network never has to do anything special to get onto the network.

An example of typical AUTOEXEC.BAT file for a network might look like this:

```
@echo off                              ;don't display commands
prompt $p$g                            ;modify dos prompt
path c:\dos;c:\network;c:\utility      ;establish search path
ne2000 /irq=5 /iobase=360              ;load NIC device driver
netbios                                ;load NetBIOS extensions
redir                                  ;load network redirector
net login \\server myname secret       ;logon to network server
net use e: \\server\mystuff            ;set up logical E: drive
net use f: \\server\deptstuf           ;set up logical F: drive
net use lpt2: \\server\@laser1         ;access laser printer
menu                                   ;run menu program
```

Electronic Mail/Messaging

Most LANs will include some type of electronic communication facility. One of the great advantages to a LAN lies in the ability to communicate electronically with other members of your organization. Furthermore, electronic mail works much more quickly and efficiently than paper memos. Coworkers can often exchange information more easily through electronic mail than over the telephone. Electronic mail software may come bundled with the network operating system, or it might be an optional feature purchased separately.

One of the issues relevant to selecting electronic mail systems involves its capabilities for interfacing with other mail systems. If the network connects with other networks, then network planners should make sure that the mail systems of each network can accept and receive messages from the others.

Application Software

Even though a computer operates on a network, the tasks required of the computer remain much the same as stand-alone systems. Applications software such as databases, word processors, and spreadsheet will need to operate on the network. However, software exhibits various levels of compatibility with networks. Some software packages do not tolerate a network as well as others. For example, many software packages that employ a copy-protection scheme will run only from a local hard disk and cannot be loaded from the network. Given the current proliferation of LANs, most software developers make great efforts to ensure that their products will run on all the popular networks. In fact, many software applications have special network versions specifically designed to take advantage of network services.

Backup Subsystem

Network administrators should take special care to provide for frequent backup of data stored on network file servers. Once a network user stores data on a file server, it generally becomes the network administrator's responsibility to ensure the security of the data. Floppy disk backup may be inadequate for many large file servers. When network data exceeds 20 megabytes or so, some other media should be used for backups.

A very common method for backing up large file servers involves magnetic tape cartridges. A single tape cartridge can hold over 100 megabytes of data. Not only do tape backup subsystems store large amounts of data, but most can be programmed to backup the server automatically and unattended. Thus, a network administrator could configure the backup system to perform the backup each night after the users are off the system.

Good backup procedures will include multiple copies of the backup data. This adds another degree of data security since it takes into consideration the possibility of both a disk failure and a defective tape cartridge. Another safeguard involves storing a copy of the backup tapes in some building other than the one that houses the file server. If a fire or other catastrophic event destroys the file server, at least a copy of the data would be preserved.

Network Concepts and Models

While the preceding section described the more tangible pieces that come together to form a network, this section aims to highlight some of the concepts that apply to local area networks.

LAN Models: Server-based vs Peer-to-Peer

LANs come in many varieties. Some LANs are patterned after a centralized model while others follow a more distributed approach. For example, peer-to-peer networks work quite differently than server-based networks.

Peer-to-Peer networks operate democratically. In these networks, each workstation has the option of both contributing resources to the network as well as using resources on the network. Printers and hard disks attached to any workstation in the network can be defined as a network resource to be shared by all workstations.

One of the greatest advantages that peer-to-peer networks hold over server-based networks lies in their great flexibility. Any system on the network can contribute its drives and printers to the service of the network. This capability, for example, allows network administrators to establish network printers in many locations throughout the physical layout of the network.

Large peer-to-peer networks can become very complicated and difficult to manage. When each system on a large network potentially contributes disk and printer resources, the process of defining, maintaining, and organizing these resources can become unmanageable. Without high-performance servers, the load of a large network exceeds the capabilities of many peer-to-peer networking products.

Server-based networks, on the other hand, follow a centralized model. Computers in these networks are either workstations or servers. A server provides resources to the network while workstations use the network without contributing resources. In a typical large server-based LAN one might find a large central file server, one or more print servers, and dozens of workstations.

These distinctions are not absolute. It is possible to have a server-based network where some servers can double as a workstation. It is also common to have non-dedicated print servers in a server-based LAN where some individual workstations can have their printers defined as network resources.

The OSI Layers of a Network

No discussion of local area networks would be complete without mentioning the Open Systems Interconnect (OSI) model of network functions. The International Standards Organization created this model in order to promote the interconnectivity of networks through the standardization and isolation of network functions. This model divides the many tasks that comprise a network into distinct, clearly defined, layers.

In addition to its intended function as a tool for network designers, the OSI model has become a great pedagogical tool. With this model in mind, one can better understand the functions of the various components of a LAN. The OSI layers provide a reference in which to compare one network with another and to conceptualize how network communications operate.

The OSI model divides network functionality into the following seven layers:

Layer 1: Physical. This layer defines the characteristics of the raw electrical signals that travel across the network. It includes properties such as the voltage used for the electrical signals and the length of signal pulses. This layer does not concern itself with specifications of cable types and connectors. These issues fall outside the scope of the OSI reference model.

Layer 2: Data Link. These definitions concern the basic rules for the sending of information across the network. Basic error checking and correction occur on this layer, but the processes that occur within this layer are totally unaware of the content of the transmitted information. The data stream is broken down into blocks and each block is encapsulated with header and trailer information so that other data link layer processes can recognize the block, verify its integrity, and move it through the network.

Layer 3: Network. The main concerns here relate to establishing the routes that data blocks can take across the network, or from one network to another. In some networks the routes that the data blocks may take are static and require very little activity on the network layer. Other networks may have multiple routes possible between nodes and may change these routes dynamically according to the current load of network traffic.

Layer 4: Transport. This layer ensures that data get all the way from the source to the destination intact. This is the lowest layer that deals with end-to-end transmission of data.

Layer 5: Session. The session layer defines the rules for how two machines can communicate with each other across the network. It determines how systems can establish, maintain, and terminate communications between themselves. The session layer represents what goes on when a user logs into a file server, for example.

Layer 6: Presentation. One of the main concerns of this layer lies with conventions used in the representation of data. Issues such as the transmission of textual information in ASCII or EBCDIC, the format of integers and other abstract data types belongs to this layer. Services such as the encryption/decryption of information and data compression also belong here.

Layer 7: Application. This top layer of the OSI model is the only one that the users of the network see. This layer includes network services such as file transfer, electronic mail, remote printing, and terminal emulation.

Although future networks may eventually strictly follow the OSI model, the networks described in this book do not. The network components found in most current network products may span multiple OSI layers, or perform part of one layer and part of another. As network products emerge conforming to the OSI standards, a much greater degree of interconnectivity among networks can be accomplished than is currently possible.

Network Topologies

The physical layout or topology of a network can take several forms. Different network products require different methods for connecting the nodes on the network together. In some networks each of the systems connect to each other, and in others each system connects only to a central hub. Network implementors need to know the various options concerning network topology and the advantages and disadvantages that correspond to each type.

One possible network topology is that of a bus. With this topology, used widely in Ethernet networks, each node on the network attaches to a single cable that spans the length of the network. Each end of the bus will have some type of terminating device and each node on the network must tap into the central cable that forms the bus. Figure 1.1 illustrates the simple bus topology.

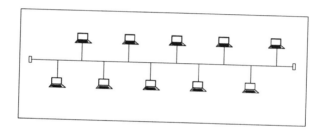

Figure 1.1

Illustration of Simple Bus Topology

The bus topology works well for a cluster of network nodes located in close proximity to each other. But as networks become larger and more complex, a simple network bus may not be adequate. Limitations apply to the total length of bus cable segments and to the number of network nodes that can exist on any one cable segment. To alleviate these limitations, most networks allow branching of the bus or allow multiple busses to be combined into a central hub. Figure 1.2 shows multiple bus segments combined through a multi-port repeater.

One of the disadvantages of the bus topology relates to cable failures. When connected in a bus topology, all the systems on the bus segment will fail in the event of a cable break. Strategies such as network segmentation can allow network planners to mitigate the number of systems affected from any given cable problem.

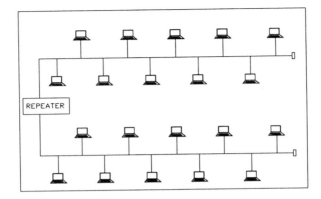

Figure 1.2
Bus Segments connected through a Repeater

The star topology requires each network node to connect to a central hub. One of the significant advantages of this topology is that most cable problems will affect only a single system. Since each network node connects directly to the central hub independently of the other nodes on the network, a single broken cable will affect only one system, and will be easy to isolate. This network topology does, however, involve the installation of significantly more cable than a bus topology. Figure 1.3 shows a star network, illustrating that each system on the network connects to some central communications device.

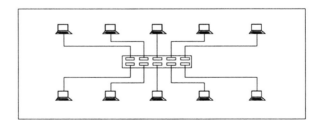

Figure 1.3
Illustration of a Star Topology Network

A third network topology, that of a ring, consists of a bus network that has its ends connected to form a complete circle. Figure 1.4 shows a ring network.

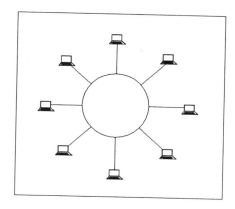

Figure 1.4
Illustration of a Ring Topology Network

It is fairly rare to see a network cabling system follow a ring topology. Although Token Ring networks require that the nodes of the network combine into a logical ring, the ring exists within the communications equipment, usually a MAU. Most Token Ring networks follow a physical star topology even though the network protocol requires a logical ring.

Access Methods and Protocols

In order for a network to work smoothly, certain rules must govern how each workstation behaves on the network. These rules, or access methods, are transparent to users of the network, and are usually implemented in the network boards themselves. These access methods concern the rules that the network hardware must follow in order to transmit data on the network. The three most common access methods are Carrier Sense Multiple Access with Collision Detection (CSMA/CD), Carrier Sense Multiple Access with Collision Avoidance (CSMA/CA), and token passing.

Three main types of network implementations prevail in the case studies in this volume, Ethernet, Token Ring, and LocalTalk. Each of these network implementations uses a different access method, Ethernet uses CSMA/CD, Token Ring networks use token passing, and LocalTalk networks use CSMA/CA. Besides these mainstream protocols, some network vendors may use their own proprietary protocols with nonstandard NICs and cabling.

Ethernet. Ethernet emerged early as a standard protocol for computer networks. The IEEE issued a standard, known as 802.3, that defines this type of network. Ethernet and 802.3, though very closely related, differ in some subtle aspects.

Especially in cases where one network will interconnect with other networks, network implementors need to know whether their network follows the Ethernet conventions or the 802.3 standard, or whether it supports either. For the broad, nontechnical discussion of this chapter, the differences are insignificant, and the term Ethernet will be used consistently.

One aspect of the theoretical operation of a network protocol has to do with its access method. When multiple computers need to communicate simultaneously over the same piece of cable, some set of rules must govern the communication.

When sending data over Ethernet, the network takes the content of the data and encapsulates it with codes that will address it to its correct destination. The encapsulation process also incorporates codes into the packet so that the recipient will know that the network transmitted the data correctly. If the receiving machine detects an error in transmission, it automatically requests retransmission. These encapsulated blocks of data are called datagrams.

A broad characteristic of Ethernet is that it uses broadcast transmission techniques over a bus topology network. Computers communicate by broadcasting datagrams onto the entire network. The sending computer broadcasts its message throughout the network, but only the addressed recipient node pays attention to the content of the message.

The broadcast messages that Ethernet uses follow an access method called CSMA/CD, meaning Carrier Sense Multiple Access with Collision Detection. Under this access method each machine senses for the presence of an active signal on the network, and may broadcast at any time. When multiple computers, also called nodes, attempt to broadcast on the network at the same time, the datagrams become garbled, much like two people talking at once on the telephone. Although any machine may broadcast at any time, the rules of the CSMA/CD cause each sending node to test to see whether their message collided with another. If a collision occurs, then each node that contributed to the collision waits a random amount of time and then retransmits its datagram.

More practical characteristics of Ethernet relate to transmission speeds and cable types. Ethernet comes in several varieties. The two main divisions of Ethernet cable types are broadband and baseband. Broadband technology allows for using a wide bandwidth of transmission frequencies. Data transmission and video transmission may be performed over the same broadband cable. Further, separate, independent data channels may also exist on the same broadband. The characteristics of broadband Ethernet are defined by the IEEE standard 10Broad36. The more common form of Ethernet is Baseband Ethernet. Baseband Ethernet is limited to a single data channel. Baseband Ethernet may use one of several cable types, thick Ethernet (IEEE 10Base5), a thick rigid coaxial cable, thin Ethernet (IEEE 10Base2), a thin flexible coaxial cable, fiber optic cable, and recently, unshielded twisted-pair cable—the same cable used by telephone systems (IEEE 10BaseT). Ethernet's transmission speed and distance limitations and cost vary according to the type of cabling implemented.

Token Ring. Another widely used network protocol is called Token Ring. The IEEE defined this type of network in the 802.5 standard. All the nodes on a token ring network interconnect to form a logical ring. Token ring protocol use an access method called token passing to govern network transmission. A special transmission packet is passed from one node on the network to the next, and continuously cycles through all the nodes on the ring. A node may broadcast data only when it receives the token. It broadcasts by adding its data to the token as it passes it along the ring. Along with the data, the transmitting node marks the address of the intended recipient. Each node examines the token as it is passed to check whether or not there is any data marked with its own address. When the token arrives at the destination node, the recipient extracts its data and flags the token with an indicator that the data was received. The token is then available for additional data transmissions.

Token ring networks generally use shielded twisted-pair cabling. Each node on the network is cabled to a Multi-user Access Unit (MAU). As mentioned in the above discussion of network topologies, even though the logical organization of Token Ring networks is a ring, the physical topology is usually a star. The logical ring that the token cycles through resides in the Multiple Access Unit, not in the main cable system that connects the nodes on the network.

Proprietary. Besides the industry standard protocols described above, some network vendors may elect to use alternate methods. These nonstandard networks may perform well enough, but users of these networks will find it more difficult to interconnect with other types of networks.

Apple's LocalTalk is one of these proprietary networking implementations. Macintosh systems use a set of network protocols called AppleTalk that can be carried over Apple's own LocalTalk, Farallon's PhoneNet, or over Ethernet. Macintosh computers come with a built-in LocalTalk port, avoiding the need to install a network interface card. The LocalTalk cabling system uses shielded twisted-pair cables terminating with special connectors.

LocalTalk uses CSMA/CA access method protocol. CSMA/CA differs from CSMA/CD in that it uses a scheme to avoid collisions of data transmission on the network instead of correcting them after they happen. To avoid collisions, the network assigns each node a time sequence in which it is allowed to transmit. When a node needs to transmit, it must wait until its turn before it is allowed to access the network. Thus, there is a built-in delay for every transmission. LocalTalk transfers information through the network at about 230 kilobits per second, and requires a bus topology network. Apple's specifications limit the network to 32 nodes per zone and suggest a total cable length of less than 300 meters.

Farallon's PhoneNet network system has also become quite popular for networking Macintosh systems. This network takes advantage of the built-in LocalTalk ports in Macintosh, and uses the same CSMA/CA access method as LocalTalk, but provides interface devices that allow one to use standard telephone wiring and connectors for the cabling system. In this way, Macintosh networks can be established in buildings without new cable installation by taking advantage of existing unused telephone wiring.

Ethernet may also be used to network Macintosh systems. Although this means that the network implementor will need to purchase an Ethernet NIC for each system and install an Ethernet cabling scheme, the resulting network will perform significantly faster than the LocalTalk or PhoneNet networks, and will have more options for communicating with other networks. More importantly, it allows Macintosh computers to use one of the well-recognized network standards described above.

This introductory chapter on network concepts certainly has not been an exhaustive discussion of the topic. Readers interested in acquiring additional information will find many books and articles devoted to LANs, ranging from general practical guides to in-depth technical works. The following publications listed sample some of the available literature.

Additional Literature

Archer, Rowland. 1986. *A Practical Guide to Local Area Networks.* Berkeley, California: Osborne McGraw-Hill.

Bulette, Greg and Chacon, Michael. 1991. Understanding 3COM Networks. Plano, Texas: Wordware Publishing, Inc.

Comer, Douglas E. 1988. *Internetworking with TCP/IP: Principles, Protocols, and Architecture.* Englewood Cliffs, New Jersey: Prentice Hall.

Desmarias, Norman, ed. 1989. *CD-ROM Local Area Networks: A User's Guide.* Westport, Connecticut: Meckler.

Derfler, Frank J., Jr. 1991. *PC Magazine Guide to Connectivity.* Emoryville, California: Ziff-Davis Press.

Durr, Michael and Gibbs, Mark. 1989. *Networking Personal Computers.* 3rd Edition. Que Corporation.

Fortier, Paul. 1989. *Handbook of LAN Technology.* Intertext Publications. New York: McGraw-Hill.

Fritz, James S., Kaldenback, Charles F., and Progar, Louis M. 1985. *Local Area Networks: Selection Guidelines.* Englewood Cliffs, New Jersey: Prentice-Hall.

Hancock B. 1988. *Designing and Implementing Ethernet Networks.* Wellesley, MA: QED Information Sciences.

Laubach, Edwin G. 1991. *Networking with Banyan VINES.* Blue Ridge Summit, PA: Windcrest.

LaQuey, Tracy L., ed., 1990. *The User's Directory of Computer Networks.* Digital Press.

Madron, Thomas W. 1991. *Enterprise-Wide Computing: How to Implement and Manage LANs.* New York: John Wiley & Sons, Inc.

Marks, Kenneth E. and Nielsen, Steven P. *Local Area Networks in Libraries.* Westport, Connecticut: Meckler.

Martin, James. 1989. *Local Area Networks: Architecture and Implementations*. Englewood Cliffs: New Jersey: Prentice Hall.

Quarterman, John S. 1991. *The Matrix: Computer Networks and Conferencing Systems Worldwide*. Digital Press.

Ranade, Jay and Sackett, George C. 1989. *Introduction to SNA Networking: A Guide for Using VTAM/NCP*. New York: McGraw-Hill.

Sandler, Corey and Badgett, Thomas. 1990. *Mac to VAX: A Communications Guide*. Glenview, Illinois: Scott, Foresmann and Company.

Shatt, Stan. 1991. *Linking LANS: A Micro Manager's Guide*. New York: Windcrest. McGraw-Hill.

Sheldon, Tom. 1990. *Novell NetWare: The Complete Reference*. (Covers through Version 2.15.) Berkeley, California: Osborne McGraw-Hill.

Tanenbaum, Andrew S. 1988. *Computer Networks*. Second Edition. Englewood Cliffs, New Jersey: Prentice Hall.

Network-Oriented Publications:

Datamation: For Mangers of Information Technology Worldwide. Newton, MA: Cahners Publishing Associates.

LAN Technology: The Technical Resource for Network Specialists. Redwood City, California: M&T Publishing.

LAN Times: McGraw Hill's Information Source for Network Managers. Midvale, Utah: McGraw Hill, Inc.

Network Computing: Computing in a Network Environment. Manhasset, New York: CMP Publications.

Network World: The Newsweekly of User Networking Strategies. Framingham, MA: International Data Group.

Telecommunications. Norwood, MA: BPA.

Part One:

Networking the Macintosh in the Library

2

A Macintosh LAN for Library Staff

Henry R. Harken
Fletcher Library, Arizona State University West

ABSTRACT

In a new institution, planning a Macintosh network proceeded in step with planning a campus and a library building. The initial installation connected twenty-five Macintosh and DOS computers, and four network printers using Farallon Computing PhoneNet system LocalTalk hubs, wiring, and connectors. After three years of growth. the network consists of over fifty devices, including servers, netmodem, router, and Internet gateway. Migration toward individual microcomputer connections to Ethernet and CD-ROM servers is under development.

Introduction

Arizona State University West (ASUW) is a new campus of Arizona State University (ASU). Started in 1984, its embryonic beginning evolved from the off-campus programs offered on the West side of the Phoenix metropolitan area. The West campus was formed to meet the higher education needs of the growing west side of the Phoenix metropolitan area and to relieve enrollment pressures at the Tempe campus located just to the east of the Phoenix city limits. The ASUW library as an institution opened in temporary quarters in 1985 with a small cadre of staff to begin offering basic library services, plan development, and begin planning for design and construction of the permanent building. The Fletcher Library was the first building constructed on a campus expected to handle 5,000 students in its first stage of development by 1995, and 10,000 by the year 2000. Curriculum based collections were expected to expand to 300,000 volumes in the first phase. Personnel was anticipated to be 35 FTE upon occupation. In 1991 after three years in the building, staff was approximately 45 FTE of which 12 were professional. Future building expansion was planned in the site and building design. Estimates made in 1991 project that collection and service growth will fill the building by 1995.

The frequently used cliche of building an airplane while flying it is still the most accurate metaphor to describe the situation of providing basic library services and technology while planning a building, forthcoming library services, and the integration of technology into those areas. Decisions on library services and collections were closely tied to curriculum planning and developments as the model was not to duplicate existing research collections at ASU but to rely on technology developments in information provision. Planning and implementation also had to continue while advances in computing and networking were being announced or expected. Answers to questions about building and technology requirements were occasionally best guesses on current information when flexibility could not be built in. Redundant solutions to questions such as what sort of cabling to install were usually the only way to handle technology changes that were occurring. In some technology arenas like data communications, the direction seemed apparent but staff needed to know when the building opened not several years later, when the new technologies in networking (like 10BaseT) would be available.

In early spring of 1988, two major decisions on technology were made for the occupation of the new library facilities being completed for this campus. The first decision made by the management team of the Library was to install new technology for library staff based on Apple Macintosh equipment. With this major technology agreement, the conclusion was to proceed with the installation of a LAN that would connect these computers and take advantage of the networking capabilities that were inherent to the Macintosh.

Networking the Macintosh

Networking Assumptions and Decisions

Many assumptions were made regarding the initial LAN installation, its services/devices, and clientele but, given the rapid changes in technology, no application was discounted for the future and planning proceeded accordingly. Because Macintosh networking does not require a server nor the loading of any special software to implement local area networking, the LAN was therefore viewed as a network that was not dependent upon any particular device or hardware to make it function other than the built-in networking capability of the Macintosh platform, and the physical wiring that would be required. Within this framework, devices connected to the network would be installed, updated, or removed with little or no impact on the operation of other network devices.

While the initial focus of this particular network was to be for staff use, it was anticipated that the services of this LAN might be extended into the public service area in the future. When the plans for equipment and LAN installation were being worked on, there were few applications available that would be appropriate for what libraries would typify as public access use, but when physical connections were made they were spread widely through the building into nearly every part of the library except for areas clearly designated for stacks and general seating/reading spaces.

While the Library was planning for its new building, campus administration was searching for a new home for a student computer access center that was in temporary quarters on a leased site. The Library believed that this was an opportunity for a partnership between traditional library services and computing services, and offered space for the public service and staff activities of this unit. Network connections for this area was included in the installation of the physical wiring and associated equipment.

Apple Computer refers to their standard networking protocol as AppleTalk. It is a standard that is independent from the physical medium over which the protocol runs. The standard Apple-supplied cabling at that time consisted of shielded twisted-pair cabling and is referred to as LocalTalk. The term is often extended to refer to unshielded twisted-pair cabling. In a typical networking configuration, Apple supplied LocalTalk connectors attach to the LAN port on the rear of the Macintosh and the shielded cabling would be connected from one computer's LocalTalk connector to another in a "daisy-chain," one cable for each pair of computer/connector combinations. This arrangement is very simple but unsatisfactory when a LAN must stretch between four floors of a building as was the case in the new installation.

There was an alternative available to the Apple supplied LocalTalk connectors, the PhoneNet connector, produced by a Farallon Farallon has now used the umbrella term PhoneNet for all of its networking products, LocalTalk or Ethernet. This product, like the Apple-supplied product, attaches to the Macintosh network port, but instead of shielded cabling, employs unshielded twisted-pair cabling with standard RJ-11 connectors. This is the standard modular cabling available at any telephone store in varying lengths. Since the PhoneNet system used standard unshielded telephone wire it was possible to use the installed telephone wiring in the building. The use of modular telephone wiring in some areas greatly simplified installation and kept costs down.

Telephone lines as installed by telephone companies typically include two pairs of wires but analog telephone service uses only one pair of these. The Farallon PhoneNet system employs the pair unused by standard telephone service (the pair the telephone company will typically use to provide second lines for residential service), and therefore analog telephone service and the LAN may actually reside on the same two-pair cabling without interfering with each other.

Cable Installation

Arizona State University has a standard cabling plan for new construction regarding basic telephone wiring. At each point where telephone service or jacks are planned a duplex jack block is installed. The first or "A" jack receives a 4-pair connection and the second or "B" receives a 2-pair connection. The other end of the connections terminate in a wiring closet. In the Fletcher Library, the cables connect back to a wiring closet on the same floor and down to a lower-level wiring closet designated for building-wide connections.

To accommodate use of the installed telephone wiring for networking, Farallon StarControllers were ordered and installed. These network hubs are cabled to punch-down blocks that are in turn connected to the house wiring punch-down blocks. The typical telephone wiring duplex at a workstation was wired with the "A" jack for use with digital telephones and the "B" jack for use with the LocalTalk LAN. Network devices plugged into the LAN "B" jacks joined the network via the hub circuitry. Unused ports require termination at the wiring punch-down blocks using resisters provided with the StarControllers. Unused jacks connected to the network were terminated with RJ-11 connectors that had resisters soldered onto the appropriate cable pair. These were included with every PhoneNet connector from Farallon.

When the Fletcher Library building was designed, it was believed that we had installed more than enough wiring throughout the building to anticipate all forthcoming technology. What we had not truly expected was the extent to which the Library may actually be caught in the transition from old to new technologies. Local area networks had emerged and were beginning to exhibit the promise of interconnections to a multitude of possible devices. However, there were many communication services that were not yet available at a reasonable cost on local area networks but were offered through other communications media. At Arizona State University the existing medium for computer telecommunications was an ASCII broadband system (here on referred to as the Broadband) that used hardware and software provided by Sytek. Connections to this system were serial and each microcomputer independently connected. Among the critical services connected to the Broadband was mainframe electronic mail through which much of the Library's professional and administrative staff communicated. These computing services required that each reference librarian have ASCII broadband access. The reference staff also needed locally connected modems to be used for access to online services. In all, each reference librarian needed four communications jacks to accommodate the digital telephone, analog telephone line for modem, ASCII broadband, and local area network; but only two jacks were available at each reference librarian desk. The University telecommunications personnel accommodated the analog telephone line and the broadband connection by extracting existing wire pairs within the "B" jack and adding a third jack to the jack duplex installation. The local area network was installed in these areas by bringing in live connections nearby and taking advantage of the PhoneNet capabilities by daisy-chaining from office cubicle to office cubicle using standard modular telephone cable.

Installing the LAN

The initial installation resulted in the connection of 15 staff Macintosh computers (Macintosh II, SE and Plus), 4 staff DOS computers, 2 staff laser printers, and eight networked impact printers. One port of a StarController was designated for use with the public access computer center and ten daisy-chained public access Macintosh and DOS computers, and two laser printers extended off this port. The connections between the LocalTalk LAN hubs and the individual jacks were made by the University telecommunications personnel on a time and material basis. Jacks to be connected to the LAN were specified by number in the work documents to the telecommunications department. It is very important to have qualified personnel perform the actual "punch-downs" in the wiring closet. Every telecommunications environment is different but especially in a setting where many types of connections are using the house wiring, professional telecommunications personnel should be used. In the Fletcher Library there are six other types of connections that pass through the building wiring closet: the online catalog system, acquisitions system, ASCII broadband, digital phone line, analog phone lines, Ethernet, and IBM 3270 connections.

DOS computers were connected to the AppleTalk LAN using network boards and software supplied by Tangent Technologies. These products were eventually acquired and marketed by Daystar. Apple Computer also developed products for connecting DOS computers to AppleTalk networks. The Apple products for DOS networking, especially the software AppleShare PC, were considerably easier for users to understand and use for connections to network printers and AppleShare file servers. The Apple products are now handled by Farallon Computing. It is also possible to connect Apple IIe and Apple IIgs computers to an AppleTalk network, and this was done by the administration of the public access computing area.

As noted above, wiring and hardware costs for the initial LAN installation totaled less than $5700. The installation costs involving time and materials by University Telecommunications Services brought the total cost to under $6000. Today's 1991 costs of purchasing and installing twisted-pair Ethernet (10BaseT) equipment instead of LocalTalk is not much more. Ethernet hubs are in the $2000 range, Ethernet interfaces, board or SCSI type, are available for $300–$500 and typically include jacks for direct connection to house wiring using commercial telephone-type cabling with RJ-45 connectors (household telephones use RJ-11 modular wiring connectors). The use of the 10BaseT standard and the inclusion of built-in jacks make the use of other connectors unnecessary. Connections to other types of Ethernet using coax or thin coax cabling typically require an additional connector between the computer's Ethernet interface and the cabling. Based on current networking standards and pricing, twisted-pair Ethernet should be seriously considered for any new LAN installation connecting computers of any type. A LAN may also be planned to initially install LocalTalk with later migration to Ethernet planned into the installation.

The public access computers and printers were separated from the rest of the network using a Hayes Interbridge, a network bridge, which served to divide the LAN into two zones and segregate network traffic. This was important for several reasons. First, Apple does not recommend having more than 34 devices in a single zone. Though this number was arrived at somewhat arbitrarily and a zone may function normally with a greater number of devices, there is a limit to traffic density in all networks. The standard LocalTalk network is less expensive compared to Ethernet, and its 234,000 BPS speed/bandwidth is much faster than typical telephone line modem speeds with which many computer users are familiar. However, any speed network may reach a point when network traffic may overwhelm it through the cumulative effects of too many devices, or heavy network traffic. The figure of thirty-

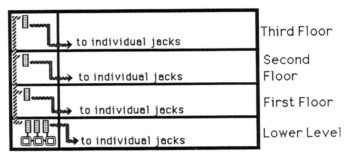

Fletcher Library, ASU West

General wiring scheme

Wiring distribution closets on each floor

to individual jacks — Third Floor

to individual jacks — Second Floor

to individual jacks — First Floor

to individual jacks — Lower Level

LAN hubs connected to house wiring in main wiring closet

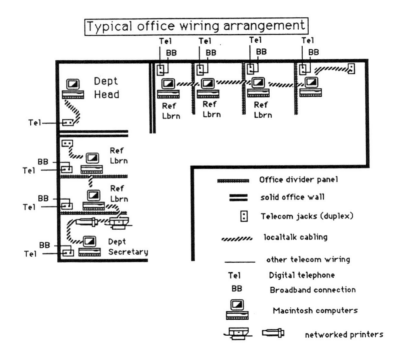

Typical office wiring arrangement

Office divider panel

solid office wall

Telecom jacks (duplex)

localtalk cabling

other telecom wiring

Tel   Digital telephone

BB   Broadband connection

Macintosh computers

networked printers

Figure 2.1
Network Wiring Schemes, Fletcher Library, ASU West

four devices provides the typical network manager with a planning number that could be higher or less depending on the type and patterns of activities that occur on a particular network. Additional zones may be created to keep network traffic local that should be local and a network bridge or router will allow traffic to pass into other zones for access.

Number	Description	Price	Total
41	Farallon PhoneNet connectors Mini DIN-8	37.35	$1,531.36
9	Farallon PhoneNet connectors DB-9	37.35	$ 336.15
3	Farallon Star Controllers	1,194.12	$3,582.36
3	Star Controller wiring kit, punch down block	67 .00	$ 201.00
Total			$5,650.87

Table 2.1

Initial Lan Hardware Costs for Fletcher Library
(1988 prices from original Farallon order)

Two years after installation of the LAN, a slight alteration of the LAN connections for the public access computers and printers eventually made the connection of the public access computing area and the Fletcher Library network unnecessary. This area was administered separately from the Library and therefore it was decided to completely sever the connection. This simplified the networking configurations for both segments and also made the Hayes Interbridge available to further divide the Library side of the LAN. These decisions allowed more efficient operation of the LAN and segregated network traffic to help prevent network overload. How important this was was demonstrated earlier when the two LAN segments were connected for a time with no bridge. Network traffic density caused by a particularly heavy period of public access user printing, the Library's networked database software and own print jobs, and the overall mass of network devices actually brought the network down.

The Functions of the LAN

Printer Sharing

The first purpose for which the Fletcher Library LAN was employed was the sharing of Postscript laser printers: two Apple LaserWriters II (NT and NTX) in staff office areas on different floors, and one LaserWriter NTX in the public access computing area. Demands in student computing needs led to an additional printer being installed soon after on the public access side of the network. Over a period of three years three additional laser printers were added to support library staff.

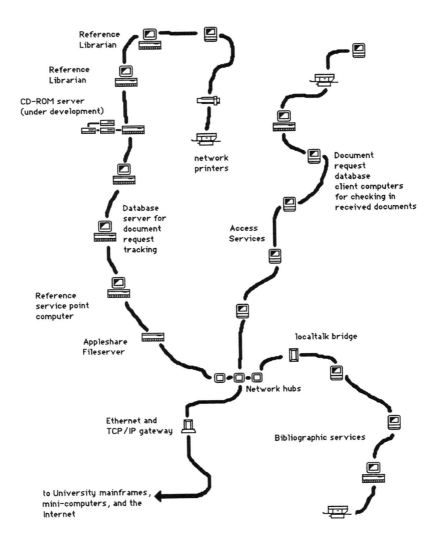

Figure 2.2
Simplified LAN Diagram for Fletcher Library

Database Server

A document/book request service, complementing the Fletcher Library's collection, is a key function that has been in operation since 1985. This service allows students and faculty to request books housed in the Tempe campus libraries to be delivered to the Fletcher Library for pick up and checkout, and the delivery of photocopied articles from those collections. For over two years while the library was housed in temporary quarters, the requests for the service and the tracking of those requests had been handled on a single "stand-alone" DOS computer.

The installation of a LAN allowed greater capabilities in the fulfillment and tracking of these requests. A Macintosh II was designated as a "database server" and a database was defined using Double Helix, a relational database program for the Macintosh. The key reason for the use of this program was its then unique standing as the only Macintosh database program that offered a LAN-based multiuser module. When the defined database was mounted on the multiuser version of the program, staff maintaining the service could access the database from anywhere on the LAN as long as they were using the "guest" program provided and were issued an appropriate password. Users submit their requests at the reference service point. Staff there verify that request details are complete, and the forms and printouts from the online catalog and/or CD-ROM indexes are forwarded to personnel who enter the new requests into the Helix database. These new requests are exported into text files that are transmitted electronically to the ILL department of the ASU-Tempe libraries. The department there, under contract for the service, fills the orders and sends materials by scheduled courier to the Fletcher Library. These materials are received by the circulation staff and checked into the database that they access through the LAN.

For the academic year 90/91, requests for over 15,000 books, journal articles, and government publications were made and handled by this system, with a turn around time between request and arrival of materials as short as the same day but typically within two days or less. This speed and volume would not have been possible on the stand-alone system that was in previous use.

When the library moved into its new building there was the single LAN "aware" database program. This feature is now becoming a common feature in Macintosh database programs, and software publishers are competing to provide increasingly better implementations. The document request service is in the process of changing to another database program, FileMaker Pro from Claris. Though not fully relational, this program includes features not found or easier to implement compared to Double Helix. Chief of these is the easier maintenance and modification of the working database by library personnel. Almost as important was the ability to perform this work without making the working database unavailable to the personnel creating and updating document request records. FileMaker Pro is fully network capable and has security features that are relatively sophisticated but easy to implement. It also includes "look-up" functions that is expected to expedite the compilation of statistics useful for service and collection development decisions. With the "publish and subscribe" features of the Macintosh newly released System 7 allowing interactive updating between programs, we expect to see additional capabilities among the Claris products. The transition between programs should be complete in July 1991.

Sharing Files on the LAN

The third major LAN installation was a file server. A networked computer with a hard drive with special network and security software, a file server allows individual computer users on the network to easily make files available to other computer users, collaborate on documents, access files made available to file server users, and run programs that reside on the server. Earlier experiments with TOPS on DOS platforms provided experience with the distributed file server model but it was decided that this would not be cost effective when mounted on over twenty microcomputers, nor practical in an environment where there would be individuals sharing computers at service points and within some departments. From the LAN maintenance point of view, the thought of "riding herd" on over twenty separate file servers and administrating access privileges for all of them was quite daunting. The TOPS hardware and software, from the TOPS company (now called Sitka) was an early entrant into AppleTalk networking and its major strength is connections between Macintosh, DOS, and SUN platforms. Computers of any combination of these three types or of the same type may make available portions or all of their disk drives available to other computers running TOPS. With the May 1991 advent of System 7 from Apple, peer-to-peer networking is included: Macintosh computers running this new version of the Macintosh operating system may make parts or all of the disk drive accessible to Macintosh computers on the network.

With these factors and experiences in mind, it was decided to implement a central file server using AppleShare, Apple Computer's file server software. AppleShare requires a dedicated Macintosh computer on which to run the file server software. This computer may not be used for typical user functions like word processing, for example, but other network services such as print servers (spoolers), LAN-based electronic mail servers, or software gateways may share the computer. The file server may make various drives or volumes on the network including internal and external hard disk drive, CD-ROM drives, and removable media. Much flexibility is provided by the hardware as every Macintosh model has a Small Computer System Interface (SCSI) port. This high speed port allows the connection of up to six SCSI devices to a Macintosh computer with the devices cabled in daisy-chain fashion. Many products have been designed for SCSI connections with Macintosh computers but it is the file storage device that is typically connected to a file server.

The administration of an AppleShare file server is based on defining users and groups, and individual membership within these groups. A file server user may be a member of multiple groups. Defining individual users as members of groups is not mandatory but group membership is essential for shared access to Macintosh folders (directories) on the file server. File server folders are assigned owners, and various degrees of access are allowed to groups or all file server users. For example, an owner of a particular folder may be able to read or write (and therefore also delete) files to a folder. A particular group may be allowed to read but not be allowed to make changes to these files. It is possible to prohibit entry to a folder to non-members of a group. In this manner, varying degrees of security are assigned to folders created by the file server administrator.

In the Fletcher Library, initial accounts and group membership was based on the Library organizational structure. For example, circulation personnel were made members of the circulation group but also members of the Access Services group with their counterparts in the department that handled journals, microforms, and media (JMM). The latter were also members of the JMM file server group. The Access Services department head was assigned membership to all three of these file server groups. This model was used for the entire library organization.   All Library personnel were made members of the Library Staff group regardless of their library department assignment. This facilitated the definition and use of "dropboxes": folders owned by an individual that any staff member could save files to but only the owner had the privileges to open the folder.

Accounts and initial passwords were at first issued to all personnel. Later this was changed to exclude part-time personnel because of a generally greater turnover rate, except for librarians and individuals whose position or duties required access. A general account and password was issued for each major department to allow part-time personnel to view critical files such as service point logs. Most individuals are assigned server "drop boxes" that allow other library staff to securely send sensitive documents that may only be retrieved by the "drop box" owner. Other folders (directories) on the server have been defined for shared use among work groups. The most common use is the viewing and contributions to logs maintained by service points and departments to share information and solve problems that arise.

The file server itself was a Macintosh II initially with a 40MB internal hard and 1MB RAM. This was later expanded to 2MB RAM, and an external 80MB hard drive was attached using the Macintosh SCSI port. Further RAM expansion is anticipated to accommodate added network services such as a software router or a LAN-based electronic mail server that may also reside there. The external drive was used by the Library's computer and network personnel for the loading of software to user's individual hard drives and the temporary storage of backed-up files when doing computer maintenance. The file server is "headless": it has no monitor but for administration of the software the program Timbuktu from Farallon is used to remotely control the file server from another Macintosh.

The network and file server provided a great service to the library staff but despite the great advantages of low cost and ease of installation there were some compromises and limitations in using the physical networking standard of LocalTalk: it was not as fast as Ethernet. Therefore this limited the number of devices in a single zone, and amount of traffic that could share the network at one time. The standard of Ethernet over unshielded twisted-pair wiring was not available as yet. The initial storage space available on the file server was also a factor. At first the file server had the limitations of only a 40MB hard drive and 2MB RAM.

With these factors in mind, users were provided the following guidelines in the use of the file server with the objective of getting the best performance for the longest period of time from the installed LAN and file server:

o   The file server is a shared resource for the entire library.

o   The file server is not meant for permanent or long term storage of personal files.

o   Move files from any of your personal folders or drop boxes to your local hard disk (the one on your computer) or a floppy disk, then delete the file from your dropbox.

o   One of the nice uses of the file server is the ability to share drafts of documents. Please, when the project has reached fruition, delete unneeded items.

o   If there is a large document being distributed and referred to, copy it from the file server to your computer's hard disk or to a floppy disk. Refer to the copy on your computer. This way the item is copied once per person rather than referred to on the file server multiple times per person.

o   We do not run programs (word processors, database programs, spreadsheets, etc.) from the file server. They are run from your hard drive.

These guidelines were designed to prevent unnecessary network traffic and to make efficient use of shared space on the file server. Running programs from the file server over the LocalTalk network offered no benefit to the user. It was slower than running it off their own hard drive and created additional network traffic. The disadvantage was the time and efforts for the Fletcher Library computing personnel in maintaining and tracking software on many hard drives. With a faster file server and faster network, networking licenses or multiple copies of software would be obtained by a single copy maintained on the file server for users to access and run. Updating applications software would involve no more than updating the file server copy. Major upgrades would still involve distribution of manuals and user instruction but would still save time and effort.

NetModems

Within a year of occupation of the new building, the ASCII Broadband system discussed earlier had added a dial-out modem pool that replaced the use of analog telephone lines and modems directly connected to most of the reference librarians' computers within the Fletcher Library. The same communication system that provided mainframe and electronic mail access became the conduit for online searching for the reference staff. However, other library departments were developing a need for access to outside data services where dial-out capabilities were not originally foreseen or additional personnel were added requiring such services. One solution was to add additional broadband connections. While these were priced by the University telecommunications services at a very reasonable, even cheap, flat fee of $500 with no maintenance costs, other factors came into play. The dial-out requirement was typically an occasional need by these other departments or individuals. Even more important was the shortage of jacks or cabling in some areas. Adding more broadband connections meant either having more cables pulled through the building (a somewhat costly proposition) or having the University telecommunications services perform the wizardry of using unused pairs in available jacks, a skill demonstrated in the past. Just as important was the cumulative costs of filling an occasional need for several stations throughout the building with additional dedicated connections. Technology developments at the University, particularly in TCP/IP Ethernet networks, were also casting doubts on the long term viability of the ASCII Broadband system. The costs of moving or requesting analog telephone lines, and acquiring modems for these areas were additional factors. Since all these points were already connected to the LAN the decision was made to purchase and employ a Shiva NetModem.

The Shiva Netmodem is a 2400 BPS modem, also now available in the international V.32 (9600 BPS) standard, that has an analog telephone line connection but also a LocalTalk port and software for use by Macintosh computers on the LAN. With this device in place, any LAN user would have access to standard dial-out services if provided with communications software and with the netmodem driver installed on their computer. With these in place, the netmodem user merely starts his/her communications software and tells it to use the network printer port on the Macintosh computer, and the driver establishes and maintains the connection between the netmodem and the computer. Selecting the second serial port on the Macintosh after completing online transactions disconnects the communication between the computer and the netmodem freeing the modem for use by other networked computers. A basically simple procedure, it was automated through the use of procedure scripts with the communications software (White Knight from Freesoft).

Interconnecting the LAN beyond the Fletcher Library

Advances in technology have added another dimension to the local area network within the Fletcher Library. The University Data Communications extended an Ethernet channel to ASU West, and the Fletcher Library was provided with an Ethernet Point of Presence (EPOP). At the University an EPOP was defined to compose of an Ethermodem, Ethernet router, and a twisted-pair Ethernet concentrator. The Fletcher Library ordered a Cayman Gatorbox and it was installed between the EPOP and the LocalTalk LAN. The Gatorbox is a gateway and router that may be used to connect AppleTalk LocalTalk LANs to AppleTalk Ethernet networks. Just as important is its capability to route TCP/IP communications. The University telecommunications community recognizes the developing OSI communications standard and has adopted the use of TCP/IP as an interim standard until OSI has matured and more vendors' products support it. Both TCP/IP and OSI are protocol standards that define how dissimilar computing systems may still communicate between them.

In the Fletcher Library, the Gatorbox is being used to provide communication links to the mainframes and other University computing resources. Using nothing more than public domain software such as NCSA Telnet from the National Center for Supercomputing Applications and Brown University's Telnet 3270, LAN users may communicate with computers anywhere in the University and the world. Over time, we expect the TCP/IP Ethernet connections to replace the ASCII Broadband system as more services are converted to Ethernet. With the Gatorbox AppleTalk routing capabilities turned on, users may access Macintosh file server, printing, and other network services anywhere among more than a dozen zones on the University Ethernet. The Gatorbox also supports IP tunneling. This allows AppleTalk packets to be conveyed within IP packets on networks that permit only TCP/IP networking. These "tunnels" are established between two or more Gatorbox routers.

Future Developments

The public within the Fletcher Library currently search CD-ROM databases on a CD-ROM server via a separate twisted-pair Ethernet LAN using DOS network stations. One of the interests of the Library is to explore expansion of the access to network CD-ROMs, and easy staff access to them without disrupting public access. To this end, CD-ROM network on AppleTalk LANs are being examined. As library software publishers expand into the Macintosh environment, more of them have made their products more functional as LAN products. While taken for granted by most Macintosh software publishers, only recently have some CD-ROM publishers made their products aware of network file servers on AppleTalk networks. During the summer of 1991, the Fletcher Library will be experimenting with access to select CD-ROM disks mounted as AppleShare volumes on the library server. This will be done by attaching SCSI CD-ROM drives to an AppleShare file server and registering the disks with the administrative AppleShare software. Library staff running the search software should expect to have those volumes available through the network.

Even more desirable is campus-wide access to CD-ROM databases, a technological development that is currently in its early stages. There are different models for accomplishing this and we expect to be seriously considering implementing this during the 92/93 academic year.

During the 91/92 academic year parts of the LAN will be converted to Ethernet. It is envisioned that the high traffic density sections of the network will be converted first, in our case it is likely to be the regular users of the document request system networked database. We also expect to place central network services such as file servers in their own Ethernet zone. To accomplish this we expect to use a combination of Farallon twisted-pair Ethernet hubs, Farallon Ethernet boards, Nuvotech SCSI Ethernet interfaces (for connecting Macintosh SE computers to Ethernet), Farallon StarConnectors EN (to connect the Nuvotech interfaces to twisted-pair Ethernet), Apple Ethernet thin coax transceivers, Apple Ethernet thin coax cabling, and Farallon's Liaison software routing software. The Apple thin coax equipment permits the "daisy-chaining" of Ethernet connections in places where there is a shortage of RJ-45 network jack connections. The software router will likely serve to unite the dissimilar networking media and provide additional network support. All components have already been acquired and testing has begun.

The Fletcher Library is expected to outgrow it's current facilities in less than five years and major remodeling and construction is an ideal time for the installation of network cabling. Cabling and conduit is relatively expensive to install after completion of a building and the installation of seemingly unneeded cable during construction may even be considered to be an investment. Because of the major costs in cable installation the technological developments in the network standard of FDDI is very important to watch. This network standard that handles speeds of 100 MB/second, is primarily for optical fiber networks. Costs are steadily declining and one can speculate that extension of such connections to the individual computing station is only a matter of time. Progress has been made in development of plastic fiber which is less expensive and less fragile compared to glass fiber. Even more exciting are the proposed standards of FDDI using shielded and unshielded twisted-pair cabling.

Network Products and Suppliers

The following list represents the major products and suppliers used in the Fletcher Library for networking.

Apple Computer

20525 Mariani Ave
Cupertino, CA 95014
Telephone: 408-996-1010
Macintosh computers
AppleShare file server software
Ethernet thin Coax transceivers
Ethernet thin coax cabling

Claris Corporation

5201 Patrick Henry Drive
Box 58168
Santa Clara, CA 95052-8168
408-727-8227
FAX: 408-987-7447
Internet: CLARIS.TECH@applelink.apple.com
America Online: CLARIS
CompuServe: 76004,1614
FileMaker Pro

Cayman Systems

University Park at MIT
26 Landsdowne Street
Cambridge, MA 02139
617-494-1999
FAX: 617-494-5167
support@cayman.com
Applelink: d0523
Gatorbox
LocalTalk/Ethernet AppleTalk and TCP/IP
router.
Also hardware and software products for links
to Unix computers, and for internet mail

Farallon Computing

2000 Powell Street, Suite 600
Emeryville, CA 94608
415-596-9100
FAX: 415-556-9020
FARART@applelink.apple.com
Applelink: FARART
CompuServe: 75410,2702
StarController LocalTalk networking hubs
LocalTalk network connectors (PhoneNet and
Star Connectors)
Star Controller EN Ethernet networking hubs
PhoneNet Ethernet boards
Liaison software router
Timbuktu software

Nuvotech

2015 Bridgeway, Suite 204
Sausalito, CA 94965
800-4nuvotech or 415-331-7815
FAX 415-331-6445
nuvomktg@applelink.apple.com
Applelink: NUVO.MKTG
TurboNet ST self-terminating LocalTalk
connectors
SCSI Ethernet connectors
LocalTalk hubs
Ethernet hubs
Ethernet boards

Odesta Corp

4084 Commercial Ave.
Northbrook,IL 60062
708-498-5615
FAX: 708-498-9917
Double Helix

About the Author

Henry (Hank) Harken has been the Electronic Systems Librarian, at the Fletcher Library, Arizona State University West in Phoenix, Arizona since January 1986. Before that he was a reference Librarian and coordinator of the online searching program at the M.I. King Library, University of Kentucky from 1982 to 1986; a reference librarian at Tennessee Technological University, Cookeville, Tennessee, 1979-1982; and a reference and serials Librarian at King Faisal University, Dammam, Saudi Arabia, 1977 to 1979. He received his M.S.L.S. at the Palmer School of Library and Information Science at C. W. Post Center, Long Island University in 1977.

3

The DONALD Network: A Macintosh-Based Reference Information Service LAN

James Alloway and Robert Schwarzwalder
Engineering/Transportation Library, University of Michigan

ABSTRACT

DONALD, a HyperCard program to provide reference and instructional information at the University of Michigan's Engineering/Transportation Library, was networked AppleShare software. The network uses a Macintosh 30/SE as server with two Macintosh Plus computers as workstations. Librarians and library school students programmed, installed, and manage the system. DONALD fulfills user demands for assistance that cannot be met by current staffing levels and offers a number of options for future networking of electronic information resources. The importance of library staff involvement in networking efforts is stressed as a vital element of developing networks in the library environment.

Introduction

Universities, libraries, and librarians across the country are setting up in-house, local networks to expand or provide new services to their patrons. In many instances the work is actually performed by non-librarians due to the nature of the software and hardware involved. For the network at the University of Michigan's Engineering/Transportation Library, the work for both software development and hardware set-up was done by librarians and library school students. We established a network in order to expand access to DONALD, a HyperCard reference and guide tool, created to support our public services. We chose the name DONALD because our server and workstations are named after Huey, Dewey, and Louie, the three nephews of Disney character Donald Duck. Those involved with DONALD acquired new skills in microcomputer technology, user interface design, and human-computer interaction. The system will be expanding to other University of Michigan libraries with continued emphasis on direct librarian involvement.

Goals

The primary goal of the Engineering/Transportation Library's network mirrored the goal of the University at large. That is, expanding the services and capabilities of existing resources through the use of automation. The decision to develop a LAN as opposed to self-contained workstations hinged upon several factors: cost, security, and expandability. It also fulfilled a goal to develop in-house expertise in software development and other automation skills. In considering cost, we measured the expense of separate units with hard disks versus the cost of a LAN. As demonstrated in our discussion of network costs, we achieved significant savings by using a local area network. Since our staff completed the necessary wiring for the system, labor costs were kept to a minimum. In addition, the possible availability of used microcomputers without hard disks from future equipment upgrades in the Engineering College would increase the cost advantage of a networked system.

Any discussion of cost would be incomplete if it did not emphasize the real impetus to develop DONALD: the need to increase the availability of user assistance in an atmosphere of decreasing staff support. Unable to augment our reference hours in response to increasing use and user requests, we saw the development of an information network as providing a much-needed increase in available assistance without incurring a corresponding increase in staffing costs. As human costs increase and hardware costs decrease, we see networked information systems as an excellent approach to the expansion of library services.

Another important concern was that of system security for DONALD. In serving a major engineering college, our library staff have experienced a number of incidents wherein users have reconfigured software and hardware on CD-ROM workstations, public access terminals, or staff microcomputer workstations. In developing DONALD we were, therefore, alert to possible user tampering. The LAN configuration allowed us to grant slave terminals read-only access, thus removing the opportunity for users to alter the system. We removed the keyboards from the file servers to prevent unauthorized access to programs and files on the network.

The development of DONALD is phase one of a three phase program to develop user-assisted informational systems in the University of Michigan Libraries. In designing this prototype, we chose an approach that would be expandable to accommodate additional terminals and added functions. Hence, while cost and system security were important criteria in choosing a LAN, this third factor was the consideration of greatest importance. The University of Michigan Libraries, like other large academic libraries, are exploring ways to enhance the accessibility of their Online Public Access Catalogs (OPACs). With the investment of millions of dollars to develop MIRLYN, an online catalog and multiple database system utilizing NOTIS software, the University of Michigan Libraries face the difficult task of providing assistance to remote users who know the Library through a computer, rather than a human, interface. DONALD provides a system that can provide these users with needed assistance on a point-of-need basis, though the system does not have access to MIRLYN at this time. The heavy use of networked Macintosh microcomputers on the Michigan campus means that our system can be installed in library and non-library LANs across campus to provide much needed remote reference to campus users.

This venture allowed us to develop new roles for librarians and library school students in innovating projects in automation. To this end, several members of the team attended classes on HyperCard programming, networks, and other areas of automation as a first step in beginning the project. This core group of individuals with the interest and desire to develop skills needed for this particular project will continue to learn and gain experience. These human resources provide contacts and trainers for others in the library system who wish to pursue similar efforts. In addition, further creative and significant endeavors can now be developed by these individuals and others in the University of Michigan Libraries. Staff education in microcomputer technology continues to be an emphasis, both for team members and others in the Engineering/Transportation Library.

User Definition

The network provides multiple patron access to a HyperCard reference support application. Patrons at the Engineering/Transportation Library fall primarily into three groups. Students and faculty from all of the departments of the Engineering College use the library for research, instruction, online searches, materials requests, and a number of other services. Individuals or companies from the large local business community rely on the library to supplement their own resources, as well as to supply instruction in searching patents and other literatures. Lastly, private individuals often use the library's resources to access our special collections, such as patents and standards, or to use MIRLYN. Their needs range from starting their own business to repairing a radio.

The College of Engineering at the University of Michigan relies heavily upon Macintosh microcomputers in computer labs and in classroom instruction. As a result, our primary users have a higher level of ability in using computers and a well developed sense of their information needs. Later, a new group of users consisting of staff and librarians will arise as more applications and workstations are added to the network for training and administrative tasks.

Networking with Macintosh: Overview and Equipment Used

Apple provides its users with a powerful, yet easily-managed system for networking, called the AppleTalk Network System (ANS). The ANS hardware and software standards allow Macintosh computers to interconnect with each other, printers, and other peripherals. LocalTalk is only one of the network types available in ANS. All Macintosh systems include built-in ANS and LocalTalk support. Computers using ANS may use ordinary unshielded twisted-pair cabling—the type of wiring available in most buildings for the telephone system.

AppleShare

A Macintosh network may also include a server to facilitate the administration of the network and to provide network users with additional disk storage for data files and software. We used AppleShare as our server software, though there are others from which to choose. AppleShare requires a Macintosh system that is dedicated as a server. No other program can be running or accessed by the operator at an AppleShare server. Other workstations on the network can be set to access any of the programs or files on the server. Mark Veljkov has written a very good book called *MacLANs: Local Area Networking with the Macintosh* (1988) which provides reviews, addresses, and comparisons for a wide range of Macintosh networking products. Also, see our discussion of network installation for more detail.

CSMA/CA

On a technical point, it is important to note the way all information on the network is handled by LocalTalk and Farallon's PhoneNet systems. ANS uses Carrier Sense Multiple Access with Collision Avoidance (CSMA/CA) to manage access to the network. All the nodes or attachments to the network compete for the ability to transmit over the network. Controlling and organizing access is necessary to allow data to be transferred in an error free and uniform manner. CSMA/CA performs three main functions; it checks for ongoing transmissions before sending information which is divided into parts called packets (carrier sense), allows multiple users to access the server, and generally prevents more than one node from transmitting at the same time (collision avoidance). This works well, but plain ANS, LocalTalk, and Farallon's PhoneNet (which we use with DONALD), are comparatively slow in data transmission. They only transfer data at 234 kilobits per second. ANS can also be used with an Ethernet, which, at 10 megabits per second, is a faster network protocol, and it can be used with many different machines. However, an expansion board and additional software are needed for a Macintosh to be able to use Ethernet.

LocalTalk vs PhoneNet

The distance either LocalTalk or PhoneNet can be used in a network without repeaters is limited. Repeaters reamplify a signal and must be used when the total length of a cable segment exceeds the limitations of the network equipment. Farallon's PhoneNet wiring system supports greater cable lengths without repeaters than does Apple's own LocalTalk scheme. Whether you have a LocalTalk or PhoneNet system depends upon the type of connector box you buy. Connector boxes attach to a node at a printer port and allow a cable to be attached linking the node to the network. LocalTalk is limited to 1,000 feet in total network length without repeaters; PhoneNet can be extended to 3,000 feet in a star topology, or 2,000 if used in a serial topology.

Due to the size of our needs and relative uniqueness of the system chosen, the task of equipment selection was fairly simple. We identified our hardware and software needs after brief consultation with our library systems staff.

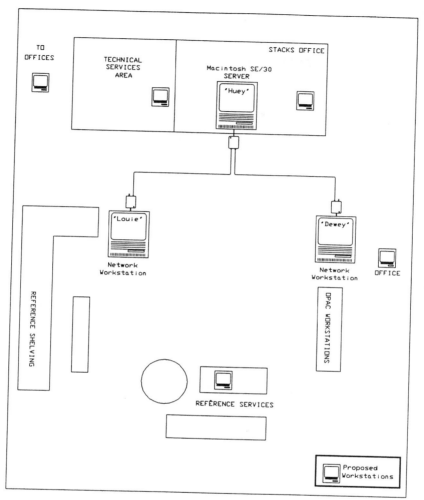

Figure 3.1
The Donald Network:
University of Michigan Engineering/Transportation Library

Network Topology

As illustrated in Figure 3.1, our network is organized in a bus configuration in which the two user stations are connected directly to the server. The center of the network consists of a Macintosh SE/30 with 5MB of RAM and a 40MB hard disk acting as the server, running the AppleShare server software. The twin user stations are Macintosh Plus computers, each with 2MB of RAM, connected to the server by Farallon PhoneNet connectors and regular telephone cable.

Equipment Security

Equipment security is of continuing concern. To protect our workstations, we chose the Qualtec Mac-Kit which fastens securely to the back of each Macintosh and then to the table on which the server or workstation is located (see appendix at the end of the articles for a listing of products and vendors).

Selection and Evaluation Process

Software and programming concerns were the primary factor in the design of DONALD, and the network. As mentioned above, we selected HyperCard for the creation of the reference application. That choice necessitated the use of the Apple Macintosh system. Since most of the other applications we use on a day-to-day basis are also Macintosh based, we can now consider additional networking options.

The skills of the staff factored into the decision as well. None of the individuals involved had experience in setting up a local area network. Our Computing Center personnel recommended the AppleShare network system as being an easy system for individuals new to the process of network creation. This was very important, for it is essential that librarians and interested staff members be able to set up and troubleshoot the network. The AppleShare software takes individuals through installation on a step-by-step basis and provides excellent manuals to answer the majority of the questions that might arise. Also, most of our staff had experience with the Macintosh and felt comfortable using them. As mentioned above, we discussed the costs and memory requirements of the network with our systems department staff. They modified our plans based upon the needs we had presented.

As described above, we chose Farallon PhoneNet connectors since they enable a network to expand over a greater physical distance. This will enable us to expand DONALD as necessary or desirable. The expansion of both the size and the scope of the network is one of our goals.

HyperCard

HyperCard itself incorporates many features of the more common applications available on the Macintosh. It also provides a very good medium for including text and graphics as well as the incorporation of other media. Due to these factors, the simplicity of its programming language (HyperTalk), and its cost, or lack of cost, we selected the HyperCard interface for this project. HyperCard is bundled as a free piece of software for purchasers of Macintosh computers .

Other libraries and library schools have used HyperCard for a number of applications ranging from front ends to public catalogs to managing multimedia presentations. Library tours are also a popular use of the application. We see our project as the first step in combining some of the more beneficial uses of HyperCard into a truly unique and integrated reference tool for the user and staff. Since HyperCard can be easily networked, the large number of Macintosh networks in public sites offer us the opportunity to reach a very large number of users.

How the System is Used

In March 1990 the Engineering Library decided to begin a project using HyperCard which would provide information and instructional reference. As the system neared completion, we decided to make the application available through a network, for the reasons stated in our goals above. The system runs the HyperCard application created by librarians and library school students in the Engineering/Transportation Library. It provides reference support in a number of areas relevant to our library. Most notable are sections on the use of our online catalog, patent and standard literature, and the locations of materials and special collections within the library.

Macintosh SE/30 computer including keyboard and memory upgrade	$2300.00
Macintosh Plus computer (as above)	$1625.00
Installation of memory upgrades	$ 180.00
Farallon PhoneNet connectors (3)	$ 00.00
400 ft. of telephone wire and 10 connectors	$ 45.00
HyperCard version 1.2.5 (Bundled with computers)	$ 0.00
AppleShare LAN software	$ 420.00
Qualtec Mac-Kit security kits (3 kits)	$ 90.00
TOTAL	$4660.00

Table 3.1
Donald Network Costs

The need to evaluate the system and generate data on how patrons use it prompted us to develop several evaluation criteria. By having the HyperCard application create a new file every time the main body program is opened, and closing when the idle screen signals a resetting of the system, we can determine a number of important points about both the application and the network. The application creates different files for each of the two workstations, with beginning and ending times and paths individuals take within HyperCard to find information. We thus are able to determine:

1. how many times a particular section or card has been used,
2. the amount of time for each session, and
3. how a particular user followed a path or sequence to get information.

The data will also tell us which terminal gets more use and may prompt our moving a workstation to a place of higher traffic. In the future, we plan to partition the hard disk and include a number of applications for staff use. These will include word processing, graphics, database, and spreadsheet applications. By placing the

HyperCard application on a network, we will significantly increase the utility of our existing resources.

Costs of the Network

We present a breakdown of the approximate hardware and software costs for the network in Table 3.1. Librarians performed the actual installation of the network and its wiring, avoiding considerable labor costs.

Installation and Implementation of the Network

Network installation began with the readying of the SE/30 to act as a server. Our Systems office had already set up the hard disk, so we needed to install the AppleShare 2.0 server software. AppleShare is relatively easy to install. It comes with two main installation disks, the AppleShare File Server: Server Installer and the AppleShare File Server: Server Administration disks. To install the computer to be used as a server, it must first be booted from the Server Installer disk. The desktop for the disk appears on the screen, and the Installer application must be chosen. A screen asks what items need to be installed. The choices include the server software itself, the system (though ours had already been installed) and EtherTalk. EtherTalk is provided to enable the network to be an Ethernet instead of LocalTalk or PhoneNet, but a card is still needed. That is all that is involved for the first stage of installation.

The server then needs to be restarted from the Server Administration disk. The program presents a short series of questions and messages which allows you to prepare the startup volume for the server. It then asks you to create a Users and Groups file to save information concerning those accessing the network. You are then queried as to the name which you wish the server to be called, and prompted for an Admin key. This password is very important for it allows the system operator to enter the administration module of AppleShare and modify access privileges. You are also asked to prepare other volumes such as hard disks or CD-ROMs if you have them available on the network. Three windows open on the screen at this point: the User List, the Group List, and a user information window. You are prompted to enter the system administrators name and password, so that the administrator can access the system and all the necessary files from the network. This also prevents others from seeing or modifying files in files and folders other than those they are authorized to use. Two options are also presented. "Login enabled" allows the administrator to access the network, and "All Privileges" provides the administrator with the ability to make changes to any folder or volume. The choice of this option may cause interference with other users if they are using a file that the administrator is trying to modify.

At this point, the server needs to be restarted once again so that the administrator may add users or groups and folders. The machine reboots with the server status window up, which lists the server name, a list of volumes, the current date, users, and an activity meter. Choose Administration from the Server menu, and you are then prompted for the Admin key. From the User's menu, select Create User or Create Group. Enter the user's or group's password, and make sure the Login Enabled option is selected. If you are creating a group, you will need to create the individual user files first, then drag their icons into the members box of the group window. Saving the changes made as you go along is important, and should be done after any addition to the Users and Groups file.

Creating folders is done by selecting File & Folder Info from the Folders Menu, and then clicking New Folder. The administrator automatically becomes the owner. A name needs to be assigned to the folder, and access privileges assigned. A group can be assigned at this time by dragging the particular group icon you want to the group box under the owner name, just as you did to assign users to groups. There are three user categories and three privileges, and these can be combined any number of ways. The three user categories include the owner of the folder, the group assigned to it, or everyone that can log in to the server. The three privileges are See Folders, which allows one to see all other folders in a particular folder, See Files, allowing a user to see files in the folder and copy and open those files as needed unless they are copy protected, and Make Changes, which is the privilege to change the folders contents by such means as moving, deleting, or creating files. AppleShare also provides reports concerning how the server is being used. It is useful for keeping track of traffic on the network and the particular activities of the users.

We loaded our programs and HyperCard applications onto the hard disk before loading the server software. We needed two copies of the HyperCard programs, one for each workstation. This was needed because a program cannot be in two places at once if it is being used to run a file. Our actual application was in a folder that allowed no changes to be made, so it could be accessed at both terminals.

We discussed the best locations for the workstations and ordered security cords to protect them in the public area. We located our server in the Engineering / Transportation Library's Technical Services area to protect it and placed a sign on it warning individuals to keep away from the machine. We decided to place the workstations at opposite ends of the reference area where reference staff could see patrons in case they were having trouble with the system.

We also considered contracting for system wiring, but decided that Engineering / Transportation Library staff would install the wiring themselves. We accomplished this in about 4 hours, running the wire above the ceiling tiles. We then tested the network and connections in the Technical Services area and familiarized ourselves with accessing the server from the workstations.

After the server is set up, the workstation boot disks needed to be prepared. We copied the very basic system files onto the disks. Next, we booted the server from the AppleShare File Server Workstation Installer disk. After selecting the Install application, we copied an AppleShare Chooser application into the system folder of the disks. This allows the systems on the workstations to access the server by using the Chooser under the Apple icon menu on the extreme upper left corner of the Desktop menu. The left part of the window shows both the icon for AppleShare and icons for any printers on the network. To connect to a server, the person setting up the connection must click on the AppleShare icon, and a list of available servers appears in the upper right corner of the window. After highlighting the server name, clicking the OK box prompts the system to ask for a password. A user can login under a name or group if they are registered on the server, or as guest if they are not. Guest users have no ownership of the folders or files they create, so anyone can delete or change them. After logging in, you are queried to select a volume. With this done, a server icon appears on the right side of the desktop under the startup disk icon and can be accessed like any other Macintosh disk. We took some time to learn more about the system, train staff, and pretest the system down prior to making DONALD public. We installed the workstations in the public area approximately two weeks later when the security cables arrived.

Evaluation

The system has lived up to all of the expectations. Patrons have been using the tool extensively and feedback from our evaluation forms has been good, both in terms of positive responses and suggested changes. A more complete study of both the forms and statistics files generated by DONALD is underway at the time this article is being written. Presently in-house seminars are planned to involve more individuals in understanding the actual administration of the network. The application and the success of the network itself has attracted the support of the administration and the Undergraduate, Chemistry, and Medical Libraries have been targeted as sites for expansions of the system. This was a major goal in bringing customized technology into the library system.

Future Developments

With the development of Phase I of the HyperCard Project we submitted a budget initiative proposal to the library administration to fund future expansion. In Phase II, we will develop HyperCard modules for the Undergraduate, Chemistry, and Medical Libraries. These branches vary greatly in target clientele, size, and reference/instructional needs. We plan to include in Phase II a feasibility analysis of expanding the system to include the Graduate Library, which houses the bulk of Michigan's 6.3 million titles. We envision Phase II as creating three new LANs in these dispersed libraries, but plan to consider options for bridging the LANs to each other or to other university networks. Also in Phase II, we begin to consider how we might interface these HyperCard networks to the MIRLYN system and provide a constantly available reference window for users of the University of Michigan OPAC. This type of workstation we termed an "information kiosk."

We ultimately aim to provide an informational interface to the electronic resources at the University of Michigan as Phase III. The development of assistance programming establishes the basis of a platform which might eventually link MIRLYN with other campus databases, electronic mail, Internet databases, and other electronic resources. For our staff, the establishment of a small local area network provides the first lessons in system management and distributed information systems.

We believe that this project and future plans will enable our libraries and librarians to continue to play a major role in the ongoing development of the information infrastructure at the University of Michigan. For the University of Michigan Libraries, it offers a new approach to assisting the growing number of remote users. For the campus as a whole, it offers a readily exportable short-term project and a new way to help manage the morass of databases and data files now clogging the University network.

Vendors and Products

Apple Computer, Inc.
20525 Mariani Ave.
Cupertino, CA 95014
AppleShare File Server software
HyperCard
AppleTalk Network System
LocalTalk Macintosh
SE/30 Macintosh Plus

Farallon Computing, Inc.
2000 Powell Street
Suite 600
Emeryville, CA 94608
PhoneNet connectors

Qualtec Data Products Inc.
47767 Warm Springs Blvd.
Fremont, CA 94539
Qualtec Mac-Kit

Bibliography

AppleShare File Server Administrator's Guide. 1988. Cupertino, Ca: Apple Computer.
Macintosh Reference. 1989. Cupertino, Ca: Apple Computer.
PhoneNet Connector User's Guide. 1988. Emeryville, CA: Farallon Computing.
Veljkov, Mark D. 1988. *MacLANs: Local Area Networking with the Macintosh.* Glenview, IL: Scott, Foresman and Company.

About the Authors

James Alloway received his B.A. (History) from the University of Kansas in 1986 and his M.L.S. from Emporia State University in 1989. He is presently in the position of Assistant Librarian, Basic Science and Engineering Libraries Cluster and a member of the University of Michigan Library Resident Program.

Robert Schwarzwalder received his B.S. (Botany) from Louisiana State University in 1979, M.L.S. and Ph.D. (Biology) from Indiana University in 1986. He has held the position of Information Services Coordinator for the University of Michigan Basic Science and Engineering Libraries since December 1990.

4

Networking from the Ground Up: Implementing Macintosh Networks in a Newly-Constructed Arts Library

Robert Skinner
The Jake and Nancy Hamon Arts Library, Southern Methodist University

ABSTRACT

The construction of a new arts library provided librarians at Southern Methodist University with the opportunity to articulate in three dimensions many of our views of what libraries should be as we near the beginning of the twenty- first century. Computers and networks were integral to this project, and built upon our existing experience and satisfaction with Macintosh equipment. Plans were developed for a library information network, and a variety of options were explored related not only to internal communication, but also connectivity with the campus online library system and the Internet.

Introduction

The building of a new library offers a variety of opportunities related to computer networking which may never be accomplished so effectively again in the life span of the building. First, and most obviously, the facility can be designed in such a way that computers can be interconnected at any point in the building. Second, the design process will encourage librarians to identify what networks are needed now and in the future, not only because of the impact of these decisions on the building design stage, but because considerable start-up money may be available now as part of the construction process. At Southern Methodist University, the construction of the Jake and Nancy Hamon Arts Library provided both these opportunities.

Description of the Hamon Arts Library

The Hamon is a four floor facility of approximately 10,000 square feet per floor. The Library employs nine full-time staff including three professional librarians and approximately five F.T.E. student workers. The majority of the staff are located on the first floor in two main areas: Circulation/Information Desk/Workroom and an Office Library Suite. On the second floor is a Special Collections unit. The basement houses an Audio Visual Center and a Computer Lab. The Library contains a rapidly growing collection of some 70,000 books, scores, and bound periodicals, 16,000 recordings, and 100,000 pieces of special collections materials in the areas of art, cinema, dance, music, and theater. The Hamon provides space for 300 readers or about 40 percent of our primary user population.

The Hamon is part of the Central University Libraries which includes the main library supporting humanities, business, and the social sciences, Science/Engineering library, Special Collections, University Archives, and the Institute for Study of Earth and Man. The Central University Libraries provides centralized ordering and cataloging for all member libraries, as well as interlibrary loan and bindery assistance for the Hamon. Three other parts of the SMU library system which are not part of the Central University Libraries are the Theology and Law Libraries and an automation department which currently consists of a director, an assistant, and one programmer.

The Hamon Library is a wing off of the Owen Fine Arts Center which houses classrooms, offices, studios, and performing spaces for the Meadows School of the Arts. When the Hamon was built, extensive remodeling was done in part of Owen, including adding electronic mail capabilities with the Hamon.

Network Design

A primary concern for our network was that it be based on the Macintosh family of microcomputers. Although the ideal in any networking project would be to start without any preconceptions or constraints, reality probably always dictates otherwise. In our case, because of the amount of existing software supporting our arts curriculum, some of which we had developed internally, we were committed to Apple equipment in general, and the Macintosh environment in particular. The Macintosh's built-in networking capability made them especially appealing.

Second, our campus has the NOTIS automated library system which is available to us via a fiber optic campus backbone and various communication devices in our campus computer center. This also dictated some of our decisions, since we wanted NOTIS to be available, at least potentially, on any networked computer in the library.

Third, we wanted every staff person to have a computer, which suggested that we should explore electronic mail and other workgroup oriented software. Concomitantly, because our library is a wing on a classroom building, we wanted to interconnect our staff via electronic mail with existing departmental and administrative networks.

Finally, we were strong believers in the workstation concept for public computers: i.e., combining as many functions, NOTIS access, online and CD-ROM services, information directories, tutorials, electronic mail between staff and patrons, and such, at one terminal. While many of these functions have yet been implemented, we do currently have three local area networks running with a fourth scheduled to come online by 1991-1992.

Planning of the system was done by the Head of the Hamon Arts Library and the Director of the Meadows School of the Arts Computer Lab. Valuable help was supplied by the Director of Campus Automation, and several members of the staff of our Campus Computer Center.

Building Wiring

Since our networking project was integrated with the construction of a new library facility, specification and installation of cabling was a primary concern from early in the schematic phases of the design process. Both the campus computer center and the architect's engineers agreed it was important the Hamon conform to the accepted standards defined by AT&T. The Premises Distribution System (PDSP) standard is the design concept used commonly by all AT&T voice and data communication products. Following this standard, data and voice lines connect the building to the campus fiber optic Information Systems Network (ISNP, an AT&T network environment) via a utility tunnel connecting with the basement. In addition to the ISN distribution, all internal networks and the building telephone system in the Hamon feed via conduit through the riser closets. A series of four riser closets distribute cabling vertically. Horizontal distribution is accomplished by several means: where possible, conduit is run directly through all exterior and interior walls. To allow for future expansion in open areas, such as stacks, conduit was run to every column. Where structural supports precluded routing conduit to areas where we knew there would be a large concentration of computers, such as the OPAC terminals in the stacks, floor trenches were installed.

Expansion space was also allowed in the riser closets by using four six inch sleeves punched into the flooring and ceiling. This should be more than sufficient to install fiber optics later. We were advised to run fiber vertically from the very beginning even though the horizontal distribution would be via twisted-pair. This decision, however, somehow got lost in the shuffle.

Installation of the conduit and trenches was the job of the building contractor. Pull strings were left in the conduit for the use of the wiring contractor. AT&T was hired by us to do the actual wiring to current and future locations of computers and telephones.

We chose to use unshielded twisted-pair wiring which would accommodate both the AppleTalk networks initially planned as well as 10BaseT Ethernet in the future. As we suspect that it may be desirable to convert eventually to fiber optics, we provided extensive amounts of conduit, even though we could have used plenum rated twisted-pair at less cost.

In most cases, the wiring terminates in what we call "superboxes." A "superbox" consists of a five-gang box containing three sets of power duplexes and two sets of voice data jacks (RJ-45). Of the power outlets, one pair provides clean power, the other two, normal. The four RJ-45s can serve as voice, data, or ISN connections, depending upon whether we pulled two or four pair of wire. Because we had some 115 data/voice outlets in the Hamon, even twisted-pair running over four floors could be quite expensive, so we carefully identified what wires were required to each box, leaving pull strings in place for pulling wire for future needs.

With only a few exceptions, we did not use superboxes in public areas. Our OPACs are all located in carrels: built-in millwork carrels on the main floor, and modified study carrels on the other three floors. All use divided gateways for power and data/voice, which run underneath the carrel surfaces. From the OPAC terminals, data wires go down through a grommet in the carrel surface to a surface mounted jack box which has been attached over a punchout at the appropriate place on the raceway. The surface mounted box takes an RJ-45 connector, providing complete compatibility with the rest of our wiring. Cable comes into the raceway via flex conduit going down to a floor box which penetrates one of the previously mentioned floor trenches. One problem we had with the "superboxes" was finding a cover plate that would work. Since the architect's engineers had designed the "superbox," we set them to finding one which they eventually did.

If we had this stage of the process to do over again, we would have tried to settle upon a network wiring system earlier in the design process. In our Computer Center, for example, the engineers designed floor trenches to accommodate twisted-pair for every one of our 16 computer stations going back to the riser closet and on to other locations in the Lab. In actuality, each of the computers is daisy chained to the next, rather than back each time to the riser closet. Initially, no provision was made for floor outlets for our second and third floor OPACs because the trenches were somehow perceived as being there to cover future rather than current needs.

Although the riser closets seem to be sufficiently large (3 feet wide by 6 feet long), we unknowingly approved two design mistakes. Had we known the amount of data and telephone equipment which would go into the riser closets, particularly in the basement, we would have installed at least two power duplexes on the top three floors, and four duplexes in the basement. Second, none of the riser closets are air-conditioned spaces, which posed ventilation problems considering the amount of data and telephone equipment in the basement. Actually, in our defense, we had planned to use an adjacent area behind some stairs for an equipment room until we found that this violated fire code.

The jury is still out on whether the "superboxes" are overkill. While several of us have had our power needs already exceed, at least temporarily, the six outlets provided, we should have priced adding the third duplex versus an external power strip individually as required. The four data/voice jacks are also questionable in light of future developments such as ISDN. While most staff are using three of the four jacks as described below, the campus is considering a new telephone system which will offer ISDN-like capabilities by simultaneously accommodating both data and voice over the same line, consequently allowing one or two jacks to do the work of four. Our problem was that we had to have three jacks now in order to function, and it may be several years before the new phone system is installed. Nevertheless, there may have been a cheaper compromise between current and future needs.

Campus and Internal Network Protocols

Our connection to the mainframe allows us to provide NOTIS for the public and NOTIS and Internet access for staff. The public NOTIS connections are currently handled via a concentrator located in the basement riser closet. The concentrator is connected via SMU's fiber optic network to the Main Fiber Cross Connect in the Physical Plant and from there to the campus computer center.

An alternative connection for staff is through the Ethernet portion of the fiber optic network. A Shiva FastPath 4 Gateway, again in the basement riser closet, allows computers on an AppleTalk network access to an Ethernet network running TCP/IP. Why the FastPath box? While several reports rated it the best of the Ethernet gateways, in actuality, the FastPath box was supplied by the computer center as its part in standardizing networking across campus.

Staff Macintosh systems interconnect via an AppleTalk network, using Farallon StarControllers to link computers in an active star topology. Instead of LocalTalk cabling between our data jacks and the computer, the Hamon chose to use the equally reliable but much less expensive PhoneNet connectors, also from Farallon. As described in the Apple Multivendor Work Solutions Guide, Apple Computer, 1990:

> . . .the PhoneNET StarController Series 300 hub is a multi-port LocalTalk repeater users mount in the telephone wiring closet. The hub connects all network devices together in a star configuration, repeating and amplifying signals over existing telephone wire or ordinary twisted-pair cable. The StarController is managed with StarCommand 2.0 software, and runs as a background application under MultiFinder, automatically notifying network managers of problems.

Although we had no idea when we were first thinking about the system, it eventually became apparent that we would need four StarControllers—one in each riser closet. Distance limitations required this, particularly those connections which go outside the Library to other parts of the Arts School. Additionally, multiple StarControllers allow for one user per port (there are 11 ports per controller) which the manufacturer recommends for optimum network performance. It also allows for considerable expansion and for ease in troubleshooting.

Wiring is distributed via three 110 blocks on every floor: one for data (that is, internal LANs), one for voice (that is, our Merlin II telephone system), and one for ISN connections via the fiber optic concentrator back to our campus computer center. Every connection on the block is clearly identified by a number which is also repeated on the jack where the connection terminates. Jacks which are data are prefixed by a "D," voice by a "V," and ISN by an "N" (for NOTIS). These prefixes represent how the jacks are currently being utilized. The 110 blocks together with the number of wire pairs pulled allow us to easily change a data jack into a voice or ISN connection as required in the future.

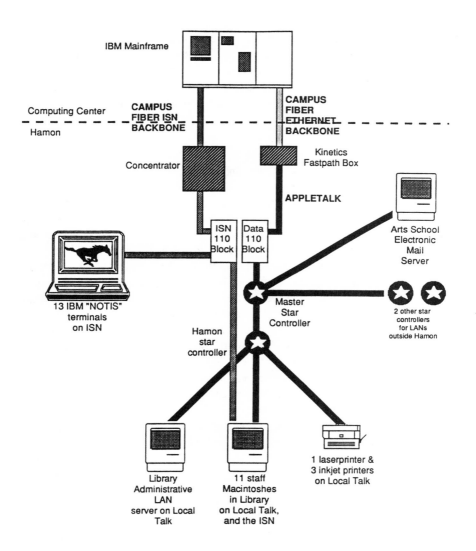

Figure 4.1
Hamon Arts Library Network

File servers use AppleShare 2.0 which was our networking software of choice. Each file server is a Macintosh SE/30 with 4 megabytes of RAM and an 80 megabyte hard disk drive. All are protected by uninterruptible power supplies with 20 minutes of backup power. In our previous experience, AppleShare has proved remarkably robust, even after unexpected shutdowns.

Local area network administration is the responsibility of the Director of the Computer Lab. All servers are contained in a single room to facilitate management and troubleshooting. The Director can run from his computer the program Star Command Traffic Watch to monitor network activity and identify problems. In its first nine months of operations, the network has been relatively trouble-free since installation.

OPAC

Currently, we have six OPAC terminals which are networked to the NOTIS system on the campus mainframe. We initially used Macintosh computers in anticipation of adding the public LAN. In recognition of the time this is likely to take, we have just made the decision to replace all of the existing OPAC Macintoshes with IBM 3151 monochrome terminals This will give us a total of eleven OPAC terminals, five on the first floor, two each on the remaining three. In addition, we will have four Macintoshes with color monitors (one IIcx on the first floor, and one Mac LC for the rest) on which to run our public information network as portions of it come online.

When the Hamon first opened, we opted to have the OPAC Macintoshes use dedicated connections to NOTIS which always went through the same port in the computer center. This method requires a more complicated login procedure and caused fairly constant problems. We eventually switched to a simpler connection method which uses any available port. This is not a problem in the mornings when few users are competing for mainframe resources, but can prevent us from logging on later in the day. Fortunately, there are a variety of ways to gain access to a port on the system, so this has rarely been a problem.

For NOTIS connections on the ISN which use the Macintosh, we run Tincan, a low cost telecommunication program developed at Yale University. Tincan is robust, allows printing, supports the ALA character set, and provides eight buttons which can be programmed to duplicate function keys. We used the capabilities of Tincan itself to disable all of its buttons (except on OPAC stations connected to printers) and the program ResEdit 2.1 to disable all of the menu options except for Quit. We also stripped the system files down to the bare minimum although every couple of weeks we find that someone has played around with the settings and these have to be reset. The program Pyro! published by Fifth Generation Systems is used as a screen saver set in the marquee mode to scroll the message "Welcome to PONI. Press any key to continue." PONI is SMU's name for our NOTIS implementation.

Public LAN: A Future Project

Our original goal was to have a public local area network supplying a variety of services (see below). Unfortunately, lack of staff time caused by chronic understaffing has delayed this project.

Once implemented, the public LAN will integrate a variety of information resources, including building directories, guides to area arts events, extensive tutorials on the use of the library and its collections, and electronic mail between patrons and staff and students and faculty. The electronic mail capability will allow patrons to send interlibrary loan and new acquisition requests automatically to the appropriate department. A community bulletin-board will sport such features as a "For Sale" section. Faculty will be able to electronically post assignments and reading lists for students. And, in the near future, it should be possible for students to send completed class assignments electronically to faculty. Some machines will allow patrons access to several popular software programs, such as Microsoft Word, in the library's stacks as well as the computer lab. One Macintosh will support CD-ROMs and, eventually, public access to remote commercial databanks which patrons can search themselves.

CD-ROM Applications

We would like to network CD-ROMS and online access as soon as feasible. Online access is easily solvable through networked modems such as the Shiva NetModem V2400 which we already own. Networking CD-ROMs, indeed even running library-related CD-ROMs in a Macintosh environment is a difficult proposition in comparison to the PC world. As long as the CD-ROMs are ISO 9660 compliant, Insignia Solution's SoftPC EGA/AT will run most of the MS-DOS based search engines. This software allows the Macintosh to run transparently MS-DOS software as if it had a 80286 CPU and an EGA graphics card. For example, we have successfully run the Wilson Index CD-ROMs using SoftPC and an Apple CD-ROM player. We are currently experimenting with the Pioneer 6 CD-ROM changer which will at least allow access to multiple CD-ROMs from multiple sites. This player may exhibit speed problems, since only one user can access the changer at anyone time.

Access to NOTIS Through the Macintosh Interface

We had originally envisioned HAL, the Hamon Arts Library information network, as allowing access to NOTIS. Although we were aware of the work done at Cornell University with MacPac, it appeared that the MacNOTIS HyperCard based software being developed at Texas A&M University would be best.

The appeal of MacNOTIS is two fold: (1) It substitutes an event-driven system for the more cumbersome command-line based interface that characterizes NOTIS. Such a system can have the effect of simplifying the use of NOTIS while at the same time offering the opportunity of adding enhancements; (2) Because MacNOTIS is a HyperCard stack, it is possible to integrate MacNOTIS into a larger information network. In the Hamon, this information network will provide building directories, events calendars, online tutorials, e-mail between patrons and staff, and other enhancements. The ease of making modifications in HyperCard has, in fact, allowed us to experiment with a slightly different front-end metaphor, and we are now testing a version of MacNOTIS which we have modified to substitute buttons for menus, and which appears to be more intuitive for users not familiar with the Macintosh.

We have not yet implemented MacNOTIS, however, for a variety of reasons. MitemView is intended to hide communications from a host mainframe behind a Macintosh-like front end. The MitemView system interprets mainframe data by matching to previously identified screen patterns. The NOTIS screens are in considerable flux on our campus and MacNOTIS has not functioned well here as of yet. Because NOTIS 5.x makes radical changes in screen design, we have also delayed implementation because so many of the patterns will have to be redone.

MacNOTIS desperately needs to be ported to HyperCard 2.0. The X-Commands currently used by the MitemView component of MacNOTIS do not function with HyperCard 2.0. Texas A&M is currently working on the modifications to MacNOTIS so that will run with the new release of HyperCard. Once complete, the upgraded MacNOTIS system should add considerable robustness to the interface in an unsupervised public setting because of HyperCard 2.0's greater error-trapping facilities. For example, under HyperCard 2.0 one can disable the Command+Period interrupts, the standard key combination in the Macintosh world for canceling functions. HyperCard 2.0 should also allow MacNOTIS to run faster. Currently, MacNOTIS performs poorly on 68000-based Macintoshes. It runs satisfactorily only on systems such as our Mac IIcx's and SE/30's with 68030 processors with 9600 baud connections to the NOTIS system. With the possibility of the Mac Classic functioning as a diskless workstation, the possibility of using Mac Classics as OPAC terminals is highly appealing. Through educational discounts, Apple makes these systems available to the University at a cost of under $800 each.

There are several ways to improve the performance of the MacNOTIS interface. One would be to break up HyperCard's own HyperTalk code to take advantage of the program's native compiler. Improved X-Commands could be used to speed up bottlenecks. Furthermore, we encourage MitemView to add direct support for TCP/IP networking protocols into their software to take advantage of the faster networking throughput. MitemView has recently added IBM 3270 terminal emulation to their product.

An alternative Macintosh interface to NOTIS, not based on HyperCard, which we are currently investigating is Connectivit 3270. As their brochure states, it is a "front-end development environment for mainframe applications [which] enables the user to customize any IBM 3270 program into a user-friendly Macintosh application in a matter of hours." This specialized 4GL (Fourth Generation Language) program would probably be most useful for providing a user-friendly front end to the technical service side of NOTIS, particularly Circulation, but we will also test it on the public OPAC side, as well.

In both cases, the initial cost for a developer's package is around $1000 plus approximately $100 each per OPAC station for run-time versions.

Staff LAN

All staff, professional and support, have their own microcomputers, minimally, a Macintosh SE with two megabytes RAM and a 40 megabyte hard disk drive. The amount of RAM was chosen in consideration of the memory requirements of System 7.x which was introduced in 1991.

Systems available to staff are: NOTIS, the Internet, internal electronic mail, an electronic in/out board, shared laser printers, and access to file servers for common data files and lesser used application programs. A networked modem was purchased but has not yet been installed because of lack of a phone line.

For connections via the Ethernet, several of the more technically-oriented staff use the NCSA TN3270 program developed by the National Supercomputing Center for normal communication and Brigham Young University's BYU Telnet for anonymous file transfer. Both of these are public domain. These also allow us to transfer our files from the campus Computer Center, allowing, for example, a file of 700K to be received to our local hard disks in approximately one minute.

We carefully evaluated available electronic mail programs, and eventually chose CE Software's Quickmail over its nearest competitor, Microsoft Mail. Quickmail was the system most often used by larger organizations, including Apple itself, and offered numerous gateways to other networks. Since then, Microsoft Mail has become much more competitive. Although we have heard complaints about Quickmail at other sites, the system has worked well enough for the 50 or so of us on it. We estimate that we have cut down on the use of paper memos by at least 90 percent. For practical purposes, all memos, all phone messages, and most drafts of reports and other paper work are handled by electronic mail. Telephone "tag" internally is non-existent. The last category illustrates that electronic mail is more than the name implies, and it is possible to include enclosures (files) with your messages. We also use e-mail to schedule our conference rooms and group studies, by simply updating and forwarding the last schedule as a mail message to everyone concerned.

The most pleasant surprise about electronic mail was how easily all of our staff were able to adapt to it, including those who were new to the Macintosh. File transferring does take some extra training, however, for those not familiar with the Mac. Especially surprising was how well our student workers adapted to it. We depend upon students to take most of our phone messages and this has gone largely without a hitch. They also use it to send messages to the other student workers, for example, when they need to trade hours. Library staff use the system to communicate library policies and procedures to students.

Staff also use CE Software's In/Out program which is available on every computer, and shows which staff are in and which are out, and when they will be returning. While student staff are not included, they do have access to the program which runs as a desk accessory and can tell visitors when staff will be back.

Computer Lab Network

The Hamon Arts Library also houses the Meadows Computer Lab. The Meadows Lab consists of 12 networked Macintosh workstations, including a high-end graphics workstation, high-end music workstation, and multimedia station. The remainder of the machines are Macintosh SEs, each with 2MB of RAM and a 40MB hard disk drive. A variety of software are available in the lab, including three-dimensional graphics packages, music composition and printing software, HyperCard development tools, and packages such as Microsoft Word, Excel, Claris FileMaker Pro, and MacDraw II. Laser, dot matrix, and color inkjet printers are available. The Macintosh LAN functions as a print server, a means of distributing messages to all lab users, and for providing some networked software. In addition to Macintosh computers, the lab also houses six Apple IIe/Apple IIgs computers on a separate LAN to run an impressive library of music theory instructional software (much of which was developed at the Meadows School) that the lab has collected over the past five years.

Adjacent to the Lab, a seven-Macintosh-training facility is available for purposes of training. During the hours when training is not being conducted, faculty may use this area for computing and research. In addition, the training room serves as classroom space for two graduate courses on the role of microcomputers in the fine arts. The Meadows Computer Lab serves as the central facility for the new Center for Instructional Technology in the Arts (CITA).

As of now, the lab is not interconnected to the other networks in the Hamon or Meadows. Eventually this will occur, and at that time we expect to offer a wide range of functions, such as students being able to complete and return computerized assignments to faculty from the lab through the e-mail capabilities that are part of the Meadows computer networks.

Costs

We estimate so far that a little over $70,000 had been spent for our computer network as it relates specifically to the Library. This includes wiring the library proper for 200 voice and data lines (approximately $20,000), three file servers and related equipment ($8000), two StarControllers and network administrative software ($1500), twelve IBM 3151 terminals ($7000), two IBM 3164 color terminals ($2600), eighteen staff and public Macintoshes outside the computer lab with software ($22,000), and additional equipment required either in our riser closets or at our computer center to become part of the campus fiber optic network and insure access to twenty-six ports on the mainframe ($10,000). It does not include expenses related to the building project, such as providing conduit or floor trenches, or for furniture and millwork built-ins.

One on-going expense associated with networks is equipment replacement and maintenance. Because of the robustness of Apple equipment, we have not kept separate maintenance contracts on these, but instead allocated a fixed amount for repair work as the warranties expire. This was done because to keep them under AppleCare, Apple's maintenance agreement, would have been prohibitive. A three-year warranty was negotiated and paid for by the Campus Automation Director for the IBM terminals. Campus automation also rebates maintenance costs for NOTIS related equipment in the Campus Computing Center.

Within the past few months, our Campus Computing Center has been instructed to pursue cost recovery to support maintenance and other expenses through increasing the monthly fee for line charges significantly beyond the $10 per line we have been paying. This is not represented above because line charges are being rebated by the campus automation project. Although nothing yet has been decided, one disturbing aspect is that Ethernet connections may be charged at several times the charge for our ISN connections, making these prohibitive. Regardless, it may be necessary to cut back on the number of lines in the Hamon, including staff stations, which may reduce access to the Internet which these days is a necessity for those librarians intent on staying current.

Evaluation

Networking in libraries can be divided into three stages. The first pre-networking stage is largely characterized by separation of function: that is, one must go to one computer to use the OPAC, a second computer for online searching, a number of computers for CD-ROM, another computer for OCLC or RLIN. The second stage is consolidation, where more than one function is available on a computer, but not necessarily related to one another in any way. The final stage is integration—the scholar's workstation paradigm—where information is shared between all resources, there is a common user interface, multimedia is exploited, and eventually even an artificial intelligence component is incorporated. The Hamon's networks have given staff a partially-integrated system, and every service we initially planned to have available has been accomplished. The equipment we chose has worked well, although only time will tell whether we used more conduit than was necessary or we could have saved money through fewer data jacks. Design flaws in the Premises Distribution System have proven solvable at little expense. Although we recognize the need to provide for going with a faster network than AppleTalk (230.4 KBs), so far we have had no complaints about slow network traffic.

We have not met any of our goals for the public network for the variety of reasons detailed above. This perhaps has been the most important lesson for us: we have failed so far not because we did not have the money for equipment or the expertise to do what we wanted, but because we cannot find the time required. There is reason to believe that we can at least partially achieve our goals for HAL within the 1991-92 school year, but fulfilling the networking needs for the Hamon requires a staffing component that is unlikely to be in place for many years to come. This does not mean that the goals should have been any less worthy; only that we should have been more realistic in which goals could be accomplished.

About the Author

Robert Skinner is Assistant Director for Fine Arts at Southern Methodist University and Head of the Jake and Nancy Hamon Arts Library. He also holds an adjunct teaching appointment in the department of Music where he team-teaches a course on Microcomputers in the Arts. He received degrees in music and librarianship from the University of North Texas where he is currently working on a doctorate in Information Science. Before coming to SMU, he was Recorded Sound Librarian at Harvard University. He has authored a number of articles and papers related to computers and media technology, and is currently editor of the Music Software column for the journal *NOTES* of the Music Library Association.

Skinner has recently accepted a position at the University of California at San Diego as Assistant Head of Research Services where he will be developing interactive multimedia library training software.

5

A Multi-Purpose Macintosh Network in a Health Science Library

Lois M. Bellamy and John T. Silver
Health Science Library, University of Tennessee, Memphis

ABSTRACT

Librarians at the Health Science Library of the University of Tennessee (UT), Memphis use the Macintosh for such functions as word processing, electronic mail, and external and internal database access. These Macintosh microcomputers are networked together in a LocalTalk local area network (LAN) to share a Macintosh II file server, LaserWriters, an ImageWriter II, and a Shiva NetModem. Chained to the file server are six Apple CD-ROM players. These players contain six years of the Macintosh version of MEDLINE on CD-ROM called Knowledge Server. Macintosh workstations located in the library reading room and connected to the LAN are used by the public for searching the Knowledge Server database. A Kinetics FastPath bridge connects the library's LAN to the campus-wide Ethernet network, NetOne. Any Macintosh on the campus connected to NetOne by a FastPath bridge or by an EtherTalk interface card can access the library's file server and search the Knowledge Server database.

Introduction

University of Tennessee (UT), Memphis is the medical center campus in the state-supported UT system, which consists of four campus sites. UT Memphis was founded in 1850 and established as an independent campus in Memphis in 1911 by merging the health science schools of the University previously located in Knoxville and Nashville with several private schools of medicine. Today, UT Memphis is composed of seven colleges: Allied Health Sciences, Dentistry, Graduate Health Sciences, Medicine, Nursing, Pharmacy, and Social Work. Approximately 729 faculty members serve a student body of 1,747 and a house staff of 547. Faculty, students, and staff may work in any of the twenty-six campus buildings and the seven local hospitals affiliated with UT Memphis. The UT Memphis affiliated teaching hospitals, which include more than seven thousand beds and two thousand physicians, serve the population of more than three million people in the counties of five states contiguous to West Tennessee. These medical facilities have made Memphis the regional medical center of the Mid-South area.

The Health Science Library of UT Memphis was established in 1913 with a collection of four hundred medical books. Today, the collections of the UT Memphis Health Science Library and its clinical branch library, Stollerman Library, support the programs of the seven health science colleges and consist of 162,089 bound volumes and 2,111 current journal subscriptions. Since 1985 the Health Science Library has been housed in a building that is completely wired for voice, data, and video transfer. The library shares the building with others, including the computer center. The clinical branch library, Stollerman, is located in a building that houses the clinical faculty and is near the teaching hospitals. Stollerman's users include third and fourth year medical students, residents, fellows, and faculty. The functions of both libraries have been automated using Georgetown University's integrated library system, Library Information System (LIS). In 1990, the libraries were merged with the Departments of Education and Computer Science to form the Department of Health Informatics. The mission of the new department "is to bring together the functions of information technology, scientific communications, and educational technology and allow the synergy among these three functions to strengthen the service base, create an active research program, and improve and enhance the teaching effort." [1].

The computer center, called the Biomedical Information Transfer (BIT) Center, supports the computing, networking, and telecommunicating needs of the university through its two units, Computing Systems and Telecommunications Systems. In 1984, the BIT Center began installation of an Ungermann-Bass Ethernet network, NetOne, to provide access to institutional computing resources. Over 1,750 ports in fifty campus and affiliated hospital buildings are now served by the network. During this same period, the university began to encourage and support the use of the Apple Macintosh microcomputer for local data and word processing. Departmental Macintoshes are in many instances networked together to share resources such as file servers and laser printers. In addition, Macintosh microcomputers across the campus are linked together for resource sharing. This is accomplished by connecting the Macintosh to the campus-wide NetOne network via an Ethernet bridge. Approximately 400 Macintosh microcomputers are connected to NetOne in this manner.

The Apple LocalTalk Network

All Macintoshes contain a hardware interface to a low-speed network called LocalTalk.[2] LocalTalk is similar to Ethernet in that the network consists of a linear bus, with taps for each network station. However, LocalTalk is much slower than Ethernet, with a 230 kilobits per second transfer rate; Ethernet transmits at 10 megabits per second. It is also possible to connect and disconnect stations to LocalTalk without bringing down the network. A LocalTalk network consists of three elements: the interface, the connector box, and the bus (See Figure 5.1). The LocalTalk interface, consisting of electronics and a serial port connector, is built into all Macintosh workstations, most Apple printers, and the Apple IIgs. LocalTalk boards are also available for MS-DOS machines with the original PC bus or the PS/2 bus. The serial port plug is a simple eight pin type, designated DB-8. A LocalTalk connector box plugs into the serial port. The box is about as big as a soap bar. It has a short "pigtail" cable which plugs into the serial port of the network station and two connectors for network cabling. The actual network bus consists of a series of twisted-pair cables running between the connectors.

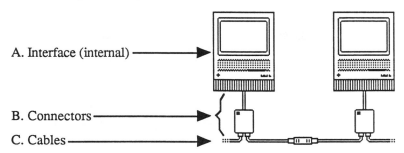

A. Interface (internal)

B. Connectors

C. Cables

Figure 5.1
LocalTalk Network Components

The simplest possible LocalTalk network is a daisy chain in which network connector boxes are attached to each workstation or printer and connected to form the bus. All Apple dealers supply the necessary components and cabling, and the connections can be made in a matter of minutes. The cabling provided by Apple corporation, although functionally the same as the twisted-pair wiring used for telephone wiring, uses non-standard materials and connectors. Consequently, many institutions use components supplied by other vendors, such as the PhoneNet wiring system sold by Farallon Corporation, which allows telephone wiring to be used in the network. UT Memphis has some LocalTalk networks consisting of Apple cabling, others consisting of PhoneNet equipment, and some which are mixtures of the two.

The PhoneNet version of the LocalTalk connector has the RJ-11 modular connectors used in telephone equipment, and the network proper consists of telephone wiring.[3] If the network is a simple daisy chain, the network bus consists of telephone extension cords. The Health Science Library network is too spread out for a simple daisy chain, so the network wiring is installed in the walls. The connection for each network device plugs into a modular jack mounted on the nearest wall. The wiring in the walls is connected in a passive star arrangement by using "punch down blocks": standard telephone wiring equipment that allows many telephone wires to be connected within the telephone switch box (See Figure 5.2). Because the library was able to take advantage of the wiring installed for telephones, it was relatively simple to connect workstations on all floors of the library.

The Health Science Library network is one of forty LocalTalk networks linked by the University NetOne backbone. Gateway devices, consisting of either a dedicated workstation running a bridge software program, or a hardwired device such as the Kinetics FastPath box, are used to link each LocalTalk network to the NetOne backbone (See Figure 5.3). The Macintoshes on all these LocalTalk networks and Macintoshes attached to NetOne directly via an EtherTalk card can access library network services, using AppleTalk networking software.

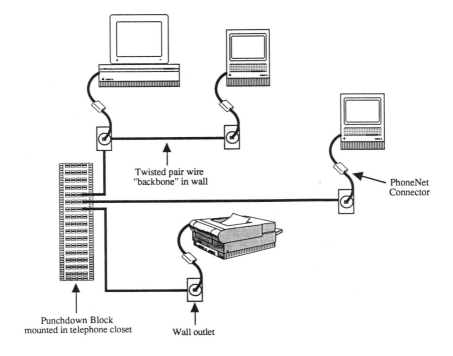

Figure 5.2
Use of Telephone Wiring System for LocalTalk Network

The term "AppleTalk" originally referred to the combination of LocalTalk cabling and the network software which permitted Apple users to share a laser printer. AppleTalk has evolved into a networking system which follows the OSI (Open Systems Interconnection) reference model proposed by the International Standards Organization (ISO). AppleTalk is a hierarchical system in which only the lowest layers of the system need to be aware of the physical characteristics of the network. Thus, most Apple system and application software works the same way with either LocalTalk or EtherTalk connections.

AppleTalk provides for each network device or node to have a user designated name and a unique network number, which the software selects automatically. Apple's LocalTalk cabling has a practical limit of 32 devices. Other types of wiring can handle a larger number of devices; PhoneNet cabling can handle up to 48 devices. Gateway devices also impose limits; the equipment used at UT Memphis handles a maximum of 32 nodes per network.

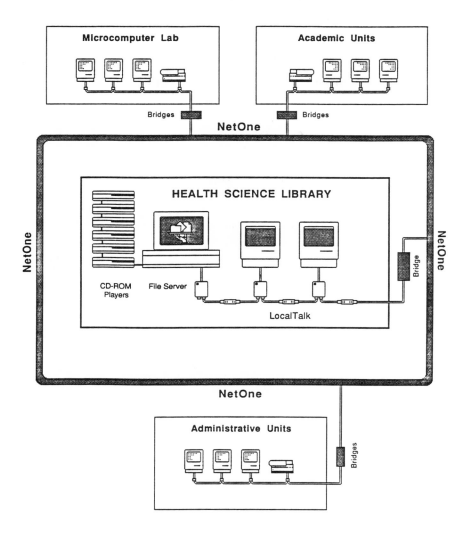

Figure 5.3
UT Memphis NetOne Network System

Although the number of stations per network is limited, a very large number of networks can be linked together through gateways. AppleTalk permits such an internetwork system to be divided into zones. Each zone consists of one or more subnetworks and has its own logical name. UT Memphis has forty-one zones; one for each LocalTalk network and one for EtherTalk users. At UT, a network services group in the BIT Center is responsible for designating network zones and configuring the gateway devices to address them. The numbering of individual network devices, however, is handled automatically. When a network device is turned on, it "broadcasts" a proposed node number to all devices in its zone. If the number is already taken, it randomly chooses a new one. This process guarantees that each station will find a usable number within a few seconds of startup. When a network process starts up, such as transfer of text and graphics from a station to a network printer, a socket number is randomly assigned in the same way.

The easiest way to see the services provided by AppleTalk is to open the Chooser, the standard Macintosh program for handling network and serial connections. Chooser is a desk accessory, so it can be accessed while the user runs other programs. As shown in Figure 5.4, Chooser allows the user to make or break the AppleTalk connection and to type a name for their station ("Tardis"). In addition, Chooser has three windows for selecting network zones and devices. The upper left window displays icons representing different types of network devices, with each icon corresponding to a network driver program in the user's operating system. In the figure, icons for file servers (designated "AppleShare"), a dot matrix printer, a messaging system ("Broadcast"), and a laser printer are shown. The file server icon has been selected, so it is darkened.

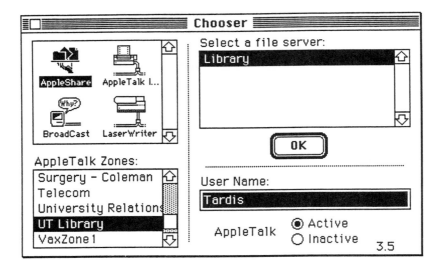

Figure 5.4
An Example of the AppleTalk Chooser

The window on the lower left provides a list of all the current zones, including the Ethernet zone. A zone can consist of one or more LocalTalk networks or a group of Ethernet users. In Figure 5.4, the zone for the UT Library has been chosen. The zone list is constructed dynamically when the user opens Chooser. It provides a quick way for the user to scan new additions to the network (for example, at this writing the Chooser lists a "Pathology–Baptist" zone that is new to the author) and have a laugh (the list currently includes an "End Zone" and an "Ohzone").

The user operates Chooser by selecting the icon of a particular type of device and the name of a particular zone. The program responds by listing all devices of the designated type in the designated zone in a window in the upper right corner. In the figure, the Library file server has been selected. Not shown are windows in which the user enters a network name and password, if necessary, and selects the server volumes to be mounted. Selections made in Chooser are stored by the operating system and used until new selections are made or the station is disconnected from the network.

AppleShare is an extension of AppleTalk that allows a user to access a file server. AppleShare provides special options to the user designated as network administrator. The latter user can create a list of network users and groups, assign network passwords, and provide access to filespace. File access is controlled by creating folders (the Macintosh equivalent of a subdirectory) with appropriate user ownership and privileges. Users can be granted the right to see the files in a folder and to change the contents of a folder. For example, each member of a working group sharing a file server can be assigned a folder with full read and write privileges, read only access to a public area managed by the network administrator, and write only access to folders owned by other members, which thus serve as mailbox type "drop boxes."

The Telecommunication Systems staff of the BIT Center installs and maintains all network wiring at UT Memphis. Each university department manages and maintains the devices including file servers connected to the network. Each LocalTalk outlet installation costs the library approximately $100.00, and each PhoneNet connector from a device to the outlet cost $50.00. The Health Science Library installed 7 outlets and purchased 23 connectors for a total cost of $2850. The Stollerman Library installed 3 outlets and purchased 4 connectors for a total cost of $500.

The installation costs, however, were incurred incrementally. The Health Science Library acquired its first Macintosh in 1987 and installed LocalTalk network connections for 4 Macintosh SE microcomputers in 1988. As of May 1991, there were five public access and three staff Macintosh Plus microcomputers, nine staff Macintosh SE microcomputers, a Macintosh IIsi, a LaserWriter II, a LaserWriter Plus, an ImageWriter II, a Shiva NetModem, and a Macintosh II file server with six Apple CD-ROM players connected to the LAN. Table 5.1 shows the evolution of the library's network. The installation charges for network connections are one-time charges, but the leasing of the Kinetics FastPath boxes is an ongoing cost. Both LocalTalk networks of the Health Science Library and Stollerman Library are connected to the campus-wide NetOne network by FastPath boxes. The BIT Center charges $14/month/device up to a maximum of $168/month for the lease of a FastPath box. The Health Science Library leases the FastPath box for $168/month, and Stollerman Library leases the box for $56/month.

1987	Stollerman Library acquires 2 Macintosh SEs and the Health Science Library acquires 2 Macintosh SEs.
1988	Health Science Library acquires 3 Macintosh SEs and networks 4 Macintosh SEs with the Department of Computer Science LocalTalk network to share a LaserWriter Plus. LocalTalk network is connected to Kinetics FastPath box.
1989	Health Science Library adds 2 Macintosh SEs, 5 Macintosh Pluses, 1 Macintosh II file server with 6 Apple CD-ROM drives, LaserWriter II, and a Shiva NetModem to the LocalTalk network.
1990	3 Macintosh Pluses and 3 Macintosh SEs are added to the Health Science Library LocalTalk network.
1991	Stollerman Library acquires a LaserWriter II and a Macintosh Classic and networks all Macintosh resources. Stollerman LocalTalk network is connected to a Kinetics FastPath box. Health Science Library adds 1 Macintosh IIsi to its network.

Table 5.1
Evolution of the UT Memphis Libraries LocalTalk Networks

Library Uses of the Network

Initially, the library joined the Department of Computer Science's LocalTalk network composed of one Macintosh microcomputer and a LaserWriter. This network was connected to the campus-wide NetOne network by a FastPath bridge. The library installed LocalTalk network connections so that individuals using Macintosh microcomputers would be able to share the use of the LaserWriter for printing teaching materials, letters, and other reports. Because there is a bridge linking the LocalTalk and the NetOne networks, the library staff can also access networked computing resources outside the library without using a modem. We regularly use our networked Macintosh microcomputers to access electronic mail and the library's automated system on the DEC VAX. In early 1990, UT Memphis joined the national network, Internet. Using PacerLink TCP/IP or Mac IP, we are able to access resources such as other university's online catalogs on non-local computers.

Coincident with the installation of the first LocalTalk connections, the library staff began to review MEDLINE CD-ROM products for the purpose of end-user searching. We wanted to install a networked version with multiple CD-ROM drives for the following reasons: (1) more than one person could search MEDLINE simultaneously; (2) disks would not have to be checked out; (3) disks could remain in the drives in a non-public, secure location. Since any Macintosh on the campus connected to NetOne by an Ethernet bridge could access resources on the library's LocalTalk network, the library decided to limit its choice to those CD-ROM products that were compatible with the Macintosh. In 1988, Knowledge Finder produced by Aries Systems Corporation was the only Macintosh MEDLINE CD-ROM product on the market. In February 1989, the main library installed the Macintosh version of MEDLINE on CD-ROM, Knowledge Server. Knowledge Server is the networked version of Knowledge Finder. The system includes six CD-ROM disks, each containing one year of bibliographic entries with abstracts, and Macintosh style search and retrieval software, installed on the library's file server, a Macintosh II. Initially, the file server had 4MB RAM and a 40MB hard drive. Since then we upgraded the file server to 5 MB RAM and a 330MB hard disk. We used the larger hard drive to offload more indexes from the CD-ROM disks in order to speed up access time. Chained to the file server are six Apple CD-ROM players. Five Macintosh workstations and a public access LaserWriter II have been available for use with the system in the library since May 1989. According to Aries, the networked system supports six to twelve simultaneous users without serious search time degradation. A complete account of the system as implemented at UT Memphis has been reported elsewhere .4

Since the file server's 330MB hard disk is not completely filled with Knowledge Finder MEDLINE data, it can also be used for staff functions. The Department of Health Informatics is divided into divisions, the Health Science Library and Educational and Research Support Services. The two divisions are located in two different buildings. Staff of the two divisions communicate daily using electronic mail, but often staff from both divisions must work on reports together. Instead of sending the reports back and forth on paper copy or on diskette, the document files are deposited on the file server. The server administrator set up "drop folders" on the file server that can only be opened by the folder owner. Anyone in the department, who is a registered user of the file server, can deposit a document in any folder for retrieval by the owner of the folder.

The reference staff also uses the file server in the billing of computer searches. Search requests are received either over the telephone, by walk-in, or electronically via the VAX. Information about the search and the search requestor are included on a search request form. The searcher uses the form to formulate and perform the search, and the reference library assistant prepares a statement using the request form. Until the fall 1990, the library assistant prepared a multi-part statement on a typewriter. One part was given to the requestor; one part was kept in the reference office; and two parts were sent to the library's business office. When a search was charged to a university account number, each account number also had to be checked against a master paper list to determine whether it was a valid account. Since the manual billing system was very time consuming and tedious, we decided to design a microcomputer based billing system using the Macintosh and Claris' FileMaker II. The system consists of four files: ACCOUNTS, USERS, DEPARTMENTS, and SEARCH REQUESTS. The SEARCH REQUESTS file is used for entering information about the search request and the requestor . The ACCOUNTS and USERS files serve as lookup files for the file, SEARCH REQUESTS. When the library assistant enters a requestor's last name into a record of the SEARCH REQUESTS file, the status, department, and college of the requestor is automatically entered if the name is in the USERS file. When the library assistant enters an account number into a record of the SEARCH REQUESTS file, the account name and its valid dates are automatically entered if the account number is in the ACCOUNTS file. The ACCOUNTS, USERS, and DEPARTMENTS files are maintained on the file server. Data are added to and deleted from these files as appropriate by authorized individuals. The DEPARTMENTS file is used as a lookup file in entering information into the USERS file. The SEARCH REQUESTS file resides on the Reference Office Macintosh. With this system, the account numbers do not have to be manually checked for accuracy, because they have been verified during data entry.

Until late 1988, the reference librarians used a Texas Instrument dumb terminal for online searching. Searches were performed and the results printed on thermal paper. The searches were then picked up in the library or sent by campus mail to the search requestor. Now each online searcher has on her desk a Macintosh connected to the LocalTalk network with access to a Shiva NetModem also connected to the LocalTalk network. The searcher using communications software performs the search and downloads the results. She may then add notes to the search and edit extraneous material from the search. The results may be mailed electronically, printed, or copied to the user's diskette or file server. If the search requestor wants to receive the search results by electronic mail, the searcher logs into the DEC VAX via LocalTalk, uploads the search file, and sends the search file via VAX Mail to the search requestor. If the search requestor wants to receive paper copy, the searcher puts the search into a drop box on the Library file server and sends a Broadcast message to the reference library assistant. The reference library assistant retrieves the file and prints it.

Evaluation and Plans for the Future

The LocalTalk network has made it possible to share hardware and software resources that would have been too expensive to purchase for each Macintosh workstation. For example, the cost for a networked version of the Knowledge Finder Unabridged MEDLINE for the current year and five prior years was $4,495 in 1990. The same subscription for a single non-networked library workstation was $2,395 in 1990. Since 400 workstations can potentially access Knowledge Finder across the campus network, the cost per workstation is about $11. A file server on the LocalTalk network has reduced the amount of time staff spend in clerical activities by making it possible for them to easily share documents with each other. For example, each year the library produces an annual report. Each unit in the library submits a report to be included in the final report. Before librarians had access to a Macintosh and a file server, each unit submitted a typed report, and the final report was re-typed. Now we produce all reports using the same word processor and deposit them in a drop folder on the file server. The reports are collected from the file server and cut and pasted together electronically to form a final library report.

LocalTalk is easy to set up and use, but it cannot deliver optimum performance. LocalTalk can transfer data at approximately the rate of transfer obtained with a floppy disk. We have found that LocalTalk handles laser printing excellently and file transfer adequately. However more intensive uses of the file server, involving server based applications and server based databases, are badly degraded if the level of network usage is high or if the data has to go through a gateway device. For example, LocalTalk runs Knowledge Finder on six or more systems within the library and a few stations linked to the library by FastPath boxes, but it fails to deliver acceptable performance on ten stations in a classroom linked to the library by a FastPath box. Put another way, LocalTalk is comfortable for users who have ever owned a Volkswagen Beetle.

Traffic on the library's LocalTalk network has also grown tremendously since its installation in 1988. The number of devices on the library network has grown from six to twenty-five. The number of LocalTalk zones linked to the library network has grown from four to thirty-seven. Users both inside and outside the library are noticing the slow response time of file server based resources. Plans are under consideration to connect the library's file server and five Macintosh workstations directly to NetOne Ethernet. This would increase network throughput five-six times on the Knowledge Finder workstations, and reduce the load on the LocalTalk network serving the other library devices. Network performance is also limited by workstation hardware. The library chose to use the Macintosh Plus with 1MB RAM and one internal and one external floppy drive for the public stations. We realized immediately that the stations should have had hard disks. Since Knowledge Server requires at least 1MB RAM and the software takes up 600K, this limited the public Macintoshes to accessing Knowledge Server only. As a first step in making these workstations multifunctional, the library has upgraded the RAM in these Macintoshes to 4MB. Our next step is to add hard drives so that a HyperCard interface can be installed. The interface will allow the user to select the HyperCard library information stacks, Knowledge Server, or the library's integrated system, LIS, that resides on the VAX. This will eliminate the need for separate stations for separate functions. (We have described the HyperCard library information stacks in a previous report .5)

A final limitation is found in some Macintosh software. Because LocalTalk does not provide high performance for server based applications, many application developers do not provide an option for server based operation. The library's plan was to launch all programs from the file server, but it was soon discovered that many Macintosh programs cannot be used by multiple users. AppleTalk also has some security deficiencies. AppleShare provides adequate security for most file server operations, but no restriction can be placed on printers. A student using a library workstation can select a printer in another zone, for example, the Office of the Chancellor, and direct all printing from his workstation to that printer. Usually, this operation is done unintentionally, and the user cannot understand why no printing occurs locally. We hope that future releases address this problem.

Many users have expressed the desire to access Knowledge Server from home. While the library does have a Shiva NetModem connected to its LocalTalk network, it is too slow at 2400 baud to offer access to Knowledge Server over a telephone line. Although the newest modems provide an effective transmission rate of 9600 baud, this is still less than 10 percent of LocalTalk's modest 230 kilobaud rate. Work is in progress with Bell Communications Research (Bellcore) to test the use of ISDN (Integrated Services Digital Network), with a transmission rate of 64-128 kilobaud, for accessing information from the library's file server.

The library's network began as an attempt to gain access to a laser printer, and evolved into an integral part of the University information network. It has increased productivity within the library, and by motivating other units of the University to link their networks to the library, it has stimulated the overall growth of University network activity. We are more aware of its deficiencies now, but this is a healthy result of growth and the increase of our awareness of how much more it can do.

Notes

1. T. Singarella, Mission statement for the Department of Health Informatics, University of Tennessee, Memphis, December 1990.

2. M. Rogers and V. Bare. *Hands-On AppleTalk.* (New York: Brady Books, 1989).

3. *PhoneNet Connector User's Guide.* (Berkeley, CA: Farallon Computing, Inc., 1988).

4. J. T. Silver, L. M. Bellamy, S. A. Selig. "Use of a CD-ROM based searching tool on local area and campus wide networks." *Proceedings of the Fourteenth Annual Symposium on Computer Applications in Medical Care*, (1990), 384-8.

5. L. M. Bellamy, J. T. Silver, S. A. Selig, J. K. Givens. "Linking information about the library to the library user through hypermedia. " *Proceedings of the Thirteenth Annual Symposium on Computer Applications in Medical Care*, (1989), 853-7.

About the Authors

Lois M. Bellamy, M.S., is Systems Librarian, Health Science Library, Department of Health Informatics, University of Tennessee, Memphis.

John T. Silver, D.V.M., M.C.S., is Educational Computing Specialist, Educational and Research Support Services, Department of Health Informatics, University of Tennessee, Memphis.

Part Two:

CD-ROM Networks

6

Networking CD-ROM with Meridian CD Net

C. Anne Turhollow and Michael J. Perkins
San Diego State University

ABSTRACT

In the latter part of the 1980's the service options available to academic libraries increased at an exponential rate, driven by technological advances. Online vs. CD-ROM, mediated vs. end-user searching, stand-alone vs. networked; the pros and cons of these choices and their consequences had to be evaluated and a unified direction chosen. At San Diego State University the choice was made to go with CD-ROMs from various vendors on a local area network. This chapter describes the environment (user, professional, and administrative) in which this choice was made, the criteria used, and how each option fared against those criteria. Also discussed are the decision to use a consultant, the bid process, installation and evaluation of the LAN. Detailed technical specifications and costs are also provided. Finally, our plans for the future expansion of the LAN, based on the lessons learned from living with the existing LAN for two years, are outlined.

Introduction

Computer literacy is fast becoming an essential work skill, and using a computer to rapidly access vast amounts of information stored electronically is an essential part of computer literacy. The education of many professionals now includes instruction in these systems. Law students must learn to use LEXIS and/or WestLaw if they hope to work in any large law office. Physicians and public health workers need to be familiar with MEDLINE, AIDSline, and other health related databases. Even business education has recognized the need to integrate computer/telecommunications literacy into their curriculum.

At the same time, the quantity and complexity of electronic information is requiring greater and more sophisticated search engines and techniques to offer some semblance of control.

For these reasons it is now more important than ever that academic libraries provide not only the information students need, but also opportunities to familiarize themselves and use in meaningful ways the types of computer search systems that they can expect to find in the workplace. Without these opportunities, today's students will be unprepared to perform or compete in tomorrow's world of work.

Access to information stored on electronic media has been around for over twenty years. However, since these services are fee-based, they have most often been used by faculty and graduate students, who can call upon departmental or grant funds to pay the high costs of these services. And even faculty and graduate students have not used them to the extent they would like, due to these high costs. Only one profession, the law, has been graced with subsidized access to relevant databases. Other professions and disciplines have not convinced the information industry of the efficacy of policies like Mead Data's and West's. The situation for undergraduates is even worse, since they don't have faculty or graduate student's access to funding.

For years librarians have searched for an efficient and effective way to bring the power of online searching to undergraduates, and to better control costs. Here at SDSU, the recent convergence of technology and unique funding opportunities has made a realistic attempt to make this possible.

First, we will describe the environment in which the various options available to us were evaluated. Our users, professional staff and the administrative climate (library, university, system, and state) will be outlined. Next, our unique needs were translated into criteria, and we will show how each of the options fared under these criteria, and explain our choice. We will describe the LAN, both hardware and software, and provide detailed specifications and cost figures. The baroque constraints of the bid process, and the use of a consultant are highlighted. Finally, the installation, evaluation, and plans for the future will be discussed.

Environment

There are three state-supported systems of higher education in California; the University of California, the California State University, and the California Community Colleges. The CSU system's primary function is to serve as four-year comprehensive teaching institutions for undergraduates. Twenty campuses make up the CSU system, and each is a very different and unique institution. System-wide coordination of resources is rare. The CSU system is an agency of the State of California and must comply with all rules and regulations regarding access and competition incumbent upon a state agency. Funding for the system comes from the state of California (80%), student tuition and fees (15%), and other (5%). Most of the 5 percent designated other is from the California State Lottery instituted in 1988. The budget is driven by enrollment-based formulas developed by the Department of Finance and line items in the budgets may be removed by the State Legislature or line vetoed by the Governor. State law requires large contracts (over $10,000) to go out to bid, and with poor system-wide coordination, this has resulted, for example, in four different vendors supplying online catalogs to the twenty campuses, and a pattern of automated services (online, CD-ROM, etc.) reflecting the needs and preferences of each campus's needs and users.

San Diego State University is the largest campus of the twenty-member California State University system, with over 35,000 students and over 2800 full and part-time faculty. It offers bachelor's degrees in 76 majors, master's in 56, and doctorates in 7. The campus is served by one central library as mandated by the system charter. The library has a professional staff of thirty, twenty-two of whom are public-service librarians. There are three reference desks (General Reference, Science Reference, and Government Publications) staffed by librarians, and several other assistance desks staffed by paraprofessionals. In addition to staffing the reference desks, librarians are expected to do computer searching, bibliographic instruction, collection development, and committee work. Since librarians at SDSU are faculty, participation in professional organizations and professional publishing are also expected.

The majority of our 35,000 students are undergraduates and like most undergraduates in the United States today, enter the university with few of the library research skills necessary to succeed in a college career. With a librarian/student ratio of 1 : 1750, any new service offered by the library must meet the criteria of being able to be used by these undergraduates with a minimum of training and assistance by librarians.

The above mentioned budget formulas were developed in the 1960's and 1970's, and reflect library conditions at those times. Thus money for automated services has either come out of book budgets or been close to self supporting. Since the introduction of the State lottery in California, these funds have become very important to automation efforts in the CSU for those libraries which are considered eligible to receive lottery funds. This determination is made on a campus by campus basis. SDSU has allowed the Library to compete for lottery funds since 1987. Unfortunately, the campus will only support "one-time purchases," not on-going expenses (re: subscriptions). However, if the library can convince the campus lottery committee that a project has a sufficient *instructional* component, they are very generous with their monies.

The administration of automated services at the SDSU Library is shared by the Electronic Reference Services Committee (E-Ref), the Library Systems group, and the Library Management group. E-Ref is composed of the Coordinator of Electronic Reference Services, three Public Services librarians, and the Head of Public Services, and has the responsibility for planning, introducing, and overseeing the use of all automated reference services in the public area. The Library Systems group is responsible for the online catalog as well as the technical support for all automated systems in public and technical services. The Library Management group is comprised of the director, the heads of public and technical services, the personnel librarian, and the budget officer, and has overall responsibility for strategic library planning.

Criteria

What are we looking for in a system? First, and most important, we look for ease of use. We had to have a system that students could reasonably be expected to access on their own, or at least with minimum assistance. Second, we wanted a system that new users could quickly reach a reasonably high (50%) success rate.

Next in importance was cost, since lottery funds, while generous, were not infinite. Also, as mentioned above, lottery funds may not be used for on-going expenses such as online vendor contracts or CD-ROM subscriptions. Costs needed to be low and controllable. Until this current fiscal year (1991/92), funding specifically for automated reference services has not been provided. Any money for these services must be taken from other parts of the budget, usually the book budget. Chargeback to users is not an option since the CSU system does not permit charging for searches if the patron performs the search. Libraries are allowed to charge for paper and equipment use, but not search costs.

Third, we wanted to design a system that would require readily—and competitively—available equipment. We wanted the simplest and the least number of components necessary to do the job.

Fourth was space. With a library designed for 15,000 students serving over 35,000 students, space is at a premium. Our system could not cut into student study space any more than was absolutely necessary. And fifth, our building has constraints in power, wiring, and such; our system could not place too much additional stress on, or require significant upgrading of the infrastructure.

Options: Pro and Con

The Electronic Reference Services Committee carefully evaluated the options that were available in 1987: front-end systems, gateways, user-friendly vendors, full-service vendors, and CD-ROM. These options, other than CD-ROM, are discussed in greater detail in Buckingham (1985).

Front-end Systems

The front-end system provides a "user friendly" interface between the user and the database, and is usually menu driven. Searches are composed offline, and the software dials up the remote vendor, uploads the search, and downloads the results. Searchhelper, from IAC, was an early example, but in 1987 such systems as Grateful MED and WilSearch were also available.

The obvious advantages of front-end systems are their ease of use and low per search cost. Being menu-driven, they walk the user through the construction of a search strategy, allow them to review and modify it, and then execute the search swiftly and efficiently. The equipment costs are fairly low, since it needs only a bare bones PC with one disk drive and a modem, which doesn't take much space and requires only a standard telephone line and a grounded power plug.

The disadvantages are not quite so obvious. While easy to use, front ends are slow, and a user may enter inappropriate or overly complex search strategies that result in zero hits. Also, once online, the user has no control over the search. The interactive nature of online searching is lost. A user may wind up repeating the search process several times to obtain any results.

Gateways

With gateways, again a user-friendly interface is provided, but this time the software is mounted on a remote mainframe, provides access to multiple vendors, rather than just one, and does require a contract with each vendor. While most gateways are menu driven, a few do allow more advanced command-driven options. Easynet is one example.

Like front ends, gateways are easy to use, but unlike front ends, they reside on the vendor's computer, so there is less chance of patrons messing up the software or worse yet, stealing it. Equipment costs are lower as only a dumb terminal is needed, along with a modem and its attendant telephone line.

However, search costs are high, since the menu-driven systems are slow and many layered. Also, while a uniform search language is convenient, it is also less flexible. Much of the power and sophistication of online searching is lost.

User-Friendly Vendors

Here the database provider has mounted a menu-driven or simplified command system geared to the inexperienced or infrequent user on their own mainframe. Examples are BRS/After Dark, Knowledge Index (Dialog), and PaperChase (MEDLINE).

User-friendly systems are even less costly than front ends or gateways since there are usually reduced rates, direct access to databases is preserved, and they don't require a PC.

However, in exchange for the lower rates, vendors usually limit searching to off-peak hours and allow access to only a subset of databases. There is staffing impact since a significant amount of training is required before a user can search independently. Success rates are again low(Ankeny, 1991; Janke, 1984).

Full Service Vendors

These are the systems that our online searchers use, such as Dialog and BRS. Instead of performing mediated searching, the library would offer training and advice on searching these services and instead of performing mediated searching, would allow patrons to perform their own searches.

The advantage full-service vendors offer is full service. All the power, all the flexibility, and all the interactive features are available for the user. Of course, search costs are high and open ended. A PC and a modem are required, and training is costly in online and staff time. Also, the long learning curve keeps the success rate low until users are reasonably proficient searchers (Starr and Renford, 1989).

CD-ROM

The CD-ROM option, just coming into its own in 1987, had the potential to bring the database itself into the library and allow users to access it directly with software and hardware provided by the library along with some training and advice. Examples include InfoTrac, WilsonDisc, and SilverPlatter.

While the subscription costs of CD-ROMs may be quite high, it is a fixed (and thus budgetable) cost, a desirable feature for a state institution. The real disadvantage of CD-ROMs is the equipment costs. They require not only a full PC with enough RAM to run complex search engines, but also a CD-ROM drive, an expensive and sensitive device. Costs are moderate in terms of training and staff time.

On the other hand, the advantages are many. You get the full power of the online system, flexibility, interactivity, field searching, and more. Since you are not "online," there are no telecommunications charges. Also, you can customize your system to your user needs. We don't have much feedback on success rates, but since users have time to learn the system (without charges stacking up for each mistake) success rates should improve dramatically over the learning curve.

Criteria	Front End	Gateway	User-Friendly	Full Service	CD-ROM
Search Costs	low	low	low	high	none
Equipment Costs	medium	low	low	medium	high
Telecom Costs	high	high	high	high	none
Training Costs	low	low	medium	high	medium
Interactivity	none	none	low	high	high
Flexibility	low	low	low	high	high
Success Rate	low	low	low	low	???
Cost Control	minimal	minimal	high	low	high

Table 6.1
Comparison of Options

This comparison table presents an overview of the advantages and disadvantages of each of the options. While each system has features to recommend them, we chose CD-ROMs because of the low (per unit) search costs, the controllability of those costs, and because it retains all the interactivity and flexibility of full-service database systems.

Choice of Configuration

By mid-1987 we had identified CD-ROM as the most cost-effective way to provide end-user searching. The system would run entirely in the library incurring no telecommunication costs and none of the attendant telecommunication problems. Costs were up front and fixed. Patrons could search as long as they liked without incurring charges by the minute. The terminals could be placed in the reference areas, rather than trying to find an available room to house terminals for dial-up searching. However, a major hurdle existed in terms of attempting to find equipment money. We then learned two weeks before the closing deadline for proposals, that the Library was finally eligible to compete for lottery funds. A proposal was written quickly, outlining a system of eight stand-alone CD-ROM workstations on which would run several Wilson indexes, ERIC and MEDLINE. We waited to find out if we would receive funds to spend for the fiscal year 1988/89.

Although we had decided to purchase stand-alone workstations, we knew early on that would not be a satisfactory solution. We could already imagine the lines of students waiting to use the single terminal for Business Periodicals Index or MEDLINE. We knew that a product which allowed multiuser access to multiple products was a better solution, but did not know of a system or a vendor who could supply this at a price we could handle, nor were we certain that the technological breakthrough would occur in time.

Meridian Data

While we were waiting for word on the lottery funds, Meridian Data announced a network for CD-ROMs. We saw the system demonstrated at ALA in New Orleans and decided that this could be the multiuser system we envisioned. Called CD Net, the Meridian network offered several advantages over stand-alone systems. It allowed more than one user to access the same CD-ROM product at the same time. Users would not have to move from terminal to terminal (perhaps waiting in lines at each terminal) to search related but separate CD-ROM products, or different years of the same product. In addition to user convenience, it also meant that staff would not have to change discs for patrons or check out discs to patrons. The network would allow for the CD-ROM players and the network server to reside in a secure area and for terminals to be placed throughout the library building. It also allowed us to have terminals at reference desks, exclusively for the use of librarians. This would allow librarians to access any CD-ROM on the server, without bumping a user off a terminal, and we hoped it would greatly ease instruction in their use. Additionally, with menu software, it allowed us to customize which CD-ROMs could be accessed from which workstation on the system. This way, we could tailor the selection of products to the reference area in which the terminals were located. Considering these facts, we decided that if we were awarded the lottery funds, we would pursue the purchase of a CD-ROM LAN as opposed to stand-alone workstations.

Final word on the lottery funds arrived a year after we had submitted the proposal. We received $34,000 to purchase equipment. Because we were switching from a collection of stand-alone workstations to a LAN based system, this amount of money was no longer sufficient. The library administration agreed to provide some additional funding. However, after costing out the hardware and the LAN software, our initial plan of an eleven-slot player and eleven workstations (five in General Reference, three in Government Publications, and three in Science) had to be scaled back to only the eleven-slot player and five workstations, all in General Reference.

The remaining six workstations were eventually purchased with regular equipment money in fiscal year 1989/90.

The Consultant

After attending a demonstration at a Meridian office, we realized that we were entering new and unknown areas. No one in the library (or on campus, for that matter) had the necessary software or hardware skills to pull together and install the desired CD-ROM LAN. It was at this point that we decided to bring in an outside consultant/installer.

Meridian provided us with the names of several firms in the San Diego area including one which had already installed a LAN (without CD Net) on our campus. This consultant, Vortex Data Systems, provided us with assistance in selecting and specifying equipment and came in to install the system, providing training in the use of the network software. This arrangement was of benefit for several reasons. It provided us with the expertise we needed and provided an introduction to what networks are all about from an "expert" rather than books and journals. Also, by installing the system for us, it meant that they were responsible for seeing that the system worked as specified. Any software or hardware problems for the first year were to be handled by Vortex. This is a standard installation agreement for the State of California. The contract also provided for training—both on-site and formal classroom training— which allowed our technician to hone his skills. The result is that the library has been able to handle all further expansions, improvements, and installations in-house with little difficulty.

The Bid Process

Patience is a major requirement when attempting any large project in the CSU system. Timelines are long, and projects must be examined by many units on campus. For purchases over $10,000 but less than $100,000, an Invitation for Bid (IFB) must be written. An IFB is an elaborate document which sets forth in extreme detail what equipment and functions are sought (a specific brand must be given for each product desired), which requires sending for, and constant reference to manufacturer's specifications. The IFB is reviewed by the Library, various campus units such as University Computing Services, Physical Plant, and finally Purchasing, where it is assigned a purchasing agent. This person adds all material and contract language specified by the State of California (a not inconsiderable task) and serves as the primary contact person for the bid process.

Normally, the names of at least three vendors must be sent to the purchasing agent. In the case of our first system, we had to fill out "sole source" justification forms as there was only one vendor we knew about. The IFBs are mailed out to be returned one month later as sealed bids. However, before the vendor can submit a bid, they must attend a mandatory walk-through. The walk-through for this product required the presence of the Online Coordinator, our systems hardware technician, the library building supervisor, library contracts officer, representatives from Physical Plant and Health Safety, and the vendors. The walk-through allows the vendors to see the worksite and determine if there will be any problems and it allows Physical Plant to determine if any upgrades of wiring or other construction work is necessary. (Our Physical Plant requires three months to act on a work order.) As a result of the walk-through, we made some minor changes in the bid and sent in work orders for both an electrical upgrade for the installation area and drilling to allow the LAN wires to run from the first to second floors. When a bid is returned by a vendor, the purchasing agent determines if a bid is "compliant" (meeting all State requirements) and the lowest compliant bid is awarded the contract. Installation is usually scheduled one to two months after the award. In our case, the process from initial request for funds to actual installation took two years.

Installation

Prior to installation, a great deal of coordination was necessary. The University's Department of Physical Plant had to be consulted, since holes would have to be drilled in floors and structural walls, and we needed to know if the envisioned system would require electrical upgrades. Vortex Data needed to observe the site prior to bid and our systems people needed to know just how long the cable from the file server and towers to the workstations would be since distance was a factor in signal strength. Thus, representatives from Physical Plant and Vortex, and our systems people held a walk through inspection in May of 1989, worked out all parameters of the LAN's configuration, and agreed on the plan for site preparation and installation.

The heart of the LAN consists of a Meridian Data CD Net Model 100T-80286 tower base unit with an 80286 microprocessor and five CD-ROM players plus an expansion tower (Model X20-286) of six CD-ROM players. A 286 AT file server (NCR PC 810 with 72MB hard drive) runs all the software, including CD Net and Novell NetWare 286 All of these components are located in Systems, away from public service areas. The first workstations installed numbered five, and were located in General Reference. Four were placed in a cluster about thirty feet from the reference desk, while the fifth was placed at the right end of the reference desk for the exclusive use of the librarians The cluster of four is readily visible from the reference desk, so any problems or a need for assistance can be spotted quickly The workstation at the reference desk has two uses. Since it has a modem attached, it can be used for ready reference searching; but more importantly, it can be used for instruction when people approach the desk with a question about an individual CD-ROM product's operation.

The workstations are PS/2 clones—Acer 710's with 8088-2 microprocessors, EGA monitors, 20MB hard drives, and Western Digital Ethernet cards. The Novell NetWare software runs over a twisted-pair wire network with Thin Ethernet. The first products on the LAN were Dialog ERIC On Disc and SilverPlatter PsycLIT, which are accessed using Direct Access menu software.

The actual installation took place on two days in August 1989, and was available for public use immediately, two years after the initial proposal.

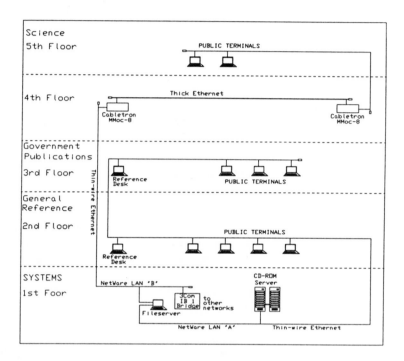

Figure 6.1
UCSD Library Network as of July 1991

Second Phased Expansion

Over the next eighteen months, the system was expanded up to Government Publications and the Science Reference area. In Government Pubs, the Marcive version of the GPO Monthly Catalog is available on three public workstations, and the workstation at the reference desk has access to all CD-ROMs on the server, and also has a modem for online access. In Science, Dialog MEDLINE and PsycLIT are available on two public workstations. At this writing, we are waiting for the PC (presently used for ready reference searching and Internet access) at the Science reference desk to be hooked up.

Type of equipment	Number of units	Total cost
Meridian Data CD Net Model 100T-80286 with five CD-ROM players	1	$7395
Expansion tower (Model X20-286) with six CD-ROM players	1	$6595
NCR PC 810 with 72 MB hard drive)	1	$4500
Acer 710 with EGA monitor, 20 MB hard drive	5	$9000
HP ThinkJet Printer	4	$1900
Western Digital Ethernet Card	1	$3300
Software - MS DOS 3.3, Norton Advanced Utilities, Fastback+,MS CD-ROM Extensions		$549
Novell NetWare 286	1	$2800
TOTAL		$36,039

Table 6.2
Equipment and costs of Meridian CD Net LAN

Evaluation

Our Meridian CD Net system has more than met our expectations and it is certainly a success with our patrons. PsycLIT had been run on a stand-alone workstation several months prior to the LAN installation, and on the day it moved from the stand alone to the LAN, patrons hovered over the technicians from VORTEX and Systems as they attempted to bring it up on the LAN, and were on the terminals searching as soon as they were able. The LAN is so popular that one and occasionally two of the workstations have to be designated for "sign up" so that students who come from far away and can only come on specific days of the week can assure themselves of getting a workstation. As it is, there are often two or three people waiting to use the next available workstation in the cluster. Most have little or no problems learning the mechanics of searching, but there are those that find the different vendor's software confusing, and are frustrated by the number and the complexity of the choices available to them.

The Systems group has been very pleased with the LAN, from a variety of standpoints. While they had few technical problems, they did discover that cheaper workstations (XT-class microcomputers without hard drives) are sufficient, and some problems occurred because Meridian and the CD-ROM vendors were occasionally less than forthright about their software's limitations. The size and scale of the configuration has allowed Systems to learn about LANs and CD-ROMs without feeling overwhelmed by either hardware or software problems. As with other CD-ROM LAN systems, the problem of RAM cram is an ongoing issue, solved by installing one megabyte of RAM, and attendant memory management software, on every workstation and using our menu software to reboot the workstations each time a user selects a new CD-ROM product. Sloan (1990) provides a more detailed description of this problem and its solutions.

Librarian's reactions have been mixed. Most are pleased to be able to offer access to CD-ROM's in such a useful and flexible manner and very much like having access through the workstation at the reference desk. But like our users, librarians also find learning different search software for each CD-ROM confusing and time consuming. Also, we use Hewlett-Packard ThinkJet printers because of their quiet printing ability, but are appalled by the costs of ink and paper. Patrons will print out hundreds of citations if they can. On a slow day in the General Reference area, one enterprising student commandeered all four workstations and set them to printing out inch thick stacks of citations. We have a sign announcing a limit of fifty citations, but it really has little effect. Management Group intends to install Venda-Card meters on all printers and we do offer the alternative of downloading the results to disks.

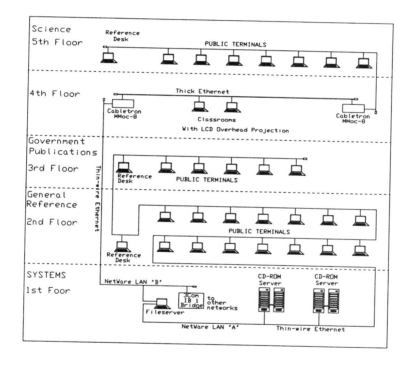

Figure 6.2
UCSD Library Network by Summer 1992

But the biggest issue with which librarians are grappling is instruction. Most patrons do not read instructions, either in the form of handouts or on-screen. Many of them figure things out eventually, but there are also those who get frustrated easily, and just "want to know what button to push when." Many are overwhelmed by computers, and Boolean logic is a major stumbling block for all. However, if a student is willing to be patient, ask questions, and work at it, they can become extremely proficient searchers. Currently, we provide handouts, one-on-one assistance from the Reference desks when possible, and class instruction as part of our regular bibliographic instruction program. The class instruction is not as strong as it could be, because we do not have workstations yet available in our library classrooms. Installation is scheduled for the summer of 1991.

The Future

Even before the system was installed, we felt that it was too small. Six months after its installation, another lottery proposal was submitted to significantly enlarge and upgrade the system. With experience gained from writing other proposals, we were able to provide a more generous cost estimate of $110,000. Several months later, we received notification of full funding. Even though this award was subsequently reduced due to a downturn in lottery revenues and other budget problems of the State of California, we were able to purchase the size of system that we needed and wanted. The new LAN will consist of two file servers with twenty-eight CD-ROM players and twenty-four additional workstations. This will bring the total number of workstations to thirty public, three reference desk, and two workstations for bibliographic instruction. The workstations will be in three clusters with one cluster in General Reference, one in Government Publications, and one in Science. Each cluster will have its own menu and only the reference terminals will be able to access all the products on the network. This allows us to control the number of users on any given product, and assures us that the patrons are in a reference area where the librarians are extremely familiar with the subject content of those databases. Additionally, if we had all terminals the same, certain large classes would swamp out all other users on the system for several days. This would occur, for example, when the 1500 students of Speech Communications 103 have their first assignment due on the same day. The expanded PIN will run ERIC, MEDLINE, PsycLIT, Marcive GPO Monthly Catalog, UN Index, Statistical Masterfile, Readers' Guide Abstracts, Applied Science and Technology Index, Business Periodicals Index, General Science Index, Humanities Index, and Social Sciences Index.

One of our key concerns in expanding the system was the issue of compatibility. There were now several vendors on the market providing similar systems (Thomas and Maxwell, 1990). And given our state of funding there is no guarantee that we could afford Meridian's new equipment line. However, with the Government Printing Office now issuing a large number of products on CD-ROM, including significant items such as the 1990 Census and the Congressional Record, our

Government Publications Divisions had decided that a mixture of stand-alone and networked workstations would best meet their needs. After studying the situation, the Online Reference Services Committee decided to move the present Meridian Data systems into Government Publications, where it would run independently of the new system, thus sidestepping the compatibility issue and allowing us to conduct a normal IFB process with a minimum of three vendors. This was pragmatic planning as the contract was awarded to CBIS.

Obviously, a major concern of this upgrade will be providing patrons with adequate signs, so they know what system they are on, and what products that particular terminal can access. Probably the best example will be the Government Publications Division where there will be OPAC terminals, PIN terminals, which serve as the catalog for United States documents, GP networked workstations, and stand-alone workstations, all with different products and different types of information. It would be helpful if microcomputers came in more colors than simply grey and beige.

Another issue will be increased instruction needs. This will be increasingly difficult for us as the number of librarians has been slowly decreasing due to budget cuts. The major change that will occur with the installation of the expanded PIN will be the switch over from InfoTrac to the WilsonDisc products. This switch over has been very carefully considered since WilsonDisc is slightly more difficult to use than InfoTrac. However, on the basis of subscription costs, quality and depth of indexing, and a better reflection of our journal holdings, which should lower interlibrary loan costs, we have decided to make that change. With the addition of two terminals for instructional use in combination with the use of overhead display units, we will be able to do actual demonstrations of the databases rather than using overhead transparencies or having twenty students crowd around a single workstation in the already crowded reference areas.

We will also be improving the menu interface that patrons use to choose their product. Direct Access is useful, but one is restricted to an entry of twenty-five characters to describe the menu choice and we have found that simply listing the name of the database is insufficient. While there is descriptive material available which describes the different databases, most patrons will not take the time to read it. A librarian who is adept in Prolog programming is beginning to write a simple expert system/menu system for the PIN, to help patrons get to the right database for their topic. This system should cut down on the number of students who search for marine biology or Microsoft Windows on PsycLIT, for example.

An alternate possibility we had to address in expanding our CD-ROM LAN is that of locally mounted databases. While we would like our patrons to be able to search from one terminal with one common interface, it is not a cost effective solution for us at this time. Running a product on a CD-ROM network is approximately 10 percent of the cost of mounting the same product on our OPAC. Mounting Wilson's Social Sciences Index on our Innopac system would cost $41,500 in start-up fees and close to $8,000 for subscription costs after the first year. On the other hand, we can run the WilsonDisc version for $1300 a year. It will reach a smaller number of users and will have a different user interface, but given the state of our budget, it is the only responsible choice.

For the future, once our new system is up and running, we will be carefully evaluating new products to add to the LAN, to correspond to this future expansion. Currently, new subscriptions entail cancellation of printed reference tools, serials, or reduction in book purchases. The next system issue that we will focus on will be providing dial-up access, should this turn out to be an option we can afford.

There are many questions unanswered, and some even unaddressed at this time. What do we do when our CD-ROM drives are full? How will we finance new CD-ROM subscriptions? Can we, and do we want to interface with a planned campus-wide network on campus? Will the current LAN be technologically and logistically obsolete in five years? Will our OPAC be able to access our CD-ROMs finally providing our users with one common interface? These and questions unthought of today will have to be addressed. We can only hope that we have designed a system flexible enough to allow us to move in the direction dictated by developments in information science and librarianship.

Bibliography

Ankeny, M. L. 1991. "Evaluating end-user services: success or satisfaction?" *Journal of Academic Librarianship*. 16: 352-356

Buckingham, S. 1985. "Choosing an end-user on line searching system." *Education Libraries*. 10(2-3): 41-44.

Eddison, E. B. 1989. "A LAN Toolbox." *Database*. 12(3): 15-21

Janke, R. V. 1984. "Online after six: end user searching comes of age." *Online*, 8(6): 15-29.

Sloan, S. 1990. "Expanded memory: one solution to networked CD-ROM memory problems." *Computers in Libraries*, 10(3): 21-23.

Starr, S. S., and Renford, B. L. 1987. "Evaluation of a program to teach health professionals to search MEDLINE." *Bulletin of the Medical Libraries Association*, 75: 193-201.

Thompson, M. K., and Maxwell, K. February 27, 1990. "Networking CD-ROMs." *PC Magazine*, 9(4): 237-260.

About the Authors

C. Anne Turhollow is a science reference librarian in the Science Division of the San Diego State University Library. She is also Coordinator for Electronic Reference Services, and serves on the Library Automation Planning Committee. In addition to her work with the CD-ROM LAN she participated in the selection and implementation of the Library's Online Catalog. Ms. Turhollow has a B.S. in Biology from Loyola Marymount University in Los Angeles, and an M.S. in Biological Sciences from Stanford University. Her M.L.I.S. is from UC-Berkeley.

Michael J. Perkins is a business reference librarian in the General Reference Division of the San Diego State University Library. He also serves on the Electronic Reference Services, and the Library Automation Planning Committees. Mr. Perkins has an undergraduate degree in business, an M.L.S from the University of Wisconsin–Madison, and is currently working on an M.B.A.

Acknowledgements

Ms. Turhollow and Mr. Perkins would like to acknowledge the assistance, encouragement and technical expertise of Helen Henry and Kirk Grier of the Library's Systems Group. Without them, none of this would have been possible.

7

Implementing a LANtastic CD-ROM Network

Martha Chantiny
Sinclair Undergraduate Library, University of Hawaii at Manoa

ABSTRACT

A LANtastic network to provide access to shared CD-ROM drives was installed at the University of Hawaii Sinclair Undergraduate Library in early 1990. In this chapter, background on related CD-ROM projects at the University of Hawaii Libraries is provided. Reasons for choosing LANtastic and an overview of the installation, upgrading and maintenance of the network are discussed. LANtastic network products, equipment and specific experiences related to the use of LANtastic for access to networked CD-ROM drives are described. Future plans for expanding the number of shared CD-ROM drives and evaluation of the system are presented.

Introduction

Sinclair Library is designated the Undergraduate Library and Learning Resources Center and has a collection geared to serving the needs of students in all basic baccalaureate programs. Sinclair Library serves as the principal library and research center for the nearly 13,000 undergraduates attending the University of Hawaii at Manoa. Sinclair Library also houses all library holdings for the music and architecture collections as well as the audio-visual center and a large microcomputer lab, the Computerized Learning and Information Center (CLIC), managed by the University Computing Center. One of the missions of CLIC in conjunction with Sinclair Library is to expand the availability and usage of Computer-Aided Instruction. Installation of the LANtastic network to provide access to multiple CD-ROM databases in the Reference Room of Sinclair Library supported this mission by making another technology-based information access system available to library patrons.

LANtastic is designed to be inexpensive, easy to install and maintain. It is a peer-to-peer system which does not require the use of a dedicated file server. The workstation which acts as a file or network resource server may also be used as a fully functioning network workstation, or node. LANtastic is one of the few network software package which offers built-in and virtually transparent support for CD-ROM drives.

The Sinclair Library LANtastic network currently consists of three workstations and five chained CD-ROM drives and provides access to CD-ROM databases for general undergraduate research as well as specialized information to support students in the Music Department. The network workstations are located near the Reference Desk and are available all hours the library is open.

Background Information and Related Automation Projects

The University of Hawaii Libraries at the main campus in Manoa Valley in Honolulu serve a diverse clientele. In addition to the over 20,000 undergraduate and graduate students and the faculty, staff, and researchers associated with the University, the libraries are heavily used by members of the general community as well as the students from the four Community College campuses on the island of Oahu and students from several private colleges.

The Library Systems Office is located in Hamilton Library and is responsible for all automation-related support for both libraries. This includes support for terminals, minicomputers, microcomputers, and any related networks.

During the summer of 1989, material containing asbestos was scheduled to be removed from water-damaged ceiling areas in Hamilton Library. The building was to be off-limits to the public and most staff during this process. In preparation for this project, the University of Hawaii Libraries began planning in August 1988 to move over 100 staff and most services and operations from Hamilton Library to Sinclair Library for the duration.

It was immediately apparent that the miles of printed reference and index materials located in Hamilton Library could not possibly be accommodated in Sinclair along with the additional staff. Therefore, a subcommittee of the Library Microcomputer Council began to investigate CD-ROM indexes as an alternative means of providing access to reference materials which would be unavailable in their printed format.

Until this time the libraries had not been utilizing much microcomputer-based information technology, nor were there many CD-ROM products available for patron use. Hamilton Library had been leasing a four-workstation InfoTrac system (the 12-inch optical disk, daisy-chained version) for several years. Information Access announced in early 1989 that the 12-inch optical disk version of the product would be phased out and replaced by a CD-ROM version before the end of the year. The original version of the CD-ROM replacement was not networked, but would require separate CD drives and disks in each workstation. Because the InfoTrac database would not be an adequate replacement for the many types of indexes that would be unreachable over the summer as well as for a number of other reasons related to collection development and budget, it was decided that the InfoTrac subscription would be cancelled on June 30, 1989 at the end of the fiscal year contract period.

The summer of 1989 marked a major turning point for the Libraries with regard to the use of new information technologies and CD-ROM. The MultiPlatter network system sold by SilverPlatter was installed temporarily in Sinclair Library in June. For five weeks prior to the MultiPlatter installation, the Library was fortunate to be able to borrow three single-user, XT-type workstations, each with an internal CD-ROM drive, from the University's School of Library and Information Studies. The Reference librarians were then faced with the logistics of handling five databases spanning eight CD-ROM disks and three workstations while they learned the search software and attempted to adjust to the new technology.

Naturally, everything that could go wrong with a single-user workstation did go wrong. A CD-ROM disc was inserted into the floppy drive, a CD disk was inserted into the CD-ROM drive but without a protective disk caddy, and a disc was stolen. Innumerable swaps were made as patrons used one disk after another. The network system was greeted with great relief and appreciation when it was finally installed.

At the end of the asbestos-removal project, the staff and the MultiPlatter network moved back to Hamilton Library. All that remained in the Sinclair Library Reference department was a single-user workstation with one external CD-ROM drive. The discs once again were swapped in and out of the drive by the Reference and Circulation staff. The wear and tear on the disks was extensive. It was often the case that within six weeks of receipt of a new disk deep scratches would develop causing retrieval errors. Discs updated quarterly often had to be replaced before the next update arrived. The wear and tear on the staff was also tremendous. Almost immediately they began to ask when Sinclair was going to get their own CD-ROM LAN. Many patrons use both the Hamilton and Sinclair Libraries and were very fond of the MultiPlatter LAN and also waited impatiently for a similar system to be installed in Sinclair.

Network Goals and Objectives

The MultiPlatter network system had been chosen to satisfy two primary objectives—to provide a replacement for as many types of printed indexes as possible and be a system which would be up and running without any false starts or a lot of time spent installing programs and/or configuring menus, software, access levels, and so forth. Cost was not a major consideration because of the need for timeliness and maximum functionality. Our goal was to provide as much shared access to as many CD-ROM databases as quickly as possible.

Unfortunately, there was no special project (or large amounts of special funding) to provide a similar justification and motivation for acquiring a LAN for Sinclair Library. However, the University of Hawaii Libraries had recently been permitted by the State Legislature to retain monies collected for fines and fees in a Library Revolving Fund. Before 1989 these monies were to be returned to the State General Fund. The Legislature specified that the retained fines and fees should be used to enhance public services. In January 1990, the University Librarian asked the Coordinator of Public Services and the Library Systems Office to develop a proposal to expand the number of library CD-ROM workstations using this money. The goal of the proposal was to provide a range of equipment to several library departments for under $18,000. In order to meet the proposal requirements and also fully fund a microcomputer-based LAN to share CD-ROM drives in Sinclair Library, a low-cost CD LAN product must be identified.

The Library Systems Office had gained more experience supporting CD-ROM applications and the MultiPlatter CD-ROM LAN, therefore it was relatively easy to formulate the basic criteria for the proposed Sinclair CD-ROM LAN. The system must use low-cost, highly-rated network software which would allow shared access to CD-ROM hardware. With no deadlines governing installation and functioning, and a limited budget, a complete support and maintenance package was not required or practical. However, because support and maintenance would not be purchased from the vendor, a system which was easy to install and use was highly desirable. Ideally, to simplify support of another LAN, the system should also match the MultiPlatter configuration with regard to the same types of workstation hardware, network protocol, and interface cards. LANtastic fit the bill perfectly.

Selection and Acquisition

Prior to the installation of the MultiPlatter system, the Library Systems Office Microcomputer Support Librarian attended a week-long workshop "Networking Personal Computers: Selection and Management of PC Based Networks" presented by the Personal Computer Group, a division of the American Institute. The workshop covered the theory and implementation of microcomputer- based local area networks. This overview of the available types of network configurations served as invaluable background for decision making prior to the selection of LANtastic.

Citations to reviews of LAN software were obtained by searching Computer Library, one of the CD-ROM databases available at Hamilton Library. LANtastic received excellent ratings from several PC journals and has continued to do so (see Bibliography). In addition, contributors to the BITNET discussion group PACS-L (Public Access Catalogs in Libraries) were reporting good experiences and low cost implementation with LANtastic.

Preliminary calls to the vendor, Artisoft, and the local dealer in Honolulu proved that the costs for the actual network hardware and software would be less than the price of one workstation. LANtastic was chosen primarily because it was low-cost yet promised to be an effective means to provide shared access to databases located on CD-ROM discs.

The Library Systems Office Microcomputer Support Librarian prepared a proposal and budget for the Coordinator of Public Services and the University Librarian. The proposal was accepted and Requests for Written Quotations were sent to the three nearest vendors.

Hardware Configuration

The LANtastic network was originally configured with two microcomputer workstations each with a printer, Ethernet interface cards, and thin coaxial cabling. A daisy-chained stack of four CD-ROM drives was installed on one workstation.

The Library Systems Office wished to avoid adding any unnecessary unknown elements to the new network in order to simplify support as much as possible. Therefore, the same type of microcomputers that had been installed for the MultiPlatter system were purchased for the LANtastic network. IBM PS/2 model 50z workstations with 12-inch VGA color monitors were chosen because they had adequately fast processors and color screens to display the software to best advantage and were easily purchased because they were listed on an official State Price List.

Technical specifications for the IBM PS/2 model 50z microcomputers include: a 10MHz Intel 80286 microprocessor with zero wait-states, 1MB of memory on the system board, a 30MB hard drive with a disk access speed of 39ms, a VGA port, 3 expansion slots, a 1.44MB 3.5 inch diskette drive, and a standard IBM enhanced keyboard.

Again, to simplify support and troubleshooting, the same type of CD-ROM drives already in use in several other library departments on single-user workstations were chosen. By early 1990, Hitachi 1503S drives were no longer state of the art but they were proven workhorses with still-acceptable access speeds. Since CD-ROM drives for library applications are not available locally in Hawaii, the library had already developed a satisfactory mail-order relationship with the Missouri Library Network Corporation and again ordered the drives from them.

The same Hewlett-Packard ThinkJet printers used on all of the terminals which access the main Library Online Catalog were chosen for the network workstations because they could be easily added to an existing maintenance contract. Parallel models were selected so that printer redirection wouldn't be needed and possible incompatibilities with CD-ROM search software could be avoided.

The IBM PS/2 model 50z workstations purchased for the network required the use of MicroChannel Architecture (MCA) interface cards. At the time of purchase, Artisoft did not offer their lower-priced starter kit for equipment with MCA expansion slots.

Starter kits are now available for both standard and MCA microcomputers and consist of: two LANtastic 2Mbps adapters with cable and terminators, the LANtastic Network Operating System (NOS) software and documentation. The starter kits use proprietary LANtastic-brand network interface cards and must be used with the LANtastic-specific network software. Ethernet starter kits are now offered as well, using LANtastic-brand Ethernet interface cards.

LANtastic also sells a version of their NOS which is adapter independent (LANtastic/AI) and may be used with a wide range of Ethernet interface cards which are NetBIOS (a widely used LAN operating system interface standard) compatible. The LANtastic/AI NOS currently costs twice as much as the Starter Kit NOS per node. This was the only type of Ethernet product sold by LANtastic in early 1990 and was called NOS 2.57g (generic).

Purchase of the higher-priced generic Ethernet product was acceptable because this product used the same protocol and type of interface as that installed in the Hamilton Library MultiPlatter network. The major drawback of using MCA-based equipment is that add-ons, including Ethernet interface cards, cost at least $100.00 more than the standard type. The library purchased the LANtastic Network OS version 2.57g and Western Digital Ethercard Plus (MCA) interface cards.

Network Software Installation

Installation and configuration of the LANtastic NOS is performed using a series of menus invoked by the NET_MGR (Network Manager) program. Initial installation of the server and workstation software is accomplished easily, in a step-by-step process begun by selecting the menu option "Install Software." The entire installation procedure is explained clearly in the LANtastic Network Operating System User's Manual.

The NET_MGR program maintains a special directory on the server where network information is stored. This directory is created when the server software is installed and it is updated whenever network resources are modified, added, or deleted.

When setting up the network, users and shared resources are described and defined. A user may correspond to a particular workstation or individual user accounts may be created if a number of different people with varying access privileges use the same workstation. Users may have different account privileges which control what type of functions the user can perform and network resources have associated access levels which control what any user may do with a given resource.

Before a user can access a network resource it must also be defined. This is accomplished by selecting "Network Access Information" from the installation menu. Resources must be named, have a link path or location identified, be described and have a level of access specified. Access types include (R)ead, (W)rite, (C)reate directory, (M)ake Directories, (L)ookup directories, (D)elete files, (K)ill directories, re(N)ame files, (E)xecute programs, (A)lter attributes, and (P)hysical access to resources. This information is input via a screen which contains the following prompts:

```
Description
Link path
CD-ROM Drive
Access Control
```

For example, the network access information for the root directory of the server might be:

```
Description :        Main Root path
Link path :          C:
CD-ROM Drive :       No
Access Control :     MANAGER              RWCMLDKNEAP
                     NUMBER1              ----L---E--
                     NUMBER2              ----L---E--
```

To insure that a CD-ROM drive is treated appropriately by the network, all that must be done when defining the CD-ROM drive as a network resource is enter "YES" at the "CD-ROM Drive" prompt on the menu and insure that the link path defined for the CD-ROM drive corresponds to the drive letter defined by the /L: switch of the Microsoft Extensions for CD-ROM (MSCDEX) setting in the CONFIG.SYS file of the CD-ROM server.

Implementation

The hardware and network software were installed in mid-April 1990. The local Artisoft dealer who submitted the lowest bid for the network software and Ethernet interface cards was intrigued by the fact that we planned to install a LANtastic system in a library and use it for multiple access to CD-ROM drives as network resources. We were apparently the first local LANtastic installation purchased for use specifically with CD-ROM drives. The vendor provided free on-site installation because he wanted to see how the CD-ROM aspect of the network software worked.

Prior to the installation of the LANtastic software, Ethernet interface cards and thin coaxial cables were installed. The Ethernet version of LANtastic uses a bus topology; workstations were linked to T-connectors on each interface card. The workstation software setup was updated to account for the new hardware. IBM PS/2's were configured by using a setup disk. After any new components are added, setup must be rerun, with any necessary device drivers copied to the setup disk, in order for the machine to recognize the existence of the new component. The process to this point was virtually trouble-free.

The Library Systems Office Microcomputer Support Librarian also installed the specific CD-ROM drive device driver for MCA interface cards and Hitachi model drivers (HITACHIB.SYS) and the Microsoft CD-ROM Extensions (MSCDEX. EXE) on the workstation which would function as the server for the CD-ROM drives. This process was the same as for a single-user workstation, and also went smoothly.

The LANtastic vendor installed the network software and explained the configuration process as he performed it. The LANtastic network software for both the non-dedicated server and the additional node was installed and functioning perfectly in less than two hours. The four daisy-chained CD-ROM drives were defined as network resources available for read/execute procedures only. The network configuration was tested by listing the directory of each CD-ROM disk from the DOS prompt of each workstation.

The CONFIG.SYS and AUTOEXEC.BAT files, after installation, contained a number of network settings as follows:

Server CONFIG.SYS

```
files=50
buffers=30
lastdrive=z
device=\drivers\HITACHIB.SYS /D:CD_0 /N:4 /P:300
```

Node CONFIG.SYS

```
files=50
buffers=30
lastdrive=z
```

No device driver was needed for the workstation which did not have the CD-ROM drives physically attached to it.

Server AUTOEXEC.BAT

```
cls
echo off
prompt $p$g
path c:\;c:\drivers;c:\lantasti;c:\util;
wd8003
ailanbios
redir server1 buffers=1 size=1024 logins=2
mscdex.exe /D:CD_0 /M:8 /L:L
server
cls
menu
```

Node: AUTOEXEC.BAT

```
echo off
cls
prompt $p$g
path c:\;c:\lantasti;c:\util;
wd8003
ailanbios
redir numbr2
net login \\server1 numbr2
net use L: \\server1\cd1
net use M: \\server1\cd2
net use N: \\server1\cd3
net use O: \\server1\cd4
net use D: \\server1\drive_c
net use B: \\server1\\floppy_B
menu
```

The WD8003 statement invokes the Ethernet interface card device driver. The AILANBIOS statement starts the LANtastic operating system software. The REDIR statement invokes the program REDIR.EXE and allows network resources to be used by any workstation as if they were physically attached to the workstation. The REDIR setting must be present in every workstation AUTOEXEC.BAT file, however, the SERVER setting is only required in the boot file of the workstation which acts as the network resource server. The NET USE settings define the path to resources on the server, for example, from the workstation node identified as "numbr2" one would type "L:" to access the CD-ROM drive defined as "cd1".

After defining the network resources and testing access to the contents of each CD-ROM disk the installation was declared a success. The LANtastic vendor left— he now knew that adding CD-ROM drives to the network was not much more complicated than defining a system printer. However, one more step was required before the network would be useful to the library. The search software for each CD-ROM database still had to be installed and configured to function on each workstation. True success from the patron or librarian's point of view had not yet been attained.

The CD-ROM drives on the server are accessed via the use of an interface card device driver and the Microsoft CD-ROM Extensions (MSCDEX.EXE) software. The MSCDEX program allows DOS on the microcomputer to act as if a CD-ROM drive is a type of large, read-only hard disk drive. The MSCDEX program communicates with CD-ROM applications and with device driver software. The device driver software in turn communicates with the physical interface card which controls signals sent to and from the CD-ROM drive. When the microcomputer is booted, the MSCDEX /D: switch in the AUTOEXEC.BAT file identifies and points to the device driver. Therefore, the HITACHIB.SYS device driver and the MSCDEX software were installed only on the server because the interface card and CD-ROM drives were physically installed only on that microcomputer.

The network was intended to be a CD-ROM disk-sharing system, rather than an application server in part because CD-ROM search software is not written in network versions which easily allow multiple use of one copy of the program. Therefore, the search software for each product was loaded on each workstation. All the search software functioned correctly from the workstation with the device driver and MSCDEX software and the actual interface card, but wouldn't work from the other workstation node.

The MSCDEX were not loaded on the other workstation because there was no physical connection to the CD-ROM drives. Unfortunately, the database search applications were configured to expect to find the MSCDEX and driver software loaded on each workstation. When attempting to search a Wilson Company product from the workstation which was not the CD-ROM drive server, the Wilson search software would return either the standard Wilson error "Serious Error 901" or a mysterious message which said "Error with Disk (A) Hit any key to continue." However, the software worked perfectly from the server workstation.

An online plea for help sent out to Artisoft and CD-ROM network users identified among the PACS-L contributors yielded the solution within a week. The Library Systems Programmer at Virginia Polytechnic Institute and State University revealed that the Wilson software should be configured for a DOS drive not any particular model of CD-ROM drive. The server had already loaded the MSCDEX settings and LANtastic NOS had defined the CD-ROM drives as DOS-type network resources. Therefore, the application software for the other workstation should not be configured for CD-ROM drives.

The Wilson application software is installed or modified via a menu-driven Install program. The Install program prompts for information on the hard drive and boot drive, the location of the Wilson software and the CD-ROM model and number of drives. In order for the Wilson search software to function, the workstation(s) which did not have a physical connection to the CD-ROM drives were configured for a CD-ROM model of "Magnetic drive" rather than "High Sierra Drive/Microsoft Extentions" [sic]. Success at last! Patrons could then search any of the four Wilson CD-ROM disks from either of the workstations.

A similar problem was encountered when a fifth chained drive containing the OCLC Music Library database was added. When trying to search the Music Library CD from any workstation other than the server, the error message "Problem 1720, Software was unable to access Compact Disc Drive—Program requires MS-DOS CD-ROM Extensions" would display. The installation program for this product did not include an option to define a CD-ROM drive type. After several calls to OCLC the solution was obtained. The configuration file updated by the software installation process (MUSICAL.DB) had to be edited at the DOS level so the software would work correctly on the workstation(s) which did not have a physical connection to the CD-ROM drives. The parameter in the MUSICAL.DB file which contained the default information "location: cd_rom" had to be changed to "location: local".

Costs

The proposed budget for the original configuration of the LANtastic network made use of the existing equipment: one PS/2 model 50z and ThinkJet printer with a single Hitachi 1503S drive and interface card. The proposal called for obtaining an additional microcomputer and printer, three more CD-ROM drives, two Ethernet interface cards and the LANtastic software for $6,081. Actual costs were within $50.00 of the proposed budget.

Ongoing costs for the original installation are negligible. However, it seems that no matter what size the network is it is never big enough. Fortunately, the University of Hawaii Computing Center (UHCC), whose mission is to support student/faculty access to computing resources, has become a strong supporter of public-access microcomputers in the library.

The Reference department wanted to make more databases available on the LAN, therefore the original four Hitachi 1503S CD-ROM drives were replaced in mid-June 1990 by five faster Hitachi TCDR 6000 drives. The 1503S's were recycled and chained to existing installed drives on single-user workstations in other library departments. In addition to expanding the number of drives, another network workstation was added. The purchase of the new CD-ROM drives and the workstation and printer were made by the UHCC on behalf of the library.

Each of the workstations has its own printer. The patrons love the print capability but many seem to use it to excess. The problem of coping with the increasing cost of providing print capability is the only major ongoing cost. The library uses the Hewlett-Packard plain paper ink cartridge so that the lowest price continuous feed paper may be used in the printers, but each ink cartridge costs nearly $12.00 and each printer uses two or more cartridges per month.

Network Use

Both of the library CD-ROM networks are used extensively by students. The Hamilton Library MultiPlatter LAN is used by researchers and faculty to a greater extent than the LANtastic network in Sinclair because of the types of databases available. The databases currently available on the LANtastic network are: Readers' Guide Abstracts, Art Index, Biography Index, and Book Review Index, all produced by the H.W. Wilson Company, and Music Library, produced by OCLC. Users generally print out their search results, but may also download to diskettes.

Patrons unfamiliar with the downloading function seem to be confused about what is happening when they choose that option and therefore a dozen or so files per week are saved on the hard disk of each workstation.

Regular preventative maintenance on these machines includes the deletion of extraneous files, searches for lost clusters, and optimization of the hard disk. This is done by the Library Systems Office using Norton Utilities such as Disk Doctor and Speed Disk.

Another aspect of usage is one common to nearly all public-use microcomputer and CD-ROM situations. Patrons tend to reboot or turn the micros off whenever they have problems or are finished with the machine. These abrupt terminations cause the hard disk to clutter up with potentially damaging lost clusters and can cause damage to the equipment over time. To circumvent this the Library installed locks over the power switches. A key is now necessary to turn the workstations off and on.

RAM-Cram

LANtastic has been touted as requiring the lowest RAM to run a network. However, a number of library CD-ROM products are notorious for requiring rather large amounts of RAM. Wilson CD-ROM search software, at least through version 2.21, are among the most RAM-intensive programs. In addition to the RAM requirements for the network software, the MSCDEX require 8k of RAM for each CD-ROM drive. When the number of CD-ROM drives were increased, these competing RAM requirements clashed.

Eight Hitachi TCDR 6000 drives may be chained on a standard interface card, however, an MCA interface card for this model drive was only capable of supporting four chained units. When the library wished to expand the number of CD-ROM drives from four to six, two interface cards were required and the dreaded "RAM cram" problem arose. The amount of RAM needed did not leave enough for all of the search software to function.

After some study of the LANtastic manual, the network parameters were reduced from the standard defaults to the absolute bare minimum and all other system configuration files were reduced to the minimum. Even with the pare-down parameters, five drives was the maximum number which could be used and still leave enough RAM for the Wilson CD search software to run from all workstations.

With only five drives rather than six, further balancing of RAM requirements was still needed. Music Library had files and buffers requirements that were too high in combination with the server software requirements to leave enough RAM for the Wilson search software to run on the server workstation. If the files and buffers were reduced to free enough RAM for the Wilson software, the Music Library software would not function. The server workstation could only be used to search four of the five databases; Music Library was available only at the other workstations. Therefore, the boot files of the server were modified to the following settings:

```
files=20
buffers=20
lastdrive=Q
device=\drivers\HITACHIB.SYS /D:CD_0 /N:4 /P:300
device=\drivers\HITACHIB.SYS /D:CD_1 /N:1 /P:360
```

The files and buffers statement were set to the minimum that would allow the software to function. The lastdrive was set to only one drive beyond the letter of the last defined CD-ROM drive (P). An additional device driver statement was required for the second interface card for the fifth CD-ROM drive and the addresses of the controller cards were supplied via the /P switch.

Server AUTOEXEC.BAT

```
cls
echo off
prompt $p$g
path c:\;c:\drivers;c:\lantasti;c:\util;
wd8003
ailanbios
redir server1 buffers=1 size=512 logins=1
mscdex.exe /D:CD_0 /D:CD_1 /M:8 /L:L
server
cls
menu
```

As shown in the above example, the REDIR settings for the server were set to the minimum values of 1 buffer with a size of 512 and 1 login.

The RAM cram issue is one that would probably not become a problem when using LANtastic for standard PC application programs. However, the addition of multiple CD-ROM drives with the associated MSCDEX driver makes memory management issues a serious concern. The Library plans to deal with this problem but it will involve some additional costs. Most probably a dedicated, AT-type server will be used to off-load the network and CD-ROM control programs to a workstation that is not used for database searching. Perhaps in conjunction with a memory management program, this should allow the expansion of the daisy-chained CD-ROM drives to a maximum of eight. This expansion will cost approximately $3,000. The UHCC or a special grant may be used to acquire this additional functionality within the next six months.

Evaluation of the System

The LANtastic system has lived up to its high ratings and to the library's original goals and expectations for it. Because LANtastic was installed to provide access to shared CD-ROM resources, integrating the CD-ROM equipment into the configuration has been the only factor which has required extra thought and effort. The LANtastic manual is quite good and specifically addresses configuring CD-ROM drives as part of the network setup. The glaring lack of an index is the only major fault of the documentation.

The functionality expected has been fully delivered, and the RAM limitation is a relatively easily solved problem which cannot be directly attributed to the LANtastic system but to our particular use of the network.

The MultiPlatter system in Hamilton Library is fully supported by SilverPlatter, and maintenance fees commensurate with such full support are paid. On the other hand, the LANtastic network in Sinclair Library is supported only by the Library Systems Office and any hardware warranties that may be in effect. Initial installation and configuration of the menu system and search software required quite a bit of time and effort on the part of the Microcomputer Support Librarian, and upgrades of CD-ROM search software often require further file tweaking and phone calls to the various database vendors. This type of work has a hidden cost which is difficult to quantify. However, evaluation on the basis of the initial purchase price and upgrades has proved LANtastic's claim to deliver an inexpensive high-value network system. From the Libraries' point of view it has indeed been cost-effective and there is nothing that would have been done differently.

Implementation and support of the LANtastic network for the purpose of sharing CD-ROM drives has been fairly simple and straight-forward partly due to prior experience with the MultiPlatter system. However, even if a library is going to install a first network, LANtastic may be one of the easiest to work with. To install any microcomputer based network, any library will need at least one support staff person on hand with experience with DOS, microcomputers, and CD-ROM installation issues. If a minimum level of expertise is available, LANtastic represents an excellent network system suitable for many types of libraries.

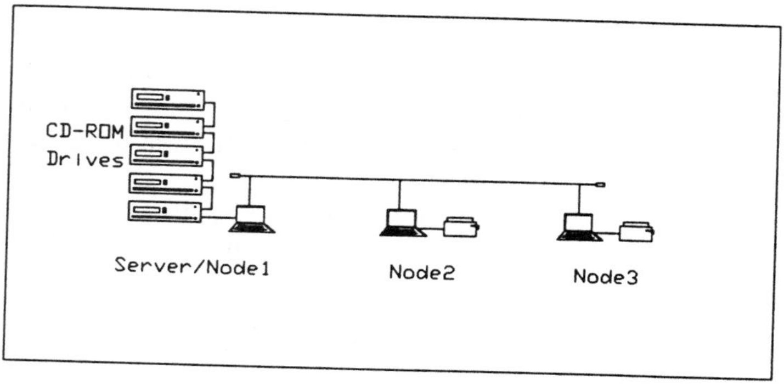

Figure 7.1
Network Layout for Sinclair Undergraduate Library LAN

List of Vendors and Products

Artisoft

Artisoft Plaza
575 E. River Road
Tucson, AS 85704
(602) 293-6363
(602) 293-8065 (fax)

Missouri Library Network Corporation

10332 Old Olive Street Road
St. Louis, MO 63141
(800) 444-8096
(314) 567-3799
(314) 567-3798 (fax)

American Institute

55 Main Street
Madison, NJ 07940

Bibliography

Chandler, Doug, Gerber, Barry, and Zimmerman, Michael. January 8, 1990. "Software broadens access to CD-ROM," *PC Week* 6(1): 23-27.

Ferrill, Paul and Derfler, Frank J. March 28, 1989. "Building workgroup solutions: low-cost LANs," *PC Magazine* 8(6): 94-116.

Lauriston, Robert. November 1989. "No pain, big gains: five low-cost LANs." *PC World* 7(11): 160-168.

Morrow, Blaine Victor. November 1990. "Do-it-yourself CD-ROM LANs: a review of LANtastic and CD Connection." *CD-ROM Librarian*, 12-24.

Sherman, Chris. 1988. *The CD-ROM Handbook*. New York: McGraw-Hill.

Thompson, M. Keith and Maxwell, Kimberly. February 27, 1990. "Building workgroup solutions: networking CD-ROMs." *PC Magazine* 9(4): 237-260.

About the Author

Martha Chantiny is the Small/Microcomputer Systems Support Librarian for the Sinclair Undergraduate Library at the University of Hawaii at Manoa and is responsible for all aspects of microcomputer support in the Library and serves as the automation liaison with the six Community College libraries in the University of Hawaii System.

She received her B.A. in Anthropology from the University of Hawaii at Hilo and her M.L.S. from University of Hawaii at Manoa. In her varied and itinerant professional library career over the last ten years she has been at different times cataloger, bibliographer, Science Reference Librarian, and Systems Librarian at the Manoa Graduate Library.

8

An Off-the-Shelf Solution:
A MultiPlatter CD-ROM LAN

Bonnie R. Nelson
John Jay College of Criminal Justice

ABSTRACT

At John Jay College of Criminal Justice the decision about whether or not to set up a network for CD-ROM access was more difficult than the actual implementation. Librarians had serious concerns about the cost in terms of both money and staff time. When money became available SilverPlatter was awarded a bid to set up a four-workstation CD-ROM network. One workstation on the network provides access for the visually impaired.

Not all networks are the result of careful planning and meticulous research. Some are put together in a rush because suddenly money has become available and must be spent quickly. It was in such a manner that the John Jay College of Criminal Justice Library acquired its CD-ROM network.

Background

John Jay College of Criminal Justice is one of the senior colleges of the City University of New York. Its 8,000 students major in criminal justice, fire science, public administration, and related fields, on both the undergraduate and graduate level. The Library maintains a good undergraduate liberal arts collection and an excellent and well-known collection of criminal justice materials. Its holdings total just under 200,000 volumes, with 1400 periodical subscriptions.

The policy of the Library's reference department has generally been that, even though we could not provide our students and faculty with as complete a collection in all fields as we would like, we would try to provide the bibliographic tools necessary at least to identify what materials were needed. It was with that philosophy that we began offering free online bibliographic searching to our faculty and graduate students in 1980. That same philosophy prompted us to acquire indexes on CD-ROM as soon as we were able.

Although John Jay is one of the smaller of the senior colleges in CUNY, it has been among the leaders in automating services. It was the first unit of CUNY to offer online searching, and when the University committed itself to a university-wide integrated library system John Jay was one of the first three libraries to convert to the new system (NOTIS) in 1987/88.

At this same time, the College was planning a new building to replace an outmoded and leased facility. The Library was to be the centerpiece of the new building. And, along with the new building came money for new equipment.

When the new library opened in September 1988, two CD-ROM work- stations were in place. Each workstation consisted of an IBM PS/2 Model 30 with color monitor, a Hitachi CD-ROM drive, and a Hewlett-Packard ThinkJet printer. Our first databases were SilverPlatter's PsycLIT and Sociofile, with each workstation being dedicated to one database. This worked quite well initially, but as the CD-ROM workstations became more popular we found that students often had lengthy waits for a workstation. The reference staff also found that there were many fascinating CD-ROM products available and the initial databases were soon followed by the MLA Bibliography, the Constitution Papers with Wordcruncher software, and Food Analyst Plus from Hopkins Technology. Changing disks in the drives now became a problem for the reference staff.

When we were told that there was still money available in the new building fund, we immediately decided to order two more PS/2s and three more CD-ROM drives. The extra drive would be connected to a computer in the Library classroom and used for teaching purposes. We did not at this time consider a CD-ROM network.

Pros and Cons of Installing a Network

By 1989 and 1990 CD-ROM networks were becoming a very hot topic in the printed library literature and on computer network discussion lists, such as PACS-L. SilverPlatter had come out with its MultiPlatter system, originally using Meridian drives, and later CBIS equipment. Shortly thereafter the literature was full of talk about lower-cost solutions that systems people could build, using CD-ROM networking systems such as LANtastic and Opti-Net.

The benefits to us of a CD-ROM network were fairly obvious—and considerable:

o   numerous users would be able to access each database at the same time.
o   librarians would no longer need to spend their time changing disks, and could spend it helping users instead.
o   CD-ROM drives and disks could be kept out of the public area in a secure location; this is of particular importance since the Library had already experienced the theft of one drive with a disk inside.

The drawbacks of a network were not all as obvious, but were also considerable:

o   the high cost of a turnkey system or of the equipment required for some network configurations.
o   the considerable staff time that might be involved in implementing such a network.

o   the staff time required to maintain the hardware and software on a network.

o   the additional charges assessed by the database producers for databases mounted on a network.

o   the uncertainty of the real need for a network in the future: NOTIS Systems, Inc. unveiled its MDAS (Multiple Database Access System) to allow access with NOTIS software to online indexes mounted on the mainframe, rendering the need for further development of CD-ROMs on campus questionable.

The chief librarian and collection development librarian were particularly concerned about the network charges levied by the database producers. While the hardware costs of a network might be picked up by the money now available for capital expenditures, the subscription costs of the data come out of the library's book budget. The additional charges for putting Sociofile and PsycLIT on a network come to about $2500 per year, a considerable sum for a library the size of John Jay. For quite a while this cost was the deciding factor in saying no to networks.

As Systems Librarian, however, my major worry was the commitment of staff time a network might take. The professional staff of the Library numbers eleven, and with a staff that size I can be a systems librarian only half the time, the other half of my time being devoted to reference work. Furthermore, since John Jay College has no computer science major, low-cost, technically competent students would be hard to come by. From the library literature and from assorted queries and answers on PACS-L, it was clear that implementing and maintaining a network was fraught with perils and highly time-consuming. The challenge was exciting, but realistically, the time was simply not available to learn what was needed about networks, to determine the proper configure of hardware and software, to make it all work together, and to troubleshoot it on an ongoing basis.

The Decision

In June 1990 the Library once again heard from the College's business office that there was money from the building fund available for equipment, but that there would be no more after this. By this time it was clear that New York State was in a recession, that a major budget crisis was coming, and that money for new equipment purchases would not be available for some time. Ready or not, if the Library wanted a CD-ROM network within the foreseeable future, it would have to invest in one now.

It was at this point that reasoned planning left off. The Business Office wanted purchase orders for equipment within a week. I put out frantic phone calls to every computer guru I knew in the College and the University. Most were happy to give me names of hardware and software to buy and in some cases the names and telephone numbers of vendors; most assured me that I could put together a network (they knew because they were working full-time, with their assistants, on putting one together right now), and most advised against buying a complete system from a vendor like SilverPlatter.

Their arguments against purchasing a turnkey system were reasoned and good. The major piece of equipment involved in such a system, the tower, might quickly become obsolete, rendering the whole network a dinosaur. Such a network would not be flexible enough to allow for change and expansion and the incorporation of new technology. Finally, such a network would be overpriced.

I managed to persuade the Business Office to extend their deadline for a week, during which I went to the ALA annual conference and attended a pre-conference on CD-ROM networks. Here I had the opportunity to hear about the time and effort that had gone into developing some very impressive CD-ROM networks. I was also able to talk to vendors of both turnkey systems and components to find out what level of support I could expect from them. It became obvious to me that the John Jay Library simply did not have the staff resources to attempt to put together a network from component parts.

The Bidding Process

Consequently, upon my return from ALA I consulted with the Business Office and we decided to put out a request for bid for a complete CD-ROM network with hardware, software, and maintenance to be provided by one vendor. Specifications were based upon some of the systems I had seen demonstrated at ALA, adjusted for what we felt was important to John Jay. On-site installation, maintenance, and training were stipulated. We briefly described what functions the menuing and statistics software must provide. We also listed all of the CD-ROM products that we wanted to mount on the network, and specified that the vendor must make sure they worked with the winning system.

As I should have expected, after I had been given no more than ten days to research and write a request for bid, the bid itself didn't go out until October—about three months later.

Part of the bidding process at John Jay involves checking references. Besides allowing me to verify the qualifications of the bidders, I learned an enormous amount from speaking with the librarians and systems people that the vendors recommended, and I was confirmed in my judgment that we needed a turnkey network. The library community is extraordinarily friendly and willing to help, something I had learned from the various electronic lists to which I subscribed. I had thought I would need an hour or two to check references, but the process wound up taking days. Partly this was a result of playing telephone tag, but for the most part it was because almost every person I contacted had a great deal of wisdom to impart and were more than happy to share it with me.

In the end, SilverPlatter was awarded the contract for their MultiPlatter network. The price they bid for our system was $26,196. This included a 286 network server, four Ethernet network interface cards, system software, an expansion unit, statistics software, onsite installation and testing, shipping, and the addition of non-Silver-Platter titles to the network.

Installation

SilverPlatter contacted me almost immediately to set up a date for installation. Any delay after that was only on the Library's part, since we needed to install a 200 ft.-long cable, which SilverPlatter provided, from the workroom where the CD-ROM tower was to be, to our CD-ROM workstation area. The College's own electricians did the work. In the workstation area the PCs are contiguous and no special electrical work was needed.

The equipment was shipped and arrived at John Jay before the promised date of installation. Also before installation, a technician contacted me and sent the forms that he needed filled out in order to know what equipment and what CD-ROM products we had. The forms were well designed and required us to specify exactly how the various software products were invoked. On the day of installation the technician arrived, installed the Ethernet network cards in all the workstations, installed the tower, installed the software, tested it, and gave four of us some basic training. This was accomplished in one day, and went off with hardly a hitch.

The Network

There are four workstations in our network. All are IBM PS/2 Model 30s with 640K RAM and 40MB hard drives. All have color monitors. Each workstation is also equipped with a Hewlett-Packard ThinkJet printer. This equipment was provided by the Library and for the most part has worked reliably.

The network card which SilverPlatter installed in each workstation is an EtherCard Plus made by Western Digital. The workstations are chained together with thin-wire Ethernet coaxial cable attached to the back of each workstation with a BNC T-type coaxial connector. The first workstation is attached in the same way to the CD-ROM server, which is kept in a separate, more secure area.

The network software that SilverPlatter provides with this system is called Network-OS, from CBIS, Inc. Network-OS is a peer-to-peer DOS-based LAN with NetBIOS compatibility. Its sole function on the LAN at John Jay is to provide access to the CD-ROM drives on the dedicated CD-ROM server, but the software itself does provide for setting up workstations as file servers and print servers.

The major hardware element provided by SilverPlatter is the dedicated CD-ROM server, a tower of seven CD-ROM drives made by CBIS, Inc. This formidable-looking piece of equipment is basically a microprocessor with a monochrome monitor, a keyboard, one 1.2 megabyte floppy drive, no hard drive, and up to seven Toshiba model 3210B CD-ROM drives stacked on top of each other in a chassis. The server at John Jay has an Intel 80286 12MHz CPU; a 386 version is also available. The system provided by SilverPlatter comes with two megabytes of memory but the unit may be customized to include up to 16 megabytes of memory. The CD-ROM host adaptor has a SCSI interface with connectors for seven internal drives. These drives are stacked from top to bottom and set to SCSI interface numbers from 0 to 6 according to dip switch settings on the drives themselves. Also installed in the Server is the same type Ethernet card as on the workstations.

Up to two expansion units can be ordered for the server, with up to seven drives in each, for a maximum of twenty-one CD-ROM drives. In our case, we ordered one full tower of seven drives plus one expansion unit with just one drive. We had planned to use all eight drives, but, as expected, the budget took a sharp turn for the worse and we were not able to order all the products we had wanted.

Provided with the CD-ROM Server is CBIS's CD Connection software. This adjunct to the network operating software enables the individual workstations to access the CD-ROM drives. CD Connection provides a substitute for the Microsoft extensions for CD-ROM while supporting all MSCDEX calls. It eliminates the need for installing the CD-ROM extensions on each workstation. The CD Connection software also provides for disk caching on the extended or expanded memory of the CD-ROM server.

The MultiPlatter system makes efficient use of DOS memory. Together the device driver, the Network-OS software, and the CD Connection software use only 40K of memory on a workstation.

SilverPlatter provides its own menuing and statistical software setup in a directory called MPLATTER. The menus appear quite attractive on a color monitor and are easy to set up with a program called MENUEDIT. Menuedit allows you to change the order of the items on the menu, to change their names, to provide password protection for any application, and to group menu items for statistical purposes. It is with Menuedit that you provide the DOS commands to load the appropriate software for each CD-ROM application, or non CD-ROM application, if you desire. Menuedit is also the program that you use to identify new CD-ROM disks to the system when new or update disks are received. On a simple set-up screen the system administrator indicates the number or letter of the CD-ROM drive in the tower where the disk is currently installed. The software searches that disk and finds the volume identifier on the disk, which it uses thereafter to identify that disk to the system, even if the disk has been physically moved to another drive.

The MultiPlatter software also allows for setting time-outs on the system to revert back to the menu if no use is recorded for a specified period of time, and provides warnings on screen to users that they have exceeded their allotted time (e.g., 30 minutes at John Jay), and should yield the workstation if other users are waiting.

MultiPlatter's statistical package, which is a separately priced option, provides the general statistics needed on CD-ROM use. The statistics are maintained on each workstation and can be accessed at each workstation at any time through the main menu. On a color monitor, the histograms displayed by the package are very pretty. For reporting purposes, however, the statistics package also comes with a program, called Absorb, which enables the library to collect and cumulate the statistics from each workstation onto one disk for a specified period of time (e.g., one month) and produce printed reports. It is possible to find out the total hours of use of all menu items, of particular CD-ROM titles, or of groups of titles. Statistics are also provided for number of users, for average length of use, and for number of simultaneous users.

There is no file server on our system, so all CD-ROM software must be installed on each workstation that needs to access it. This has a few drawbacks. When new versions of software are released they must be reinstalled on each workstation, a time consuming operation. The other major problem is that MultiPlatter's menuing system can limit the number of users of a product only if there is a file server that can keep track of each workstation. Since we did not have the money to purchase site licenses for our CD-ROM products, we wanted to limit the number of users at a time to one. However, this was easily resolved by simply limiting the number of workstations that offered that product on their menus.

Access for the Visually Impaired

One of the Library's goals is to be completely accessible to the handicapped. We had been working on making our OPAC accessible to the visually impaired and had decided to try to combine in one workstation the online catalog and access to a CD-ROM player. With the purchase of the CD-ROM network came the challenge to put this workstation on the network and have all CD-ROM products and our catalog available to the visually impaired.

We were working with a speech synthesizer called VERT Plus by Telesensory Systems, Inc. VERT Plus consists of an internal board with software that enables a PC to speak what is displayed on the screen. We also purchased software called 3278 VERT, which works with an IRMA board (by DCA) to allow a PC to function as a 3278 terminal for the blind. Since our OPAC terminals are 3278-type terminals this was ideal for displaying our catalog. After a little bit of work we were also able to get regular VERT to work with our CD-ROM products.

When we put this workstation on the LAN, one interrupt had to be changed to avoid a conflict; otherwise the change was transparent. The only thing that was a challenge was to configure the menu so that VERT was not invoked with every use. We have very few blind students at John Jay and the workstation would have to be used by sighted students as well. VERT slows down the system while it speaks everything, and it is a bit disconcerting to hear a voice suddenly coming from the cabinet above the computer where the earphones are kept.

The solution was to make the VERT program a separate menu item and to have it password protected. Once it is turned on by a blind user it will read the screen for whatever product is invoked afterwards. It is worth pointing out, however, that the fancy color graphics used by many of the CD-ROM vendors are extremely confusing to VERT and it is often necessary to turn the voice off and then on again to make any progress through the program.

Evaluation

On the whole, we are very satisfied with our network. Once the contract was signed we were up and running within a month, and most of that time was spent waiting for our own electrician to run a cable. We have had no hardware problems, and very few software problems, which have been easily resolved over the telephone. The only part of the package that did not work as promised was the Absorb program for the statistics package. This did not work at all initially, but we have been given a replacement version that appears to do most of what we need.

Our patrons love having four workstations and not having to ask the librarians for help in changing disks. The librarians love not having to change disks, and having the drives in a secure place. Our statistics indicate that we are getting a tremendous amount of use of our CD-ROM products.

While the cost of the MultiPlatter system was high there was very little staff time involved in implementation, and even less, so far, with maintenance. At the John Jay Library, which is chronically understaffed, this has rendered the system almost priceless.

What is disappointing, however, is that because this year we could not afford the multi-user licensing fee on our most popular CD-ROM products, PsycLIT and Sociofile, we must still limit access to these CD-ROMs to only one user at a time. Although we could afford the capital expenditure of $26,000 for the network, we could not afford one-tenth of that cost from our operating budget to make it fully functional. That is our top priority for next year, if the budget situation improves at all.

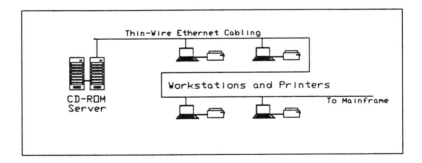

Figure 8.1
Network Diagram of John Jay College of Criminal Justice
MultiPlatter Network

We would also like to add two more workstations to the network. CD-ROMs are very popular tools which really do make research easier and more efficient for our students and faculty. As new titles become available that are crucial to the mission of the school, we would like to be able to offer them without forcing our patrons to wait long periods. Without a doubt, the CD-ROM network has provided improved service to our users; however, we still must work to stay ahead of their needs.

Vendors and Products

SilverPlatter Information, Inc.
One Newton Executive Park
Newton Lower Falls, MA 02162-1449
617-969-2332

Telesensory Systems, Inc.
455 North Bernardo Ave.
Mountain View, CA 94043-5274
800-227-8418
VERT Plus speech synthesizer

DCA
1000 Alderman Drive
Alpharetta, GA 30201-4199
IRMA 3 Convertible 3278 emulation board.

About the Author

Bonnie R. Nelson is Deputy Chief Librarian and Systems Librarian at John Jay College of Criminal Justice, City University of New York. She holds a B.A. from City College of CUNY, an M.S. in Library Service from Columbia University and an M.A. in Anthropology from New York University. She has previously written on library automation and published library catalogs.

9

A LANtastic CD-ROM Network with Remote Access through a Campus Digital Voice/Data Network

Harry M. Kriz, Nikhil Jain, and E. Alan Armstrong
University Libraries, Virginia Polytechnic Institute and State University

ABSTRACT

We describe a remotely-accessible CD-ROM network implemented in a large research library. Within the library building, the LANtastic-based network connects eight public workstations which are distributed between two different floors of the main library building. A ninth workstation on the network is operated as a host under the remote PC operating software package PC Anywhere III. A caller at a remote PC, which can be located anywhere that a phone line or a campus data connection is available, can call the host using suitable terminal emulation software. The remote user's workstation is then virtually indistinguishable from a workstation connected directly to the CD-ROM network.

Goals of the LAN

This paper describes a LAN which was implemented to provide multi-user access to CD-ROM databases in a large research library. Before installing the LAN, it was necessary to determine what problems were to be solved and what services were to be offered by the LAN. Because it is all too tempting for computer enthusiasts to call for the implementation of elegant, expensive solutions, it is important for librarians to define the parameters which will determine the success of any computerized system. Brainstorming sessions involving computer specialists, librarians, and those with enough knowledge in both fields to forestall misunderstandings over goals and techniques, led to three goals for the LAN:

1. To improve library service by providing shared, multi-user, simultaneous access to CD-ROM databases so as to eliminate disc swapping and user scheduling.
2. To further improve service by providing access to CD-ROM databases from branch libraries and from offices.
3. To maintain maximum hardware and software flexibility and hardware interchangeability which would allow the LAN to evolve into a generalized reference service system involving additional shared database applications.

Users of the LAN

The LAN is used by patrons and staff in the University Libraries at Virginia Polytechnic Institute & State University (Virginia Tech) in Blacksburg, VA. A brief description of the university and its libraries is useful in gaining perspective on the network.

Virginia Tech is Virginia's largest university, offering over 200 degree programs. With more than $100 million per year of funded research in agriculture, biotechnology, computer science, engineering, architecture, energy management, and other fields, Virginia Tech is also the state's primary research institution.

The University Libraries consist of the centralized Carol M. Newman Library and four branch libraries. The Veterinary Medicine Library, the Art and Architecture Library, and the Geology Library support specialized areas on the Blacksburg campus. University programs in the Washington, D.C. metropolitan area are served by The Northern Virginia Graduate Center Library in Falls Church, Virginia. Collections of the Libraries include about 1.7 million volumes (829,700 titles), nearly 18,000 current serials, and 5 million microforms. The Libraries receive most series of depository U.S. government documents. The Special Collections Department houses rare books, manuscripts, and realia, and serves as the home of the Archives of American Aerospace Exploration and the International Archive of Women in Architecture. The Libraries' interlibrary loan operation is the most active in the state, with over 24,000 transactions completed each year.

The Libraries' staff of 50.5 faculty, 106 classified staff, and 47 FTE student assistants provide service to Virginia Tech students, faculty and staff, to the broader Blacksburg community, and to the commonwealth as a whole. On-campus enrollment at the university totals about 22,900 students, 19 percent of whom are graduate students. Full-time instructional faculty members number approximately 1500.

The Reference Department provides public services at three reference desks on the second floor of Newman Library and at one reference desk on the fourth floor. The second floor desks include the Information Desk, the Main Reference Desk, and the Electronic Reference Area (ERA) desk. These are staffed 104 hours per week and handle more than 70,000 questions each year. The Science Reference Desk on the fourth floor of Newman Library is staffed 72 hours per week and handles almost 20,000 questions during the year. In the past year, more than 3400 patrons used CD-ROM databases in the ERA, first at stand-alone workstations, and later via the CD-ROM network.

The Electronic Reference Area provides access to InfoTrac, NewsBank, and Autographics (government documents) CD-ROM databases at stand-alone workstations. Two online systems, WestLaw and Dow Jones News/Retrieval Service, are also available. The CD-ROM network was made available to the public in mid-1990 and is the most recent addition to the ERA. It provides shared access to Agricola, CIRR, ERIC, MLA Bibliography, NTIS, PsycLIT, and other databases.

Network Selection and Remote Access

Choosing the LANtastic network operating system

Articles in the microcomputer and library literature, and the recommendation of a satisfied user, led us to investigate LANtastic as the basis for the Virginia Tech CD-ROM network. Important arguments in favor of LANtastic are the following:

o A LANtastic starter kit with hardware for 2 workstations can be purchased for well under $500. This cost is so low that it can be fully justified as a cost for training in networking fundamentals even if the product is not used later in a production network.

o LANtastic specifically supports CD-ROM drives as network devices, in contrast to other network operating systems which do not recognize CD-ROM drives.

o LANtastic reduces system complexity and expense by eliminating the need for an additional layer of CD-ROM networking software running on top of the network operating system software. More workstation RAM is available for use by the CD-ROM application software.

o LANtastic's use of small device drivers frees more workstation RAM for use by the CD-ROM application software.

o LANtastic requires the use of the Microsoft extensions only on the CD-ROM drive server, which further reduces expense and frees still more workstation RAM for use by the CD-ROM application software.

o LANtastic works with any brand of CD-ROM drive that works with the Microsoft extensions, whereas some turnkey systems are limited to using a single brand of drive supplied by the system vendor. CD-ROM drives from existing stand-alone workstations can be incorporated into a developing network.

o LANtastic is especially well-suited for use in small installations. As a peer-to-peer network operating system, it allows each and every PC on the network to be used both as a searching workstation and as a CD-ROM drive server.

o LANtastic allows a single microcomputer to be used both as the network file server and as the CD-ROM drive server, thereby reducing expense and complexity in smaller networks.

Finally, it should be noted that LANtastic is perhaps the easiest network operating system to install and maintain. Initial installation was accomplished by following the straightforward instructions in the manual. Soon after initial installation, day-to-day maintenance was taken over by Reference Department personnel who are not professional programmers. LANtastic's ease of use results in part from the excellent design of Net Manager, a comprehensive network management tool. Net Manager enables the network administrator to install new users, change passwords, regulate access, install new devices such as printers and CD-ROM drives, and keep audit trails. These functions are menu-driven with online help.

In addition, LANtastic's NET command allows the user to connect with network resources using interactive commands, menu-driven commands, or DOS batch files. NET commands issued from a workstation allow a user to login to the server, look at the print spooler, change passwords, connect to network resources, converse with other users, and send mail. Implementation of NET commands through batch files allows workstations to interact with the network in a manner transparent to the public.

Choosing a Remote Access Method

The term "remote access" refers to using the networked CD-ROM applications from terminals or microcomputers which are not part of the network. Remote users access the CD-ROM applications via telephone lines or from other networks which can be linked to the CD-ROM network through communication lines. On the CD-ROM network itself, database application software runs on an IBM compatible PC, or it could be run on a virtual machine implemented on an 80386-based PC running under a multitasking operating system such as DESQview. Either type of machine, real or virtual, can function as a host for implementing remote access to the CD-ROM drives attached to the network.

Remote access to the CD-ROM network can be implemented by enabling a remote user to operate the host machine from a remote terminal using appropriate communications software. The host PC on the network must be running communications software which can communicate with the remote terminal, and which can pass commands and responses to and from the applications software running on the host. The host must be connected to a communications line, typically a modem connected to a phone line, which will allow it to receive incoming calls from the remote PC.

PC Anywhere is a remote access software package that enables a remote terminal to call a host and run applications on that host PC. The remote terminal must be able to accurately emulate both the keyboard and the screen functions of the host. PC Anywhere allows the host PC to be accessed by many different types of terminals, or by PCs running a variety of terminal emulation software. In practice, the choice of terminal emulation is limited by the way in which the CD-ROM applications software uses the PC keyboard and screen.

Keyboard emulation is not a particular problem for CD-ROM applications. Screen emulation, however, can cause problems. Many CD-ROM applications take full advantage of the complete IBM PC character set, and they use color to aid the user in interpreting what is on the screen. Dumb terminals cannot reproduce the

IBM PC character set, and translations of that character set to the characters available at the terminal may not provide usable screen emulation. The terminal emulation package ATERM is provided with PC Anywhere. It provides essentially perfect screen and keyboard emulation when a remote PC is used to call the host on the network. For Macintosh users, a product called PC MacTerm is available from the manufacturer of PC Anywhere to allow remote operation of a PC from a Macintosh computer. We have not tested this system, however.

IBM/ROLM Digital Switch

Description

The major campus communications network available at Virginia Tech for the provision of library services is an IBM/ROLM digital switch, popularly referred to as the CBX (Computerized Branch Exchange). This digital voice/data network is the campus telephone system, as well as the most generally available data communications network. Because it is the campus telephone network, and because physical data connections are made through the telephone itself, connections are readily available in every office and dorm room. Callers from off-campus, which includes the majority of Tech students who live off-campus, can connect to the CBX through normal phone lines. In addition to data communications to the campus IBM mainframe, the CBX provides access to the Library's VTLS online public access catalog. It was natural to consider the CBX as the most desirable means of providing a communications link between a host PC on the CD-ROM network and a remote PC.

Remote Access Problem

There is a problem when a caller at a remote PC on the CBX tries to open communications with a host PC on the CBX using commercially available remote PC operating software such as PC Anywhere. In such a configuration, the remote caller will usually get a busy signal from the host PC, even when the host is not in use. Thus, it is not possible to use this popular type of commercial software in a routine manner to operate a PC remotely over CBX lines.

The problem originates in the fact that the commercial software packages assume that the PC is connected to a modem which is connected to an analog phone line. In this case the modem acts as an intermediary between the host and the remote PC. The software assumes that the modem will receive an incoming call and establish the communication link before transferring control to the software. In this arrangement, the software on the host tells the modem of its readiness to communicate by setting DTR high at the PC serial port and sending an initialization sequence to the modem. The modem then waits for an incoming call. When an incoming call is received, the modem uses RS232 pins 5, 6, and 8 on the serial port to do the handshaking with the host software to establish communication between the host and the remote PC.

When the host is connected directly to the CBX, the remote operating software on the host still sets DTR high and attempts to send an initialization signal to the modem. The sending of this signal causes the line to appear busy while the CBX is waiting for further transmissions from the host. This would not be a problem in itself because after transmitting the initialization signal the host would be waiting for an incoming call. In the absence of further transmissions, the busy condition would time out after a brief interval so that incoming calls could be received.

However, the CBX works in such a way that setting DTR high on the host immediately causes pins 5, 6, and 8 to be raised also. The host software interprets this as an incoming call. The host then stands by for the caller to logon. When no logon occurs, the host software resets itself, sends another initialization signal, and again places the line in a busy condition. This cycle repeats endlessly. Anyone attempting to connect to the host will get a busy signal unless the call happens to be received during the very short interval while the host software is resetting itself.

Remote Access Solution

Library staff solved the remote access problem by developing a device dubbed the PC Host/CBX Interface. This electronic circuit is installed between the host PC and the CBX connection. It can be constructed at a cost of a few dollars from parts readily available from electronic outlets such as Radio Shack.

The PC Host/CBX Interface is inserted in the communications line between the host PC and the CBX. The DTR pin from the host, and the DTR pin and ring indicator pin from the CBX, connect to the circuitry in the Interface. All other pins are connected as indicated in the manuals for the remote software being used on the host.

The DTR line on the CBX side of the Interface is set low while waiting for an incoming call even though DTR on the PC has been set high by the host software. This causes pins 5, 6, and 8 on the CBX to stay low also until an incoming call is received.

When a remote PC makes a call to the host, the CBX attempts to ring the phone. The incoming call sets the ring indicator (pin 22) high on the CBX side of the Interface. The circuitry in the Interface detects the high ring indicator and sets DTR high on the CBX side of the Interface. The host software can then proceed to open communications with the remote PC.

The Interface performs its task by ANDing the DTR from the PC with the ring indicator from the CBX. The result is passed through a flip-flop to the DTR line on the CBX. When there is no incoming call, the CBX sees the host Interface with DTR low. However, when an incoming call sets the ring indicator high, the circuit causes the flip-flop to change states. This causes the CBX to see DTR high on the CBX side of the Interface, allowing a connection to be made.

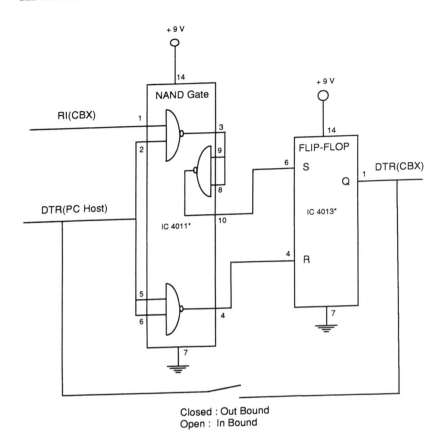

Figure 9.1
Host PC / CBX Interface Box

When breaking a connection, the host software drops DTR temporarily before resetting it high to await another call. The reset of the flip-flop in the Interface is connected through an invertor to the DTR pin of the host. When the host DTR is dropped, the circuitry resets the flip-flop so that DTR is dropped on the CBX side of the Interface. The system can then await another call.

An external switch on the Interface allows the DTR signal to bypass the Interface circuitry to enable an operator on the host to make outgoing calls.

Long Distance Access

The Northern Virginia Graduate Center has direct 9600 baud access to the campus CBX in Blacksburg over a distance of about 250 miles through a T1 communications line. A problem was encountered when using PC Anywhere to access the Blacksburg host from Northern Virginia through this line. The problem was overcome when the Northern Virginia branch was assigned to use a dedicated channel in which flow control protocols have been turned off.

LAN Components

The Virginia Tech University Libraries CD-ROM network was assembled from a mixture of new equipment purchased specifically for the network and older equipment transferred from other library units. It includes some hardware formerly used in stand-alone CD-ROM workstations. On the basis of published reports and vendor literature, the Libraries had expected to spend several tens of thousands implementing the CD-ROM network. However, by judicious choice of networking options, and by "trickling down" older PC and PC XT computers from offices which were upgraded with more modern equipment, the total direct costs of implementing the CD-ROM network were held to just under $19,000.

The following is a list of the major hardware and software components that comprise the Virginia Tech CD-ROM network.

Hardware

o   One 25MHz 80386 DTK Keen 2503 microcomputer with 110MB hard drive, one 3.5" 1.44MB floppy drive, 5MB RAM, Super VGA adapter and monitor, two Hitachi CD-ROM controller cards. This computer functions as a network file server and CD-ROM drive server. Cost: $3,253

o   Sixteen Hitachi Model TCDR 6000 CD-ROM drives, daisy-chained in two groups of eight and connected to the network server. (Existing Hitachi 1503S CD-ROM drives used at stand-alone workstations in the reference area were released for use in branch libraries.) Cost: $9,552.

o   Eight network workstations, six on the 2nd floor of the library in the Main Reference Room, two on the 4th floor of the library in the Science & Technology Reference area. IBM PC or PC XT with 20MB hard drive, two floppy drives (each has at least one 5-1/4" floppy drive. Some machines have a second 5.25" drive, while others have one 3.5" 720KB floppy drive). A ninth machine in the Main Reference Room serves as a host for remote access. These workstations were assembled from existing equipment transferred from elsewhere in the library following several years of use. Cost: $0.

o   Ten Western Digital EtherCard Plus network cards, one in each workstation and one in the server. Cost: $1,900.

o   Eight printers, one for each station. Hewlett-Packard ThinkJet or Epson dot-matrix impact printers. Cost: $2,320.

o   Ethernet wiring and connectors. Cost: $540.
o   Security hardware, including cables, anchors, locks. Cost: $300.

Software

o   LANtastic Adapter Independent Network Operating System and Adapter Independent LANBIOS with drivers for Western Digital Ethernet cards. Cost: $790.
o   PC Anywhere III. Cost: $84.
o   DirectNet menu, security, use-tracking software. Cost: $250.
o   MS-DOS or IBM PC DOS version 3.3. Cost included with workstations.

Installation and Implementation of the CD-ROM Network

Personnel Requirements

All network design, including hardware and software specifications, as well as all hardware and software installation, setup, configuration, testing, and user-instruction, was carried out by the Libraries' in-house staff. These included a full-time electronics technician who maintains library computer equipment, a part-time programmer, and two full-time librarians, one of whom is assigned to manage network operation and software applications. While each of these individuals has several years of experience in dealing with microcomputer hardware and software, most of their knowledge of microcomputing was gained through self-study. Their knowledge of networks was acquired while working on the CD-ROM network, which is the first microcomputer network ever installed in the Libraries. Total time devoted to development and implementation of the network amounted to no more than 0.5 FTE.

It is clear that a person who is very familiar with DOS, adept at creating batch files, and comfortable with installing cards, figuring out interrupts, and configuring jumpers can learn enough to establish a small CD-ROM network based on LANtastic. As the network grows in complexity, additional skills related to trouble-shooting and system debugging are necessary, as is increased understanding of the Ethernet network protocol. The ability to visualize the complex interaction among the various hardware and software components in the network becomes important because error messages issued by the software often do not make sense or may not be related to the problem which gives rise to the operating symptom. For instance, poor cable connections can cause intermittent problems that can be difficult to isolate, and that could be attributed to the CD-ROM drives, the software, the network cards, the PC workstations, or the server. Defects that developed in some of the CD-ROM drives did not result in any clear indication of the origin of the problem. Should the network grow very large, a technician dedicated to managing the physical integrity of the system would be necessary.

Ergonomics and Space

While planning the software and hardware aspects of a CD-ROM network, it is easy to overlook the physical and electrical requirements in the area chosen to house the network. Older buildings, already filled with library materials and having inadequate electrical wiring, require special attention.

In Newman Library, the Main Reference Room on the second floor was completely rearranged to provide space for the network workstations. Much planning was devoted to the arrangement of furniture and equipment so that traffic patterns were not impeded. The area was originally designed for book stacks, not for power-hungry electronic equipment. Power poles and outlets had to be installed, phone lines and data lines had to be moved, books had to be shifted, and reference desks and index tables had to be relocated. Of course, user guides and signs for the existing Reference Room arrangement all had to be revised. Disruption to public services was kept to a minimum because it was possible to carry out all the changes during the summer sessions when enrollment is only about 1/3 the level during the normal academic year.

Timetable and Procedures

Installation of the network proceeded in a phased manner. A small working network consisting of the server and two workstations was installed first. Once the operation of that system was stable and routine, one additional workstation was installed and configured approximately every third day. The guiding principle was to proceed slowly and verify that each new addition to the network was working properly. This provided time for the staff to become familiar with increasing complexity, and it usually assured that any newly observed problem resulted from some aspect of the most recently installed workstation.

Server Hardware Installation

After the server was set up to run as a normal PC with DOS installed and the hard disk configured, Ethernet cards and two CD-ROM controller cards were installed in the server. Each type of card requires assignment of an interrupt and an I/O (Input/Output) base address. Availability of unused interrupts and I/O base addresses was determined from the server's hardware manual. After the cards were installed, a diagnostic program was run to ensure that there was no hardware conflict and that the other components in the computer system worked normally. User's manuals supplied with the Ethernet cards and with the CD-ROM drives adequately described the hardware settings for these devices.

The CD-ROM drives were physically attached to the server in two groups of eight daisy-chained drives. In each daisy-chain, the first drive is connected to the adapter card in the server, and the seven additional drives are connected in sequence to each other.

Installing the Server Software

The LANtastic software was installed using the supplied installation program. Then the Microsoft CD-ROM extensions were installed following the instructions in the manual which was supplied with the drives. During installation, logical drive letters are assigned to each drive. Successful installation can be checked by using the DOS command DIR to verify that each drive can be accessed.

At bootup, the server with its two chains of CD-ROM drives is initialized by the following CONFIG.SYS and AUTOEXEC.BAT files:

CONFIG.SYS

```
lastdrive=z
files=51
buffers=30
fcbs=16,8
device=\cdrom\hitachia.sys /d:mscd001 /n:8 /p:320
device=\cdrom\hitachia.sys /d:mscd002 /n:8 /p:340
```

AUTOEXEC.BAT

```
@echo off
cls
path c:\;c:\dos
prompt $p$g
c:\lantasti\wd8003 irq=7 iobase=220
c:\lantasti\ailanbio retry_period=5 ack_timeout=5
c:\lantasti\redir serv1
c:\mscdex\mscdex.exe /d:mscd001 /d:mscd002 /s /m:80
c:\dos\share /1:200
c:\lantasti\server
```

Workstation Installation

Workstation installation procedures were similar to those followed for the server. However, since the workstations were older IBM PC and PC XT machines, they used different interrupts and I/O base addresses for the Ethernet cards.

LANtastic is a peer-to-peer network operating system which allows any workstation on the network to be used simultaneously as both a server and user workstation. However, this option was not implemented, and only the workstation portion of the networking software was installed on the individual workstations. This reduced the amount of processing done on each workstation, reduced the complexity of the network, and maximized the available RAM on each workstation. Since there were no CD-ROM drives attached to any workstation, the Microsoft extensions were not installed on the workstations. Other than DOS, only the CD-ROM applications software and the menuing software had to be installed on each workstation.

Workstations are initialized at bootup using the CONFIG.SYS and AUTOEXEC.BAT files listed below. Device drivers are loaded for ANSI.SYS and for a 720KB 3.5-in floppy disk drive. Then the system clock is set from the battery clock. NETWORK.BAT is executed to initialize the network adapter card and to login to the network. Finally DONE.BAT is executed to display the DirectNet menu. These three files are the same on each workstation.

CONFIG.SYS

```
lastdrive=z
files=51
fcbs=16,8
buffers=30 +
device=ansi.sys
device=c:\dos\driver.sys /d:1 /t:80 /s:9 /h:2
```

AUTOEXEC.BAT

```
@echo off
cls
 \util\readdclk
call c:\network
done
```

DONE.BAT

```
@echo off
cls
path c:\menu;c:\util
c:
cd c:\menu
dnet
```

In addition to these three files, each workstation has a DNET.BAT file to display the particular workstation menu, and a set of application menus for the applications used on that workstation. For example, on Workstation 6, the DirectNet menu and access to the ERIC application software and CD-ROMs are controlled by the following batch files:

DNET.BAT

```
@echo off
cls
c:\lantasti\net
logout \\serv1
c:\lantasti\net login \\serv1 dnet network
c:\lantasti\net use f: \\serv1\dnet
f:
f:\dnet2\startdn work6
```

When the user selects ERIC from the DirectNet menu, the following batch file is executed to access the appropriate CD-ROM drives and to call the SPIRS.BAT file which starts the SilverPlatter applications software:

ERIC.BAT

```
@echo off
cls
echo.
echo Loading ERIC. One moment, please...
c:\lantasti\net logout \\serv1 + c:\lantasti\net
login \\serv1 work6 cdrom +
c:\lantasti\net use e: \\serv1\cdrom1 cdrom
c:\lantasti\net use f: \\serv1\cdrom2 cdrom
c:\lantasti\net use g: \\serv1\cdrom3 cdrom
cd \spirs
call spirs
cls
cd \menu
done
```

Cabling

A very critical part of the network is the cable and all the connections. Extra money spent on high-quality cables, BNC connectors, and a good crimping tool will eliminate many problems as the network grows in size. Bad connections and poorly made cables cause problems that can be hard to isolate. It is best to take every precaution to prevent the occurrence of cable problems.

Thin-wire Ethernet cabling was used for the network. In the Main Reference Room on the second floor of the Library the workstations are located as close as a couple of feet from one another, and none is further than about 25 feet from the server. Cables are strung loosely behind the tables containing the workstations. For neatness, security, and cleanliness, these should be bound together and run through conduits. To reach the workstations on the fourth floor, the cable is run about 100 feet through existing conduit in the walls and over the top of the suspended ceiling tiles.

Bringing Up the Network

After the server and the workstations are installed and physically connected, the network components must be logically defined in order to establish communications among the network operating system, DOS, and the Microsoft extensions. In particular, each workstation must be able to logon to the network and execute the DOS command DIR on any of the CD-ROM discs on the server.

To achieve this, the network administrator uses the functions of the server software to assign logical names to the physical network devices, such as the workstations and the CD-ROM drives attached to the server. Details of the process for configuring the network are described in the LANtastic manual, but some points are worth emphasizing.

As an example, assume that the server's logical drive K: is assigned the name CDROM5. The network workstation of interest is named Station2. The network administrator assigns access privileges for Station2. When Station2 logs in to the server, it can issue commands to access CDROM5. Although Station2 needs to access the CD-ROM disc assigned to the logical drive K: on the server, when Station2 issues the login commands and accesses the physical drive known as CDROM5 that drive will be assigned to the first unused DOS drive letter on the workstation. If the workstation has only one hard drive C:, and if it is not accessing any other CD-ROM drives, then the first available drive letter will be D:. In principle, all CD-ROM drives on the server could be accessed simultaneously by the workstation when it logs on to the network. However, it is preferable to reduce network overhead by accessing only those drives needed by the specific application to be used at the workstation. When changing to another application, the drives used by the first application can be released and the drives required by the second application can be accessed. All of this can be handled through DOS batch files in a manner transparent to the user.

Installing Applications

To reduce the load on the server and to reduce the amount of data flowing through the network, all application software was located on the workstations. This complicates maintenance to some extent, since every time an application is updated it must be installed on all workstations. The benefits on a small network override the inconvenience.

Menu and Application Management

Starting an application is a two-part process. First, the appropriate CD-ROM is accessed by the workstation and then the application is started. These commands can be issued through DOS batch files which can be executed from the DOS prompt. An appropriate menu can be displayed indicating which command corresponds to which application. As complexity increased and security became an increasing concern, the DirectNet commercial menuing application was installed to manage access to the applications from each workstation.

DirectNet allows the network administrator to create a single menu that will run on all stations, including the capability to distribute menu changes across the network. Individualized menus can be created for special requirements on each workstation. DirectNet also includes security features such as password protection and user privilege assignment. Access to DOS operations can be suppressed, but it is possible to allow users to perform some DOS operations such as checking floppy disk directories or formatting floppy disks. A usage-tracking utility in DirectNet records date, time-in, and time-out for each use of each application. The utility prepares usage reports from these data. Other features of DirectNet include a color customizer, and a screen blanker to prevent menu burn-in. DirectNet is not RAM-resident, so it does not conflict with the operation of any application nor does it consume system resources needed by the CD-ROM applications.

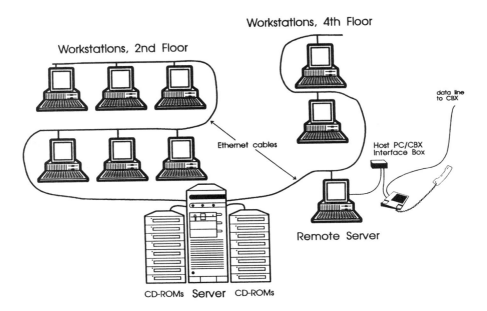

Figure 9.2
Virginia Tech Libraries CD-ROM Network Diagram

Installation Do's and Don'ts

Do not install the whole network at once. It is very hard to debug a large system, but it is relatively straightforward to resolve problems if the network is installed incrementally. Debugging is easier when only the latest addition to the network needs to be considered. Also, on a working network, any addition which leads to a problem can be removed until the problem is solved while the network can remain in operation for the users.

Do plan the user interface in advance and avoid making changes after the network is made available to users. A surprising number of questions were received from dozens of regular users of the network and from library staff when even minor changes were made in the appearance and operation of the workstations. For example, the installation of screen blankers confused several people who thought the network was down.

Do remember that people will become dependent on the network. Use can become so heavy that routine network maintenance which requires shutting down the network will have to be done during hours the library is closed, or will have to be scheduled some days in advance to avoid disrupting the work of individuals who have scheduled searches.

Do use the best quality Ethernet cables, cards, crimping tool and BNC connectors.

Do call vendors when there are problems. Vendors of the products used in the network have been very helpful in resolving the inevitable problems that arise in any complex system.

Staff and User Training

Our emphasis on technical aspects of the LAN should not overshadow what may be the far more important human aspects of the LAN which can be summarized in an Overriding Implementation Principle: when any new technology is introduced into a library, a proportionate amount of attention must be directed to assuring that the human elements receive as much attention as the machine elements.

If the ways in which humans interact with the technology are ignored, the technology will be rejected and the goals of the technology will not be achieved. Several areas need special consideration.

Communication

Effective communication (the key word is effective) is the primary means by which the balance between technological and human elements are maintained. Every change in the technology must be accompanied by communication, and a great deal of it. Indeed, the amount of time spent on communication may exceed the time devoted to development of the specific technology. Implementing the CD-ROM network required formal training sessions and presentations for all those who would be supporting the network in the reference areas, but these were only the beginning. Communication is needed long after the network technology is functioning routinely. The extent of communication may at first seem surprising, until it is recognized that the network affects the work of almost every reference librarian in every subject specialization. Only the online catalog is more pervasive as a reference tool.

Electronic mail is used almost daily to notify reference staff of the status of existing and updated applications on the network. Solutions to problems arising with procedures or with hardware are also circulated electronically. Announcements and queries about the network are recorded in the Reference Desk notebook to provide continuity of information between changes in shifts at the desk. Announcements about the network are made at semi-monthly Reference Department meetings and at meetings which include library administrators and personnel from other library departments. Finally, many direct informal conversations and demonstrations take place with individuals.

It turns out that what works best of all is communication between individuals. In theory, group sessions have all the advantages of efficiency and consistency of information. In practice, group sessions fail miserably in some manner directly proportional to the size of the group. Effective communication requires extensive repetition in informal encounters between individuals. It is useful if one individual is assigned responsibility for seeing that information reaches all those who need it.

Maintenance

Perhaps nowhere is the need for communication more obvious than in the area of network maintenance. Once staff and users become accustomed to the availability of the network and it becomes part of their normal expectations for service, then any problem which prevents access can be frustrating. Unfortunately, there is a tendency to attribute all CD-ROM database problems to "The Network." In fact, most problems we have encountered have been specific to an individual workstation, printer, or CD-ROM drive. Most problems would have occurred if the equipment was not connected to the network at all.

Although problems directly attributable to the network are infrequent, the effects of the occasional network failure can be very disruptive when sessions of all users, including a remote user, are likely to be aborted. Even planned maintenance, for example, replacing a CD-ROM drive, may require shutting down the entire network for a period of time. While such maintenance on mainframe systems is normally conducted at hours when most offices are closed, this requirement has not yet been introduced for our CD-ROM network. Thus, most maintenance occurs during times when walk-in users are likely to be searching. Repair technicians may not always be sensitive to the needs of users, and it is important that some public service person be assigned to arrange all scheduled maintenance. Technicians should work on the network only after the LAN manager has completed preparations for an orderly shutdown.

Instruction and Staffing

In a busy library, matters relating to patron use of the LAN will be of more concern than will technical matters relating to hardware and software maintenance. In particular, supporting users of the network will consume more time of public service personnel than most libraries expect.

The CD-ROM network tripled the number of workstations available to users in Newman Library. This made use of the databases much more convenient when compared to the stand-alone workstations previously available. As a result, demand for access to CD-ROM databases increased, as did the need for instruction, for routine attention to network maintenance, and for provision of supplies such as printer paper and ink cartridges. These factors alone put more demands on staff time following introduction of the network. Instructional needs also increased demand for professional librarian services in relation to the network resources.

Library patrons seem eager to conduct their own electronic database searches. As is well known, however, patrons are seldom aware that their skills in electronic information retrieval are deficient. Many, if not most, end users of computerized reference tools walk away satisfied by the ease and rapidity of retrieval, and by the fact that a printout has been produced. They frequently do not realize that they have not necessarily retrieved what they need, that they have retrieved many irrelevant references, and that many relevant references have been missed. Even worse, if they have not discussed their requirements with a reference librarian, they may not realize that they did not define their information needs and did not ask the right questions and did not search the best database. When the number of patrons using CD-ROM databases was limited to a few stand-alone workstations, instructional and support needs could be handled by available reference staff. Following introduction of the network, this was no longer possible.

The increase in the number of computer workstations, and the increase in the number of simultaneous users of a single database, brought a proportionate increase in the amount of instruction that must be provided to library patrons. There is the potential for as many as nine people searching at the CD-ROM stations simultaneously, and each person may need help with search strategies simultaneously. We have only begun to consider how instructional support might be provided to remote users.

Following introduction of the CD-ROM network it became necessary to staff the Electronic Reference Area almost all hours that the library is open. For the most part, staff for this purpose had to be taken from those already staffing the Main Reference Desk, although some relief was found through hiring a wage employee and sharing hours from two library assistants. A long-term solution has yet to be found for satisfying the increased staffing needs and meeting increased demands on the time of professional librarians generated by introduction of the LAN.

Evaluation

The network was made available for public use in July 1990, about seven months after the initial purchase of LANtastic for testing. The main reason for the delay was the time involved in going through the bidding procedure on some network components and in the time it took to obtain release of older equipment from offices which were being upgraded during this period.

The network clearly satisfied its original goals as stated in the beginning of this article. Selection of appropriate hardware and software allowed these goals to be accomplished for considerably less money than would have been required to purchase a vendor's turnkey system. Shared, multi-user, simultaneous access to CD-ROM databases is now available, with as many as nine individuals able to search a single database from locations within the main library and from branches or from offices. With most discs permanently installed on the network, there is greater convenience to patrons who no longer have to exchange an ID card for a disc. Reference personnel no longer have to run a disc circulation system. Since discs are no longer being handled, there is far less damage to the CD-ROM discs, which are actually quite fragile in the context of a public service area in a large library.

The use of in-house staff for the LAN implementation was of great value due to the practical and theoretical knowledge and experience we on the Library staff gained by doing the work ourselves. This knowledge will be useful as networking becomes more important in other areas of the library in the future. Successful implementation of a CD-ROM network as the Library's first microcomputing networking project has greatly increased the staff's confidence in their ability to manage and control computerized systems. Tentative plans call for developing a more broadly based reference network which would incorporate microcomputer workstations at the reference desks into a network providing access to in-house databases and to the CD-ROM network, as well as to the CBX and to external databases.

Reference staff were initially skeptical about the network implementation, and some early hardware problems did not build confidence. There was an early tendency to attribute all problems to the network when in fact the network itself operated nearly flawlessly. As mentioned earlier, constant communication with staff throughout the implementation assisted in building confidence. After almost two semesters of relatively smooth network operation, most early skepticism has faded.

Most library staff now acknowledge that the network is a great improvement over stand-alone workstations. However, they frequently feel frustrated or overwhelmed by two concerns. First is the time required for minor routine maintenance chores such as loading printer paper, clearing printer jams, and replacing depleted ink cartridges. Second is the number of different application interfaces with which they must become familiar in order to assist patrons even at the most basic level. Vendors should pay special attention to the issue of the user interface if they wish their products to be used. Interfaces should be standardized, or at least simplified, so that their use is more transparent to users in complex environments where many different applications are available.

Library patrons are enthusiastic about the network, although rising expectations lead some patrons to complain when some particular database product is not owned by the library. With most of the heavily-used databases simultaneously available, patrons need no longer wait in line nor handle discs nor forfeit id cards when checking out a disc from the Reference Desk. Waiting in line and advanced scheduling have been significantly reduced. However, scheduling has not been eliminated because the convenience of using the network has led to a large increase in the demand for access to CD-ROM applications.

The Virginia Tech CD-ROM network currently has only a single host for remote access so that only one remote user can access the system at a given time. Three additional host PCs are being prepared for installation at this writing. These are being installed to facilitate remote access from the branch libraries, including the branch in Northern Virginia. It is expected that network access will be restricted to the branch libraries, and perhaps a few other offices, for the forseeable future. The Virginia Tech campus has about 15,000 microcomputers, and large numbers of off-campus students also have computers. Although many of these users, and the hundreds of others connected to dumb terminals on campus, can access the Library's online public access catalog, it appears impractical at this time to provide similar unrestricted access to the CD-ROM network. In part, remote use is limited by the number of available hosts on the network, although the number needed to provide adequate service may not be large. Indeed, there are only eighteen ports available for remote use of the online catalog, and this number appears to be nearly adequate.

Rather, the number of remote users is limited by the problems of terminal screen emulation, by the monthly cost of additional dedicated CBX connections, and by the cost of acquiring and distributing suitable terminal emulation software such as ATERM. In addition, CD-ROM applications are considerably more complex than the online catalog, so that a substantial program of user education and support would have to be implemented to support unrestricted remote access to the network.

The most significant professional problem remaining with the network is that of delivering adequate instructional and support services to the numerous users of the CD-ROM applications. It is worth nothing that this and other unresolved problems are those that would exist even in the absence of a CD-ROM network. They are problems that appear to be inherent in the interface between users and electronic information sources, and they are not characteristic of some particular electronic information technology.

About the Authors

Harry M. Kriz is Automated Systems Research and Development Librarian in the University Libraries at Virginia Polytechnic Institute and State University. He received a Ph.D. in physics from Brown University in 1970 and an M.L.S. from the University of Pittsburgh in 1975. From 1971 to 1979 he was Agriculture-Engineering Librarian at West Virginia University. He moved to Virginia Tech in 1980 as Head of the Science & Technology Department. In 1986 he became Head of the newly formed Automation Services Department. He assumed his present position in 1990. His publications in librarianship have been in the areas of citation analysis, engineering education, collection management, staff training, and library automation.

Nikhil Jain is a programmer in the Automation Services Department of the University Libraries at Virginia Polytechnic Institute and State University. He received his Bachelor's degree in electrical engineering from the Indian Institute of Technology in 1985 and an M.B.A. in finance and information systems from the University of Rochester in 1987. In May, 1991, he received an M.S. in Industrial and Systems Engineering from Virginia Polytechnic Institute and State University. He is now a student in the Ph. D. program where he conducts research on the logical design of communication and computer networks.

E. Alan Armstrong is Electronic Reference Services Librarian in the Reference Department of the University Libraries at Virginia Polytechnic Institute and State University. He obtained his M.L.I.S. degree from University of Texas at Austin in 1987. That year he moved to Virginia Tech in position of Automation Services Librarian, and he assumed his present position in 1990. Previously he worked for the Aurora Public Library System in Aurora, Colorado, and he was an instructor of English for English Languages Services at Loretto Heights College in Denver. He also taught English and English instructional methodologies in Chung Nam Province, South Korea, while serving in the Peace Corps.

Communications to the authors may be addressed to: University Libraries Virginia Tech Blacksburg, VA 24061-0434 or to the authors' BITNET addresses: KRIZ@VTVM1, NIKHIL@VTVM1, and ARMSTRNG@VTVM1.

Acknowledgements

The authors wish to thank Mr. Al Wagner, Lab Mechanic in the Automation Services Department, for his continuing support in the installation and maintenance of hardware associated with the Virginia Tech CD-ROM network. We also wish to acknowledge Ms. Laura Craighead of the Automation Services Department for her imaginative work in developing the library's equipment reallocation plan which led to the release of hardware used in the network.

10

Husky Hoops and the University of Connecticut CD-ROM LAN

David W. Lewis and Terry Plum
Homer Babbidge Library, University of Connecticut

ABSTRACT

Using $54,000 donated by the 1989/1990 Husky basketball team, the University of Connecticut Library created a CD-ROM LAN. The LAN has ten public workstations—either IBM PS/2 Model 30s or Zenith 286 clones—and runs Novell NetWare software over IBM Token Ring hardware. The LAN file server is an IBM PS/2 Model 80. The CD-ROM server is a CBIS CD Server 386 with seven disc drives running CD Connection software and a second, seven drive, expansion chassis. Twisted-pair wiring, part of the university telephone system, and two multistation access units connect the network. The Saber LAN Administration Pack provides menus, metering and statistics. The LAN supports 10 CD-ROM products: ERIC (three discs), PsycLIT (two discs), Sociofile, CINAHL, Agricola, Disclosure, ABI/Inform, MLA, Humanities Index, and the OCLC version of the Monthly Catalog. Our experience leads us to conclude that a stable system in a high-use environment can be created and supported without special expertise or undue effort. CD-ROM LANs are not rocket science; you too can do it yourself.

Husky Hoops

It is March 22, 1990 in the Brendan Byrne arena in East Rutherford, New Jersey, and Clemson University is playing the University of Connecticut in the NCAA Basketball Tournament. With 1.6 seconds left and UConn down by a point, Scott Burrell stands 94 feet from the opposing basket. He throws a perfect pass to Tate George, who collects the ball, turns to his left, squares to the basket, and swishes a jump shot! In what most observers concede was the best game of the tournament, UConn has defeated a courageous Clemson team 71 to 70 and advances to the final eight. There, Duke defeats UConn, also with a shot at the buzzer, and continues on to the finals where they are beaten by UNLV. For Connecticut the victory by Duke did not really matter in the long run, because Tate's shot completed a UConn "dream season." In addition to earning the respect of many new fans, the basketball team also earned $514,000 for the University from NCAA tournament and television funds. The Homer Babbidge Library received $100,000, and allocated $60,000 to enhance CD-ROM services, primarily through the creation of the local area network (LAN).

Eight months later at the end of November, head basketball coach Jim Calhoun dedicated the LAN by noting that basketball players were just like other students, although fortunately for him, generally taller. By this time the CD-ROM LAN was operational and had significantly expanded the University of Connecticut's CD-ROM service.

The University and the Library before the LAN

The University of Connecticut is the state's comprehensive research university. The main campus at Storrs serves 13,000 undergraduates and 4,000 graduate students, and has a faculty of 950. The Homer Babbidge Library provides library services for all academic disciplines and contains 1.7 million volumes and has a staff of 120. The Research and Information Service Department (RISD) has a staff of 14 librarians and 8 other professional staff. It provides reference service and contains microform and documents collections.

The library adopted CD-ROMs early and by the beginning of 1990 had over fifteen products running on eighteen stand-alone workstations each with its own printer. The products included: four InfoTrac workstations; the SilverPlatter versions of Agricola, CINAHL, ERIC, PsycLIT, and Sociofile; ABI/Inform; Disclosure; Dissertation Abstracts International; the Humanities Index; MLA; the OCLC version of the Monthly Catalog; Newsbank; PAIS, and the Science Citation Index. Except for InfoTrac, Newsbank, and PAIS—which operated on a first come, first served basis— users signed up for half-hour blocks of time, and are theoretically limited to one half hour slot per day. During February and March 1990 the workstations had an average sign-up rate of more than 35 percent for the 96 hours per week that the library was open and the CD-ROMs were available. In February we logged almost 2,700 half-hour sessions and in March over 2,200. PsycLIT had a utilization rate of near 70 percent and was often booked solidly for days in advance. ERIC, MLA, the Science Citation Index, and Sociofile had utilization rates in the 40 percent to 60 percent range. Because of the high use, reference staff could rarely gain access to the most used CD-ROM products, and so CD-ROM databases were difficult to use as part of routine reference work.

By the spring of 1990, it had become clear that even though our CD-ROM service was extensive, its capacity could not keep up with demand. As the word spread, and as students, faculty, and the outside community discovered the power of CD-ROMs, lines grew longer and users could not gain access to the sources they needed. We had to provide multiple access to heavily used products and to better utilize workstations. The obvious solution to these problems was a CD-ROM LAN. We were fortunate that the basketball team's success provided the required funds and allowed us to move quickly and decisively.

Project Development

Based on preliminary investigations we established an initial budget of $60,000. The proposal called for the purchase of six new workstations and creating a LAN with ten workstations—eight in the CD-ROM area, one "express" station adjacent to the reference desk, and one workstation at the reference desk for staff use. The CD-ROM server was to have fourteen drives. At this stage, neither RISD staff, nor staff from the library's Microcomputer Support Unit had any LAN experience.

We immediately turned to the Computer Center's administrative support group, because they had staff with LAN experience. They also needed to sign off on all of our equipment requests. The Computer Center set a number of hardware constraints. First, it is their established policy to discourage turn-key solutions or custom hardware. They wanted to know how the system we were to purchase worked, and they did not want to be dependent on a single outside vendor. These constraints lead us to construct our own CD-ROM LAN rather than to turn to a turn-key system such as MultiPlatter. Secondly, the Computer Center is an IBM shop. The established LAN standard was Novell NetWare running over IBM Token Ring using the university's new telephone system for wiring. We decided on NetWare SFT 2.15C, giving us a fault tolerant system that is very stable and that has a "hot fix" feature for locking out bad sectors on the hard disk of the file server. Although SFT software can be set up to create identical, dynamically changing copies of the information on the network, this feature is usually implemented in networks with two hard drives or two servers, not our situation. They also specified an IBM PS/2 Model 80 server and strongly recommended a 320MB hard drive. This was the LAN configuration they would support and the one they would approve for purchase. It was an expensive solution, but one that was within our reach.

With the decisions on the LAN made largely outside the library, the final piece was to choose and purchase a CD-ROM server. Because of state purchasing procedures and because there were at the time only two vendors of suitable equipment — CBIS and Meridian — this choice was also easy. The CD-ROM server was put out to bid, and CBIS came in with the lowest price.

The initial project budget and the actual costs are shown in Table 10.1. We needed to add several items to the budget as the project progressed, however, none was major. Because of our unfamiliarity of LANs, we did not anticipate the need for multistation access units, nor did we project the need for menuing software. We paid CBIS for installation, which we had not projected, but this was balanced by an unanticipated educational discount. We purchased an additional Token Ring card to add a staff workstation to load and test system. All in all, our actual budget was only a little less than $2,000 over the projected budget. We used the remainder of our $60,000 allocation to purchase an additional workstation and two six-disc Pioneer CD-ROM players.

Also at this time we established the list of CD-ROM products to place on the LAN and built the expected additional cost of LAN rights into the RISD budget for electronic sources. Our projections were that the additional costs would be approximately $10,000; in fact, the increase cost was closer to $7,000 or just over a 30 percent increase. (See Table 10.2.) The decisions on which products to bring up on the LAN were based upon three criteria: use, LAN license cost, and the number of disks the database required. Thus, the heavily used PsycLIT, ERIC, Sociofile, Disclosure, and ABI/Inform were selected. The Science Citation Index was rejected because it required too many slots on the CD-ROM server despite its almost constant use. After the most heavily used products were chosen, we looked at cost. Agricola, CINHAL, the Humanities Index, MLA, and the Monthly Catalog were logical to add because there were no additional fees. Finally, we selected PAIS. We did not consider ease of installation. We were confident we could get all of the databases up and running, a confidence that proved correct in all cases but one.

The two Pioneer DRM-600 six-disc CD-ROM players run two ISI databases, the Science Citation Index and the Social Science Citation Index, which, were it not for the number of CD-ROM drives they consume, might well have been on the LAN. The Pioneers sit next to dedicated workstations, and have worked out very well. In the case of SSCI, the Pioneer is responsible for greatly increased demand. Prior to the six-disc drive, patrons searching SSCI had to check out the disc for each year from a service point. Now that all discs are resident in the Pioneer, SSCI is searched much more often. As an added benefit we have loaded Current Contents—Social & Behavioral Sciences, a floppy disk product representing about .5 megabytes each week, onto the SSCI workstation so patrons can seamlessly search social sciences citations from last week through the six year coverage of SSCI. Pioneers are a little slow, but the benefit of having all of the discs resident and their cost (roughly half that of an equal number of CD-ROM drives) far outweigh the minor inconvenience.

Except for ABI/Inform, all of the LAN fees were based on simultaneous users. Since we were building a large LAN with many workstations and many products on it, we had a strong preference for this fee structure. One vendor, PAIS, developed a simultaneous user price at our request. Because our menuing software includes the capability to control the number of users accessing a particular product, we can limit simultaneous users and live up to the stipulations imposed by the publishers.

Implementation

Structure and Strategy

To begin implementation, we made two framework decisions. Because the LAN was new and cut across already existing job responsibilities, we decided to designate on paper a LAN administrator and a back-up administrator, but in actuality, to share the LAN knowledge we were gaining across three positions. As we moved forward, three people knew where we were at all stages of the implementation. Ongoing installation, upgrading, and maintenance is also shared across positions, although one person is finally responsible. We value this redundancy.

The second decision we made was to schedule, shortly after all the equipment had arrived, a LAN christening ceremony to which the basketball coach, the university president, and various other notables outside of the Library were invited. The date was announced and publicity was sent out, long before the CD-ROM LAN was actually operational. Indeed, at times it felt as though we were spending more time on the LAN ceremony than on the LAN itself. By announcing a non-postponable date for completion, we created pressure and excitement about bringing the CD-ROM LAN in on time. While there was risk, there was reward as well.

Topologies, Protocols, Cards, and Wires

The topology or way in which the microcomputers are connected, the transport protocols or the language in which information is moved on the network, the access method or card that is placed into the microcomputer, and the cabling connecting the micros can be best thought of in groups of three. There are three basic network topologies; ring, star, or bus. At present there are three popular transport protocols; NetBIOS (or Network Basic Input/Output System), TCP/IP (Transmission Control Protocol/Internet Protocol), and IPX/SPX (Internetwork Packet Exchange/Sequence Packet Exchange). There are three common access methods; Ethernet, Token Ring, and Arcnet. And there are three cabling choices for connecting the network devices; coaxial cable, twisted-pair—shielded and unshielded (telephone wire), and fiber-optic cable. These choices can be combined, for example, cascaded star topologies or a fiber optic backbone cable with twisted-pair connections to the individual microcomputers.

The Computer Center guided us through a potentially confusing situation, and we elected to run IBM Token Ring Network 16/4 Adapters, requiring IBM Local Area Network Support Program, using telephone wire in a star topology with Novell NetWare which runs IPX on each workstation. Token Ring is a star wired ring topology in which all computers are directly wired to a multistation access unit (MAU) as the hub. Each MAU can accept eight connections, so we purchased two, permitting some expansion. Token Ring is reliable, easy to maintain, and can transmit at 16 megabits per second (Mbps). The MAU star hub allows dead micros to be disconnected from the network without bringing down the network.

The requirement that we use the university telephone system meant that $2,500 had to be spent to pull a 50-pair cable to the CD-ROM area. This was more capacity than we required, but will allow all of the workstations in this area to be easily placed on the LAN in the future. Phone jacks were installed by Southern New England Telephone and connected to the MAUs by the university's data communication staff. Jacks are connected to T3 Media Filters and then to the Token Ring installed in the workstations. IPX, Net 3, and Net 4 were installed on all workstations connected to the LAN. Net 3 and Net 4 work with DOS 3.x and DOS 4.x, respectively. At the time, we were uncertain if all applications would run under DOS 4.x on the two different types of workstations that we were integrating. There were the inevitable bureaucratic problems, but the installation was straightforward.

LAN Server

Bringing up the network software required generating shell software that is specific to the Token Ring cards and configuring the network operating systems to the file server. A Comprehensive Surface Analysis prepares the hard disk of the server, and took roughly ten hours to run. The Computer Center generated our LAN off of an already existing LAN—one of the advantages of using Computer Center support for a system they recommended. All NetWare diskettes were loaded onto an existing Novell file server in the Computer Center. The files were configured there and then transferred over to our server. The Computer Center provided instruction in Novell NetWare commands and utilities, made decisions at the configuration stage, and advised us concerning supervisor privileges and responsibilities. Their support was excellent. Working with the Network Operating System (NOS) has not been difficult. It is similar, though not identical to DOS. After the expected period of learning, the adjustment has not proved to be difficult.

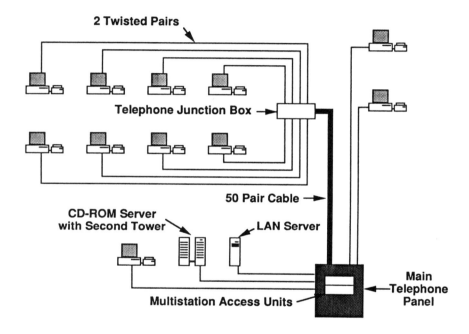

Figure 10.1
University of Connecticut CD-ROM LAN Network Structure

Workstations

The workstations we use are Zenith 286 clones and IBM PS/2 Model 30s. After considering several LAN workstation configurations, we settled upon one which balanced several considerations. To place the LAN in one area concentrates service aspects and is easier to wire, but it defeats the purpose of LANs which is to decentralize activity while centralizing maintenance on the server. A single area for the LAN also intensifies printer noise and consultation discussion, making the area noisy at times. Each workstation was configured with a local printer, rather than using a shared LAN printer. Local printers are easier to install, and we were cautious about queuing problems with shared printing among patrons who do not know each other. We felt that shared printing would involve a staff attendant sorting output.

The LAN should also be in sight of the reference desk so that reference librarians can service it. We felt it was important to integrate the CD-ROMs into our standard reference activity, and therefore placed a LAN workstation at the reference desk. (The CD-ROM LAN configuration is shown in Figure 10.1.)

The supervisor's workstation became necessary when we discovered that the LAN had been generated so that the server could not also serve as a workstation. The supervisor's workstation, dubbed the Super Station, has FPROT, a virus protector installed, so that all softwares that have rights to the server are checked for viri. We have plans to install virus protection on all workstations on the LAN. We encourage downloading and sell formatted disks in the library to make it easier for patrons, and to guarantee at least some clean disks..

The Library Microsupport Unit and the Computer Center Data Communications section installed the Token Ring 16/4 Adapters and added the IBM Local Area Network Support Program, v. 1.2 to all workstations on the LAN. Each Token Ring card is dropped into the workstation. The T3 Media Filter connects the card to the phone jack. Phone wire goes through a telephone junction box to the MAUs at the main telephone panel, completing the ring. To run the LAN Support Program, the CONFIG.SYS file of each workstation must be altered to reflect the chosen device driver, which in our case was DEVICE=DXMA0MOD.SYS 001 and DEVICE=DXMC0MOD.SYS. Microsoft Extensions (MSCDEX) is located on the CD-ROM server software, and not on local hard drive. The CONFIG.SYS on each workstation is the following:

```
LASTDRIVE=Q
BREAK=ON
DEVICE=DXMA0MOD.SYS 001
DEVICE=DSMC0MOD.SYS
FILES=30
BUFFERS=30
DEVICE=C:\DOS\ANSI.SYS
SHELL=COMMAND.COM /P /E:2048
```

Installation of the CD-ROM Server and Applications Software

A variety of hardware problems prevented the CBIS installer from completing the installation. She did, however, get us started and showed us some tricks, such as placing UMI's ABI/Inform in the first drive on the CD-ROM tower, drive D. Rather than summon her to return to Storrs, we completed it ourselves and learned much about the CD-ROM Server software, and various CD-ROM application softwares in the LAN environment. The size of our hard disk permitted a certain freedom, and we elected to create a directory for each workstation on the hard disk on the recommendation of the CBIS installer. In each workstation directory are all of the CD-ROM application softwares. We also created a supervisor's directory, identical in content to the workstation directories, to run tests, installations, and upgrades. We have therefore encountered no software conflicts as multiple users search a CD-ROM. Response time, because of the 386 server, is, in most cases, better than it was on stand-alone workstations.

In each case, we placed the CD-ROM in the CBIS server, ran the software from the C drive of the supervisor's station, copied the software over to the supervisor's directory on the server and ran it, copied it over one of the public workstation directories, ran it, and then copied it to all of the workstation directories and a backup directory on the C drive of the Super Station. Typically, at each level, with every piece of application software, there were unexpected problems. Some involved networked CD-ROM applications, some involved trustee rights differences between supervisors and patrons, some involved mappings or paths on the server. Some application software rewrites the maps or paths to suit its own selfish purposes. For security reasons, we wished to limit patrons to read, open, and close rights on the server. In the end, only Wilson software required full rights except for parental on the server. Our menuing software, to track statistics, also requires full rights for public workstations to a directory on the server.

None of the application software is on the patron workstations, although the AUTOEXEC.BAT's of these workstations contains a number of temporary file specifications to encourage caching on the workstation hard drive, such as SET RTEMP=C:\RTEMP (for UMI software) and SET SCD450TMP=C:\ (for OCLC). The AUTOEXEC.BAT, after running IPX and NET4, then runs a login script specific to each workstation. The AUTOEXEC.BAT on each workstation is the following:

```
PROMPT $P$G$E [44M$E [1M
CLS
SET RTEMP=C:\RTEMP
SET SCD450TMP=C:\
CLS
ECHO OFF
NETWORK
```

NETWORK runs the following batch program:

```
C:\IPX
C:\NET4
R:
LOGIN PCXX
```

NETWORK exists as a separate batch because during installation we would bring up workstations in either a network or dedicated mode.

We identified each workstation, each login script, each user, and the specific directory on the server as the same entity, that is, PC01 through PC10. CD Connection, the CBIS software, writes a network logical drive to each CD-ROM product and tricks NetWare so that it can identify up to 21 logical drives. It runs CDREDIR which redirects the drives and runs MSCDEX. Up until two days before the LAN christening, every time a workstation was rebooted, we lost a drive from the CBIS server. We finally found the right software switch to correct this problem. The login script runs up a file called HUSKIES that calls up CD Connection software for the CD-ROM server, redirects the drives, sets Saber Meter, and calls the Saber Menuing program.

Interestingly, in the dedicated mode with a CD-ROM drive attached to a workstation, Wilson software had a propensity to fill up the hard drive with fragmented files that had to be removed with CHKDSK every few weeks. On the server under the Network Operating System it no longer fragments files, or if it does, we cannot find them. NetWare SFT NOS appears to be more stable and more powerful than DOS.

By the date of the LAN ceremony we had all of the databases running but one—PAIS will not run under our configuration. Unfortunately, PAIS software is designed by Online Computer Systems, who market Opti-Net, a competitor to CBIS. When we called Online Computer Systems for help, we received a lesson in the delicate demarcations that occur with networks. If a software will not run, whose problem is it? Is it the server software? Unfortunately Novell charges $50 per quarter hour for support, and the Novell list server, will bury all but the most diligent in days. One can join the Novell list server on BITNET (NOVELL@SUVM with log files stored at NOVELL@UIUCVMD), and it is free, but because of the cost of Novell technical support, the list server is extremely active. Perhaps the best way to handle the list is to join, but then to elect NOMAIL so that one is spared the daily deluge of messages. Then, when faced with a particular problem, one can search the list server archives for the answer.

Should the problem go to the CD-ROM server support? CBIS was helpful, but had not brought up PAIS. Is it the responsibility of the database software? No, if they also market a CD-ROM server. Our conversation ended with the not-very-helpful advice that we should have purchased Opti-Net since PAIS will run there.

Menuing Software

For most patrons, the initial menu is the LAN. The menuing package we chose was the Saber LAN Administration Pack. Saber Menu is a powerful, but initially complex, menuing program. The LAN team had some previous experience with DOS menus and Automenu. Still Saber Menu took some thought, but the end result was very satisfactory. The menu has one screen, help screens for each database, describing what the database is and how to enter and exit from it. Exiting from each database returns the patron to the menu, although we were initially plagued by SilverPlatter software's insistent efforts to create its own menu at restart. A call to

SilverPlatter solved this problem. We have now set up SilverPlatter and OCLC products to time out to the menu, a nice touch. The menu runs in batch and not TSR mode, so it consumes no memory, theoretically. Wilson needs all the memory it can hog, and would not run when the menu was in memory. The menu does not permit exit to NOS, although the supervisor's menu has a password-protected exit option.

Saber Secure was disappointing. It would disable control-break and thus prevent patrons from breaking out of the menu or aborting the workstation boot. However, disabling control-break introduced some amazing problems, including invisible characters, alternative character sets, pauses, and other unwanted fallout when a patron pressed control-break as all SilverPlatter software suggests. We were not interested in screen blanking, preferring to show patrons a menu at all times, or disabling local drives, since we encourage downloading. Saber Meter, a dBase program, counts usage in almost any way you can imagine and meters software from the menu so that we can comply with simultaneous user licensing agreements. It also has a menu driven dBase browser and predefined report formats for easy extraction of simple reports. At present we have deleted no part of the Saber Meter usage file, no doubt due to our reverence for statistics, so it is growing like a cancer on the server drive. We have not yet used Saber File Manager.

Vendor Agreements and Vendor Support

We went ahead and scheduled payment for LAN licenses based upon an expected LAN implementation date. We also asked for a second copy of the CD-ROM for each database so that we could run the LAN in a test mode, while offering the database to the patrons on the dedicated CD-ROM workstation. In all cases the vendors, once they understood that we were not trying to cadge a second subscription for free, were supportive and forthcoming.

Switching over to LAN licenses is fairly complicated. The acquisitions or serials staff should be given plenty of warning and lead time, and a thorough understanding of what is going to occur. Most vendors prorated subscription costs from single to multiple users, and so can handle implementation on any date.

Cut Over Strategy

One decision LAN administrators must face is what point to go live with the LAN. If all applications and databases on the LAN are new, the decision is less crucial, but as with most libraries, if the LAN replaces some existing databases, then the live LAN has more far reaching consequences. There is always more to do, but at some point the LAN needs to be offered to the public. At that point, it become much more difficult for the administrator to work on the LAN, since the fooling around may bring the LAN down. However, in the month we switched over, PsycLIT was reserved 93.6 percent of the time the library was open, so there was real pressure by the patrons.

The LAN added five new workstations. Five old workstations were already running dedicated CD-ROM databases. While we met our goal of a complete CD-ROM LAN in time for the LAN christening, in fact, there were still some problems with CBIS CD Connection software and with specific application softwares. For the rest of the semester, we offered the new LAN workstations as a LAN, but used the five older IBM PS/2 30s in either dedicated or LAN mode, depending on what problem we were working on. In one of the weirdest problems we faced, one of the PS/2s would not run OCLC SCD450 (GPO) from the LAN menu. The solution—we replaced the workstation battery! Then it ran fine.

LAN Backup and Ongoing Maintenance

The Microtext/CD-ROM area where the CD-ROM LAN is located is staffed by students at all times. The students have been trained to reboot microcomputers when faced with software problems on dedicated CD-ROM drive microcomputers. Therefore, any LAN problem-solving must initially begin with rebooting the system. We hid the keyboard for the LAN server, and then instructed the students that when faced with a hung microcomputer to reboot the individual workstation. If all LAN workstations are down, they should reboot the CBIS CD-ROM server to bring up CD Connection. If that fails to work, they have been instructed to remove certain CD-ROMs from the CBIS towers and transfer them to CD-ROM drives on specified dedicated microcomputers. We have placed the software for the most popular of the LAN products on five microcomputers with a menu selection titled "LAN Back-up." Should the LAN go down, the students can bring most of the databases up on dedicated microcomputers by simply removing and inserting a CD-ROM and pressing a menu selection. They service other CD-ROMs every day in this manner as part of their regular duties, so nothing unusual is demanded of them, and training is minimal (just show them which CD-ROM goes where). The scheduling problems could be nasty, as, for example, the five users who were searching ERIC when the LAN went down vie for the one dedicated microcomputer offering ERIC.

The rest of our backup procedure is primitive but we think effective. The applications directory is copied over to the Super Station hard disk in a backup directory. If the applications software for any or all workstations becomes corrupted, we can copy over the backup directory and bring up the applications. The Novell software, Saber LAN Package software and other networking softwares are copied over to the reference workstation hard disk. We do not have an ongoing backup procedure with tape files or automatic backup since we are not creating data files that need to be saved on a timely basis. We also elected not to purchase an uninterruptible power supply. Should the LAN crash, and rebooting does not revive it, we hope to copy over the softwares from the workstation hard drives to the server hard drive, and come back up.

User Training and Documentation

As is all most always the case this aspect of the project was treated as an after thought. We collected our user guides for the CD-ROM products on the LAN and put them in a notebook at each LAN workstation. We are in the process of revising the guides. We collected all of the thesauri and placed them in a central location. Our only training was the one-on-one training that resulted from reference transactions.

Moving from stand alone workstations to a LAN presents a documentation problem because it is no longer possible to have specially marked keys or templates. The manuals, thesauri, and other guides for all of the systems will no longer fit at a given workstation, nor are there sufficient quantities. The patron is confronted with a "naked" workstation at which there is only a single black notebook. Fortunately, it turns out that most CD-ROM interfaces have good help, and navigation through the systems is generally possible by observing on screen instruction. Except for exiting the system—which is required to call the LAN menu—most command options are found on the screens. Patrons seem untroubled by our limited documentation.

We have, however, not cut the patrons completely adrift. Because the CD-ROM LAN is located at some distance from the reference desk, we have established a CD-ROM reference desk nearer the LAN, staffed during the busy times. The librarian at this desk is expected to be intrusive, asking patrons if they need assistance. and regularly patrolling the area to see if patrons are in trouble. For example, the librarian would offer help upon seeing a patron patiently plowing through several thousand citations, the result of a poor search.

The CD-ROM reference desk has caused much discussion among librarians. We elected to try it for a year, and then evaluate the service. The desk is wasteful of staff resources, creates another service point, logs fewer questions per hour than the reference desk, and defines a mode of library service that contrasts somewhat with service offered at the traditional reference desk. On the other hand, librarians have learned CD-ROM databases and softwares on the LAN and are becoming familiar with the more arcane GPO offerings on CD-ROM. The service is appreciated by all patrons, except for perhaps mating couples who are only using the discussion of the CD-ROM screen to mask other intentions. On tours of the library by student tour leaders to groups of parents and prospective students, we have heard statements like, "The librarians even come over and ask you if you need help on the CD-ROMs," followed by sounds of astonishment and professions of disbelief from the tour.

The CD-ROM desk may not survive a more level-headed evaluation, but it may be replaced by a rover librarian so that the service aspect is not lost.

Evaluation

Network Performance and User Reaction

It took several weeks to stabilize the LAN, but since that time we have had only one crash. This was the result of an electrical failure which occurred when the library was closed. The system came up smoothly the next day. CBIS, Novell, and the Token Ring access method have proven to be stable and fast, requiring little maintenance. We have had no hardware problems with packet throughput, cable echoes, faulty LAN adapters, or like occurrences.

We have done no tests, but it is our clear sense that with a single user the LAN is faster than a stand alone workstation. At times of heavy use we have observed slower response, especially when retrieving citations, but these delays are slight and do not seem to bother users.

In the first four weeks of the 1991 Spring semester—the first time the CD-ROM LAN was fully functional—the workstations were booked on average 40 percent of the time and 10 percent of the time all of the workstations were booked. We believe these to be a conservative figures since they are based upon sign-up records, and often users will simply walk up to the workstations, especially if the LAN is not full.

If figures from February 1990 are compared with February 1991 (see Table 10.3), we see an increase in overall CD-ROM activity of over one thousand booked half-hour slots, despite the library being open 20 fewer hours. The easiest explanation of this overall increase is to look at the number of workstations available; we went from 10 to 14 booked workstations. If we look only at the products which are on the LAN and compare their use on standalone workstations with the LAN activity there is an increase of almost 600 slots reserves from 2,139 to 2,714 or more than a 25 percent increase. The percentage of the available slots reserved was up over 17 percent from 44.2 percent to 52.0 percent. This does not include the use at the "express" workstation or at the reference desk.

By March 1991 we were able to get reasonably reliable statistics on use of individual products on the LAN and of the activity at the different workstations on it (see Tables 10.4 and 10.5). We were able to log the number of times a database was opened and the number of minutes that the database was open. The latter figure is suspect for the non-SilverPlatter databases because in March and April they did not timeout to the main menu. Since all the SilverPlatter products timeout and because many users return to the main menu when they complete their searches, we do not think these figures are too far off. We believe the number of logins is a solid indication of use. We had 6,040 databases opened in March 1991, or 194.6 databases opened per day or 19.5 databases open per day on each workstation, and one week was spring break! In April without spring break the figures are comparatively higher. The total time in March was 1,783.5 hours or 57.5 hours per day or 5.8 hours per day on each workstation. The pattern of use across databases is similar to the pattern before the LAN.

When the use on the workstations in the CD-ROM area is compared with the express workstation and the workstation at the reference desk, the results are not surprising. In March the CD-ROM area workstations averaged 20.5 logins per day; the express workstation averaged 21.4 logins per day, and the reference desk workstation 10.6 logins per day. The rate of use at the reference desk might be viewed at low, but we do not take this view. We handled 3,539 reference questions at the reference desk in March of 1991. If each login represents a different question, then we used the LAN for 9.3 percent of our reference questions. In fact, this total is low because reference librarians often use the express workstation with reference questions. It is more convenient for instructing users, and the user can be left in the database to search for other citations. Another way to look at the activity at the reference desk workstation is to consider each search as a ready reference search. In March 1991 we did 111 ready reference searches on BRS, Dialog, EPIC, and RLIN. From this point of view the CD-ROM LAN accounts for about 75 percent of our total ready reference searching.

Effects on Service

There has been a clear increase in access to and use of our high-use products and that users were more likely to do multiple database searches. Patrons are using the LAN workstations for longer periods of time, and it is not unusual for someone to block out a two hour slot during the slower times. Reference librarians now have easy access to the most popular CD-ROM databases.

One way to look at the value of the CD-ROM LAN is to consider how its use and cost compares with an alternative way of acquiring the same information—online searching. In March 1991 recorded 6,040 logins to the databases on the LAN. The average number of minutes in a data base was 17.7 for all databases and 13.4 minutes for the SilverPlatter database which have been set to timeout. If one assumes that each of our searches would have taken 15 minutes online—at total of 1,510 hours—and that the average cost would be $15 per hour, the cost of our searching would have been $22,650.

The existence of the "express" workstation and the workstation at the reference desk meant that rarely would a user, especially someone asking a question at the reference desk, be shut out of our most used CD-ROMs.

Lessons Learned

When we look back at our experience we believe there are several lessons to be learned. We do not suggest these lessons out of a sense that we made that many mistakes or that we were particularly insightful, but rather we offer them as a result of our experiences.

1.   LANs are not rocket science. Building and managing a network, while a more complex task than working with stand-alone equipment, is well understood and

involves stable technology. It should not be beyond any library to apply it. If you can do DOS, you can learn to do a LAN.

2.   Do it yourself. This follows from lesson #1. Our experience has been that by using standard building blocks and by putting the pieces together ourselves, we can expand and customize the system to meet our needs, and we are not dependent on any one vendor. There is a learning curve, but it is worth the effort to learn it yourself.

3.   Assume it will get bigger, much bigger. We were initially uncomfortable with our Computer Center's insistence that we use high-end, and expensive equipment, but we have come to appreciate the wisdom of this choice. Our very large hard drive provided us with options in setting up the system that have improved performance and has given us the opportunity to expand the system easily.

4.   Conform to institutional standards. Our use of Token Ring as a network hardware standard was more expensive than a number of alternatives, but we now expect, in the near future, to be able to easily bridge into the campus network and to offer the CD-ROM LAN on the same workstations that will access our OPAC. We also received important support from our Computer Center early on in the project.

5.   Put at least one workstation at the reference desk. A CD-ROM LAN is the most expensive and powerful part of the reference collection and reference librarians need easy access as much or more than library users. It is now common for reference librarians to perform ready reference searches on the LAN (e.g., what information is there about mental health care facilities in Cuba?) More extended searches are handled by setting up a search on the LAN, running off a few citations, printing out the search strategy, and then explaining to patrons how they can sign up for the LAN to replicate the search and carry on in new directions.

6.   Expect better access with fewer reference tools.   Because CD-ROM products are expensive, especially in a network environment, and because money does not on grow on trees, you will need to cancel other reference sources to pay for CD-ROM products. We have not only cancelled the paper version of the products we have on the LAN, but other more specific indexes and abstracts covered by the large disciplinary tools. We can not justify the purchase of an index or bibliography on divorce when we have PsycLIT and Sociofile available. Our LAN has made us rethink the way we build our reference collection.

7.   Allocate sufficient staff to administer the LAN. In most discussion of whether or not an institution should launch a LAN, the ease of updating software is usually presented as a justification for electing a LAN. The argument typically states that it is easier to update software on the server than to update the same software on individual microcomputers. While this may be true in large LANs that are not running CD-ROMs, in the library CD-ROM LAN environment with a relatively small number of workstations (fewer than 50), it is most definitely not true. Relatively trivial updates in a dedicated workstation mode become a half-day work session on the LAN. The myth of ease of server updating may be part of the larger myth that surfaces periodically in administrative circles, namely that higher level automation

somehow saves staff time. Working librarians know, perhaps best of all, the fallacy of this argument.

The Future

We expect the LAN to get bigger, both in terms of the number of workstations and the resources available on it. In the next year we are looking to expand the number of workstations by at least four and hope to add as many as fourteen more CD-ROM drives. It is our expectation that within a year or two 80 percent of all of our indexes and abstracts will be on the CD-ROM LAN as will a significant number of other reference sources. We foresee a 40 workstation, 40 CD-ROM drive system within the next five years.

Because of the availability of a large hard drive we are exploring the addition of several floppy disk products to the LAN. We expect to begin with the Connecticut Data Manager, a statistical source, and PCGlobe and PC USA, statistical and map sources. These possibilities have lead us to begin thinking about building a ready reference capacity on the LAN.

We hope to provide dial-in service to the LAN, though this function raises a number of questions concerning licenses. Because we can control which workstations have access to which files, and the dial-in solutions we are considering employ an auxiliary processor board (possibly Cubix) which is in essence a workstation on the network, we may be able to avoid this problem. Publishers which will not provide appropriate rights at a reasonable cost will not have their systems available to our dial-in users.

Over the longer term we expect to expand the LAN to many more workstations within the library. We are in the process of installing an integrated library system. We expect to use a Novell/Token Ring network as the basis for workstation to mainframe connectivity. We plan to have the option of accessing our CD-ROM server from each of these machines. Since we expect to migrate some of the heavily used CD-ROM products to the mainframe based integrated system, we see the combination of the CD-ROM LAN and the integrated automation as the way to create a unified system capable of providing a wide range of information resources.

	Projected Cost	Actual Cost
LAN Server	$7,000	$11,275
Novell software	3,000	2,100
Token Ring Cards (11)	5,500	7,370
Token Ring Cards (1)	—	670
Wiring	5,000	4,500
Multistation Access Units(2)	—	$1,500
SUB-TOTAL	$20,500	$26,740
CD-ROM Server Base Unit (7 drives)	$10,000	
Added Unit (7 drives)	7,000	
Software	1,500	
SUB-TOTAL	$18,500	$15,470
Installation	—	$1,550
Workstations with printers (6)	$15,000	$11,700
Menuing software	—	$500
TOTAL	$54,000	$55,960

Table 10.1
University of Connecticut CD-ROM LAN Projected and Actual Costs

	Single-User Price	LAN Price	Price Structure
ABI/Inform	$4,950	$5,325	$150 per workstation
Agricola	630	630	no additional fee
CINHAL	915	915	no additional fee
Disclosure	4,200	6,900	up to 5 simultaneous users
ERIC	570	570	no additional fee
Humanities Index	1,235	1,235	no additional fee
MLA	1,460	1,460	no additional fee
Monthly Catalog	300	300	no additional fee
PAIS	1,705	2,855	up to 5 simultaneous users
PsycLIT	3,310	4,917	up to 8 simultaneous users
Sociofile	1,882	2,890	up to 8 simultaneous users
TOTAL	$21,157	$27,997	
Increase		$6,840	
Percentage Increase		32.3%	

Note: Most prices reflect NELINET discounts.

Table 10.2
University of Connecticut CD-ROM LAN Product Costs—Single-User and LAN as of summer 1990

	February 1990 (no LAN)	February 1991 (LAN)	% Change
Hours CD-ROMs available	346	326	-5.8%
Number of Workstations available	10	14	+40.0%
Number of half-hour slots reserved	2,690	3,707	+37.8%
Percentage of slots reserved	39.0%	40.6%	+4.1%
LAN product slots reserved	2,139	2,714	+26.9%
Percentage of LAN product slots reserved	44.2% 5	2.0%	+17.6%

Table 10.3
University of Connecticut CD-ROM LAN
CD-ROM Use February 1990 versus February 1991

DATABASES	Logins	% of Logins	Logins per Day	Hours	Minutes per Login
ABI/Inform	555	9.2%	17.9	281.0	30.9
Agricola	230	3.8%	7.4	49.4	12.9
CINAHL	287	4.8%	9.3	66.7	13.9
Disclosure	401	6.6%	12.9	143.1	21.4
ERIC	89	14.9%	29.0	249.0	16.6
ERIC 2	125	2.1%	4.0	14.4	6.9
ERIC 3	91	1.5%	2.9	11.2	7.4
Humanities Index	379	6.3%	12.2	125.8	19.9
MLA	510	8.4%	16.5	262.0	30.8
Monthly Catalog	333	5.5%	10.7	109.8	19.8
PyscLIT	1,315	21.8%	42.4	300.4	13.7
PsycLIT 2	269	4.5%	8.7	29.3	6.5
Sociofile	647	10.7%	20.9	141.4	13.1
TOTAL	6,040	100.0%	194.8	1,783.5	17.7
SilverPlatter Databases					13.4
CD-ROM Workstations	5,049	83.6%	162.9		
Average	631		20.5		
Express	662	11.0%	21.4		
Reference	329	5.4%	10.6		

Table 10.4
University of Connecticut CD-ROM LAN
CD-ROM LAN Use March 1991

DATABASES	Logins	% of Logins	Logins per Day	Hours	Minutes per Login
ABI/Inform	838	11.4	27.9	400.5	28.7
Agricola	304	4.1	10.1	61.6	12.2
CINAHL	308	4.2	10.3	66.0	12.9
Disclosure	469	6.4	15.6	146.4	18.7
ERIC	808	11.0	26.9	213.3	15.8
ERIC 2	127	1.7	4.2	15.5	7.3
ERIC 3	76	1.0	2.5	7.3	5.8
Humanities Index	504	6.9	16.8	118.4	14.1
MLA	777	10.6	25.9	283.4	21.9
Monthly Catalog	421	5.7	14.0	127.2	18.1
PyscLIT	1,442	19.6	48.1	303.0	12.6
PsycLIT 2	310	4.2	10.3	45.6	8.8
Sociofile	961	13.1	32.0	184.5	11.5
TOTAL	7,345	99.9%	244.6	1,972.7	14.5
SilverPlatter Databases					10.9
CD-ROM Workstations	6,076	82.7%	202.5		
Average	760		25.3		
Express	828	11.3%	27.6		
Reference	424	5.8%	14.1		
Supervisor	17				

Table 10.5
University of Connecticut CD-ROM LAN
CD-ROM LAN Use April 1991

Products and Services

CBIS
5875 Peachtree Industrial Blvd
Building 100, Suite 170
Norcross, GA 30092
(404) 446-1332
CD-ROM Server

Cubix Corporation
2800 Lockheed Way
Carson City, NV 89706
(702) 883-7611
Dial-in access

IBM Corporation
P.O. Box 12195
Research Triangle Park, NC 27709
(800) 237-5511
Token Ring 16/4 Adapter

Novell Inc.
122 East 1700 South
Provo, UT 85601
(801) 379-3700
Network Operating System

Pioneer Communications of America
600 East Crescent Avenue
Upper Saddle River, NJ 07458-1827
(201) 327-6400
Six Disc Changer

Saber Software Corporation
P.O. Box 9088
Dallas, TX 75209
(214) 361-8086
Menuing and metering

About the Authors

David W. Lewis is the Head of the Research and Information Services Department at the Homer Babbidge Library, University of Connecticut, Storrs, Connecticut 06269, 203-486-2522, BITNET: dlewis@uconnvm. Before coming to Connecticut he held various public service positions at Columbia University, Franklin and Marshall College, Hamilton College, and SUNY at Farmingdale. He has a B.A. from Carleton College, an M.L.S. from Columbia University, and a Certificate of Advanced Study from the University of Chicago.

Terry Plum is the Coordinator for Computer Based Services in the Research and Information Services Department (203-486-2589 BITNET: hbladm82@uconnvm). He has held public service positions at Middlebury College and at SUNY at Plattsburgh. He has a B.A. from Middlebury College and a M. L. from the University of Washington.

Acknowledgements

The authors wish to acknowledge the work of Sue Gibbs, Head of the Processing Section in the Research and Information Services Department, and George Waller of the Homer Babbidge Library Microcomputer Support Unit, in setting up and maintaining the CD-ROM LAN.

11

The Intelligent Reference Information System CD-ROM Network

Thomas C. Wilson and Charles W. Bailey, Jr.
University of Houston Libraries, University of Houston

ABSTRACT

The major goals of the federally-funded, two-year IRIS Project are to: (1) network nineteen citation, full-text, graphic, and numeric CD-ROM databases in the Information Services Department of the University of Houston Libraries; and (2) create a related expert system that will identify appropriate reference materials to meet users' needs, including networked CD-ROM's, stand-alone CD-ROM's, and print reference works. This chapter examines the selection, installation, implementation, and utilization of the IRIS CD-ROM network.

Background of the IRIS Project

In the fall of 1989, the University of Houston Libraries were awarded a $99,852 Research and Demonstration Grant from the U. S. Department of Education's College Library Technology and Cooperation Grants Program to develop an Intelligent Reference Information System (IRIS) over a two-year period.[1] It is estimated that Federal funds will pay for approximately 51 percent of the IRIS Project's costs.

The primary goals of IRIS Project are to: (1) network diverse CD-ROM database resources in the Information Services Department of the University of Houston Libraries; and (2) create an expert system that will identify appropriate reference materials to meet users' needs, including networked CD-ROM's, stand-alone CD-ROM's, and print reference works. Users of the CD-ROM network will be able to consult the expert system, then connect to CD-ROM databases that are recommended by the expert system.

The IRIS Project hopes to provide some useful data about networking CD-ROM databases, test the success of such an endeavor from the user's perspective, study the effectiveness of using an expert system in such an environment, identify intellectual and technical issues surrounding the use of expert systems, and enhance the understanding of the profession in these areas.

The work of the IRIS Project is conducted by the Project Director and eleven librarians, serving on four committees: the Electronic Publications Instruction Group, the Knowledge Engineering Group, the Project Management Group, and the Research and Evaluation Group.

Prior to the project, the University of Houston Libraries had accomplished pioneering work in the area of automated reference assistance by developing the Information Machine and the Index Expert programs. The Information Machine provides general directional and library use information through a menu-driven interface.[2] Index Expert is an expert system designed to assist users in selecting appropriate indexes and abstracts based on a subject approach.[3,4] Both systems have been successfully implemented in the University of Houston Libraries.

A complete discussion of the IRIS Project is beyond the scope of this paper, which will primarily focus on technical aspects of the CD-ROM network. The reader is encouraged to consult the cited references for further information about the IRIS Project.

History of CD-ROM Use

Prior to the IRIS Project, the University of Houston Libraries had significant expertise in implementing CD-ROM technology. The Information Services Department began exploring CD-ROM databases in 1986 and served as a beta-test site for Compact Disclosure.

During the summer of 1987, the University of Houston Libraries implemented three CD-ROM workstations consisting of one IBM-PC/XT and two OCLC M300's. These machines were equipped with 640KB RAM (Random Access Memory), 20MB hard disk drives, and CGA color monitors. Each workstation was dedicated to a particular product (one for Compact Disclosure and two for Ondisc ERIC). These two databases were immensely popular with the University of Houston Libraries' clientele. Shortly after implementation, however, it became evident that a more diverse set of databases would be necessary to meet client demand.

The following year the University of Houston Libraries expanded the collection of databases to include: ABI/Inform Ondisc, Compact Disclosure, CD-Plus MEDLINE, MLA International Bibliography, GPO/CAT PAC (Monthly Catalog), Ondisc ERIC, PAIS on CD-ROM, PsycLIT, Science Citation Index Compact Disk Edition, Sociofile, and SUPERMAP. The number of workstations was also expanded from three to nine. Since there were more databases than workstations, the configuration had to allow more than one database to run on each workstation. The three dedicated workstations were retained because of heavy use, but the six remaining workstations were configured to run any of the other CD-ROM databases. The University of Houston Libraries named this service point the "Electronic Publications Center."

Quickly the use of this service doubled, then tripled. Just prior to the installation of the network, the annual cumulative use total was eight times as much as the first year. Lines and queues were common occurrences in the Electronic Publications Center. It was evident that somehow the CD-ROM resources needed to be made more widely available.

Network Requirements

In preparing to network CD-ROM resources, the University of Houston Libraries explored a variety of local area network options. It would be necessary to create an environment that could support a great diversity of data resources. Part of the project was to test access to a wide-array of databases, including citation, full-text, graphic, and numeric databases. To accomplish this end, the network environment needed to be robust. The University of Houston Libraries had installed an IBM Token Ring network running the IBM PC LAN software for shared administrative and staff functions. The Libraries were very pleased with the reliability and performance of the IBM Token Ring network; however, a more sophisticated networking operating system would be required to support IRIS.

Security was another concern. Some clients in the Electronic Publications Center had proved that, given the opportunity, they would use the workstations for whatever purpose they chose, despite reasonably restrictive security measures. Thus, to avoid an increase of these problems in a network setting, the network operating system needed to have good security features.

Given that the exact nature of the behavior of CD-ROM databases in a network was an unknown variable, the network needed to be flexible and expandable. It was also a distinct possibility that the network would be used for other types of data resources other than CD-ROM, and that over time the network would be greatly enlarged throughout the building, to the branches, and across the campus.

To the degree possible, centralizing the searching software on a file server was also desirable. This approach would make updating and maintaining the software for each database much easier. In addition, other network management software, such as menu programs, statistical packages, and utilities could be more easily used and maintained if they were available from a central file server.

Description of the IRIS Network

The University of Houston Libraries utilize an IBM Token-Ring network for the IRIS Project. The IBM Token Ring network was chosen in part because of previous experience with it and in part because of a belief that it would perform well under moderate and heavy loads. The University of Houston Libraries' network uses the IBM Cabling System, with major cables being Type 1 cable.

From a physical perspective, the IBM Token Ring network is a combination of ring and star topologies. Cable runs from Multistation Access Unit (MAU) to Multistation Access Unit to form a ring. From each MAU, cable emanates in a star pattern to individual workstations. This arrangement permits malfunctioning workstations to be removed from the network without bringing the entire network down, and it enhances troubleshooting. Logically, the IBM Token Ring functions as a ring. The IRIS Project is running Novell NetWare 2.15 revision B as a network operating system. NetWare provides high levels of reliability, stability, security, and expandability. It is considered a major player in the computing industry and is widely supported. NetBIOS is used on the network servers and workstations.

The file server is a Club American Model 320, 20MHz, 80386 microcomputer with an ESDI 150MB hard disk drive. The file server and each workstation has a Western Digital TokenCard network interface card.

Two Meridian Data CD Net Model 314 CD-ROM servers are used to provide access to 19 CD-ROM databases. Each 20MHz 80386 server houses 10 CD-ROM drives (up to 14 CD-ROM drives can be housed in each unit). The Meridian CD Net software (3.01) as well as the NetWare DOS Client software (3.01) are running on the Meridian servers.

Originally, the workstations were a mix of 80286 and 80386SX machines, but due to a need for large-body machines elsewhere in the University of Houston Libraries, the 80286 machines were replaced. All workstations are now Club American Model 316SX, 16 MHz, 80386SX microcomputers with 40MB hard disk drives and EGA color monitors. The performance of these workstations has been remarkably good.

Eight public network workstations are located in the Electronic Publications Center, one staff workstation is located at the Information Desk, and the servers as well as another staff workstation are located in the University of Houston Libraries' central computer room. The computer room provides a climate-controlled, secure location for the computing equipment. The following CD-ROM databases are currently available on the network: ABI/Inform Ondisc, Art Index, Biological and Agricultural Index, Business Dateline Ondisc, Compact Disclosure, Compendex Plus, Computer Library, Social Sciences Index, The New Grolier Electronic Encyclopedia, Humanities Index, Microsoft Bookshelf, Ondisc ERIC, Periodical Abstracts Ondisc, PsycLIT, Social Sciences Index, Sociofile, The Software Toolworks World Atlas, Statistical Masterfile, and SUPERMAP. Future plans include additional electronic publications, both on CD-ROM and on magnetic media.

Procurement Process

Acquiring network licenses for the nineteen databases needed by the IRIS project was complicated process that required about two months of negotiation with database vendors.[5] At the time, many database vendors were uncertain about what contractual terms and license fees were appropriate for network use, and the contracts that resulted from these negotiations were not very uniform. A variety of restrictions on use were included in these contracts, including number of simultaneous users, number of network workstations, location of network workstations, and end-user affiliation.

As a public institution in the State of Texas, the University of Houston Libraries were required to follow strict purchasing guidelines—a practice common to all publicly-funded agencies. The nature of these requirements determined the level of flexibility in selecting network hardware and software, not to mention workstation hardware and software. For most items, selection was limited to suppliers on the state contract; however, some of the items needed for networking could be purchased off contract.

One crucial element was the certified compatibility of the file server with the NetWare software. The most critical aspect of NetWare compatibility was the disk drive. Fortunately, the Club American vendor on state contract also handled NetWare and could guarantee the compatibility of the equipment.

Another complexity of dealing with state contract purchase was the length of time between the submission of an order and the arrival of the items. Delivery times for some needed items were sixty days or more.

The process was also slowed by the level of review necessary for a grant project. Additional paperwork was required, and the University's Office of Sponsored Programs had to review purchases to ensure that the University of Houston Libraries were following Federal government guidelines.

The University of Houston Libraries had been installing Copicard units on all photocopiers and CD-ROM workstations to assist in defraying the cost of printing supplies. Such a commitment, however, demanded that each new equipment acquisition be compatible with the Copicard units. Arrangements were made for a trial of the Club American hardware with the Copicard hardware and software. Both companies were willing to communicate with each other and were helpful in satisfying our request.

Network Implementation

Implementation of the IRIS network proceeded in two broad phases: (1) testing a small-scale prototype network, and (2) testing the full-scale network.

Small-Scale Network Test

Given the size of the IRIS Project, it seemed wise to begin by installing a test network in a staff area. This arrangement permitted ample working room, a quiet work space, and physical security. The Information Services department had available space at the time. Having the test network in this location was also convenient for demonstration purposes.

The test network consisted of the NetWare server, two Meridian Data CD Net 314 CD-ROM servers, two workstations, and one MAU. Cables were conveniently placed behind the equipment to allow for easy connecting and disconnecting, which occurred quite frequently in the test mode.

NetWare. Installing NetWare was a somewhat daunting task. Portions of the process were lengthy and complex. Fortunately, Novell provided extensive documentation; sometimes it seemed like too much documentation. Several NetWare books proved to be useful during the installation process.

One of the first challenges was the preparation of the disk drive for NetWare. A test, called COMPSURF, needed to be run to check the surface of the platters for any irregularities and to prepare the drive to receive data. This test could take 12 to 18 hours or more to complete and could be run unattended. The better part of wisdom suggested that the server be set up for the test prior to closing the department for the day to allow the computer to do what it does best on its own. In the morning, messages indicated that the process had been aborted. The next night this was done again with the same result.

Investigation revealed that the University's custodial staff were turning off the power to the Information Services department over night. This problem was resolved by taping official-looking messages to the door of the circuit box controlling this area of the building. Fortunately, the custodial staff obliged our request.

NetWare used a program called NETGEN to place the appropriate files on the file server and to configure it according to the implementer's wishes. There were many options. Fortunately, there were also defaults, but these were often not well-documented. Nonetheless, we often relied on default settings as a starting point.

NetWare used another program called SHGEN to create the "shell" for each workstation on the network. This process created the IPX.COM program and it was considerably less tedious than NETGEN, as one would expect.

In addition, installing more than one Meridian server on a network running NetWare required the use of the NetBIOS program or an emulator, which provided another level of network services. Novell provided a NetBIOS emulator with their software. This program needed to be copied to each workstation.

When running the IPX.COM network shell only, the CD-ROM drives in the Meridian servers were mapped directly to drive letters on the workstations. These drive assignments could not be changed without editing files and rebooting the workstations. Under the NetBIOS emulation, by using Meridian's MOUNT.EXE or CMOUNT.EXE mapping utilities, the workstation's logical drives could be dynamically allocated to any of the CD-ROM drives.

The NetWare implementation was a time-consuming process because there was a substantial learning curve involved. NetWare is a complex network environment that should not be attempted by the technically faint-at-heart.

Once the initial hurdles were crossed, success was evident at the network level. The small test network appeared to be communicating appropriately.

Meridian Data CD Net 314 Servers. Once the NetWare file server and the workstations were configured, the Meridian CD-ROM servers had to be installed. For the most part, these servers came ready to plug and play. Some software adjustments were necessary, such as naming each server and generating the appropriate shell for the network.

The Meridian servers connected to the network just as any other workstations would. They were not identified by NetWare as servers. It was the Meridian software running on the CD-ROM server and on each workstation that permitted mapping to specific CD-ROM drives and multiuser access to these resources.

In addition to software adjustments on the Meridian servers, each workstation required the presence of certain programs and environment variables. Each workstation needed to run the Microsoft Extensions for CD-ROM to identify what type of CD-ROM device would be used, how many of them could be mapped at once, and what size memory buffer was required. Each of the Microsoft CD-ROM Extensions settings had memory (RAM) implications. There were other variables to set in the DOS environment, such as the name and number of Meridian servers. These adjustments were fairly well-documented in the Meridian manual, and little trouble was encountered in this arena.

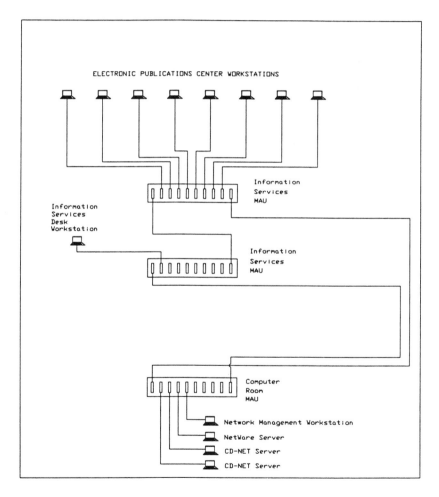

Figure 11.1
University of Houston IRIS Network

CD-ROM Databases. Since the University of Houston Libraries had purchased a number of CD-ROM databases from H. W. Wilson and UMI, these vendors' CD-ROM searching software packages were installed first on the network. Presumably, once the software was installed, all of that vendors' products would run. This approach had psychological as well as pragmatic advantages.

Another guiding principle was to install as much of the software as possible on the file server's hard disk. This arrangement would simplify maintenance and updating of the network. Several vendor products, however, did not run reliably—or at all—in this configuration and had to be installed on individual workstations instead.

The initial installation of CD-ROM products went remarkably well. Two people being able to search the same database at the same time or to search multiple databases from one workstation was an exciting prospect. Many of the staff who had followed the installation process closely were quite excited as the system unfolded. However, as was discovered later, two workstations on a small test network are quite different from ten workstations on a fully implemented network.

The CD-ROM installation process was not without its challenges. Incomplete or inaccurate documentation for network installations caused many frustrating moments. For nearly all of the products, calls had to be made to the vendors to request additional information.

Since many phone calls to a number of vendors were necessary, an accurate impression of the technical support capabilities for each vendor was attained. The quality, helpfulness, and attitudes of the technical support staff varied greatly. In several cases, vendor representatives gave prompt, accurate, and courteous assistance. Others were argumentative, ill-prepared, and non-committal. Clearly, the issue of providing adequate network support will need to be addressed by vendors in the future.

Another challenge faced in this process was caused by misbehaving or poorly designed software. Although many software sins can be hidden in stand-alone mode where only one product is running on a workstation, the network environment tended to accentuate program weaknesses. Theoretically, software that was written for a single-user environment should also run in a multiuser environment (unless the application entails transaction processing, which CD-ROM does not); however, in reality, problems arose. Some products performed poorly, required the constant attention of the network manager, or even ground the network to a halt. The nature of these problem ran the gamut from hard-coded sub-directory assignments to circumventing the Microsoft CD-ROM Extensions or other standard conventions.

Despite the challenges faced, the IRIS network had sixteen databases up and running after two weeks of intensive effort. At least, these products ran most of the time on the small test network. Minor glitches remained, such as not being able to dependably view the results of a search on one vendor's products and an occasional freeze up with another vendor's products.

Full-Scale Network Test

After the successful implementation of the test network, the time came to move the equipment to its final resting place and to connect the actual public workstations. The three servers (NetWare server and two Meridian servers) were moved to the computer room that also houses the integrated library system equipment. Eight public workstations in the Electronic Publications Center were connected to the network, the cabling and MAU's having been previously installed. One workstation remained in Information Services, intended for network administration.

Once all of the hardware was connected, it was time to test the network. The network booted the first time; however, this success was fleeting. At the observable network level, connectivity had been achieved; however, once the applications (i.e., the CD-ROM databases) were tested, new problems arose. The CD-ROM databases would work if one or two users were searching in the same product at the same time. But higher numbers of users froze the workstations and the network. Even when products did work, the performance was highly variable. Some products were more problematic than others.

Diagnosing the Problem

Diagnosing network troubles is akin to determining the desires of a new-born infant. Even with previous experience, the most one can hope for is a reasonably accurate guess. Starting from the simplest component and moving to increasingly more complex ones was the approach taken.

The Network and NetWare

Through the process of elimination, components were tested. One at a time cables, connectors, and MAU's were removed from the ring and the network was rebooted. If the same problem persisted, the component was reconnected and another removed. Several potential weak points were identified via this method, but none that yielded significant improvement in network performance.

The cable run to the Information Services department was from a previous LAN connection installed several years before. The caliber and condition of the cable were suspect, but removing it from the network did not resolve the entire problem. Nonetheless, a significant improvement in network performance occurred when the cable was disconnected. The network management workstation was then moved from Information Services to the computer room.

A cable tester was acquired. The suspect cable proved to be problematic, but other cables were fine. More sophisticated network diagnostic equipment was available, but it was expensive ($1,500 to $25,000) and topology-, NIC-, and operating system-specific. Consequently, the acquisition of this type of costly diagnostic equipment was seen as a last resort.

The network level of communication could also be tested by utilities provided with some network operating systems. NetWare came with COMCHECK.COM, a program that ran on each workstation to verify that each is sending and receiving messages on the network. Once the cabling difficulties had been resolved, this program indicated that the network itself was not the cause of continuing problems.

The Meridian CD-ROM Servers

Throughout the implementation process, representatives from Meridian were in regular communication with the University of Houston Libraries. It became evident after all of the testing that there must be a problem related to the Meridian servers. The hardware appeared to be functional, but something was not working appropriately. It seemed likely that the Meridian software was not functioning properly in the NetBIOS-oriented Token Ring network environment.

One problem was that the University of Houston Libraries had purchased "plug-compatible" Token-Ring boards on state contract, and, at that time, Meridian did not support these boards. Consequently, Meridian staff needed to become familiar with these boards before potential software compatibility problems could be addressed.

Meridian representatives were extremely helpful in resolving the server problems. The University of Houston Libraries had access to Meridian's technical support, software development, and engineering staff. Meridian sent faster, more reliable NIC's for the servers, and it provided the University of Houston Libraries with two new versions of its CD-ROM server software as well as the NetWare DOS Client software. Once these changes were made, performance improved dramatically and the network was highly reliable.

Additional Implementation Challenges

While the primary network problems were being addressed, other technical issues needed to be resolved as well. During the course of testing, a number of product errors had been linked to the lack of sufficient memory on each workstation, a common problem in network environments.

Each workstation had device drivers, Microsoft Extensions for CD-ROM, network drivers, and DOS environment variables loaded in conventional memory below the 640KB limit, leaving a fairly small amount of useable RAM. Many CD-ROM products required additional RAM in order to function properly. Fortunately, each workstation was equipped with one megabyte of RAM. With appropriate memory management software, certain portions of the these memory resident programs could be moved into high memory (the memory between 640KB and 1MB).

The AboveLAN program, which was chosen because it is a software-only solution, performed these functions easily. This program ran on each workstation and freed up approximately 37KB of RAM below 640KB.

Memory management continues to be a challenge for the IRIS Project. Additional solutions are being investigated to yield even greater RAM savings.

Another issue requiring attention was the creation of menus to guide users to available databases, to provide easy access, and to minimize security risks. NetWare came with a built-in menu program, but it was limited to fewer menu entries than the IRIS application needed and users could easily exit from the menus into NetWare. Some CD-ROM searching software would not run on the file server unless very liberal directory rights were granted to network users, creating a security risk. Thus, a different menu program option was required.

To meet this need, the Saber LAN Administration Pack was acquired. This package also included a statistics gathering program, a report generator, a metering program to ensure licensing compliance for network products, a program that prevents users from exiting the menu system, and other network utilities. The menu software permitted relatively easy modification of menu entries. Menu entries could be password protected, assigned to particular workstations, and nested. The Saber software ran on the file server, making maintenance and updating manageable.

Total Network Implementation Time

Implementation began May 21, 1990, and the network was made publicly available August 20, 1990. During that time, the equivalent of about four weeks of intensive effort was invested in getting the network up and running. The remaining time can best be described as "hurry up and wait." Obviously, other library-related tasks had to continue in the interim; no new staff were hired as a result of this project. Furthermore, technical challenges were frequently resolved at odd hours after removing oneself from the firing range. Thus, the entire period was not spent directly resolving network problems.

Network Evaluation

Based on the previous success of CD-ROM products, it was anticipated that the IRIS LAN would be a popular service; however, actual use quickly exceeded our expectations. Table 11.1 shows use statistics for the first full six months of operation. Each use represents one CD-ROM session; multiple searches may have been conducted during that session.

	Sept.	Oct.	Nov.	Dec.	Jan.	Feb.
ABI/Inform Ondisc	1,249	1,561	1,369	380	542	1,205
Art Index	59	90	85	31	22	63
Biological and Agricultural Index	84	150	123	87	69	144
Business Dateline Ondisc	602	737	567	201	269	619
Compact Disclosure	516	520	387	140	266	553
Compendex Plus	133	134	141	66	119	124
Computer Library	123	201	192	94	118	167
Electromap World Atlas	89	142	68	59	42	101
General Science Index	192	244	199	139	146	277
Humanities Index	209	241	384	125	89	274
Microsoft Bookshelf	67	108	78	52	51	88
OnDisc ERIC	749	779	781	234	323	804
Periodical Abstracts Ondisc	272	422	464	169	158	373
PsycLIT	974	1,252	1,298	288	387	1,155
Social Sciences Index	460	543	645	227	202	620
Sociofile	379	480	559	130	186	439
Statistical Masterfile	0	78	76	43	34	70
SUPERMAP	56	79	98	69	21	54
Monthly Total	6,213	7,761	7,514	2,534	3,044	7,130

Note: Electromap World Atlas is now called The Software Toolworks World Atlas.

Table 11.1
IRIS LAN Use Statistics 9/1/90-2/28/91

The IRIS Project is currently analyzing performance benchmarks for the Meridian CD-ROM network. In general, performance is quite good, even when the network is heavily loaded. The network has been rock solid since the service became public, and there has been very little network downtime. Routine network maintenance (e.g., putting CD-ROM update disks on the network) takes a maximum of two hours a week, and little other work is required to keep the network operational. Overall, the IRIS Project has been very satisfied with the network, and it would not hesitate to purchase additional hardware and software from our current vendors to support expanded CD-ROM network efforts.

Conclusion

CD-ROM networking is a relatively new technology. Unless libraries purchase true turn-key CD-ROM networks that include network installation and maintenance services, they should expect that a fairly high level of technical expertise will be required to support these networks. As the size and complexity of these networks increases, technical support needs will also increase.

This paper has provided a candid "behind the scenes" look at some of the technical issues that the University of Houston Libraries faced in its CD-ROM network implementation. Some of the challenges described here were the result of being an early user of CD-ROM networking technology, local hardware compatibility and cabling problems, and the overall scope of the CD-ROM networking effort. Some challenges were caused by the fact that, for the most part, CD-ROM vendors have not modified their single-user products to run smoothly in networked environments. Some were simply the result of the inherent complexity of CD-ROM networks.

CD-ROM networking offers libraries a powerful and effective tool for providing increased access to electronic information. For libraries with adequate fiscal resources, a desirable information provision strategy may be to put high-use databases on mainframe computers, medium-use databases on CD-ROM networks, and low-use databases on stand-alone CD-ROM workstations. Of course, some databases will only be available in CD-ROM format, and the demand for high- or medium-use databases in this category is likely to be adequately met only through networking.

Notes

1. Charles W. Bailey, Jr. and Kathleen Gunning, "The Intelligent Reference Information System," *CD-ROM Librarian* 5 (September 1990): 10-19.

2. Jeff Fadell and Judy E. Myers, "The Information Machine: A Microcomputer-Based Reference Service," *The Reference Librarian* 23 (1989): 75-112.

3. Charles W. Bailey, Jr., "Building Knowledge-Based Systems for Public-Use: The Intelligent Reference Systems Project at the University of Houston Libraries," in *Convergence: Proceedings of the Second National Conference of the Library and Information Technology Association,* (October 2-6, 1988), edited by Michael Gorman (Chicago: American Library Association, 1990), 190-194.

4. Charles W. Bailey, Jr., Jeff Fadell, Judy E. Myers, and Thomas C. Wilson, "The Index Expert System: A Knowledge-Based System to Assist Users in Index Selection," *Reference Services Review* 17(4) (1989): 19-28.

5. Thomas C. Wilson, "Zen and the Art of CD-ROM Network License Negotiation," *The Public-Access Computer Systems Review* 1(2) (1990): 4-14. (To obtain this article, BITNET users can send the command GET WILSON PRV1N2 to LISTSERV@UHUPVM1.)

IRIS LAN Components

CD-ROM Server

Meridian Data CD Net Model 314 with 10 CD-ROM drives and 1MB of memory
Proteon ProNet 4/16 Token-Ring Board
Meridian Data CD Net Server Software 3.01
Microsoft DOS 3.3
Novell NetWare DOS Client 3.01

Network Server

Club American Model 320N with 2MB memory
Club American 1.2MB Floppy Disk Drive
Everex EGA Monitor
MiniScribe 150MB ESDI Hard Disk
Western Digital TokenCard
Advanced Novell NetWare 2.15 Rev. B
Saber Software LAN Administration Pack 1.1

Network Hardware and Cables

IBM Cabling System Plenum-Grade Type 1 Cable
IBM Multistation Access Unit

Typical Workstation

Club American Model 316 SX with 1MB memory
Able Copier Service CopiCard Unit
Club American 1.2MB Floppy Disk
Epson LX-810 Printer
Everex EGA Monitor
MiniScribe 40MB Hard Disk
Western Digital TokenCard
Above Software AboveLAN 3.1B
Above Software Above640 3.1B
Meridian CMOUNT
Microsoft CD-ROM Extensions 2.10
Microsoft DOS 3.3
Novell IPX
Novell NetBIOS
Novell NET3
University of Houston Libraries Reference Expert

Vendors

Above Software, Inc.

2698 White Road
Suite 200
Irvine, CA 92714
(800) 344-0116

Club American Technologies, Inc.

3401 West Warren Ave.
Fremont, CA 94539
(415) 683-6600

IBM

Old Orchard Road
Armonk, NY 10504
(800) 426-2468

Novell, Inc.

122 East 1700 South
Provo, UT 84606
(800) 453-1267

Meridian Data, Inc.

5615 Scotts Valley Drive
Scotts Valley, CA 95066
(408) 438-3100

Saber Software Corporation

P.O. Box 9088
Dallas, TX 75209
(800) 338-8754

About the Authors

Charles W. Bailey, Jr. is the Assistant Director for Systems at the University of Houston Libraries and IRIS Project Manager. Mr. Bailey is the moderator of PACS-L, a large, international computer conference on BITNET; Editor-in-Chief of The Public Access Computer Systems Review, an electronic journal; and co-editor of Public Access Computer Systems News, an electronic newsletter. He also serves as co-editor of Advances in Library Automation and Networking, and he edits the LITA Newsletter's "Standard Fare" column. Mr. Bailey has published papers dealing with electronic publishing, expert systems, multimedia computing, and public-access computer systems, which have appeared in *Advances in Library Automation and Networking, CD-ROM Librarian, Information Technology and Libraries, Library Hi Tech, Reference Services Review*, and other publications. He holds an M.L.S. from Syracuse University as well as a B.A. and an M.A. from the University of Connecticut.

Thomas C. Wilson is currently the Head of Systems for the University of Houston Libraries. He began his work at the University of Houston Libraries in the Information Services Department as a Social Sciences Reference Librarian/Bibliographer. Mr. Wilson was later appointed the Coordinator of the Computerized Information Retrieval Services program. As such, he managed all forms of computer searching including mediated, end-user, and CD-ROM. During his tenure in the Information Services Department, Mr. Wilson guided the implementation of CD-ROM and other microcomputer-based technology. Mr. Wilson holds degrees from the Ohio State University and The University of Michigan. Since 1986, he has been involved with CD-ROM technology as a user, installer, consultant, author, and speaker. As part of a Title II-D Research and Demonstration Grant from the U. S. Department of Education, Mr. Wilson implemented and managed a CD-ROM network providing access to nineteen databases on ten workstations. He continues to provide technical support and oversight of this network.

Part Three:

Small General-Purpose Networks

12

Networking with PCSA

Dave Bloomberg
Wimberly Library, Florida Atlantic University

ABSTRACT
This chapter describes implementation and use of a PCSA-based campus-wide local area network at Florida Atlantic University, Boca Raton, Florida and in the S.E. Wimberly Library of in particular. The Library's portion consists of about 25 nodes spaced throughout the Library which use the LAN to share software, data and print services as well as for access to the Library's integrated library system.

Background

At the Wimberly Library of Florida Atlantic University, certain decisions about the Library's computer networks were made by a group of people perhaps not directly related to the Library. In this respect, we may be somewhat atypical in regards to other academic libraries. On the other hand, some libraries may indeed share our situation—that is to say, some other University organization made the major computing decisions, and we in the library were offered the choice to join or not. In our case, the benefits of joining far outweighed the price for not participating. The Library became "live" in October 1990. As of this writing, we have about seven months of experience with the network described in this article.

Why Network?

Our university plans to establish a campus-wide computer network for the use of the entire population of the university community. The long-term goal for the network is to fully implement the Fiber Distributed Data Interchange (FDDI) standard, bringing together many dissimilar computing environments under one unified system to facilitate the sharing of information.

For the Library to more efficiently utilize its existing base of installed personal computers, the decision to join in the University's effort to provide a state-of-the-art computing environment was easy. Such technology would provide the ability to exchange scholarly information via electronic means, and would provide powerful computer resources to individuals. Through the network, these resources would be shared among a large number of users, avoiding the need to have hundreds of individual copies of software, and other duplication of resources. There were still many unknown details and unanswered logistical questions at the time, but there was no question that the library needed—and wanted—to be an integral part of the campus network.

One of the benefits directly affecting the library environment relates to the access of the Library's OPAC (On-line Public Access Catalog) on the campus network via an electronic gateway. The OPAC represents the most significant electronic resource related to the Library. We in the Library saw that it was important for library users with access to the network to be able to access the OPAC electronically. This allows users of the network to gain information before they ever actually enter the library.

Network access to the library's OPAC can save time and effort for library patrons. For example, if a professor needs a particular book, rather than taking the time to come to the library—not knowing if we even own a given book, and if we do own it whether it might already be checked out—he or she simply sits down at the PC in his office and logs into the network. Within a couple minutes, the professor has the necessary information, such as the book's call number, to expedite the library trip, and may have avoided an unnecessary trip altogether.

Other reasons that favored the Library joining the campus network included the need to more efficiently use the computer resources already in place within the Library. Through a network, we could give library staff better access to various software packages, increased disk space for data storage and access to printers on the network.

Why PCSA?

Digital Equipment Corporation (DEC), well known for their VAX family of midrange computers, offers a product called Personal Computer Systems Architecture, or PCSA, that allows microcomputers to participate in VAX networks. While PC's generally use the MS-DOS operating system, VAX systems use an operating system called VMS. The networking method associated with VAX systems is called DECnet, and is based on Ethernet. PCSA uses Ethernet to allow microcomputers to use DECnet protocols to access network resources available on VAX/VMS systems.

DEC recently significantly upgraded the PCSA system and modernized the name of the product to PathWorks. The network installed in the Library uses PathWorks Version 3.1.

PCSA was selected as the campus networking platform at Florida Atlantic University (FAU) for several reasons. One of the most important considerations was its ability to bring together users from several different computing platforms under a single network environment. PCSA takes advantage of the power of an existing VAX system, combined with the personal computers already installed, to provide a cohesive networking structure for the university community.

Through the PCSA network, each microcomputer user has ready access to the computing resources and the larger external networks available through the VAX system. Network resources such as shared disk storage, print services, and gateways to other networks and systems are all performed by the VAX through PCSA. Because the VAX is a powerful midrange computer system, it can accommodate the needs of a very large number of network users. The VAX can support many more users than would be possible in networks which use a microcomputer network server.

Why the Library?

In academic settings, the library has become a hub of information flow. This may take many forms, and in order for the staff to keep up-to-date within the scholarly community, it is important for the librarians to have access to the same technology that impacts the rest of the university. We saw the implementation of the LAN in the Library as an opportunity to upgrade the level of automation in the Library and to help library staff gain familiarity with an extremely relevant technology.

Computers have taken over manual tasks in several areas of the typical academic library. The most obvious area is the Online Public Access Catalog (OPAC). Card catalogs are a thing of the past for the modern academic library. Step up to a terminal, type in your request, and almost instantly the computer matches your search criteria with the library's holdings.

Automation has also made a huge impact in the reference department. The personal computer tied to a CD-ROM player gives library patrons almost instant access to volumes of data, that would previously have taken hours, if not days, to search and organize. Although there are limits to the depth of bibliographic information available through CD-ROM products, they provide ample amounts of data for a large portion of reference patrons. There are even full text systems available so a user wouldn't even have to go find a particular journal, its right there in front of you. You can download to a diskette or get hardcopy output from a printer.

The Goals

The library has formulated short-, near-, and long-term goals for its use of the campus network. Each of these goals relates to stages of implementation in integration of the network in the library.

We have already accomplished the short-term goals. These goals center around the initial installation and implementation of the network in the library. Tasks associated with the short-term goals included the installation of cabling in the library, installation and configuration of software, and the initial training of the end-users of the network in the library. With this phase accomplished, the network was in place and ready to be integrated into the library's workflow.

Our near-term goals involve increasing access to the network to more members of the staff and the expansion of training as end-users delve into the new services available via the network. Through these goals, the network will become a tool that will help library staff better use its computer resources.

Long-term goals will be reevaluated as time goes on, but may include the addition of some type of CD-ROM network interconnected with the campus LAN, such that users could perform CD-ROM research tasks from their office or dorm room. As is the case for most libraries, budgetary constraints may cause delays in the implementation of these goals.

The Physical Installation

The network administrators in the computer center planned to connect the library to the campus network through fiber optic technology. A fiber optic cable would connect the library to the computer center, where the university's VAX host resides. Considering the 100 megabits per second data throughput possible through fiber optic link, the library would have a very fast and reliable connection to the VAX system at the heart of our network.

We used thick-wire Ethernet cabling to connect the fiber optic interconnect to the main distribution block of the library building. In this main distribution hub, a multiport repeater allows us to connect several segments of thin-wire Ethernet to our thick-wire Ethernet. The thin-wire Ethernet segments connect to the individual workstations located throughout the library building.

The progression from fiber optic cable, to thick-wire Ethernet, to thin-wire Ethernet takes advantage of the advantages of each cabling type used in Ethernet networks. These three cable types each have specific capabilities when used in an Ethernet network in regards to the total length possible per segment, the rate of data throughput, and in the minimum distance allowed between nodes. The properties of Ethernet have been defined by the IEEE 802.3 standard.

Fiber optic cable supports much faster data rates but costs more than the other cable types and involves specialized equipment to manage.

Thick-wire Ethernet, although capable of spanning greater distances than thin-wire Ethernet, requires special taps and transceivers to connect workstations. This type of Ethernet cabling is quite rigid and requires special care when installing.

Thin-wire Ethernet cable is not only less expensive, but is also easier to manage in connecting individual workstations to the network. Thin-wire Ethernet segments must be no greater than 300 meters in length.

From the fiber optic link a section of Thick Ethernet cable was run to the distribution block. Thin Ethernet cable runs were installed from this block to points throughout the library. Teflon-coated fire resistant (open plenum) cable was used throughout this process (as per building codes in effect for this location).

The Academic Computing Department provided the staff for the cable installation. The campus Physical plant provided drawings for the cable pullers to work from. The actual cable pulling took about two weeks to complete—in spite of the building's best effort to stop them. Our library is actually two buildings, an older building five stories tall, and a newer building only three stories tall, but three times wider. Also, in southern Florida there are no basements to speak of in most buildings, so any cable runs that couldn't conform to cement encased conduit in the floors or support columns had to be run in the ceilings and or the "cat-walks" that connect the two buildings.

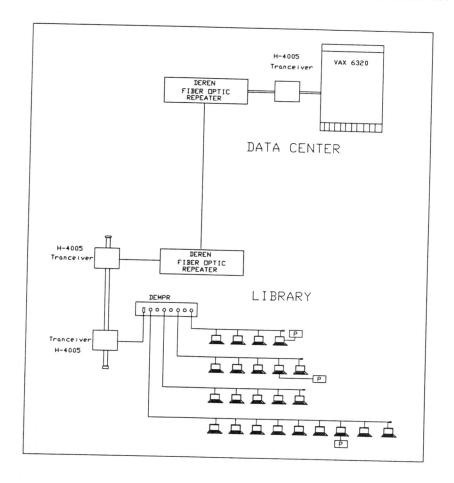

Figure 12.1
Florida Atlantic PCSA Network

There were some minor problems with the fiber optic link, and we discovered that there are very few people qualified and certified to work with it, in the case of repairs.

Once these problems were worked out, the software team from the Computer User Services Department began the workstation by workstation installation process.

We at present have about twenty nodes on our network in the library. Our workstations are primarily IBM systems—both AT (ISA) bus and MicroChannel Architecture (MCA). There are four Memorex-Telex (ISA) (model 7045) AT-clones.

We had only a few problems with the installation of the PCSA software, but the problems we encountered were mildly difficult to resolve. In two cases as noted below, the resolution was to accept certain weaknesses of hardware/software interfaces.

A few of the IBM PS/2 model 30's had interrupt conflicts between the Ethernet adapter card and the hard drive controller. Also, we have several versions of DOS currently installed from 3.1 to 4.01, and that fact made the software team's work more difficult, as PCSA has subtle differences depending on which version of DOS and on which PC it was being installed.

There were a few minor problems with the network version of WordPerfect. These were resolved by putting the setup configuration data on the local hard drives, as the software seemed to be "timing out" as it searched for configuration parameters (it was waiting for the network to supply access to these data files).

We were also instructed that any workstations currently utilizing any type of terminal emulation to support a mainframe link would have to relocate that mainframe link, if we also wanted a network connection installed on that particular workstation.

Also, we attempted to install a Toshiba XM-3201 CD-ROM player on an IBM PS/2 model 50Z that had a network connection. We were prevented from completing this task because of some deep software (perhaps BIOS level) conflicts. Again the solution was to locate the CD-ROM player at a non- networked PC.

The Emotional Installation

Computers and PC's are not new to libraries. But the speed with which they have multiplied and become entrenched is new to the library. There will always be some resistance to change in any organization, but as we in Systems have shown the user-community not only how to use the PCs, but more importantly, why to use them, the walls have been broken through.

Our university provides an excellent compliment of classes for faculty and staff who wish to enhance their productivity with computers. But there are still times when things go wrong, that a deeper level of expertise is required to effect a repair. Now that we have the network, our users can send electronic mail to us for these work requests instead of using the internal paper mail process. The systems department uses these requests to track our workload throughout the fiscal year.

The users we work with fall into roughly three categories (these are rough generalizations, and may not be completely inclusive):

1. Anxious and ready to take on a new challenge
2. I'll do it because my boss says I have to do it and
3. Computers are nice, but I'll do it my way thank you very much.

Over time, I believe that category three should disappear. The first two categories will always exist, having little or nothing to do with computers or networks.

The challenge that we have seen in implementing the network in the library relates to promoting the use of computers among these widely differing attitudes.

The people who work here are very good at what they do, and they will, over time, learn to use the computer and the network. But one of the most interesting processes that I have observed is the "How did I ever get along without this thing before?" phenomena. Even as we begin to upgrade some workstations from older models to the newest ones, that emotion is exhibited.

Comments like "That old PC was so slow compared to my new one!," or "What a dog that thing was," or "The new color display is so much nicer than that old black and white one" have become commonplace to me. This demonstrates that very often the initial resistance to change eventually becomes displaced by the practical utility that the new technology brings. Users will decide that the computer belongs on their desk top, just as much as a telephone.

Applications

Currently, our campus network offers several programs that would have previously required each PC to have its own copy. The library supports a standard compliment of software applications including a database manager, a spreadsheet program, a communications program, and a word processor. Most important, in this author's opinion, is the availability of electronic mail. The electronic mail facility is also linked to BITNET and the Internet which provide the ability to communicate with national and international systems.

Electronic mail provides our users with an incredibly powerful tool for the expedient exchange of information with virtually any person who also has access to the BITNET or Internet. As the number of network nodes is expanded within the library, more and more of our users will begin to take advantage of the capabilities presented by the network. For example, one of our users serves as recording secretary for one of the academic review committees here on campus. After the transposition of the notes from paper to electronic format, they are transmitted over the network to the various members of the committee.

As with any new product, the toughest part is simply penetrating into the thought paradigm that there may be an alternative method for accomplishing any given task. Once this mental process is accomplished, it is easy to envision a work area almost free from paper. Certainly, some items will need to be kept in a hard copy format.

In time, the number of applications available to users via the network will increase. There will come a time when the users may need to know several programs at once, and be able to move freely within any of several different applications, making changes to one document, and having that change dynamically change the affected data in the other application.

The library has recently added a network laser printer to the network facilities for library personnel use. The network shell software will be reconfigured to allow for spooling of output to that printer in the library. Currently, application output is most often printed locally at the user's workstation.

Network Security

Security on a computer network is sometimes overlooked by users when the large majority of information is not personal or confidential. The real danger for attack comes from "hackers" or people who with willful intent, attempt to break into a computer system and gain access to the data contained therein. Another possible source of entry comes from the users who are lax in their general security practices. They may bring from home or elsewhere a disk unknowingly infected with a virus. Computer viruses are real, and they can do real damage. Because some of our workstations will be for public use, this is something that has been determined as an acceptable risk. To offset this risk, anti-virus software will be installed onto these workstations.

PCSA requires each user to have a valid Userid and password. After that, users can be segregated into different areas of use as determined by the network administrator. We currently have four levels of data segregation including a personal drive, a departmental-wide drive, a college-wide drive, and a university-wide, common drive. The use of the word drive here is more of a method that PCSA uses for logical or virtual segregation of data, rather than there being four physical disk drives. For example, each user could be assigned a certain amount of disk capacity that is assigned to the drive M: that can be accessed by only that user. A drive P: would be one that all members of a department share with the ability to both read and write data. A drive O: might be a drive shared by everyone in a particular college. Drive N: might be one that is common for the entire university. It is also possible for the network administrator to establish logical drives that a user may query, but cannot modify.

The different layers of segregation make it easy for users to determine for themselves who they want to have access to certain data or other information. If the Systems Department generates a document for any library staff to view, we simply place it on the O: drive. Only users with the assigned O: drive may view that data. Conversely, another college unit will also have an O: drive, but it is not the same as the O: drive for the library.

The library has a number of public use workstations that connect to the network. For these workstations, one may access network services only by entering a valid user id and password. There is some risk involved in having these public workstations connected to the network. If some user fails to exercise proper security practices, user id's and passwords may become pirated by unauthorized persons who could then gain access to the network on these workstations. So far, the library has not experienced any serious problems in this regard.

Special emphasis was placed on this concept within the staff of the reference department, They, as part of their heavy workload, also staff the Ready Reference desk where there is a workstation with public access. One initial concern arose in that it would be very easy for a staff person to log in to the network, then get called away from the desk for several minutes to assist a patron. This situation would leave an unattended public terminal logged into the network for more than enough time for a potential attack. We worked out a compromise between security and practicality where if any staff person was going to be out of visual contact with the workstation for more than a minute after a login had been completed, they are to turn off or reboot the computer.

Performance

Evaluating the worthiness of particular computer products can be a very subjective process. It is difficult to separate one's own personal biases from objective, factual data. I consider myself a low-side power user. I don't use the computer to write programs or build huge three dimensional spreadsheets, but I do use my computer to help maintain, repair, and train other people and their computers. On one level, I can evaluate products from many subjective and practical aspects.

One means of evaluating the performance of the network was to compare the speed of loading applications over the network to the speed of loading the same software from the local hard disk.

I have dBase IV V1.1, Lotus 1-2-3 v2.2, and WordPerfect V5.1 each installed on the hard drive of my own workstation. Each of these products is also available through the network. The only significant difference is that the network offers only dBase III+ not dBase IV. Since each of these software applications is available both on my local hard drive and over the network, I was able to measure the performance of the network compared to the speed of a hard disk. The values in the table represent the total time in seconds that it takes to load the software and display the main prompt of the program.

As can be seen from this simple comparison, it takes longer to load most software applications over the network than it takes to load the same program from a workstation's own hard disk. As I mentioned above, my own experience as a microcomputer user reveals that the network is comparatively slow.

Product	Stand-alone	Network
WP V5.1	5	15
Lotus 1-2-3 v. 2.2	5	22
dBase III+	N/A	8
dBase IV v1.1	18	N/A

Table 12.1
Comparison of Software Load Times: Local Hard Disk vs Network Drive

Although this comparison of network performance against hard disk access times shows that loading software across the network can be a little sluggish, we have observed that in reality our users are very happy just to have the software available through the network. In this light, the slightly longer network load times really do not seem to cause significant dissatisfaction.

Summary

Our library is dedicated to serving the needs of our patrons and the University. As the needs of these communities expand, we must be ready to meet the challenge. Adding the network to the library staff's toolbox will help us meet that goal. It has not been entirely painless, but the aspect of cost vs value must be evaluated. Over time, our staff will come to treat the network as an extremely valued tool. Our users will become its biggest supporters. And, new users will wonder how we ever functioned (in the past) without it.

About the Author

Dave Bloomberg is Computer Systems Coordinator at the Wimberly Library at Florida Atlantic University.

13

Networking in an Acquisitions Department with Novell NetWare ELS

Mary Ann Chappell, Dan O'Brien, and Sharon Gasser
Carrier Library, James Madison University

ABSTRACT

To give multiuser access to the order database in the Acquisitions Department, Carrier Library evaluated and installed a local area network in consultation with the University's Office of Information Technology. This small, low-cost network uses Novell's ELS NetWare and includes a non-dedicated file server with two additional workstations. This chapter explores issues facing libraries installing networks, such as the need for a network manager, maintenance of the network, network standards, and tape back-up systems.

Background

James Madison University is an undergraduate institution offering a limited number of graduate programs. The University has an enrollment over 10,500. The University Library works closely with each academic department to purchase materials and to integrate the use of the library and its resources in the curriculum.

The library has a monographic budget of approximately $250,000. The acquisitions department employs three full-time, classified staff plus student assistants which are supervised by a full-time acquisitions librarian.

Automation in Acquisitions

Prior to 1987, the acquisitions department handled all transactions manually and the staff had no computer experience. In 1985 the library installed the VTLS's online public access catalog and automated circulation and reserves system. Since VTLS was still developing its acquisitions/serial system, the library enlisted the aid of programmers from the university's administrative computing office to develop its own fund accounting system. This system tracks departmental and library expenditures and encumbrances.

When VTLS finally announced the release of the acquisitions/serial subsystem, a library committee investigated it as well as alternative systems. The committee found VTLS was still working on essential features and recommended a competitor's acquisitions/serial system.

Concurrently, the library was implementing CD-ROM technology in the public service area which limited funds available for the purchase of an acquisitions/serial system. Because funds were limited, the committee's recommended system was infeasible. Although the fund accounting system worked well, the manual order system was increasingly cumbersome. As an interim solution for monographic ordering, the Acquisitions Librarian recommended Bib-Base, a PC-based acquisition system by Library Technologies, Inc. The library continues to use its in-house fund accounting system, even though it means using two separate systems. Serials was forced to wait for automation.

The library purchased an OCLC M310 terminal to load Bib-Base and to give acquisitions access to OCLC. The OCLC M310 terminal is based on a 286 Wyse PC with a 40MB hard disk. In addition, the library purchased a Maynstream 60MB tape back-up system. Two printers were attached to the OCLC terminal using an A-B switch: one for printing order forms and the second for paper. The OCLC terminal was used (1) to search and download records from OCLC; (2) to store and manipulate the Bib-Base acquisitions files; and (3) to do word processing.

Since the order database is vital to the library, protecting this database was a high priority when the library first implemented Bib-Base. The library purchased a Maynstream tape backup system to simplify and speed up the back-up process. The Maynstream was installed on the OCLC workstation. The Maynstream system comes with Tape Backup Software which backs up the entire hard disk or allow individual directories and files to be selected for backup. The software allows users to program scripts to automate the back-up procedure. Acquisitions decided to back up the Bib-Base files daily and do a weekly backup of the entire hard disk.

The Decision to Network

With one PC serving multiple functions, the staff wasted time waiting to use the PC. While an additional PC would help to eliminate some of the problems, staff members and student assistants frequently needed access at the same time to the order database to perform the traditional acquisitions functions of searching, ordering, receiving, and claiming. Shared access to the order database was essential if the department was to handle the volume of incoming orders and receipts and to meet its fiscal deadlines.

The Acquisitions Librarian started investigating networking and recruited the help of the Automation Librarian. Because of the limited in-house experience with networking, they contacted the university's Office of Information Technology (OIT) for advice. OIT was working with other departments on campus to install local area networks and was willing to assist the library.

The Office of Information Technology had taken responsibility for all computer-related offices on campus, including the administrative computing office that had helped the library earlier. It serves the university community by providing telecommunications and computing support for instruction, research, and administration. OIT offers seminars and short courses to students and university personnel to enhance computer skills. OIT personnel provide expertise to academic and other departments for planning and installing new computer systems. A Help

Desk staffed by students provides support when problems occur. An essential aspect of OIT's service is in-house maintenance and troubleshooting of current systems. This supportive environment was a positive factor in the library's decision to pursue networking.

Goals of the Acquisitions Network

The Acquisitions Department developed the initial goals of the network:

o   To provide shared access to the order database.
o   To give staff word processing capabilities.
o   To share two existing printers.
o   To explore the option of making the order database available to public service librarians.
o   To purchase the additional PC's and all the components needed for the network on a limited budget of $7,500.
o   To try to use the network file server as a workstation.
o   To purchase a network that the acquisitions staff could learn and use with limited computer experience.

Additional goals were suggested by the Automation Librarian and OIT's Network Supervisor:

o   To provide the ability to use the order database in the single-user mode in case of network failure.
o   To gain LAN experience in the library.
o   To explore CD-ROM capabilities on a network.

Selection and Evaluation of the Network Software

Since making the Bib-Base acquisitions database access to multiple users was the major goal of the network, the Acquisitions Librarian called the software maker to find out if Bib-Base had been successfully networked and what network was used. She also asked the vendor for a list of libraries with a local area network. Her research on low-cost networks identified LANtastic by Artisoft as a good candidate. LANtastic looked like a good match for the library's needs: it is a peer-to-peer network which does not require a dedicated file server; it is low-cost; and reviews report that it is easy to install and use. However, when the Library contacted the University's Office of Information Technology, it found that OIT had selected Novell as the network standard for the University.

The University selected Novell as its standard because it is the industry standard, with over 70 percent of all networks using some type of Novell software. Novell provides a rich array of features including operation in a non-dedicated mode,

Macintosh and PC connectivity, password security to the system, efficient file and print sharing capabilities, and broad compatibility with existing office and library automation software. Its high ratings for reliability, speed, and ease of use made it the logical choice for the campus standard.

While the Library was free to pursue LANtastic, OIT would only provide support for the campus standard. With limited network experience in the library, on-campus support for the network was an important issue.

Although Novell's Advanced NetWare is well known, Novell also offers NetWare for small networks. Novell's ELS (Entry Level Solution) Level II NetWare version 2.15 network software is a low-cost, small network with all the features and commands of Advanced NetWare. Unlike Advanced NetWare, which can accommodate 100 concurrent users, ELS II is limited to eight concurrent users. ELS II not only met the library's needs for an inexpensive network that would allow the file server to be used as a workstation but offered fault tolerance and security capabilities that are not available on the peer-to peer LAN's, which the library first explored.

Like Advanced NetWare, ELS II can operate with either a dedicated or non-dedicated file server and supports 80286 and 80386 server. While Advanced NetWare requires a minimum of 2M of server memory, the minimum for ELS II is 640K. The performance of the network can suffer in the non-dedicated mode because the file server is doing two jobs; yet it adds another workstation for no extra cost. With ELS II like Advanced NetWare, the library would have the option of dedicating the file server if speed became a problem on the network.

ELS II offers the advanced fault tolerance features found in Novell's Advanced NetWare. ELS II includes Novell's Hot Fix feature which checks the data written to the file server disk. Hot Fix checks to see if the data written to disk is readable, rewrites it to another part of the disk if it detects a problem, and permanently prevents data from being written to the bad sectors. Sophisticated fault tolerance features aren't available on peer-to-peer networks and provide extra protection for a dynamic database like the order file where multiple users are entering data at the same time.

ELS II also allows the Network Supervisor to restrict user access to directories on the file server and to control how a user can work with the files in a particular directory, including whether a user can read, write, or open existing files, erase files, create new ones, create subdirectories, search the list of files in a directory, or modify file names and subdirectories. These security features made it possible to give student employees access to the order database but to restrict what they could do to the files. These security features are not available on peer-to-peer LAN's.

Its low cost, advanced fault tolerance and security capabilities, as well as on-campus support made Novell ELS NetWare Level II the logical choice for the library over the inexpensive peer-to-peer networks.

Configuration of the Network

In the preliminary discussions, the Acquisitions Librarian, Network Supervisor, and Automation Librarian envisioned four workstations on the network: a non-dedicated file server that would also act as a workstation, the existing OCLC terminal, a new PC in the acquisitions librarian's office, and an additional workstation for student assistants where the CD-ROM version of Books in Print could be added. All four workstations would have access to the two printers in the department. Plans were to move the tape back-up system from the OCLC terminal to the workstation/file server.

To further contain costs, the Acquisitions Librarian, Automation Librarian, and OIT Network Supervisor scaled back their thinking and concentrated only on the minimum needs of the Acquisitions Department to perform its work and meet its deadlines. The final network configuration included just three workstations: a new 386 IBM clone to serve as a workstation and the file server, the OCLC terminal, and an new 286 IBM clone for the acquisitions librarian. The streamlined configuration continued to allow all three workstations to use the existing two printers, to provide access to OCLC only on the OCLC terminal, and to move the tape back-up system to the file server. The CD-ROM and fourth workstation became possible future enhancements.

Evaluation and Selection of the Network Hardware

As a public-supported institution, the university is required to purchase equipment, goods, and services, usually at discounted prices, from specified vendors under contract with the state. When selecting the software and hardware for the network, what was available on state contract determined what the library purchased. The state contract limited the library to purchasing an IBM clone. From previous university and library experience with this clone, the library knew it faced potential problems with compatibility, quality, and service, but there wasn't sufficient justification to purchase IBM computers for the network.

In addition to state contract limitation, cost was also a factor. The IBM clone was significantly cheaper than an IBM manufactured machine. Acquisitions needed at least three workstations to have access to the order database. Because the OCLC terminal would continue to be one of the workstations, the library needed to purchase two additional PCs.

Although the minimum requirement for the Novell NetWare ELS Level II is a 286 file server with 640K of memory, the OIT Network Supervisor suggested that the file server should be a 20MHz 386 Win Labs PC with a 80MB hard disk and 4MB of RAM, especially since the file server would also serve as a workstation. The 386 machine would cost more, but it would give the network more speed. The 80MB hard disk would insure plenty of room for the order database and other files.

Since the second workstation was to go into the Acquisitions Librarian's office, the OIT Network Supervisor suggested a 286 Win Labs PC with a 20MB hard drive,

1MB of RAM, and a modem. Although the Acquisitions Librarian would have access to the network, this machine would enable her to have files, run software, and access remote databases that are not accessible through the network.

Additional Network Costs

Software costs also had to come out of the limited funds available for the network. In addition to the Novell network software, the library had to purchase the multi-user version of Bib-Base and a word-processing package.

Cabling was another concern. A separate department at the university is responsible for cabling. However, the high volume of work handled by this department makes delays in installing cable common. Running the network cabling under the floor was going to be difficult since the acquisitions department is located in the part of the library built in the fifties. To expedite implementing the network and to save money, the OIT Network Supervisor decided to install the cabling along the wall around the perimeter of the acquisition area. Since installing the cable along the wall did not require drilling, he could do the work himself.

Standard 10Base5, or thin-wire Ethernet, cabling was chosen because of the small office size and short distances between the workstations. JMU purchases thin Ethernet in bulk at a cost of less than $0.20 per foot. Ethernet proves fast (10mb/second) throughput rate and is compatible with the planned campus network, which will allow the acquisitions department access to other services on campus.

Cost

Minimum materials and their cost to make the LAN function as a network include:

Description	COST
Novell ELS II	$858.00
Seagate 80 MB Drive with software	535.00
NE2000 Novell 16bit Ethernet	207.00
NE1000 Novell 8bit Ethernet 2 @ $108)	217.80
Bib-Base Multi-User Software	995.00
Win Labs 20 MHz 386 PC	1822.00
Win Labs 286 PC	1253.00
Cabling (80 ft. @ $0.20/ft.) & components	25.00
Total	$5912.00

Installation and Implementation

The Network Supervisor and his team of student interns took the file server, a Win Labs 20MHz 80386 PC (IBM clone), and installed Novell's ELS Level II, version 2.15, network software. The software installation procedure performs a low-level format of the 80 mb hard disk, and then runs an extensive test for bad sectors, which are marked so as not to be used by the file server.

There are two programs used in this procedure, ZTEST and COMPSURF. ZTEST checks the "track zero" portion of the hard disk, which is the area that the hard disk boots from. If this area is bad, it is necessary to replace the hard disk. The COMPSURF program, which generally runs overnight, writes data over and over again to every sector on the hard disk. If a hard disk sector fails to accurately record the information, that sector is marked as back, and is never used by the system.

The process of creating the network operating system is called NETGEN. While running this program on the new file server computer, we specified the hard disk size, printer configurations (parallel and serial ports), file server name, and various performance-related parameters. Novell's Advanced NetWare prepares the file server hard disk with this information by placing a compiled file called NET$OS.EXE on the hard disk. This program contains all the boot information for the file server.

This latest release of Novell's Advanced NetWare, version 2.2, includes a friendlier installation procedure than past releases of NetWare. In the past, the installer was required to wade through a maze of difficult questions to configure the system correctly. Many times the installer had to perform the procedure more than once to get it right. The present program is very quick, and presents the configuration questions in a much more logical format.

Although our file server PC is not Novell certified, we have used the same brand and make of computer for many file servers in the past. Novell provides a list of computer manufacturers and their computer makes that pass a rigorous testing procedure at Novell's labs. It is usually prudent to look for one of Novell's approved file server computers, unless a computer brand is found that has worked correctly in the past.

All of the Novell operating files were installed, which occupy approximately 10 megabytes of hard disk space. The network operating system was set up in non-dedicated mode, which allows the file server to be used as a workstation. A Novell NE2000 network interface card was installed, which is a 16-bit, high-performance card which provides the necessary throughput for multiple users on the network.

Use of the file server in non-dedicated mode slows down performance, but the small network size and high speed of the file server offset this performance lag. In a larger network environment, it is not wise to use a non-dedicated file server, as the performance may severely degrade. With only four or five people using a small selection of programs, the 20MHz 80386-based server does not slow anyone down.

Two parallel printing ports and two serial communications ports are standard equipment on Win Labs PC's, and two parallel ports were used for two networked dot-matrix printers attached directly to the file server. Serial ports were not specified for use by the file server for printing because a 2400 baud external modem was installed to be used with a communication program.

A total of 80 feet of standard 10Base5 thin Ethernet cable was used to connect the computers on the network. The cabling was installed by Office of Information

Technology staff, and three-piece Amp brand solderless crimp ends were used to finish the cable pieces. Each network interface card is attached to the cable with a T-type connector, and the two ends of the cable have 50 ohm terminators attached. The cable was thoroughly tested with a Time Domain Reflectometer (TDR) to test for shorts and impedance loads.

Upon bootup, each workstation uses Novell's IPX.COM and NET3.COM programs to initialize the network interface card and then attach to the file server. The file server boots up with a 5 1/4" diskette, initializes the network operating system on the hard disk, then loads DOS so it can be used as a workstation. When a user connects to the network with a login name and password, a login script is executed, which sets the proper drive letter mappings to the file server's hard disk. The login script also diverts the workstation's local printer ports to print queues on the file server. This CAPTURE.EXE command allows sharing of the printers on the file server between all the network users.

Each of the programs installed on the network operate flawlessly with Novell's NetWare. To the users, the system is transparent, and the file server acts as another hard drive on each user's personal computer. The printers are configured in each program, such as WordPerfect, and Novell's CAPTURE command redirects the printer output from each person's printer port to the network. Everyone may share files by putting them in a special directory on the network called COMMON. This eliminates the "sneakernet" method of sharing files found in most non-networked office environments.

A Maynard Maynstream 60MB streaming tape unit is attached to the file server. The software provided with this streaming tape drive allows for full and incremental backups of the file server contents. Due to the high speed of the Maynard Maynstream unit, which backs up data at a rate of 4 to 5 megabytes-per-minute, full backups are performed every day.

Tape backup provides a secure, cost-effective means of insuring data against hard disk loss. The tape software provides an easy-to-use menu system, and the library personnel simply have to choose full backup from the menu. Our Maynard tape unit has a 60 megabyte capacity, which is enough to back up the entire system on one tape. The software has built-in error checking and verification, which guards against bad data getting to the tape.

All personnel in the Acquisitions Department were given training on the basics of the Novell operating system. An introductory text that is customized to the particular network installation is provided by the Office of Information Technology for all new network users. This handout provides information about network file sharing, network printing, adding and deleting users, network drive mappings, basic troubleshooting, and introductory administration. The Acquisitions staff were given a formal half-day seminar on networking, and then subsequent one-on-one training in their office. In addition, the network administrator and her backup were given advanced configuration and management training.

Evaluation

Has the network been worth it? The answer is a resounding yes. Without the network, acquisitions could not have met its commitments. The Network Supervisor deserves much of the credit for the success. He worked closely with the librarians involved, analyzed the department, its limited computer experience, and future needs. Then he programmed the network to meet these needs, including easy-to-use menus. At the present time, simple DOS batch files are used to get to the applications programs. Since there are only several programs on the network, batch files are used instead of a more expensive and difficult menuing system.

The installation of the software onto the file server and the cabling was performed without trouble. Due to defects in the computer's power supply and hard disk, however, each expired and were replaced in the first months of use. The Bib-Base software had to be reinstalled and reconfigured for use on the network, which was fairly straightforward. WordPerfect version 5.1 is used in its network mode, and does not pose any problems on the network. Save for the computer hardware malfunctions, the Acquisitions network has been reliable, efficient, and fairly easy to use. The network provides an efficient vehicle for use with Bib-Base, WordPerfect, and the OCLC software. For a cost of under $6000, users are able to share files, programs, and printers, and the network allows multiple users access to the Bib-Base program, which was the intended goal of the project. However, we would have used a higher-quality computer as the file server, with a more reliable brand of hard disk.

Recently Novell marketed a new version of its software for small networks. Its Advanced NetWare 2.2 supports a maximum of ten simultaneous users. The Network Supervisor will be upgrading the library's network. From this library's experience, the role played by the Network Supervisor was critical and will continue to be with new developments in hardware and software.

Bibliography

Byrd, David, Mike Byrd, Frank J. Derfler, Jr., Paul Ferrill, M. Keith Thompson, and Randol Tigrett. 1989. "Building Workgroup Solutions: Low-Cost LANs." *PC Magazine* 8(6): 95-131.

Howden, Norman. 1989. "Local Area Network Management: An Unresolved Issue." *Microcomputers for Information Management* (6)4: 281-291.

Lauriston, Robert. 1989. "No Pain, Big Gains: Five Low-Cost LANs." *PC World* (7) 11: 160-170.

Lawrence, Bill. 1990. *Using Novell NetWare*. Carmel, IN: Que Corporation.

Products and Vendors

Library Technologies, Inc.
1142E Bradfield Road
Abington, PA 19001
(215) 576-6983
Bib-Base vendor

Maynard Electronics
460 E. Semoran Blvd.
Casselberry, FL 32707
(305) 331-6402
MaynStream Tape Backup Systems

Novell NetWare
CMB Computer Center
834 Tyvola Rd.
Charlotte, NC 28217

VTLS, Inc.
1800 Kraft Drive
Blacksburg, VA 24060
(703) 231-3605

Win Laboratories
11090 Industrial Rd.
Manassas, VA 22110
(703) 330-1426

About the Authors

Dan O'Brien is a 1983 graduate of James Madison University. He has five years of network and personal computer experience, and worked for such firms as Freddie Mac, The Washington Post, and the National Academy of Sciences. Dan returned to JMU in 1989 to work for the Academic Computing Department as the Campus Network Specialist.

Mary Ann Chappell has been Loan Services/Automation Librarian at James Madison University since 1988. Prior to this, she was at the Institute for Scientific Information, first as manager of Current Contents and then as Assistant Director of Production Operations. She received a B.A. in English from James Madison Univerisity and an M.S. in Library Science from Drexel University.

Sharon Gasser is Acquisitions Librarian at James Madison University. She joined James Madison as a part-time reference librarian with responsibilities including bibliographic instruction and collection development in the area of biology. Prior to this position, she worked as a serials cataloger at Virginia Tech. Sharon received a B.A. in English and history from Cornell College, an M.S. in Library Science from the University of Illinois, Champaign-Urbana, and a B.S. in Dairy Science from Virginia Tech.

14

Networking in a Serials Department:
The Installation and Use of an IBM PC-LAN

James L. Huesmann
Murphy Library, University of Wisconsin—La Crosse

ABSTRACT

Serials Control at the University of Wisconsin-La Crosse was hampered by the limitations imposed by a single-workstation system. A UW system grant allowed for the implementation of a IBM-PC LAN from OCLC which circumvented these problems. This chapter details the setups involved in setting up the network, the problems solved by conversion to a LAN, and the advantages and pitfalls of LAN selection driven by a vendor's desires instead of an institution's needs.

Background

The University of Wisconsin-La Crosse is a comprehensive institution of around 9,000 students located in Western Wisconsin at the junction of the La Crosse, Black, and Mississippi Rivers. Primary emphasis is on undergraduate education, with graduate programs in Education, Business, Physical Education, and Biology. The library contains over 500,000 volumes and approximately 2000 current serial subscriptions.

Serial information was one of the early subjects of automation efforts at UW-La Crosse. A locally-developed and maintained mainframe system was used during the early 1980's, and our SC350 system, developed by OCLC, has been running as a stand-alone workstation since 1986. The problem of maintaining all serial information on one terminal, as required by SC350, negated many of the benefits produced by leaving the old system. Contention over workstation scheduling for check-in, database clean-up, subscription control, and such, was rife. Several steps were taken to maximize access to the workstation such as scheduling, staggered shifts, and central location. However, the inherent problem of too few hours for too much work remained. Several processes which should have taken advantage of the system's capabilities were placed on hold or not even started, including subscription control, bindery, and claiming.

In 1989 the University of Wisconsin System provided grants to the eleven comprehensive universities in the state system for the purchase of acquisition and serials control systems. The software chosen were OCLC's SC350 and ACQ350, which were microcomputer-based, linkable to the campuses' OPACs (LS2000), and capable of being configured as either stand-alone workstations (one for each software package) or based on a local area network. The entire OCLC system had been previously selected by a system-wide committee, but implementation up to that time had been slow due to lack of funds, the workstation contention issue, and other problems. The LAN configuration was chosen and implemented on the various campuses.

We at the University of Wisconsin–La Crosse's Murphy Library were particularly pleased by this decision. The Serials Department was certain that adding an extra workstation would solve many of the workflow bottlenecks that were hampering full implementation of the system. In effect, we envisioned a pseudo-mainframe solution—a central database and programs with several terminals for simultaneous access. Also, we felt that expansion of the number of workstations would free up computer time for more mundane tasks such as word-processing.

SC350 is a DOS-based serials control system which includes the following functions: check-in, subscription, claiming, prediction, display, bibliographic data, copy data, binding, routing, names and address directory, record transfer, reports, and funds control.

The system is based on the MARC record and, as would be suspected of a system developed by OCLC, highly interactive with both the OCLC systems and LS2000, OCLC's minicomputer-based OPAC and circulation system. It was certainly one of the most advanced serials systems available on the market. But the same features which provided that level of functionality such as its use of full MARC records, and its links between the various subsystems, resulted in large data files and, in the case of many of the batch operations, devotion of the workstation to particular tasks for hours. For example, when a claims scan was run, SC350 would review the entire database to discover which predicted issues were not received on time, and the workstation could be occupied in this task for three to four hours. During this time it was unavailable for other tasks. OCLC originally delivered the SC350 system on an M300 workstation, an IBM-PC 8088-based computer running at 4.77 MHz. We viewed moving the program to a faster microcomputer and putting it on a network to solve the workstation bottleneck as methods to circumvent the problems inherent in the system and to optimize its capabilities.

ACQ350 was OCLC's Acquisitions counterpart to SC350. SC350 and ACQ350 can run in tandem with each other. When implemented in such an interfaced system, ACQ350 overrides SC350's Subscription and Funds Control modules, in effect replacing them with its more sophisticated control systems. While primarily used in monographic acquisitions, its funds hierarchies provide very useful information, and integrates all library purchasing activity into one system, capable of reports detailing the financial commitments of the institution.

Planning for a Network

After further consideration of the capabilities of a LAN, we added additional goals for the system. The ability to have a shared printer would mean that future workstations would not need a printer beside them. Programs that could not run on our hard diskless M300s could be accessed over the LAN. Finally, the simple transfer of files via a central server meant the death of the dreaded "sneaker-net," the sending of files from one microcomputer to another by copying onto a floppy, then carrying it by hand to the other machine.

The decision of who was to have access to the network was not a simple one. Four factors were involved: who needed access, who wanted access, how many stations could we support, and for whom it would be nice to grant access. We resolved the problem by working on the questions in reverse order.

SC350 includes a Public Access subsystem, so the question of putting a public workstation in Reference was considered, but only for a short time. While the Public Access system doesn't allow users to do anything to the records, the possibility of someone breaking through to the MS-DOS operating system and causing problems quickly led us to eliminate that option.

How many workstations could we support on our LAN? OCLC told us that we could have only seven workstations. This parameter was then combined with the number of workstations we had available. We ended up with ten workstations that were available that might want access to the LAN.

The ten workstations quickly whittled themselves down to six when the question of who wanted access was considered. When reviewed, however, we discovered that one of the workstations was in an area where it could be utilized for acquisition work, if heavy demand required another terminal. This workstation was primarily used for cataloging, and the cataloging staff feared that placing it on the network would result in it being coopted by acquisitions! A compromise was reached in the following manner: cabling was run to the workstation in question, but it was not hooked into the network. If we decided we needed an additional workstation in the future, this provided fairly immediate expansion capability.

Planned Configuration of the Workstations and LAN

Three factors were of major importance in configuring the system in this manner: equal access by department to workstations; separate access to OCLC and LS2000; and administrative control. Both political and workflow implications were inherent in the first factor; spreading the microcomputers evenly among the staff would result in greater access (it was hoped) and remove a possible bone of contention. While Serials' workflow and need for workstation time had been demonstrated, the need for computer time in Acquisitions was unknown. Thus, retaining flexibility between areas to adjust to new needs was influential in the placement decisions. Separate access to OCLC and LS2000 were important points, since the two departments are on opposite sides of the building. Finally, providing workstations in the area administrators' offices provided an easy access point for problem analysis, work review, and workstations for running the longer reports without interfering with standard workflows. They also served as backups, in case of workstation failure within a unit.

Six microcomputer workstations comprise the LAN. Two workstations (one M300 and one M310) were located in both Serials and Acquisitions. One workstation (a Zenith XT clone) was also located in the office of the LAN Administrator/Serials Librarian (me), and another in the Automation Librarian's office. Each M310 had access to OCLC, as well as both downloading and Link ports. The link ports were serial interfaces. The information was converted into files, and then processed. In many aspects, information from OCLC came into the 350 systems in much the same manner as the new Export functions on OCLC's PRISM. The two M310 workstations, both running at 12MHz and using 80286 processors, serve as the workhorses of their respective departments.

We initially planned to use the M300s, running at 4.77MHz on 8088 processors, as backups to the other machines. But, as the increased capabilities incorporated in these systems were utilized, the M300s were used less as backup systems and more for full-time operations. However, I quickly noticed that staff would arrange their schedules so that they could use the faster machines, if possible.

The network itself ran on IBM PC-LAN ver. 1.31. A 4-Mps Token Ring board distributed the signal, with an eight-port multistation access unit (MAU) physically located next to the file server and connected to the workstations using plenum-grade type 3 wiring. The workstation network cards were IBM Token Ring Network PC Adapter IIs. The hardware and software used to run the LAN came from our system vendor. OCLC decided upon all aspects of this setup. No variations were allowed. This did not sit well with our campus Academic Computing Center, who were pushing for Novell NetWare and Ethernet as campus standards. However, since they were not asked to help maintain the system, there was little they could do about the decision.

The configuration of the IBM PC-LAN software for the 350 systems was based on an earlier version of IBM PC-LAN. Thus, only the Basic Services section of the IBM PC-LAN software were copied onto the system. The Extended Services section of the software was not used. The difference between Basic and Extended Services is that Basic Services is machine-oriented, with most LAN commands imbedded in batch files, while Extended Services is user-oriented, with far more options in setting up the system. The batch files (AUTOEXEC.BAT, AUTOUSER.BAT, etc.), which contained the LAN commands, were built in the installation procedures in the 350s software. The use of LAN resources were completely transparent to the user. In effect, each user on the LAN had access to a common big hard drive, and workstations without printers were set up to send their printouts to the file server's printer. This control over options provided OCLC with a standard LAN configuration at each of its sites. Since OCLC maintenance contracts covered everything, including hardware, software, and the LAN itself, the standard configuration made their job of problem analysis, upgrades, and such, far easier than on a user-defined system.

The 350s used three levels in Basic services, Server, Messenger, and Receiver. Terminals designated as Server (only used at the file server itself) could perform the following tasks: send messages; receive and log messages; use network resources; use network request keys; receive and transfer messages; and share network resources. Messengers, used for the floppy disk workstations, could perform all Server functions except sharing network resources. Receivers, the hard disk workstations, could perform all Messenger functions except using network request keys and receiving and transferring messages. Receivers use a menu system for issuing network commands instead of entering them as line commands.

Using SC350 and ACQ350 on the LAN

The inability to vary from OCLC's standards did not prevent us from making some adaptations to the system. However, the basic system, its evaluation and selection, were never really things that we had control over. The University of Wisconsin system purchased the systems for the campuses, and OCLC did not allow variations from its standard. Since there was no other way in which to acquire the system, we took what we could get. Ameritech's acquisition of OCLC's Local Systems Division has caused this to change, however, so it is now possible for SC350 and ACQ350 to be mounted on other LANs. I know of at least two sites using Novell NetWare, and one site using StarLan.

Ameritech, the midwestern Baby Bell, acquired OCLC's Local Systems division in 1990. It has purchased another automated system (now called Maestro, developed at Tacoma Public Library in Washington), and is rumored to be considering other systems as well. The 350s products are planned to be incorporated into Maestro, which means that both SC350 and ACQ350 may be components in two separate automated systems. With the 1991 court decision allowing the companies of the old Bell telephone network to expand into information services, it is possible that this entry of Ameritech into the Library Automation market will not be alone nor limited to library automation products. The impact on the current 350 users has been minimal in the most part, although the transfer from OCLC's First System to PRISM and the needed changes in the local system products showed that the old tie-in between those systems is unlikely to be as strong as it once was.

One beneficial aspect has been the decoupling of 350s to standard hardware and network environments, even though this requires a greater level of on-site expertise to deal with the problems within these two areas, and may result in some difficulties in establishing problems as software-specific. The option to proceed in this manner loosens many of the shackles imposed by OCLC upon libraries which choose to accept these liabilities in return for greater customization and capabilities.

The initial use of the LAN was primarily for SC350 and ACQ350. OCLC designed the system to minimize LAN traffic by loading all software from the workstation hard disks and only storing data over the LAN. The two M300s, which did not have hard disks, were set up to access programs as well as data from the file server. They ran programs at a noticeably slower speed than their faster, hard disk-based cousins, the M310s. Addition of a hard disk to the Serials M300 showed us the definite advantages of having hard disks in this setup. Speed of transactions increased noticeably, and the wait time between screens decreased markedly. However, the programs were disk hogs, taking up more than 15 megabytes on the hard disks.

Other LAN Functions

Use of other aspects of the LAN quickly followed. Since all stations on the LAN were able to access a logical drive in the file server (H:\), I set up a special subdirectory on the file server (H:\JUNK). This served as an area to transfer files and to place certain programs to allow cross-LAN use. This assisted in solving our "sneaker-net" problem. Unfortunately, our only laser printer wasn't on the LAN, so some disk exchange was still needed. It also allowed for the floppy disk workstations to run certain programs, primarily word processing, that needed a hard disk to run efficiently.

Shared printer capability was and is used more as a fall-back option. When a printer is down, the server's printer is utilized as a backup, thus allowing continued, if cumbersome, operation. The file server's location, central in the building but away from the two main areas of operations, made shared used of a printer less attractive for standard operations. The only time where this was possible was with the workstation located physically within the same room as the file server. While sharing printers other than the file server's over IBM-PC LAN is possible, the setup used for the 350s did not allow for this capability.

The LAN provided some rudimentary electronic mail capabilities. These were not used to a great extent. Primarily, this was for notifying LAN users of impending backups, system maintenance, and occasionally for notes between staff. Its use, however, has been minimal due to its lack of storage for messages.

Installation of the Network

Installation of the network involved four different groups of people. Site preparation consisted mostly of pulling cable. This was done by the campus physical plant personnel, on a payback setup, in which the department requesting the services "pays back" the funds to the physical plant. Since no money leaves the institution, it is basically a budgeting tool. They pulled the cable, put in cable guides and channels, and basically installed the nerve paths for the LAN. NCR, OCLC's national service vendor, installed the network cards and the actual wall plates for the cable connections. They also set up the file server and the two M310s that came with the package, and made certain that these were running. A week later, an OCLC staff member came to our library to help with the software installation. After installing the software, she was to provide training on the LAN and ACQ350.

The software installation did not go as predicted. Three weeks later OCLC finally discovered that the problem was incorrect dip switch settings on the Tseng memory board inside the M300. Other problems installing the ACQ350 software resulted in much of the training being done "off-machine," instead of hands-on. Final installation of the software was done by myself, with help via telephone from OCLC.

Costs

Costs for the system, as mentioned above, were covered by the University of Wisconsin system. The file server, an OCLC M330 workstation (80386 based), running at 16MHz, with a 115MB internal hard disk and tape backup, cost $4,500, after the trade-in of an 80MB Tallgrass external hard drive/tape system. The M310 workstations ran $3,415 each. The LAN, including the cards, adapter cables, software, patch cables, and MAU, cost $5,609. A printer and external modem completed the hardware purchase ($475 and $550, respectively). Installation, site prep, training, and profiling costs ran another $2,050.

Evaluation of the LAN

The LAN met all of our planned goals for the system. It distributes the workload across various terminals, mitigating the bottlenecks we so frequently encountered previously. While the LAN allows for multiple workstations, it seems that the need for workstations increases as work on the system increases. The productivity of the Serials department has risen, and we have used the 350 systems to a greater extent than previously, eliminating many dual- or paper-based systems. Having workstations in the area administrators' offices has allowed for development of adjunct systems to 350s, such as an interface to a locally-developed serials use database. The functionality of the LAN has proven to be acceptable.

The major flaws we have encountered include the following. Backup requires some down time each morning, since the hard disk is so large that it necessitates a second tape. This was not a flaw of the LAN, but a flaw in the original specifications for the size of the tape drive in the file server. As it is, we needed a larger disk drive, and have sought short term relief by removing some of the software and files added to the system. We have already had to move cabling, an expensive cost if terminals have to be moved. The system drags only when being used at its fullest capacity. This diminished performance especially occurs when users of the floppy disk-only workstations load programs across the system as well as data, during the running of the large database scans for title lists, scanning for bindery items or for claims, and such, and other intensive activities.

For the most part, we wouldn't have done anything differently. Our largest problem has occurred as result of being a beta-test site for a new release of SC350, not because of the LAN.

The library is, however, planning some changes in the near future. We are currently planning on migrating over into a Novell 386 environment. Through this change, we will better match campus networking standards, allow greater access and control to our 350 services, and provide TCP/IP access throughout the building. The campus installed a university-wide thin-wire Ethernet system one year after installation of our network.

The network we installed has functioned well in the areas that we asked. The conversion to a new system is a function of new needs and desires. The pseudo-mainframe solution, while perhaps valid at the time of original development, has been superseded by advances in workstation capabilities and user sophistication and desires.

About the Author

James Huesmann is Serials Librarian at the Murphy Library of the University of Wisconsin at La Crosse.

15

Network Transitions:
The Evolution of an Ethernet LAN
in a Medical Library

Laurie Potter
Savitt Medical Library, University of Nevada School of Medicine

ABSTRACT

This chapter describes the evolution of a local area network that serves the patrons and staff of the Savitt Medical Library at the University of Nevada School of Medicine. Starting from a small LAN of four workstations using 10-Net, the network later increased to eight workstations. In its latest phase, the network has grown to sixteen workstations and uses Novell rather than the 10-Net operating system. The network supports a variety of applications including computer-assisted instruction, word processing, database management, and telecommunications.

Background

The Savitt Medical Library was founded in 1978 to serve the information needs of the faculty, staff, and students of the University of Nevada School of Medicine as well as all campuses of the University of Nevada System. In addition, it is the medical resource library for the state of Nevada as part of the National Library of Medicine's information network.

Savitt ranks as a medium-sized medical library, with holdings of 427 journal subscriptions and 7,500 monograph titles. The library serves medical students, faculty, and staff as well as graduate students in the basic sciences and is open to the general public. Another library on campus supports nursing and allied health sciences. Space is at a premium in the library which is physically located on one floor. Most of the eight permanent staff members share office space and 90 percent of the collection is made up of bound journal volumes.

In the mid-1980s the library acquired its first stand-alone microcomputers for staff and students. The two microcomputers available for students were located in a group study room. They were self-service for those students already familiar with microcomputers. Students soon, however, came to know this room as the library's computer lab.

In 1986 a formal proposal was made to obtain funding for a file server, four IBM compatible computer workstations and a laser printer. In 1987 funding was obtained. At that time, the library chose 10-Net for both the network operating system and the cabling. The rationale for selecting 10-Net was as follows: "This is a network based on the Ethernet protocol (common in many office systems). This particular network also allows for a certain amount of file security, electronic mail, print spooling (to the existing printer), and at least one port to the campus cable network (with a drop site and multiplexer "ready to go" in the library). Using a single line this network can operate over distances up to 2,000 feet and with a repeater can operate up to 2 miles ... which should meet the needs of the Medical School well into the future. The cost of this network is approximately $500 per workstation."[1]

I started working at the library in April 1990. When I arrived, the 10-Net LAN had been in place for about two years. Planning had already begun to upgrade the computer lab since a sum of $28,000 was received from university funds available for instructional computing equipment. This money allowed for the upgrade of the computer lab from four workstations to eight workstations and the addition of two more printers.

The librarian who held the position before me had moved to another state and had been gone five months before I arrived. I had no experience with any type of LAN and a graduate student was designated to train me on how the existing network was configured. He had spent many hours of his time in the past two years installing 10-Net, writing batch files, installing the menu/security system using "WONDER PLUS," loading any new programs or upgrades, and in general maintaining the system. However, this graduate student was no longer a library student employee. He was only helping out because he was a nice guy! To make matters worse, he was getting busier and busier with his research projects necessary for his M.D./Ph.D. degree. I felt like I was imposing whenever I had to call him for help but there was nowhere else to turn. The 10-Net manuals were cryptic at best and since a local vendor was not involved in the installation, there was no support available. None of the other LANs on campus were 10-Net, they all used Novell NetWare. I could not find any manuals or "how to" books on 10-Net in local book stores. In fact, noone seemed to have heard of 10-Net.

Selection Process for the Current Novell Network

The goals for the student computer lab as well as our desire to link all staff members to the network guided our decision in selecting the current configuration. The overall goals of the student computer lab, as stated in the original grant proposal, were to teach medical students the following skills:

1. how to use a computer, printer, telecommunications, and word processing software
2. how to access and effectively search MEDLINE and other databases
3. how to locate medical information to solve problems presented in the classroom
4. how to speed the process of information gathering

The reasons for establishing the computer lab in the library were stated as follows:

1. The facility would be in a permanent, accessible, and secure location.
2. The facility would be conducive to learning, as it would be properly set up and comfortable to work in.
3. The facility would be open 96 hours a week.
4. The library staff would be available for consultation.[2]

There was also a need to upgrade each staff member's office computer. After our experience with the student computer lab, we realized that linking everyone to the existing network would be the most cost effective way to do this. Purchasing cabling and network equipment is much less expensive than buying eight brand new computers with all the features that everyone wanted such as increased speed and hard disk capacity. Moreover, word processing could be made more efficient by having everyone using the same version of WordPerfect. Commonly needed files could be accessed without having to carry diskettes from micro to micro. In addition, the staff could send short messages to each other using the Novell broadcast or send commands.

The main reason that we chose to part with the existing 10-Net configuration (aside from the previously mentioned frustrations) was that there were many problems with the way the system was set up in general. The menu/security system, "WONDER PLUS" in particular, seemed to make things unnecessarily complicated. The process of loading a new program onto the network could take as many as twenty different steps!

We told our campus purchasing department these problems and right away they suggested Novell and Ethernet. There were several immediate benefits to this choice: (1) a local vendor could provide installation, training and help when needed; (2) it is a standard operating system and network; (3) many other people on campus were using it; and (4) it would be compatible with the campus backbone.

Description of the Current Novell/Ethernet LAN

The new network exhibits the typical features of Ethernet. The network follows a bus topology, meaning that the nodes all connect to a single cable trunk. We used thin-wire Ethernet, specifically 2100 feet of RG58A/U plenum coaxial cable to link the sixteen workstations on the network. Ethernet uses CSMA/CD, meaning Carrier Sense Multiple Access/Collision Detection, as its access protocol.

The file server is a CP system 386SX computer with the following features: 16MHz, 80386SX CPU, monochrome monitor, 4.0MB RAM, one 1.2MB floppy drive, AT hard drive controller, two serial ports (com1, com2), two parallel ports (lpt2, lpt3), enhanced keyboard, and a 330MB SCSI external disk subsystem. Three printers attach directly to the file server: a Hewlett-Packard LaserJet Series II laser printer, a Panasonic KX-P1124 dot matrix, and an Epson LQ850 dot matrix printer. The file server has two surge suppressors, a 1.2KVA UPS, and a 12amp line conditioner.

The sixteen workstations on the network are a variety of IBM and IBM compatible microcomputers. There are also a variety of CPUs in the stations: eight are 8088 machines, five are 386SX machines, and three are 286 machines. Due to the variety of machines, there are likewise a variety of LAN cards installed in the machines. Two of the machines have 16-bit Novell NE2000 Ethernet cards, eleven of the machines (counting the file server) have 8-bit Novell NE1000 cards, two machines have 8-bit 3Com Etherlink II cards and two machines have 8-bit Western Digital Star/EtherCard Plus cards. Five of the stations in the computer lab have modems and all eight office computers have a modem. Station #5 in the lab has a Pioneer LaserDisc player connected to it. The workstations in the lab are mounted on a QVS Vertical CPU stand with their monitors on a wall mount terminal valet (arms that extend the monitor from the wall). In addition, the keyboard drawers are mounted under the tables so that the keyboards can slide in and out. Each of the workstations has one surge suppressor.

Software

All of the workstations and the file server run the same disk operating system: v3.3 IBM PC-DOS. Five stations have this loaded on their PROMs, six have DOS loaded on their hard drive, and five stations have it on a floppy boot disk. Although only a few workstations are actually IBM, we have not had any trouble loading all of them with IBM PC-DOS. The IBM PC-DOS works with no problem on the IBM compatible stations including the two Zeniths. Our vendor has not had good luck in the past using Zenith DOS on a Novell network and has never experienced any glitches running IBM DOS on a Zenith.

LANSight is a software package that was purchased to help manage the network. It is a utility that allows the network supervisor to monitor and if needed, control other workstations attached to the Novell network. In essence, it allows the supervisor to solve user problems without leaving the supervisor workstation. The supervisor can inspect the user's hardware and software configuration, view the user's display screen, execute programs on the user's workstation, and even reboot a remote workstation. LANSight also supplies statistics about the number and types of packets passing through the node, and the number of packets lost. This information is needed to identify bottlenecks and troubleshoot hardware and software problems. The supervisor can analyze problems much easier with LANSight than with Novell's "monitor" command since LANSight tells you what type of computer you are viewing, which version of the operating system it is using, how much memory is installed, and which programs currently reside in memory.

The network operating system is Novell Advanced NetWare 286 v2.15. On the OSI model, NetWare resides in the application layer while DOS resides in the presentation layer. In effect, NetWare forms a shell around DOS so that it is able to intercept application program commands before they can reach DOS. Since the workstations and the file server must be able to communicate, this shell must be loaded into each workstation before it can function on the network. The NetWare shell has two parts. The first part is the IPX (Internetwork Packet Exchange) file. The IPX.COM file directs network messages to the file server, and in some special cases, to other network stations. The second part is either NET2, NET3, or NET4 (depending on which DOS version you are using). On our system, the NET3.COM file directs workstation requests to DOS or NetWare. When a workstation needs to perform a task, the shell decides which operating system should handle it. DOS handles workstation tasks, such as the DIR command on a local disk, while NetWare handles network tasks, such as accessing a network file. The shell sends the request to the appropriate place. On a NetWare file server's hard disk, the file storage system is broken down in a fashion similar to that of a hard disk on a microcomputer. Our file server contains a hard disk which is divided into the SYS: volume. This is created automatically when the server is installed.

Most of the software available on the network is in the form of computer-assisted instruction (CAI) for the medical students and graduate students enrolled in basic science programs. The CAI programs include: AXOVACS, CHAMP: Cholesterol Assessment & Management Program, DERMCAL, Dynamic Models-biochemistry, ENDOCAL, EPI-Info, Food Processor II, HB Kinetics, HUMAN-physiology, MICAL, MR: Modulated Receptor Hypothesis, NBME: Boards Part 1 Review, Protein Sequencing, and PSYCAL. Other programs on the network include: FREIDA (AMA'S Fellowship and Residency Program), Grateful MED 5.0, Lotus 1-2-3 2.2, PC-File 1.0, ProComm 2.4, and WordPerfect 5.1 with Bitstream Fontware.

Installation and Implementation

We chose a vendor located in the Reno area from which to purchase the new equipment and to do the cabling, system setup, system configuration, system installation, and final system checkout. The total cost (equipment and labor) to upgrade the computer lab and two staff computers was $27,350. The total cost to link the rest of the staff's office computers to the network was $6,146. This $6,146 included one new computer, a new external modem, memory upgrades for two older IBMs, cabling, network cards, and labor.

The initial planning for the computer lab upgrade was done with our purchasing department's liaison for campus computing. She had worked with other labs on campus and helped to outline a plan for switching from 10-Net to Novell NetWare. The planning started in August 1990 and the request for bids was sent in September. The actual installation for the computer lab started on December 26, 1990 and was completed on January 14, 1991. The second phase of linking all the staff's microcomputers started on April 11, 1991 and was completed on April 23, 1991.

Although the installation of NetWare was performed by the vendor's technicians, the basic steps they followed were:

1. The program called "NETGEN" is run to configure, generate, and install the NetWare operating system on the file server. NET$OS.EXE is the file created by NETGEN.
2. The program called "SHGEN" is run to generate a NetWare workstation shell. IPX.COM is the file generated by SHGEN.
3. The networking hardware is installed and tested with a program called "COMCHECK." This is a NetWare utility that performs a diagnostic communications check to determine whether a network's stations are communicating properly across the cabling system.
4. Hard disk configuration is verified, formatted, and tested with a program called "COMPSURF" (comprehensive surface analysis). The COMPSURF utility also analyzes the hard disk surface.

All the stations in the computer lab that do not have an internal modem, were set up to boot to the network automatically with a programmable auto boot chip (PROM). The PROMs had DOS 3.3 programmed onto them. The auto boot chip on the network interface card allows the computer to log on to the network without a start-up floppy disk. The user just needs to turn on the computer and enter their login name. Those stations with an internal modem and a hard disk had the network boot files loaded on their hard drive. Those stations with an internal modem and no hard disk have a network boot disk that they use in their floppy drive. PROMS are especially useful for a student computer lab because they avoid a large number of users handling floppy disks. With our previous setup, there was a floppy boot disk for each station. These had to be replaced several times (new copies made from the masters) due to the disk going bad or being misplaced. None of the staff's workstations have a PROM. They access the network from their hard drive or from a floppy.

Several unforeseen problems caused delays in the installation process. The problems related to the network autoboot PROMs, the tape backup subsystem, and the installation of the monitor supports.

The first problem concerned the autoboot PROM chip on the network board. The technician discovered that an auto boot chip will not work if an internal modem is present. We received credit for the 3 PROMs that were returned.

Some trouble-shooting was done to make the internal tape drive work as the third drive in the supervisor's machine. A special cable had to be built so all three drives could run off the same floppy/hard drive controller.

The computer lab's walls are made of cement block which does not hold bolts or apparatuses very well. The arms for the monitors required special drilling and bolts to make them stay in the wall. About a month after installation, one of the arms did come out of the wall and had to be reinstalled. So far this one has stayed in place and none of the other arms have pulled out of the wall.

I thought it was going to be a big problem to switch from one network to another, but this went quite smoothly. The 10-Net cables were removed and replaced with Ethernet. All of the programs on the old file server were backed up using the program, Fastback Plus, and then loaded on the new file server using Fastback's restore mode.

The previous menu system, Wonder Plus, was deleted. A new menu system was created using DOS' text editor, EDLIN. A batch file was written using EDLIN to display the menus and to execute each program. Our vendor had copied a template EDLIN batch file to the file server that I could customize for what we needed. The main menu that appears when a user logs on is as follows:

```
COMMAND        PURPOSE or FUNCTION

HOME           RETURNS YOU TO YOUR HOME DIRECTORY & THIS MENU
LOGOUT         LOGS YOU OUT OF THE NETWORK
CAI            GOES TO THE COMPUTER ASSISTED INSTRUCTION DIRECTORY
DOS            GOES TO THE DOS DIRECTORY - USE FOR DOS FUNCTIONS
FREIDA         RUNS THE AMA'S FELLOWSHIP AND RESIDENCY PROGRAM
GMED           RUNS GRATEFUL MED 5.0 TO SEARCH MEDLINE
LOTUS          RUNS LOTUS 1-2-3 RELEASE 2.2
LOTUS-M        RUNS LOTUS 1-2-3 RELEASE 2.2 ON MONOCHROME MONITORS
PCF            RUNS PC-FILE+ 1.0 DATABASE MANAGER PROGRAM
PROCOMM        RUNS THE PROCOMM TELECOMMUNICATIONS PROGRAM
WORD           RUNS WORDPERFECT 5.1

SPOOL0         TO PRINT ON PANASONIC PRINTER IN LAB
SPOOL1         TO PRINT ON HP LASER SERIES II PRINTER IN LAB
SPOOL2         TO PRINT ON EPSON PRINTER IN LAB
```

All of the commands such as "home", "cai", "word" and such execute batch files. For example, "word.bat" starts WordPerfect 5.1. This batch file contains the following lines:

```
ECHO OFF
CLS
ECHO ^@
ECHO ^@
ECHO ^@
ECHO         PLEASE WAIT...I'M LOADING YOUR PROGRAM...
MAP I:=SYS:WORD51  > NUL
I:
REM CAPTURE NFF TI=5 NB
WP
CLS
REM CAPTURE FF TI=5 NB
H:
MAP REM I:  > NUL
TYPE HOME.NET
```

Use of the Network

The main users of the network are the first and second year medical students. Although the lab is open to faculty, staff, medical students, and graduate students in the school of medicine, faculty and 3rd and 4th year students rarely use the lab. A user survey was distributed in May 1991 to the 93 first and second year medical students. forty-two (48% of population) questionnaires were returned. Questions were asked to determine how they use the lab. Sixty-eight percent of the respondents indicated they have used at least one of the computer assisted instruction (CAI) programs, 52 percent have used WordPerfect and 2 percent have used Lotus. Only one person used ProComm for telecommunications and no-one has used PC-File for database management. Sixteen percent indicated that they spend most of their time in the lab using WordPerfect.

According to this survey, the capabilities of telecommunications software need to be explained to the students. Although the school of medicine is not linked to the rest of the campus through the Ethernet WAN, we do have dial-up access. Macros have been written in the Procomm script language that allow dial-up access to the campus mainframes including "WolfPAC," our Innovative Interfaces online library catalog since 1989.

In April 1991, the six remaining library staff members had their office computers cabled to the network (stations 11-16). The staff is just beginning to use the network for word processing and spreadsheets. This marks a major improvement for those staff members who did not have a hard disk nor enough memory to run the more recent versions of WordPerfect and Lotus.

Network Management

NetWare basically recognizes two types of network users: the network supervisor and regular network users. The supervisor is responsible for the smooth operation of the whole network and has "rights" to everything.

I perform many of the tasks as supervisor right from my office computer. With the previous setup I had to work on the network using the file server in the computer lab. This is not recommended since any time you reboot the server, all of the workstations "lock up." Now our file server is dedicated in the sense that it is not used as a station nor is it used for network maintenance.

The network environment is organized using NetWare's methods of creating directories, login scripts, and assigning rights through SYSCON (system configuration). I decided it would be too cumbersome to make every student that might use the lab (potentially 200 different students) a "user" and assign them a password. Since we have eight workstations available for students, I created a login script for: student1, student2, student3, student4, student5, student6, student7, and student8. The student logs on according to the number on the station they are in front of, for example, if they are at station #1, they enter "student1" when prompted for their login name.

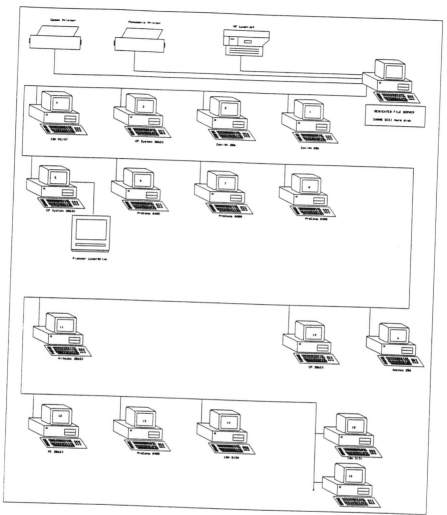

Figure 15.1
Savitt Medical Library Ethernet LAN

Security

Software

The supervisor is assigned a password and only one other staff member knows the password. So far (4 months) there have been no thefts or tampering with the system. We have ordered an anti-virus program but it has not arrived yet.

The system is backed up whenever a new software program has been loaded on the network. In addition, regular backups are done once per month using an internal tape back-up system (on 3M DC2000 mini data tape cartridges). This works rather well except that formatting a tape takes longer than backing up the entire drive. It takes 1 hour and 19 minutes to format a tape and 29 minutes to complete the backup of the entire file server. More frequent backups will have to be done when the staff starts saving important files on the network. Presently, students are instructed to save their documents to a floppy disk.

Although there are no passwords for the students, there is some control over access to the network since they have to ask someone how to logon. WordPerfect in particular was made more secure by putting the following measures in place for the group "students":

1. Subdirectories were created and named: student1, student2, student3, student4, student5, student6, student7, student8.
2. Station restrictions were put in place by entering the node addresses that correspond to stations 1-8. In other words, the only way to gain access to the network at a computer lab workstation is to enter "student1" at station #1 and "student2" at station #2, and so on.
3. The student 1-8 subdirectories contain a batch file that automatically enters st1, st2, st3 etc. as the user identification (/U) when they enter WordPerfect. These three initials direct WordPerfect to use the setup file that has been programmed by the supervisor (on the Setup: Location of Files screen, backup files and documents go to the A: drive).
4. The setup mode in WordPerfect was disabled (for anyone logging on as student 1-8) so that it cannot be changed.
5. The students only have read, open, and search rights to the WordPerfect subdirectory.

Hardware

The building which houses the library is locked everyday after 5pm and all day Saturday and Sunday. The library itself is locked at closing. The keyboard on the file server is always kept locked. None of the workstations or office computers have locks. The file server is left on at all times. Each station's computer and monitor is turned off when the library closes as well as each printer. In the event of an electrical storm, the system is brought down using Novell's "down" command, and all of the machines are turned off and unplugged. Electrical storms are very potent in Nevada and our vendor recommended this procedure (i.e., unplugging) in the event of an electrical storm. Of course, if it happens in the middle of the night, we have to hope that the UPS, line conditioners and surge protectors will work. We are just being extra cautious if a storm occurs when the library is open.

Quantity/Description	Price	Total
File Server		
1 386SX computer	1,530.00	1,530.00
1 330MB SCSI hard drive	2,329.00	2,329.00
1 disk coprocessor board	399.00	399.00
1 external drive casing	350.00	350.00
Network Equipment		
Novell Advanced NetWare v2.15	2,199.00	2,199.00
5 PROMs	50.00	250.00
2 Novell NE2000 Ethernet cards	215.00	430.00
2 WD Star/EtherCard Plus	215.00	430.00
2 3Com EtherLink II	215.00	430.00
11 Novell NE1000 Ethernet Cards	215.00	2,365.00
Workstations		
5 CP System 386SX computers	1,814.00	9,070.00
1 1.44MB floppy drive	87.00	87.00
Communications Equipment		
2 2400 bps internal modems	193.00	386.00
1 2400 bps external modem	375.00	375.00
Printers		
2 Panasonic KXP-1124 printers	335.00	670.00
Backup System		
1 80MB internal tapedrive	499.00	499.00
6 DC2000 tape cartridges	25.00	150.00
Power Protection		
1.2KVA UPS	1,195.00	1,195.00
1 12amp line conditioner	966.00	966.00
6 surge suppressors	75.00	450.00
Cabling Equipment		
terminator w/straight splice	12.00	12.00
terminator w/ground and straight splice	5.00	15.00
34 BNC 'T' connectors	6.00	204.00
2100 ft. RG58A/U Plenum Cable	.80/ft	1,680.00
Memory Upgrades		
1 AST SixPak Plus	282.00	282.00
1 Everex RAM card	189.00	189.00
Miscellaneous Software		
LANSight by LAN Systems	335.00	335.00
13 IBM PC DOS v3.3	100.00	1,300.00
Miscellaneous Equipment		
8 QVS vertical CPU stands	25.00	200.00
8 wall mounts	110.00	880.00
8 keyboard drawers	35.00	280.00
24 extension cables	10.00	240.00
Installation & Labor	3,319.00	3,319.00
GRAND TOTAL		$33,496.00

Table 15.1
Network Project Costs

Evaluation

The survey of the first and second year medical students conducted in May 1991 also measured their satisfaction with the computer lab as a whole. On a scale of 1-5 (5 being the most positive rating), they were asked to rate ease of use, satisfaction with the software available on the network, helpfulness of the staff, and overall how satisfied they are with the network. They were encouraged to write comments after each question.

Total downtime since the network was installed has amounted to two occurrences each lasting about 2-3 hours. The first time the network came up again on its own. The second time, a technician came and found that the terminator (on the last station) was bad. This was replaced.

The ongoing costs include supplies such as printer ribbons, paper and floppy disks, and one phone line. The most expensive cost is labor when our campus computing maintenance department cannot fix something and we have to call for a technician to come. The vendor's labor charge is $75/hour.

Many of the original goals of our network have been met especially since it has been upgraded from four workstations to sixteen. However, online computer searching training using Grateful MED has yet to be started for the medical students.

Problems

There were many problems at first with the way the printers were working with WordPerfect. The printer port selection was done incorrectly during installation and it required the students to select their printer at the network main menu as well as within WordPerfect. The printers were reinstalled and the corresponding "PRINTQs" were entered for each of the three printers. Previously, the printer ports were entered as LPT1, LPT2, and LPT3 instead of PRINTQ_0, PRINTQ_1, PRINTQ_2. Reinstallation solved the problem and users only have to select a printer from within WordPerfect.

The fact that we do not have a staff member assigned to the lab during all the hours it is open is another problem. As supervisor, I am the most familiar with the network but I only work Monday-Friday from 8am-5pm. The lab is open the same hours as the library (except that it closes 30 minutes before the library). The library hours are Monday-Thursday 7:30am-11pm, Friday 7:30-8pm, Saturday 9am-5pm, Sunday 1pm-11pm. Student workers cover the evenings and weekends but they can only be expected to provide a limited degree of assistance.

The lack of a full-time lab consultant relates to user training. It is difficult to train all of the students that may be using the lab. Handouts and one-on-one training is all that has been done so far. But, more formal instruction is being planned for the fall semester.

Another problem relates to ergonomic factors. The physical layout of the computer lab room is not ideal. We have eight stations and a file server in a room with a total of 96 square feet. When all stations are in use it is quite crowded. We planned for the monitors to be mounted to the wall and the keyboards in drawers that can slide under the tables to save table space. However, many students have complained that the monitors are too high and cannot be adjusted. The chairs can be raised but the tables are so low that their knees bump into it. Tall students are stuck with having to look up at the monitor. After working about an hour, their necks become very stiff. We did not think of this at all until everything was in place and people started using the facility. We plan to purchase narrower, higher tables and reinstall the keyboards and monitors to correct these problems.

What I Would have Done Differently

I do not have any regrets. Many of the problems with the previous 10-Net LAN have been solved since we switched to Novell. I do not even regret that my first experience was with 10-Net. I gained a sense of what LANs are all about and one method of how they can be organized.

Although I cannot think of anything I would have done differently, I still have a lot to learn. I attended the free Novell network class offered by our vendor before our system arrived. It was hard to grasp many of the concepts and procedures because I could not try anything until about two weeks later when everything was in place. I have taken the introductory class a second time (there is no limit on the number of times one may attend) and this has helped.

Plans for the Future

Starting with the fall 1991 semester, formal classes will be organized to orient new users to the lab. We are also going to start teaching classes on how to search MEDLINE using Grateful MED software. Another plan for the future is to have better bibliographic control of the software available on the network, namely to catalog each title. In fact, documentation in general needs to be tighter and more specific especially when upgrades and changes are made.

Possibilities for expansion have been considered such as putting our CD-ROM MEDLINE product on the network, acquiring a Macintosh stand-alone machine, collecting additional laser disks for CAI, and purchasing a communications server for dial-up access.

Final Thoughts

Networks are very complex and detailed. I thought that once we installed a more standard system (and what could be more standard than Novell running on Ethernet), everything would run smoothly and effortlessly. However, I am constantly learning new features and having to troubleshoot to fix a variety of problems. Continuing education in the form of reading and attending classes is a must. The more you read and ask questions, the more things start to make sense.

My advice for anyone considering a local area network for their library is to be realistic about the scope of the project. At the same time, you need to give yourself a break about how fast you will become an expert. I have been at it for about four months with Novell and I am just now starting to appreciate the benefits that a LAN can offer. At first everything seemed overwhelming and more trouble than it was worth!

Notes

1. Memo to the University of Nevada School of Medicine Dean from Nelson Publicover, Ph.D., Assistant to Dean for Computers, October 26, 1987.
2. Joan S. Zenan, Director of the Savitt Medical Library, grant proposal, August 11, 1986.

Bibliography

Amon E.M., Heatherington A.N., Henderson D.D. 1991. *Intelligent LAN Management with Novell NetWare*. Englewood Cliffs, New Jersey: Prentice-Hall.

Hancock B. 1988. *Designing and Implementing Ethernet Networks*. Wellesley, MA: QED Information Sciences.

Hannigan G.G., Brown JF. 1009. *Managing Public Access Microcomputers in Health Sciences Libraries*. Chicago: Medical Library Association.

McDonald T.K. 1989. *Illustrated Novell NetWare*. Plano, Texas: Wordware Publishing.

Nasatir M. March 1990. "Special Section: Local Area Networks". *Information Technology and Libraries*, 9(1): 89-108.

Novell NetWare Manuals. 1988. Provo, Utah: Novell, Incorporated.

Schatt S. 1987. *Understanding Local Area Networks*. Indianapolis: Howard W. Sams & Co.

Vendors and Products

3Com Corp.
3165 Kifer Road
Santa Clara, CA 95052
408/562-6400
3Com II Ethernet LAN Cards

3M Data Storage Products
St. Paul MN 55144-1000
800/328-9438
DC 2000 Mini Data Cartridge Tape

Archive Corporation
1650 Sunflower Avenue
Costa Mesa, CA 92626
714/641-0279
ARCHIVEXL Tape Drive

AST Research Inc.
2121 Alton Avenue
Irvine, CA 92714-4992
714/863-1333
SixPakPLUS Memory Expansion and I/O

Everex Systems Inc.
48431 Milmont Drive
Fremont, CA 94538
800/821-0806
Everex Mini Magic Memory Expansion Card

Fifth Generation Systems, Inc.
11200 Industriplex Boulevard
Baton Rouge, LA 70809-4112
800/225-2775
FASTBACK PLUS 1.5

LANSystems Inc.
300 Park Avenue South
New York, New York 10010
800/628-5267
LANSight

Novell, Incorporated
122 East 1700 South
P.O. Box 5900
Provo, Utah 84601
800/453-1267
801/379-5900
Novell Advanced NetWare 286 v2.15

Western Digital Corporation
2445 McCabe Way
Irvine, CA 92714
800/847-6181
714/863-0102
Western Digital EtherCard PLUS LAN Cards

About the Author

Laurie A. Potter, MLS, is the Medical Reference Librarian at the University of Nevada School of Medicine Savitt Medical Library. She graduated from Simmons College, Boston, Massachusetts in 1980 with an M.S. in Library and Information Science. Her ten years of library reference service have evolved from online searching via microcomputer to planning and managing the local area network at her current position.

16

The LAN as a Communications Gateway: Using a Token Ring Network to Access a NOTIS Library System

Dan Marmion
Edmon Low Library, Oklahoma State University

ABSTRACT

This chapter describes the implementation of a Token Ring LAN at Oklahoma State University, the primary purpose of which, at this time, is to provide access to the library's NOTIS integrated library system. The chapter also discusses the reasons behind OSU's decision to use this approach, the physical configuration and equipment involved, and where we are currently and where we plan to go in the future.

Introduction

The Edmon Low Library at Oklahoma State University is in the process of implementing the NOTIS integrated library system. As of this writing, we have the Online Public Access Catalog (OPAC) in production and are just beginning to implement cataloging. We will activate other modules (circulation, acquisitions) during the coming months.

NOTIS is an IBM mainframe-based automated library system that was developed at Northwestern University. When Northwestern began selling the system to other libraries, they formed a for-profit, wholly-owned subsidiary called NOTIS Systems, Inc. (NSI), to manage, maintain, and market the NOTIS system.

Until recently, NSI has aimed their marketing efforts toward larger university libraries, and especially members of the Association of Research Libraries (ARL). Today, nearly one-half of the ARL membership, including Oklahoma State and the University of Oklahoma, are NOTIS sites.

The NOTIS system software and the library's bibliographic database reside on an IBM 3090 200s mainframe computer located at the University Computing Center (UCC). The UCC building is approximately 100 yards distant from the library building. Although the library plans to use a few Telex 476L terminals connected via coax cable in cataloging areas, the majority of staff accesses the NOTIS system by means of an IBM Token Ring local area network. In addition, all of the OPAC terminals are connected through the LAN.

The decision to use a LAN dates back to a series of events that took place before I arrived at OSU, and for the purpose of this article they warrant only a cursory overview. The library had contracted with an outside vendor to develop an integrated library system. That vendor, for reasons not germane to this discussion, concluded that the system they were developing would be best suited to microcomputers connected to a local area network.

The Campus Backbone

At approximately the same time, the Computing Center was making plans for the creation of a campus-wide network backbone to facilitate connecting the local networks of various departments. The College of Veterinary Medicine, for example, was planning to implement its own LAN, and the campus backbone would enable it to communicate with other departments.

The campus backbone is a Fiber Distributed Data Interchange (FDDI) network. FDDI is a high-speed (100 million bits per second) LAN standard primarily for use with fiber optic cable. Initially, our FDDI network will have ports at fourteen buildings across the campus, allowing each site to connect Token Ring- or Ethernet-equipped devices to the backbone via a bridge.

The campus backbone connects to the IBM mainframe through a front-end processor (FEP). This is a box that identifies various physical units and logical units to the system. There are actually three FEPs in use: an aging 3705 that supports several 3270 terminals (see below for an explanation of 3270 terminals) across campus; a 3725 that is seven years old and very overworked and overloaded; and a recently-installed 3745 with substantially more memory and the capacity to add more users. We'll have more to say about the FEPs later, but for now let's return to the Token Ring.

The Selection Process

The UCC selected the IBM Token Ring as the standard networking platform for the university. The IBM Token Ring, or Token-Passing Ring, is a *de jure* standard for networking computers as defined by IEEE (Institute of Electrical and Electronic Engineers) code 802.5. Token ring runs over shielded twisted-pair cables (i.e., wire much like telephone wire that is wrapped in shielding to prevent electrical interference).

The major advantage of Token Ring is that it performs consistently under a heavy load. Our LAN currently runs a 4Mbs (million bits per second), but is capable of 16Mbs. The disadvantage of Token Ring is that its cost is prohibitive to many institutions. Be forewarned, however, that many organizations have opted for cheaper Ethernet-based LANs and regretted that decision after growth, due to the lesser throughput of most Ethernet hardware.

The Token Ring cable connects to the workstations through MAUs (Multistation Access Units). The MAU is simply a relay box; when a workstation powers up it sends a signal to the MAU, which adds the workstation to the ring.

Installation and Implementation

Because of these factors, the library began planning for its own Token Ring network. At that time, the library owned very few microcomputers. What it did have was a substantial number of Telex 476L dumb terminals connected via coax to the university mainframe. To implement the LAN, the library administrators did the following:

o   Pulled out all but just a few of the Telex terminals and associated cabling. Many of them were sold to another library in the state for use in their online system. The remaining 476Ls will be used in cataloging areas, because they are capable of displaying the diacritic marks found in the ALA character set.

o   Purchased approximately 90 microcomputers from Memorex Telex Corporation to be used as network workstations and OPAC terminals. These are 80286-based machines with EGA video displays. The administration distributed them throughout the library for staff use. Thus, the library was in the enviable position of having virtually a one-to-one ratio of full-time staff and microcomputers.

o   Purchased a like number of IBM Token Ring 16/4 (i.e., capable of running at either 16Mbs or 4Mbs) network interface cards (NICs) at $627 each, the same number of Token Ring adapter cables at $25 each, and an appropriate number of eight-port Multistation Access Units (MAUs), at $582 each, for connecting the computers to the network.

o   Contracted with the university's Physical Plant to install the shielded twisted-pair network cabling throughout the library building at an estimated cost of $16,000. It is possible to run Token Ring on cheaper unshielded twisted-pair cable, and newer chip sets for Token Ring NICs are making this option more attractive to many, but OSU would like to stay as standardized as possible, and departments are encouraged to adhere to IEEE standards.

o   Made arrangements with the UCC for the library's network to tie into the campus backbone.

That was the situation as it existed when I arrived at Oklahoma State in October 1989 to assume responsibility for what soon became the Library Systems Department. Developments over the next several months led to the decision to go with an established integrated library system rather than continue with the previous arrangement, and we subsequently signed a contract with NOTIS.

By this time, however, most of the physical components of the local area network were either in place or about to fall into place: the building was about two-thirds cabled, the Token Ring cards and MAUs were installed, and the link to the campus backbone and the IBM mainframe (via a 3725 front-end processor) was established and working. To us it made sense to utilize this existing communications framework.

Dumb or Smart—That Is the Question

One major change, however, was in the area of public access terminals. The original plan, remember, was to use microcomputers. That's why the library bought so many, and in fact that's why we put in the LAN in the first place. But the staff had been using them for some time now and didn't want to part with them. We decided to use dumb terminals for the OPAC, although that decision was not unanimous—there are some advantages to using microcomputers as public access terminals.

Microcomputers provide a level of flexibility not present with dumb terminals. You can download data to disk and then massage it or process it for use elsewhere: a bibliography list, for example. You can program function keys for patrons to use that will eliminate their needing to know various commands. You can even install a complete "front end" software package to act as an interface between the patron and the system. Several libraries are employing variations of this approach.

The current status of our LAN project is as follows: we have installed 75 copies of IBM's LAN Support Program ($46 for the first copy and $30 for the rest). The LAN Support Program provides the software necessary for the workstation to communicate with the LAN. It grabs the token when it needs to and passes information back and forth between the workstation and the ring. At the same time, we installed 75 copies of their Personal Communications/3270 terminal emulation program ($495 for the first copy and $30 for each additional license). The 3270 is IBM's full-screen terminal standard that employs escape-sequence commands to position data on the screen. It essentially treats the video screen as a complete entity, rather than the line-by-line procedure of a teletype (TTY) terminal.

Gateways

The IBM software provides for using certain microcomputers as gateways to the LAN through which we can channel other workstations. A gateway is a machine that is identical to all other PCs on the LAN in that it has a Token Ring NIC. We are using IBM PS/2 Model 30-286 machines (i.e., a model 30, but with an 80286 processor rather than the original 8088) as gateways. A gateway can be dedicated to that purpose, or it can function as a workstation simultaneously to being a gateway. We are using dedicated gateways.

The advantage of a gateway is that it enables the IBM front-end processor (FEP) to recognize only one physical unit (PU), while allowing multiple workstations to be attached to the gateway. The FEP sends a message to the gateway, and then the gateway determines which particular workstation needs to receive the message.

We are using this approach at the request of the Computing Center. We have a total of three such gateways, each supporting up to twenty-five workstations (although in order to have that many, the gateway itself would have to double as a workstation, so we are only attaching twenty-four workstations to each gateway).

The gateway and three of the workstations are in the Systems Office, which also serves as our training facility for NOTIS training.

We had one gateway functioning for several weeks, with about ten workstations attached, in order to test the viability of this setup. At that time, certain workstations were activated to provide mainframe connectivity for some administrative functions. Our personnel officer, for example, uses the LAN to access the university's personnel records on the mainframe.

This brings up the point that, although the original reason behind the decision to install a LAN was for using the online library system, it gives us access to everything on the IBM mainframe. Those of us who have BITNET accounts can access BITNET through the local area network. Our Circulation Department has access to student records. And since there is a link between the Oklahoma State computer and that at the University of Oklahoma, we can search their OPAC through our LAN without having to incur dial-up charges.

I mentioned earlier that the UCC has three front-end processors. That wasn't the case when we first began this operation. Our original gateway, with it's ten workstations, was connected to the 3725, which at that time was the second of only two FEPs at the UCC (along with that old 3705). When we tried to add the second and third gateways, the entire system crashed. (Actually, it was just everybody else on campus that crashed—we were still active, which we thought was awfully considerate of the 3725!)

This precipitated some fast shuffling on the part of the UCC. For a temporary fix, they added more memory and a software upgrade to the 3725, but it was obvious that something more would be needed. The solution was to purchase the 3745 FEP, a very expensive (around $240,000) but effective answer, and migrate the backbone to that unit. The Library chipped in a substantial portion of that purchase cost.

Additional Installations

For the public, we have installed 35 Telex 1471 dumb terminals. They were on state contract for about $500, so we didn't have to go through a bid process. Color terminals would have been nice, but they are much more expensive, and as it turns out, the orange (amber) and black screens happen to be the OSU colors.

We connected them to the mainframe via a Telex 1174 terminal controller (this unit is similar to IBM's 3174). The 1174 resides in the library and is attached to the same Token Ring LAN that connects our staff workstations to the campus backbone. In its basic configuration, this box would allow us to attach as many as 64 terminals, but we exercised an option to expand this to 96 ports. Total cost of the unit is approximately $13,000. The controller is located roughly in the middle of our six-floor library building.

The controller package we purchased includes eight Telex 1199 Multiplexer (Mux) units with eight ports each. This enables us to save on cabling in the building and give us more flexibility. Instead of running separate cables from the controller to a bank of eight terminals, for example, we will run a single cable to a Mux, and then a short cable from the Mux to each terminal. If at a later time we decide to put more terminals in the bank, we can simply attach a second Mux to one of the ports on the first one. This gives us the ability to expand that bank to fifteen terminals, all hanging from the single cable coming from the controller on another floor.

Currently, we have a cluster of terminals on the first floor and one on the second floor. These areas are near the entrances and the main reference desks. Other, smaller clusters are located in strategic areas throughout the building. Specifically, there are four in the Reading Room, where we keep current periodicals; three each on the third and fourth floors, which are stacks areas; four on the fifth floor (Government Documents); and three in the basement stacks.

The three terminals in the basement, and two at the General Reference desk, are directly cabled to the 1174. All other clusters are attached to Muxes, giving us three to four empty ports on each Mux for additional terminals if we need to add them later.

I had wondered what the LAN performance would be like when we had 75 staff workstations and 35 public access terminals all hanging from the same ring. But the people at the Computing Center didn't seem to be overly worried about it, and of course it's unlikely that all 110 of these workstations and terminals would be in use at the same time. As it turned out (at least so far!), my concerns were unfounded. Response time is as good as other terminals that are directly wired to the FEP, so we are quite happy with our situation.

Plans for the Future

Possibly the thought has struck you by now that this is not your typical LAN. We don't have a file server, we don't have Novell NetWare or some other fancy network operating system, and we are not using sophisticated groupware or networked software programs. What we have, in fact, is simply a telecommunications system—a very expensive modem, in a manner of speaking.

But we also have plans, and the skeleton is in place for all that other stuff. We intend to do all the typical LAN things. We are now making plans to buy a file server with a large, fast hard disk; we will get NetWare 386 or something comparable; we will add network versions of WordPerfect, Paradox, and we'll have electronic mail and shared printers and more. At the Oklahoma State University Libraries, we have only just begun to network. We have seen the future, and it's spelled L, A, N.

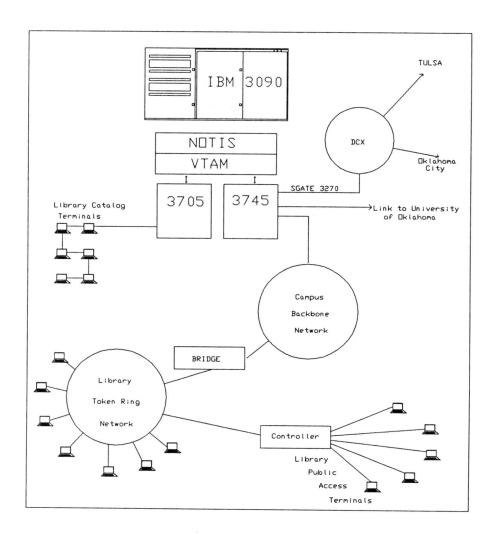

Figure 16.1
Electronic Access to the OSU Library

About the Author

Dan Marmion is Head of Library Systems at the Edmond Low Library at Oklahoma State University. In addition to this position, he is currently the Editor-in-Chief of *OCLC Micro,* the Software Review editor for *Library Software Review*, and is a Contributing Editor for *Computers in Libraries*—all Meckler publications. He authored *The OCLC Workstation* as part of the Meckler series *The Essential Guide to the IBM PC.*

Marmion has an M.S. in Information Science from the University of North Texas. Prior to accepting his current position at Oklahoma State, he was the Microcomputer Operations Manager for the AMIGOS Bibliographic Council. He began his professional career as a Reference Librarian at Southern Methodist University.

Part Four:

Large Multi-Purpose LANs

17

Project BLISS:
The Bradley Library Information Support System

Ellen I. Watson and Stephen J. Patrick
Cullom-Davis Library, Bradley University

ABSTRACT

Project BLISS is designed to provide an integrated array of information services and resources to the students and faculty of Bradley University. Five UNIX-based servers are linked in a StarLAN network within the Library, and the Library network provides bridges to the campus and national networks. Developed and implemented in close cooperation with Computing Services, the focus of Project BLISS is on information literacy, with the technology providing the delivery vehicle for expanding Library programs and services.

Introduction

The Bradley Library Information Support System (BLISS) links function-specific UNIX servers in a StarLAN network to support information services throughout the Library. The servers include the following functions:

o networked delivery of software and printing in the Microcomputer Information Center
o networked CD-ROM resources
o document delivery services based on computer-to-computer fax technology
o support of a variety of new information databases and library management activities, including an image database of the collection of historical photographs
o communications linking the Library servers with the campus backbone networks and the universe of electronic information.

BLISS workstations for both patrons and staff are located throughout the Library. A menu system lists the available resources and makes the connection to the resources transparent to the user. The Library and Computing Services jointly developed and are implementing BLISS to provide a platform for the development of cohesive electronic information services, with the Library serving as the access, training, and mediation locus.

The Bradley Environment

The University is an independent, comprehensive institution enrolling approximately 6,100 undergraduate and graduate students, located in Peoria, Illinois. In support of its mission, Bradley emphasizes appropriate applications of information technology to support instruction and research.

Bradley's information management units—including the Library as the University's information access center—were organized as Information Technologies and Resources in 1986. Included within this unit are the Cullom-Davis Library, Computing Services, the Center for Learning Resources, and Telecommunications (see Figure 17.1).

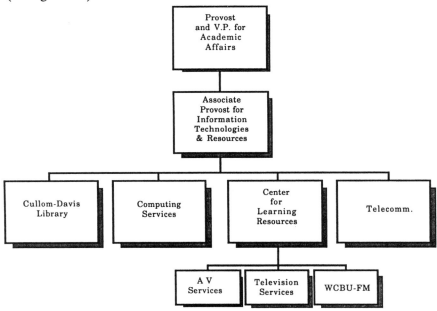

Figure 17.1
Organizational Structure of Bradley University
Information Management Units

This organizational structure has worked well for the Library, ensuring that the Library's needs are included in all university-wide planning for information resources and services, allowing coordination with other information providers, and encouraging the development of a new vision of Library programs and roles. The Library has taken a leadership role within Information Technologies, expanding and enhancing programs to become the end-user's primary contact point for information services and delivery. The University—administration, faculty, and the Library itself—views the Library as the University's information access center. The Library provides the basic collections and resources needed for the University's teaching and research activities, and enhances these collections with access to the expanding universe of information resources of all types and formats.

The focus of both current and future activities is on information fluency, rather than on hardware. While the Library has taken a leadership role, all Information Technologies units are actively involved in the "Integrated Information Literacy Program," which offers a wide range of general and discipline-specific programs to encourage both students and faculty to take advantage of all of the resources available to support research and study. Several of the programs, such as the one focusing on access to and use of the Internet, are jointly prepared and presented by Library and Computing Services personnel.

A major expansion and renovation of the Cullom-Davis Library has greatly facilitated the Library's ability to provide these new services and enhance existing programs. Completed in April, 1990, the expanded and renovated facility has provided space to house new activities and equipment. As part of the construction, extensive wiring was provided to allow every area and office access to a variety of electronic connections, both current and projected.

In the midst of these plans and activities, however, we were concerned that, as in most libraries, our electronic information resources existed as individual resources with no cohesive structure. Further, while we were emphasizing delivery of information resources and services beyond the physical confines of the Library, these resources—except for the Library catalog—were seldom accessible outside the library building. Access methods and search commands varied, making it extremely difficult for students and even faculty to identify and use the various electronic information resources available.

It was within this context that Project BLISS developed.

The Bradley Library Information Support System (BLISS)—Concept and Goals

BLISS is based on a philosophy of information outreach and delivery, with the Library as the central locus for access, delivery, training, and mediation. BLISS hardware and software are the vehicles for providing and promoting this. BLISS development has proceeded with the intimate involvement and support of Computing Services; the Library provides local information resources, as well as training and mediation, while Computing Services provides access and delivery.

The computer-assisted Bradley Library Information Support System (BLISS) addresses this philosophy and concern through four major components: distributed networked access to library information; library information creation, storage, and management; unified access to information through a networked, menu-based front-end system; and the development of ongoing user training and support programs. These major components include the following elements:

A. Distributed networked access to library information:

1. Access to the Library's online catalog and the online catalogs of several distant libraries.
2. Access to local CD-ROM databases, indexes, and text files.
3. Access to local and distant online textual, numeric, and image databases.
4. Development of an electronic document delivery system based on computerized facsimile technology.
5. Development of a uniform command syntax to standardize keystrokes required for activation of entry, help, downloading, and exit functions of specific online electronic database services.

B. Library information creation, storage, and management:

1. Development of new information resources, including indexed databases of scanned historic photographs, textual databases of institutional information, and library management tools.
2. Storage, retrieval, manipulation, and management of large textual, numeric, and image databases .
3. Linkage of existing but previously incompatible information resources, especially those currently available in the Cullom-Davis Library.
4. Use of electronic mail and voice mail as a means of coordinating information requests and deliveries.

C. Unification of the above resources through a library-based cluster of communication and applications servers, making local and distant information of various types as accessible to users throughout the campus as it is to users within the Library. A menu-based interface identifies for users the range of resources available, performs the necessary connections, and masks the varying complexities of information access and transfer.

D. Development of support programs to assist users in locating and accessing information, including computer-assisted tutorials, documentation, training programs, and individual guidance.

When it is fully implemented, Project BLISS will establish a tightly-coupled complex of networked UNIX-based communication and application servers that will become a platform for the development of cohesive electronic library information services (See Figures 17.2-17.4). Students and faculty will be linked to the world of electronic information, providing a "virtual" as well as a physical library. Building upon existing library expertise in information services and Bradley's technology infrastructure, this project will result in a platform for future electronic services development. Whenever possible, existing off-the-shelf hardware and software components are being utilized to minimize costs and maximize flexibility.

BLISS will improve library management effectiveness by creating the ability to centrally manage and distribute text and images retrieved from remote sites, to build specialized databases to meet local needs, to electronically manage the significant flow of facsimile documents between external sources and users, and to improve communication with faculty and students through electronic and voice mail. BLISS will also give specific attention to the need for multiple access to CD-ROM and other electronic databases and indexes.

At the present time, BLISS clientele consist primarily of traditional in-library users, including faculty, students, and staff, together with users out-of-the-library but on-campus, including students in the Residence Halls of the Future program and faculty and staff in their offices. In addition, as an enhanced service, we are working with distant special, system, and academic libraries to provide computer-to-computer delivery of technical information in support of interlibrary loan activities.

BLISS as a Technical Program: Bradley Computing and Networking Environment

Bradley University was an early entrant in campus-wide, fiber optic networking. In 1986 Bradley University installed a campus-wide network. This network, AT&T's Information Systems Network (ISN), was mainly an asynchronous "terminal emulation" network, providing medium- speed delivery of data over fiber optic lines, in a homogenous environment of mainframes, minicomputers, terminals, and MS-DOS personal computers emulating terminals. The ISN network also provides bridging to the campus Ethernet. Later, Bradley added two additional campus-wide backbone networks, a campus-wide Ethernet, and AppleTalk networks. In addition, StarLAN networks serve working groups and provide access to the backbone networks. StarLAN is a 10BaseT network capable of linking heterogeneous equipment in a UNIX or MS-DOS environment. StarLAN is essentially equivalent to Ethernet: the cabling used is different, but can easily be connected with cable adaptors; and Ethernet and StarLAN environments can communicate with minimal difficulty or translation.

Bradley uses a dual outlet concept in each faculty or staff office. One receptacle is used for the telephone with the other providing data service. Using the twisted-pair wiring in each building, any faculty member can be connected to the network(s) of that individual's choice. All three networks are connected by gateways to provide access to the campus mainframe, minicomputers, the Library catalog, and other services, including BLISS. The campus mainframe, which is used for administrative, academic, and research activities, is a Cyber 932. As the University moves to a distributed computing environment, more functions and services are being developed on minicomputer and server platforms, including 386 and 486 servers and AT&T 3B2 minis. The Library catalog is served from Tandem equipment located in East Peoria,

Illinois, but appears to users as a transparent component of the Bradley networks, via direct log in to the host "library," or as a menu pick on the BUINFO campus-wide menu.

Also in 1986, Bradley University began the Residence Halls of the Future project, placing networked personal computers in residence hall rooms. The University installs, maintains, and provides training for the computers in these residence halls, and students pay an additional fee each semester to participate in the Residence Halls of the Future program. By the 1990-91 academic year, Bradley had installed 600 XT-class microcomputers connected to the ISN as well as 170 386 microcomputers connected to a 10BaseT network. Approximately 80 percent of entering freshmen participate in the Residence Halls of the Future program.

In 1991 Bradley completed its "Computers for Faculty" program, providing a computer for every faculty and staff member who requested one. Most of these computers are XT-class PCs, mixed with a significant number of Macintosh and 386-generation computers. Most of these computers are connected to one of the campus networks.

The University supports several computer labs including the Microcomputer Information Center in the Library, general-purpose computer labs in Computing Services, and departmental labs for Computer Science, English, Physics, Education, Communications, Business, Art, and Engineering. The computer labs contain a variety of terminals, MS-DOS, Sun, and Apple microcomputers. Most of the computers in these labs are connected to one of the campus-wide networks.

Bradley has a leased line to the University of Illinois to provide Internet access. One use of this network is to link to other library systems including Illinet Online, and CARL UnCover.

Library Computing and Networking Environment

The Cullom-Davis Library contains the Microcomputer Information Center (MIC), online public access terminals, CD-ROM workstations (both stand-alone and networked through BLISS), OCLC workstations including an Ameritech IBM Token Ring LAN for ACQ350 and SC350 acquisition and serials control functions, and individual microcomputers for the library faculty and staff.

The Library is currently a participant in the Resource Sharing Alliance of West Central Illinois, a multitype consortium of sixteen public, academic, and system libraries that uses a Tandem-based system located at Illinois Central College in East Peoria, Illinois, to provide online public access catalog and circulation services. We are presently beginning a migration to Illinet Online for these services, which would provide Bradley patrons with access to a 19-million item database and the holdings of thirty-eight other Illinois academic and public libraries.

Each member of the Library faculty, and many staff, have personal computers, including XT-class, 386, and Apple Macintoshes, all linked to the Library and campus networks. Library faculty and staff use their computers to search online databases; use the ACQ350 and SC350 software for acquisitions and serials control; respond to document delivery and interlibrary loan requests and reference queries on local e-mail; participate in a wide variety of BITNET and Internet discussion groups; search our own and distant library catalogs; and increase their productivity with word processing and spreadsheet capabilities. The computers and networks have become an integral part of the work life of everyone in the Library.

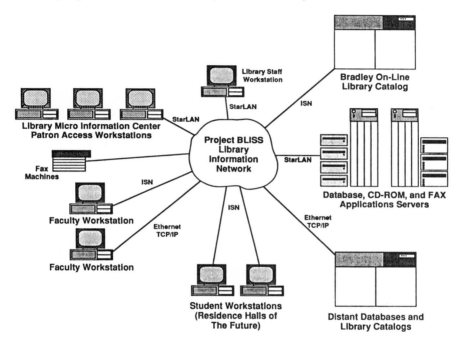

Figure 17.2
General Organization of BLISS Network

The BLISS concept was developed over a period of more than a year (1989-1990). The physical implementation of BLISS was jointly developed by the Library and Computing Services with the coordination of the Associate Provost for Information Technologies and Resources, and included twenty-eight 386-level workstations and five 33MHz 386 UNIX-based servers, together with essential software. The workstations are used both in the MIC and as public and staff workstations throughout the Library. The role of the servers is to provide CD-ROM, image, database, software, and communications services.

BLISS Activities

The MIC Server

The Microcomputer Information Center is designed to provide students with access to a broad range of information resources, as well as the computing power and productivity software necessary to manage that information. MIC hardware includes eighteen 386 and nine Apple Macintosh microcomputers. The 386 computers are equipped with color VGA monitors and are linked by a 10BaseT network to a UNIX-based file server running AT&T's StarGROUP network operating system.

StarGroup 3.4 software, in conjunction with UNIX 4.0.2, Mac Server 3.4, and TCP/IP for 4.0 UNIX software, allows the Macintosh computers, which had previously been linked to a Macintosh server through an AppleTalk network, to be linked to the Unix server, using the AppleTalk network. The software packages provide all of the support necessary to allow the various protocols and applications to coexist transparently to the end-user. Under the current configuration, all software access and network services are provided through the UNIX server.

The MIC computers are very heavily used because they are among the most advanced publicly-available computers and because networked laser printing is provided. While the heaviest use is for word processing and other productivity software, the increasing range of information services available through BLISS is beginning to change the use of the MIC to a genuine information resource. Computing Services provides a trained student as a "Computer Consultant" during the busiest hours of operation, approximately 60 hours per week.

CD-ROM Server

The CD-ROM server is a 33MHz 386 computer running the UNIX operating system. The network operating system being used is AT&T's StarGROUP. This is a LAN Manager network operating system and can support both Macintosh and MS-DOS computers. SCSI Express (Micro Design International, Inc.) software has been installed and allows the CD-ROM drives to be directly addressed through UNIX, without the intervention of Microsoft Extensions for CD-ROM on remote workstations.

Simultask, which allows terminal users of a UNIX computer to start and run MS-DOS sessions, is also supported on this server. While we hope to be able to use Simultask as the "least common denominator" to support text-based CD-ROM services to a wide audience, without having to run special adaptive software on each workstation, we are presently testing SoftPC, run on the local Macintosh, to provide the MS-DOS configuration required by the CD-ROM search software. We are using NEC CDR72 drives, which work well with the UNIX server. Bradley University is cooperating in a research and development project with AT&T Bell Laboratories to develop this networked CD-ROM service.

The networked CD-ROM server is intended to provide services in a heterogeneous environment and to provide services across the campus. The significance of the first goal is to provide the CD-ROM services across a variety of platforms to PC, Macintosh, and Sun workstation users. Since most CD-ROM products are only available within a homogeneous product line we felt this would be a difficult challenge. Provision of CD-ROM resources through the UNIX server addresses this problem for those machines connected through StarGROUP software on a 10BaseT network.

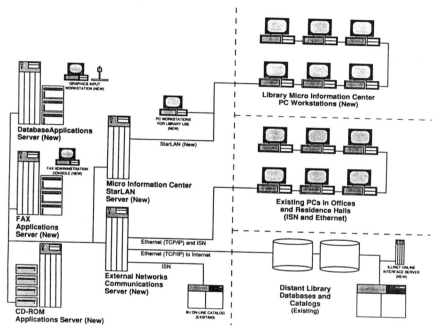

Figure 17.3

Network Servers and Workstations Related to BLISS

One complicating factor in reaching the second goal is that while the MIC consists of new state-of-the-art computers with high resolution color monitors, many faculty and students are using older, less capable, computers. We are finding in our tests that the less capable computers may support access to some but not all of the available CD-ROM resources. A second complicating factor is the cost and availability of licensing for networked access.

We are implementing the CD-ROM network capability in phases. The first phase is to network the MIC and Library faculty computers to the CD-ROM server. This phase is presently being tested, with six workstations of varying capability

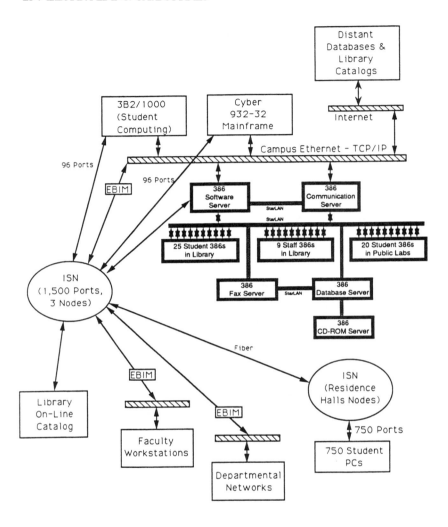

Figure 17.4
Bliss Facilities as they relate to Bradley University Campus Networks

successfully networked to ten CD-ROM databases. The databases being served as part of the test include the following: Readers' Guide Abstracts, Business Periodicals Index, Social Sciences Index, General Science Index, and Applied Science and Technology Index, all WilsonDisc; National Trade Database (NTDB), a government publication; the Dialog version of ERIC; and a variety of other databases as needed or available for testing.

We will expand access to the full library network, potentially including the Macintoshes in the MIC (although this capability has not yet been tested), during the summer of 1991, and anticipate that by August we will have a maximum of forty-two workstations able to access fourteen CD-ROM resources in a networked environment. The present network interface provides a menu (developed in-house by Computing Services staff using the C-language in UNIX) listing the available resources and making the linkage to the resource transparent. Future enhancements include the ability to maintain usage statistics and to control access and queueing for CD-ROM resources.

After we are confident that the network works within the Library, we will attempt to broaden support and provide, within licensing agreements, campus-wide access to those users with equipment compatible with network requirements. This phase will be implemented by the fall of 1992. Full access to this component of BLISS will depend, in part, on the gradual campus-wide transition to more capable equipment.

Document Delivery Server

The goals of the Document delivery server are to:

1) To collect and distribute images (from the Cullom-Davis and other libraries) in computer format.
2) To send images to the Library's patrons using the medium most convenient for that patron.
3) To reduce the time required to provide document delivery services.

The most common images entering and leaving the Library are fax transmissions based on interlibrary loan requests. This service is the basis for the document delivery server networking application.

The document delivery server, a 33MHz AT&T computer running the UNIX operating system, includes four fax boards. The fax boards allow the capture of incoming images, the storage of those images on disk, and the delivery of images to University patrons or external agencies. The network operating system being used is StarGROUP, and the server supports Simultask. The server appears to external agencies to be a standard fax machine, accepting both Group III and Group IV fax transmissions.

To capture locally-owned documents for on-campus or external delivery, the Library uses a workstation with a scanner to scan documents and transmit them to the server. Once captured, the images are stored on the server and can be examined and routed to the patron's location or routed to an external agency. StarGROUP and UNIX software allow the scanned images to be named, stored, reviewed, delivered, and retrieved on demand. The Interlibrary Loan Coordinator, a paraprofessional, is responsible for managing the delivery and receipt of documents, and for notifying patrons by either electronic mail or voice mail that a document is available.

Bradley patrons have a variety of options for receiving the documents: they can view the documents on their local workstations; print the image on a local printer; request delivery to a local fax machine; request that the Library print and physically deliver the document to a specific on-campus location; or discard the document. External patrons can request the documents either as computer files or as fax output.

As in the case of the CD-ROM server, the capability of the end-user to access the system is in part dependent upon the power of the computer the end-user has available. At present, only users with high-resolution workstations can receive and view the documents. This is a relatively small subset of the campus community. We are exploring the possibility of converting the content of the imaged document to a text file (through OCR conversion) which can be delivered to and processed by a user with a less powerful local workstation. While this is not a satisfactory solution to the delivery of illustrations accompanying the text, it would allow the end-user to store and manipulate the text with word processing software, to facilitate note-taking and manuscript development.

The document delivery server is currently in limited use, primarily among Information Technologies units. We have joined with a special library, an academic engineering library, and a multitype library system in submitting a grant proposal to the Illinois State Library to test the computer-to-computer delivery of technical information using the network resources of netILLINOIS. The Bradley document delivery server will operate as the primary server for this project. If funded, this proposal will give us a much clearer idea of the extent to which document delivery is a feasible and cost-effective mechanism for direct delivery of imaged documents both to libraries and to end-users.

By December 1991 the document delivery server should be in full operation, receiving imaged documents from other libraries for storage and delivery to Bradley patrons, and delivering imaged documents in response to standard, faxed, or computer-to-computer interlibrary loan requests.

Database Applications Server

One of the most important resources in the Library is also the least accessible: over 16,000 historic photographs and glass negatives, many of them fragile and deteriorating, and none fully indexed, are housed in the Virginius H. Chase Special Collections Center. We have hoped for some time to develop an image database of these photographs. The Library has a number of other resources, such as the syllabus and test collections, which we would like to make accessible campus-wide as image databases. In addition, there are several in-house management functions, including a check-in and record of the depository collection and an interlibrary loan record, that we would like to automate as database files. The database applications server of BLISS is making these applications possible.

The database server is a 33MHz 386 computer using UNIX as the operating system, with 32MB RAM and additional SCSI capacity for the future addition of optical or magnetic storage devices. Informix has been installed for development of the variety of databases. The database applications server will be available on the Library StarLAN, but access to certain databases will be restricted to particular users or to particular functions, such as read-only access.

Library and Computing Services staff are presently investigating the availability or portability of a selection of commercially available database programs to run under Informix in the UNIX environment. Informix is a relational database specifically designed to take full advantage of UNIX capabilities, and supports both text and image. We anticipate using graduate students in computer science to do the necessary programming for the databases that will be developed in-house. The database applications server will become active in fall 1991, providing a reserve room control database to supplement the circulation system. Other databases will be implemented in a phased manner, beginning in January 1992, with the index to the historic photograph collection.

Network Server

As stated earlier, Bradley has three different networks which require three different methods of access. Even within the Library, there are StarLAN and IBM Token Ring networks, which are not compatible. This disparity inhibits access to library and network resources. The situation is even more complex when the user attempts to access resources beyond the campus: each library catalog on the Internet has its own search protocol, and access to full-text databases or computing resources can be especially arcane.

The goal of the network server is to provide an aid to accessing library information across a variety of networks. The network server, another 33MHz 386 computer, will provide a transparent interface to the various campus networks and to Internet library catalogs and resources. A menu-based campus-wide information system (CWIS), BUINFO, is in the early stages of development. BUINFO is being developed in-house by Computing Services staff using the C-language in UNIX. In-house development was chosen because of the variety and complexity of the networks on campus, to allow maximum customization, and minimize training requirements for users. The Library has designed the specific sub-menus applicable to our services and has consulted with Computing Services on screen design and other patron-service issues. BUINFO will let patrons know what resources are available on campus networks and transparently connect the user to the resource, without requiring the patron to know specific network protocol, or even the network or host on which the service s/he is interested resides. Library resources appear as a separate sub-menu within BUINFO, but appear as the primary menu options on BLISS equipment in the Library.

Future development of the network server will include the implementation of "hot keys" for the most-used resources, so that certain critical functions such as "log-on," "help," and "quit" will be standardized, with the server providing the appropriate translation and transmission to the host service. Development of this capability will be labor intensive and heavily dependent upon hardware and software programs over which Bradley has no control, so we expect this to be the final component of BLISS to reach full implementation.

User Support and Training:

While the computer literacy level of Bradley's user population is high, and the information literacy level is increasing, the implementation of such a broad-ranging information management and delivery system requires substantial ongoing training and support. Much of the success of BLISS will rest upon the ability of the user to become aware of and to understand and control the available resources.

The Cullom-Davis Library has a strong tradition of service and end-user support in information resources, but we are finding that implementing BLISS services has overwhelmed our ability to maintain the level of documentation and training that we expected to provide. The Library organizational chart recognizes both "electronic services" and "information literacy" as critical functions in library activities. New staff members will assume responsibility for those activities during the fall of 1991. Plans call for online, interactive tutorials for the services, as well as written and online documentation, demonstrations, orientation sessions, and individual guidance in the use of BLISS and its resources.

Costs

It is difficult to assess the precise costs for BLISS. Much of the infrastructure and some of the equipment was already in place and dictated the directions in which BLISS was developed. AT&T provided much of the BLISS hardware and has

5 AT&T 6386/33S servers, in a variety of configurations	7 laser printers (variety of models and vendors)
28 AT&T 6386SX/EL workstations, with VGA monitors,	14 NEC CDR72 CD-ROM drives
	PagePower software
mouse, expanded memory, 40MB hard drives, and a variety of software	Informix software
	Variety of networked versions of applications software
StarLAN connecting hardware	1 Macintosh SE/30 server
StarGROUP operating system	9 Macintosh SE workstations
Gatorbox, EBIM and other bridging hardware and software	AppleTalk software
	Development of space to house servers
Simultask	Database design and implementation
Fax boards	Staff training and orientation
1 Hewlett-Packard Scanjet+ scanner	Development of training materials and programs

Approximate cost: $425,000

Table 17.1
Library components

provided substantial technical support as well. It is especially difficult to estimate the costs of those components of BLISS which are still being implemented. Tables 17.1 and 17.2, however, represent a general outline of the costs.

Hardware and software installation	Development and implementation of
Technical support from AT&T	document delivery
Development and implementation of MIC menu, software delivery, and linkages	Development and implementation of BU-INFO menu system
	Database programming and development
Development and implementation of CD-ROM network	Training and support for Library staff
	On-going technical support

Approximate cost: 3,000 staff hours

Table 17.2
Computing Services component

Evaluation of BLISS

Evaluation of BLISS is much more subjective than quantitative, since the goal of BLISS is to enable the Library to support all members of the Bradley community in meeting their information needs, whatever their chosen environment, format, or schedule. Usage information is being kept or will be developed for each BLISS application. While plans have been made for evaluation, implementation of evaluation is just beginning. However, evaluation will include these statistics:

Microcomputer Information Center use:
o Patrons per day
o Queuing for equipment use
o Pages printed
o Usage of individual menu choices

Using March 1991, as an "average" example, the MIC served 147 patrons per day, with a wait of .35 hours for access to the desired workstation, and a printing output of 74,200 pages.

Document delivery use:
o Annual number of document delivery requests received
o Annual number of documents delivered via the system
o Annual number of documents delivered by user (end-user or external agency) and by type of delivery
o Standard fax or computer-to-computer
[These figures will be collected in the future, but are not yet available]

CD-ROM network:
o Uses per day (total)
o Use per resource
o Queuing for resources
[These figures will be collected in the future, but are not yet available]

For other applications, evaluation is based upon factors other than quantity of use, including:

Database applications server:
o Functionality and value of application
o Timely development of application

Communications server:
o No more than 10 percent downtime annually in communication to any network or service
o Full implementation and functionality of "hot keys"
o Full implementation and functionality of menu system

Training and documentation:
o Full documentation for all services, in both print and on-line formats
o Variety of training programs and resources for all services, including interactive video, workshop, demonstration, and such.
o Development of an official credit or non-credit course on information literacy

As part of the evaluation of BLISS, it should be noted that there have been frustrations. From the Library viewpoint, one of the primary frustrations has been in the area of installation and implementation. Original timetables for installation of equipment and implementation of services have not been met for a number of reasons: delays in equipment delivery; unanticipated problems outside of the Library that sidetracked Computing Services personnel; unexpected incompatibilities in hardware and software selections; and an overly-optimistic original timetable. From the Computing Services viewpoint, the research and development component has taken more time and resources than was anticipated because some of the technology was either still in development or had not previously been implemented in our particular configurations. While all of our plans should have worked—and all equipment, software, and networks should have been compatible with minimal modification—the real world has not followed our careful plan and timetable.

Perhaps the best final measure of the success of BLISS will be the university-wide acceptance of information literacy as one of the key elements distinguishing a Bradley graduate. We have begun to use BLISS activities to create both improved campus access to information and a platform for promulgating the concept of information literacy.

Conclusion

BLISS is an ambitious effort to use the Library to provide a broad range of information resources and services in support of research and scholarship. BLISS is imbedded in technology and uses the technological infrastructure in delivery of these services. The success of BLISS, however, will be seen in the vitality and centrality of the Library to the academic life and success of Bradley, regardless of the technological platform.

About the Authors

Ellen Watson is Director of the Cullom-Davis Library, Bradley University since 1988. Previously, she was Director of the Learning Resource Center, Arkansas College and Acting Director of the Libraries, Community College of Baltimore. She received a B.A. from Wellesley College and an M.L.S. from University of Maryland. She is a member of the Illinois Valley Library System Advisory Council, the Illinois Association of College & Research Libraries/ Illinois Board of Higher Education Liaison Committee, ALA, and the Illinois Library Association.

Stephen J. Patrick is Director of Computing Services, Bradley University since 1989, managing academic and administrative computing and data networking. From 1976-1989 he worked for the University of Wisconsin-Stevens Point in a variety of roles, ranging from a trainee programmer to Director of Administrative Systems to Acting Director of General Services. He is also the founder and president of NUGATT, the international users group of AT&T networking users, and a member of the board of Heartland Freenet, a non-profit organization providing a free community service public-access electronic bulletin board.

18

A Novell Ethernet LAN at Central Connecticut State

John Rutherford
Elihu Burritt Library, Central Connecticut State University

ABSTRACT

In 1989-91 the Central Connecticut State University Library installed an Ethernet/Novell local area network (LAN) and CBIS CD-ROM server unit. The Novell file server and CBIS CD-ROM server effectively provide multi-user access to 14 discs housed in the central CBIS server. The file server stores one copy of the search software for each CD-ROM database, eliminating the need to install and maintain software on individual microcomputers. Librarians were involved with all aspects of the project from fund raising through design and installation. Issues related to equipment selection, network design, and network management are discussed.

Introduction

This case study describes the process of implementing a CD-ROM network within the Elihu Burritt Library at Central Connecticut State University. Unlike previous automation projects, where the Library contracted with outside agencies (OCLC, GEAC) for services, this project was initiated, designed, and funded entirely with library resources and personnel. The following study outlines our approach to planning, installing, and operating the LAN, and highlights key steps in the process.

Background Information

In approaching the project we realized that our proposed network would need to satisfy our immediate need for CD-ROM networking, and conform to long-range library and campus automation goals. To see how these issues affected our planning, selection, and implementation of a network system it is useful to look at our automation environment prior to the project.

Library Automation and Networks Before the Project

Central Connecticut State University (CCSU) is one of four campuses in the Connecticut State University system (CSU). Prior to installing our present network, automation at the Burritt Library consisted of a GEAC circulation system operated cooperatively by a group of Connecticut libraries including the four State University campuses, OCLC terminals for interlibrary loan and cataloging, one microcomputer used for online database searching by librarians, and four microcomputers used for end-user searching of several CD-ROM databases. Terminals connected to a network of Digital VAX computers located in the Computer Center provided local electronic mail and access to BITNET, as well as access to a few specialized databases mounted on the central VAX computer. The Faculty Computing Center, a microcomputing facility supporting courseware development, provided an additional computing resource available to librarians and CCSU faculty.

Initial planning for the installation of a fully-integrated online catalog was in progress, but issues of funding and politics among the four campus libraries made it difficult to predict when a system would be chosen and implemented. No network wiring was installed in the library prior to the CD-ROM project.

Campus Networks

For the most part, few campus buildings were wired for computer networks, though high-speed lines did connect the four campus computer centers with DECnet (Digital's implementation of Ethernet). Despite the lack of existing networks, it is clear that future networked computer applications, including the library catalog, must operate over an Ethernet network based on a combination of thick and thin coaxial wire, unshielded twisted-pair (UTP), and optical fiber cables. The choice of network protocols is less certain, but should certainly support both TCP/IP and DECnet at a minimum.

Designing the Network

Network Goals

Initially, the primary goal of our networking project was to improve access to CD-ROM databases, while laying the groundwork for an expanded library network. The following issues were considered to be key problem areas and objectives to be addressed by implementation of the network:

o To provide security for the CD-ROM discs by housing them in a network server located in our library computer lab.

o To allow multiuser access to each disc from any microcomputer connected to the network.

o To permit easy relocation of microcomputers due to planned library reorganization.

o To eliminate multiple copies of CD-ROM search software and the need to perform multiple installations when existing packages were upgraded by the vendor. Search software had to operate from the central LAN file server.

o To reduce costs by permitting the use of workstations without individual hard disk.

o   To provide access to CD-ROM databases to librarians and staff in non-public areas.

o   To permit wide area networking of CD-ROM databases over our future campus network.

o   To provide a general-purpose library network for future automation projects, including office automation, shared printing and communications, and the backbone for a building-wide cabling system.

In addition to these specific objectives, we hoped that the process of planning, selecting, and installing a local area network of this complexity would serve as an introduction to the implications of wide area networking for our library.

How the Network Works

For the network to satisfy our objectives it must allow access to centrally mounted CD-ROM discs from workstations distributed throughout the library. The ideal solution to our problem is to attach multiple CD-ROM disc drives directly to the file server, allowing the network administrator to map these drives to local PC drives with MS-DOS drive designations ranging from D: to Z:. This is difficult to accomplish since most LAN operating systems do not permit the direct attachment of CD-ROM drives to the file server and do not necessarily support the ISO 9660 file formats and Microsoft Extensions for CD-ROM (MSCDEX) required by many commercial CD-ROM search packages. To provide the functional equivalent of directly attached drives, special network software and hardware are needed to remotely map CD-ROM drives as local microcomputer drives.

CD-ROM Networking Technology

In brief, CD-ROM networking involves attaching a number of individual CD-ROM drives to microcomputers connected to the local area network cabling system. One way to achieve this is to attach microcomputers with internal or external CD-ROM drives to the network and share their drives among other network stations without CD-ROM drives. Software packages such as Opti-Net and Map Assist provide the software support for sharing CD-ROM drives over the network. This approach makes good use of existing equipment but lacks security since library patrons still have access to the computers containing the physical discs. Inadvertently removing a disk or turning off the PC will block at least one database from general network use.

A second technique is to attach a large number of internal CD-ROM drives to a relatively high performance microcomputer equipped with 2-8MB of RAM, and one or more SCSI interfaces. SCSI interfaces make it possible to attach up to seven CD-ROM drives in a daisy-chain fashion to each SCSI card. From one to three SCSI cards may be installed in one PC, permitting the connection of as many as 21 CD-ROM drives to one CPU. Additional tower-style computer cases are available that lack a central processing unit (CPU) but include built-in power supplies to operate the extra drives connected via the SCSI cables. Each server unit contains a network interface card that attach the CD-ROM server directly to the LAN. In most cases this is the only computer hardware required to build a CD-ROM server. It is also possible to assemble CD-servers using generic components for the cost of an inexpensive 80286 or 80386 microcomputer priced at $1500-$2500, and the required number of CD-ROM drives which are available for $500-$700 each. Preassembled CD-servers are also available from several manufacturers including CBIS, Meridian Data, and Online Systems. However, before the CD-ROM drives in a server unit can be shared among network users, it is necessary to purchase specialized redirector software.

Redirector software is loaded into the memory of each individual network workstation before accessing the discs in the CD-ROM server unit. This software allows remote cd-rom drives in the server to appear as local drives attached directly to the microcomputer. MS-DOS letter designations of D: through Z: are assigned to each active CD-ROM drive. During installation of the various search packages from companies such as SilverPlatter, Dialog, or UMI, the software is configured to assign one of these drive letters to the CD-ROM disc.

In addition to redirecting requests for files to the remote server, the CD-ROM networking software may also provide special caching services to speed access times, and may provide special management functions to enhance the use of the network. Depending on the vendor, this software is sold as part of a preassembled optical server unit, or may be available to install on your own CD-ROM hardware. Some vendors claim performance advantages if both software and hardware are purchased together, though, a more important consideration involves service—it is difficult for a vendor to isolate software problems from hardware problems if the CD-ROM server is home-grown.

The Design Process

The overall idea for the network developed while applying for a software grant from Novell Corporation. We applied through the Novell Educational Grants Program for a free copy of their NetWare SFT 2.15 network operating system. As part of the application, we outlined our plan for a LAN to be used specifically for CD-ROM networking. No design specifications were required at this stage beyond the general outline of purpose. After receiving notification that the grant had been approved, we were faced with developing a formal design and plan for implementation. To learn more about networking concepts and principles we studied texts on network architecture [see bibliography], spoke with other university computing departments, and consulted with several commercial networking firms. From the beginning it was clear that we could not afford to hire networking specialists to perform the entire installation. Consequently, we reduced the project to the following series of tasks that we would sub-contract to outside contractors or perform ourselves:

1. Design, install, and test the basic wiring system. [wiring contractor]
2. Install the Novell network operating system on the file server. [Novell reseller]
3. Purchase and install network interface cards in the Zenith microcomputers, and configure the network drivers. [library]
4. Select and purchase the CD-ROM server, and install it on the network. [library]
5. Install the CD-ROM search software on the file server, test for compatibility, and license the packages for network use. [library]
6. Select, install, and configure the workstation menu system, and set up the software metering system. [library]

After developing this plan, we requested vendors to submit bids for wiring and for installation of the network operating system. At roughly the same time we discovered that we had less money than originally estimated to complete the project, requiring yet further cuts to vendor-provided services. Installing the network operating system in-house would save enough money to bring the project back under budget.

Selecting and Installing Components

Wiring System

Most university computing environments depend heavily on large minicomputer or mainframe systems from IBM, DEC, or one of several UNIX-based equipment manufacturers. In most cases it is desirable to choose a wiring system that will allow maximum integration with existing campus networks and computers. For us Ethernet was the obvious choice because of our large DECnet system. However, Ethernet cabling systems can include different combinations of thick and thin coaxial cable, fiber optic cable, and unshielded twisted-pair wire (UTP), each with advantages and disadvantages under certain circumstances. However, the high cost of fiber-based systems and the lack of firm standards for unshielded twisted-pair wiring in late 1989 simplified our decision.

The price of fiber cable and the bridging components needed to connect network segments ruled out fiber for use within buildings at our university. UTP wiring was also ruled out due to the high cost of concentrator units and the lack of a standard for Ethernet over UTP wiring. Additionally, lab-style arrangements of computers are often easier to connect with linear, bus configurations than with star-based designs typical of UTP wiring.

Instead, thick-wire coaxial cable was selected for use as a riser, running vertically through existing conduit from the first to the fourth floors of the library. As the riser

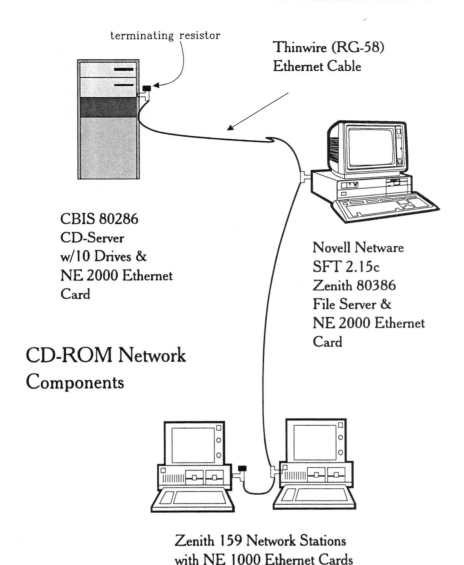

terminating resistor

Thinwire (RG-58)
Ethernet Cable

CBIS 80286
CD-Server
w/10 Drives &
NE 2000 Ethernet
Card

Novell Netware
SFT 2.15c
Zenith 80386
File Server &
NE 2000 Ethernet
Card

CD-ROM Network
Components

Zenith 159 Network Stations
with NE 1000 Ethernet Cards

Figure 18.1
Central Connecticut State Network Components

cable passed through wiring closets, several loops were made to accommodate
connection of future network components such as terminal servers, bridges and
repeaters. In two of the wiring closets (See Figure 18.1) eight port repeaters were

attached, allowing up to sixteen connections for thin-wire Ethernet segments. These segments would run from the repeaters through drop ceilings to library floors scheduled to receive network stations. Microcomputer network stations connect directly to the thin-wire cables via the BNC connectors on the Ethernet interface cards.

The bid for the wiring contract was awarded to Digital Equipment Corporation (DEC) on the basis of price and compatibility with our larger campus network. DEC sub-contracted the job to a local wiring and electrical contractor who installed and tested the cables.

File Server and Network Operating System

File Server

Selecting a file server and network operating system was easy, but installation was another matter entirely! Due to State and local university purchasing regulations, Zenith or IBM were our only choices for a file server. At the time, the cost of a properly configured IBM PS/2 model 80 and third-party MicroChannel Ethernet card seemed too expensive for our budget. Instead, we selected a Zenith 80386, 16MHz microcomputer with 4MB RAM and a 150MB Miniscribe hard disk drive with ESDI controller.

Network Operating System

A copy of SFT NetWare version 2.15, received from the Novell Educational Grants Program, was the first component of our LAN. We built our network around the NetWare operating system and selected other hardware and software components that were compatible with Novell. And while this is not necessarily the best approach to network design, conservative use of workstation memory, security, performance, and wide third party support set Novell apart from other competing systems at that time.

Most of our purchasing decisions were made in late 1989 when CD-ROM networking was not a proven technology. For the most part, CD-ROM networking in a campus environment depended on products from Meridian Data, CBIS, or Online Systems—all of which supported Novell. Additionally, Novell did not require the overhead of NetBIOS, leaving added memory for CD-ROM search software. Finally, performance, network security, and multi-protocol support provided by NetWare would permit us to build a large, general-purpose library LAN that could be bridged to the larger campus network in the future.

Our Crash Course in NetWare Installation:

The Novell NetWare series of network operating systems for 80286 systems are not designed for installation by novice users, although, as this is written, Novell has announced NetWare version 2.2 which is considerably easier to install. Installing

NetWare requires the installation of server hardware such as network interface cards and hard drives, testing and initializing the disk media, the infamous COMPSURF process, generating the network files, and finally configuring the workstation start-up files. At any point during this process hardware incompatibilities may halt the installation, generating error messages impossible to locate in any of the numerous Novell manuals. And while this may be rare, it certainly happened to us!

Novell assumes that NetWare will be installed by a certified NetWare reseller or Certified NetWare Engineer (CNE), both of which have access to Novell technical support services. Most installation problems can be quickly answered by experienced network administrators or technicians, though academic users, who typically cannot afford to pay for installation services, can easily fall through gaping holes in Novell's technical support system. We, unfortunately, were among this select group.

During NetWare installation, we encountered few problems, but later found that we could not allocate network printers properly. Naturally, we assumed this was due to our lack of experience with NetWare, and spent many hours looking for software installation problems, before finally tracing the problem to a defective parallel port on our Zenith file server. Similarly, attempts to initialize the file server hard disk drive, using the compsurf utility, failed due to inadequacies in the Novell COMPSURF program. The solution to this problem is well-documented and easy to cure provided you have access to Novell technical support, which, of course, we did not. Ultimately, we found the best source of support and technical information to be the BITNET-based Novell listserv NOVELL@SUVM, which is an incredible resource for information on all aspects of networking.

Adding the CD-ROM Server

One of our primary goals in establishing the LAN was to provide public access to CD-ROM databases while reducing the task of managing stand-alone stations. To do this we needed to concentrate the CD-ROM drives in a central server unit located in a non-public area, and to install all search software on a central file server. For this reason we decided to select a cd-server from either CBIS or Meridian Data, both of which had been successfully resold by SilverPlatter as part of their MultiPlatter configuration. And though a cd-server could have been built using Online System's Opti-Net software, it would have reduced total workstation memory due to Opti-Net's requirement for Netbios and Microsoft extensions (MSCDEX) at each workstation. For the same reason, we selected the CBIS server since it did not require the installation of MSCDEX at each workstation. Another factor that influenced our choice of cd-server units was the planned expansion of our campus network.

When the campus wiring project is complete, we will offer CD-ROM services to remote microcomputer users attached to the Ethernet. Unfortunately, in addition to standard network software, many CD-ROM systems require the installation of device drivers and Microsoft extensions at each workstation—a management problem we cannot afford under current personnel constraints.

The CBIS CD Connection software consists of a CD-ROM device driver installed on the CD-server, and the CDREDIR.EXE and CDUSE.EXE programs that redirect requests from search packages to the CD-ROM discs housed in the server unit. Since these files are executable programs, and not device drivers, they can be loaded either from the file server or from the local microcomputer floppy or hard drive. Any microcomputer, even diskless workstations, attached to the Ethernet can log into the CD-ROM network provided they have been given valid usernames and passwords. Of course, each users' machine must have the proper network start-up software, which for Novell consists of the network transport file IPX, and the NET3 or NET4 redirector programs, which can be provided by the computing department as part of the normal network installation process. Since the CBIS server does not need to access the file server, only the network transport software (IPX) is installed on the CD-ROM server.

Configuring Library Workstations

After testing the file and cd-rom servers, establishing a few basic user accounts, and installing the CD-ROM search software, it is time to do the real work of preparing the public workstations for unattended use. This involved the following steps:

1. Installation of Network Interface Cards
2. Crimping and attaching Ethernet cables to the workstations
3. Creating user accounts
4. Configuring menu software, metering, and providing network statistics

Installing Network Interface Cards

Our first workstations were 8088 Zenith 159 computers with hard disk drives, EGA monitors, 640K RAM, and Novell NE1000 Ethernet cards. Installing the Ethernet cards was uneventful (after reading numerous horror stories about interrupt conflicts between network cards and workstation hardware, we expected problems) the default settings did not require adjustments. However, when we later replaced these machines with 80286-based Zenith 212 computers it was necessary to experiment with several alternate settings before finding the correct match. After spending several hours yanking cards, pulling hardware jumpers, and regenerating network software, the conflict resolution features of more expensive IBM PS/2 computers can look very appealing, and considerably cheaper!

Attaching Ethernet Cables

Physically connecting workstations to the Ethernet should be easy, and probably is if you can find someone else to take care of the tedious job of preparing thin-net cable segments. Thin coaxial RG-58 Ethernet cable is connected to the interface cards with BNC T-connectors in a bus configuration. Each PC on the Ethernet segment is connected to the next with short lengths of cable running between the T-connectors. In addition, 50 ohm Ethernet terminators are placed at the ends of each segment and bridges or repeaters may be used to connect multiple segments. In our case, this meant outlining the exact configuration of our entire network, including the placement of workstations, in our specifications to the wiring contractor. We opted for crimping the cables in-house, which is a manageable task given the proper tools and a good deal of time. For future projects I will specify that the wiring contractor provide a number of preconfigured cables in a variety of lengths. But do not neglect to purchase crimping tools—no matter how detailed your plan—for workstations will end up in the most unpredictable locations!

Creating User Accounts

Most networks require users to have an account registered with the operating system. User accounts can be allocated to each individual user—a common solution in workgroups with a static number of users—or they may be assigned to a particular workstation. Since creating unique accounts or library users in a university environment is almost impossible, we decided to create a CD-ROM users group composed of one user id for each station on the network.

The general specifications for the CD-ROM user group include read-only rights to directories on the file server containing the CD-ROM search software, CBIS redirector software, and the NetWare network utilities. Additionally, each user account is assigned full rights to a permanent directory on the file server. This becomes the user's home directory and is dynamically mapped to the second network drive letter by the NetWare system login script. All CD-ROM programs are launched from this directory and may use this area for storage of temporary files or for downloading records to disk. The total disk space allocated to this virtual drive is limited to 1MB, and all files are deleted on a regular basis.

The Menu and Metering System

Library users cannot be expected to learn the details of launching programs from the MS-DOS prompt. Good menuing systems are essential for unattended network operations and should include additional modules for monitoring network usage statistics, and for restricting access to network software. At CCSU we purchased the Saber LAN Administration Pack, which includes a basic menu system, metering/statistical system, system security, and print management modules.

Creating menus with the Saber Software is fairly straightforward and requires that you create simple text files containing the commands needed to launch programs. After creating a menu script, it is compiled into a binary file with the Saber script compiler. To start the menu, you specify the name of the compiled menu script following the Saber Menu command: MENU CDUSERS.DAT.

On our system we use this command as the final line in our NetWare users login script, which displays the proper menu automatically on login to the network. Different menus can be attached to different groups or users. This allows us to tailor menus to the needs of different user groups or for individuals.

Description of the Current Library Network

The Burritt Library local area network now consists of a dedicated Novell file server, a CD-ROM server, seventeen microcomputer lan-stations, two networked laser printers, and four local ink-jet printers. The file server, CD-ROM server, and microcomputers are attached to an Ethernet cabling system spanning all four library levels (See Figure 182.). The specifications for the major LAN components are:

- o *File server:* 16 MHz Zenith 80386 with 150MB ESDI hard disk drive and 4MB RAM. The Zenith is shipped with two serial ports and one parallel port to which we added an additional parallel port for attachment of network printers. The VGA graphics adaptor was replaced with a Hercules monochrome card and a Zenith monochrome monitor to reduce costs.

- o *CD-ROM server:* CBIS CD Server with an 80286 CPU operating at 12MHz, 14 NEC CDR-80 half-height CD-ROM drives, 2MB RAM, two SCSI interfaces, a 1.2MB 5.25 inch floppy drive, an expansion chassis to house the second bank of CD-ROM drives.

- o *Network operating system:* Novell NetWare SFT 2.15C operating as a dedicated server. The Macintosh value added process (VAP) was purchased but has not been installed.

- o *Network transport and cabling system:* an Ethernet system was installed using a thick Ethernet backbone extending from the ground level to the fourth (highest) floor. Digital 8-port multi-port repeaters (DEMPR) are attached to the thick wire backbone at two points, with five thin net segments extending to the servers and microcomputer workstations.

- o *Ethernet interface cards:* 16-bit Novell NE2000 cards are installed in the CBIS server and in the Zenith file server. A combination of 8-bit NE1000 and Western Digital WD 8003 Ethernet cards are used in each of the microcomputer workstations.

- o *Workstations:* initially, Zenith 159 microcomputers with hard disk drives and EGA color monitors were used for network workstations. Most of these stations have been replaced with Zenith Z-212+, 80286 based microcomputers with VGA color monitors.

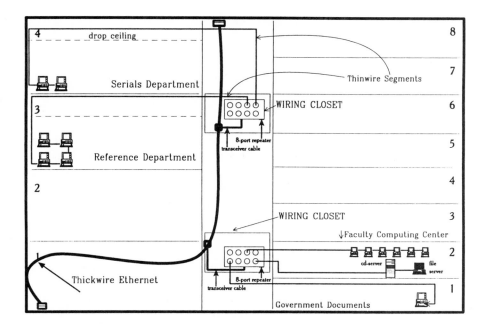

Figure 18.2
Network Diagram of Burritt Library LAN

Current Use of the Network

At present, the local area network serves two primary functions:

1. To provide access to the central CD-ROM server from public microcomputer network stations in the Serials, Reference, and Government Documents departments which are located on different floors.

2. To provide file and print services to 10-15 networked microcomputers located in the Faculty Computing Center on the second stack level of the library. Common applications such as WordPerfect, dBase IV, Microsoft Windows 3.0, Excel, PowerPoint, Quattro, and PageMaker are installed on the Zenith file server. Two laser printers are currently attached to the file server, which, to-date, are used only by the Faculty Computing Center.

The use of the network is divided between use by the library patrons exclusively for CD-ROM services, and by the faculty who use the computing center for development work, and for laser printing and desktop publishing. The dual nature of this arrangement has required special planning in the overall design of the network, choice of LAN components, and LAN administration.

How Much Did It Cost?

If any one factor guided our selection of equipment and implementation decisions, it was cost. Initially, we began the project with careful estimates of equipment and services needed to: (1) install our network with the least strain on staff resources; (2) provide maximum hardware support for future expansion; and (3) furnish adequate security equipment such as uninterrupted power supplies and tape backup units. However, after several rounds of cost reductions, we were forced to eliminate key equipment including a tape backup unit, power supply, and additional CD-ROM drives for our CBIS server. Additionally, installation services that we planned to subcontract to network vendors were ultimately performed by library staff. The first chart illustrates our original proposal prior to budget reductions, the second represents our final budget:

1. *Original Budget.* Originally the plan called for the installation of a 80386 file server with 300MB hard drive, uninterruptible power supply, Cubix modem board for remote dial-in, tape backup unit, and fourteen NE1000 and NE2000 Ethernet cards. Extra cards were ordered for future expansion, and Co/session and LANAssist software for dial-in access. CCSU would provide the Novell NetWare and the Zenith workstations. All installation, including staff training was to be provided by a Hartford-based networking firm. Ethernet cabling was to be subcontracted to a wiring firm by the network vendor and billed to the university as part of the total contract. The CD-ROM server would be purchased separately form CBIS.

File server and all network components, including all installation services	$20,352.00
14 drive CBIS CD Server w/software	$18,869.00
Ethernet wiring installation including all connectors and repeaters	$12,000.00
TOTAL	$51,221.00

Table 18.1
Network Costs

2. *Final Budget, After Reductions.* To significantly reduce costs, it was necessary to cut all nonessential equipment and services, including training. We reduced the number of CD-ROM drives in the server unit to ten, purchased a less expensive Zenith file server with 150MB hard drive, purchased only twelve Ethernet cards, eliminated the tape backup unit and all dial-in hardware and software, installed all network hardware and software in-house, and submitted the wiring contract for competitive bid.

Zenith file server, 12 Ethernet cards, Saber menu software	$ 6835.00
14 drive CBIS CD Server w/software	$16,469.00
Ethernet wiring installation (including all connectors and repeaters)	$11,436.00
TOTAL	$34,740.00

Table 18.2
Revised Network Costs

The second proposal realized over $16,000 in savings by forcing library staff to assume a much greater role in the installation and subsequent management of the network, and by limiting future expansion options. And while these reductions made it possible to obtain final approval for the network project, they were also the cause of several significant operational problems that would plague us in the future.

Evaluating the Project

Several months ago I would have rated our first network project as a complete success. We significantly reduced the time required to manage stand-alone CD-ROM stations by centralizing discs and search software, improved access to databases for library users, eliminated security problems and damage to CD-ROM discs, created a general-purpose library network for staff use, and reduced the cost of adding additional CD-ROM stations and databases. Library users have responded favorably—usage statistics continue to climb each month—and the system has been surprisingly stable for such recently developed technology. An additional benefit is the crash course we received in networking.

The process of designing and implementing a local area network has been a valuable experience for the participating librarians. Networking terminology and communications concepts are much better understood, and librarians now actively seek new projects for implementation on the LAN. However, the compromises we made to our original design specifications have now returned to haunt us!

The cuts in our original proposal are beginning to affect the reliability of our network through increased equipment-related downtime. Substituting the Zenith file server for the model recommended by the network vendor was a mistake. Problems with defective parallel ports, and an unreliable hard disk drive have caused the server to fail on several occasions. Without a tape backup unit, these failures required extensive work to reinstall software and create new user accounts. Worse yet, since we received our Novell software as a grant and did not contract with a vendor for installation services, we were on our own when it came to diagnosing and correcting specific problems. Yet another hardware problem that has recently shown up can also be attributed in part to cutting corners in our original specifications.

Our first proposal called for a CBIS server and expansion chassis with the maximum of fourteen installed drives. To save money we reduced the number of drives to ten, hoping to purchase additional drives at a later date. As Murphy's Law must predict, when we finally added the extra four drives, we discovered that one of the drives would not work. After many hours of troubleshooting and long-distance calls, it turns out that there was a problem with the server that never showed up in the factory (or in the first months of operation) because it affected only the thirteenth drive. If we had purchased the unit with all fourteen drives the problem would most likely have been caught at the factory, or soon after installation.

Looking Back

In evaluating our approach to designing and implementing our LAN, two problem areas deserve the most attention. First, allowing budget limitations to compromise the quality of key components was a mistake. Instead, we should have limited the scope of the project by limiting the number or workstations or purchasing only one bank of CD-ROM drives, rather than sacrificing quality. Each hour of unscheduled downtime we have experienced can be attributed to inadequate equipment. Second, we should have provided for technical support services from Novell or from an experienced Novell reseller. Properly installing and administering NetWare 2.1x requires information that is often available only from experienced NetWare administrators. Greater attention to both areas would have practically eliminated network downtime, reduced burdens on library staff, and saved money in the long run. As it turns out, we are now replacing our file server with a model more closely matching our original specifications, and have added tape-backup.

Overview

This was our first automation project designed and managed totally within the library. Like many projects in academic environments, our goals and objectives changed in response to available funding, and to the success of the initial phases of the operation. And, in fact, they are still changing! As technology changes and we further automate our library, I am sure that parts of our current network will take on a greater role in information sharing, and that parts will be scrapped entirely. However, the experience we gained has been valuable and will help us to better integrate library automation within the framework of a wider campus information system.

Bibliography

Bartee, T. 1985. *Data Communications, Networks, and Systems*. Indianapolis: Howard Sams.

Chou, W. ed. 1983. I, *Principles* Vol I: Englewood Cliffs, NJ: Prentice Hall.

Hancock, Bill. 1988. *Designing and Implementing Ethernet Networks*. Wellesley, MA: QED Information Sciences.

Martin, James. 1989. *Local Area Networks: Architectures and Implementations*. Englewood Cliffs, NJ: Prentice Hall.

McCusker, Tom. October 15, 1990. "Compact Disks on LANs." *Datamation* 36(20): 55-56.

Mendrinos, Roxanne. April 1990. "A CD-ROM Network Allows Multiple Users to Simultaneously Access Discs." *Electronic Learning*. 9(7): 32-33, April.

Quarterman, John S. 1990. *The Matrix: Computer Networks and Conferencing Systems Worldwide*. Bedford, MA: Digital Press.

Roberts, Lawrence G. 1974. "Data by the Packet." *IEEE Spectrum*, 11(2): 46-51.

Stallings, William. 1990. *Local Networks*. New York: Macmillan Publishing Company.

Stallings, William. 1990. *The Open Systems Interconnection (OSI) Model and OSI-Related Standards*, vol. 1 of *Handbook of Computer Communications Standards*. Indianapolis: Howard Sams.

Stallings, William. 1987. *Local Area Network Standards*, vol. 2 of *Handbook of Computer Communications Standards*. Indianapolis: Howard Sams.

Tanenbaum, Andrew S. 1988. *Computer Networks*. 2d ed., Englewood Cliffs, NJ: Prentice Hall.

Van Name, Mark L. June 1990. "A Natural Match." *Byte*. 15(6): 109-112.

Vendor Information

Artisoft Inc. (617) 969-2332

Artisoft Plaza, 575 East River Road
Tucson, AZ 85704
(602) 293-6363
LANtastic network operating systems

CBIS

5875 Peachtree Industrial Blvd.
Bldg. 100, Suite 170
Norcross, GA 30092
(404) 446-1332
CD-ROM network products, Network-OS

Colorado Memory Systems

800 S. Taft Ave.
Loveland, CO 80537
(303) 669-8000
Tape Backup

Meridian Data, Inc.

5615 Scotts Valley Drive
Scotts Valley, CA 95066
(415) 438-3100
CD-ROM network products

Novell, Inc.

122 East 1700 South
Provo, UT 84606
(800) 346-7177
Network operating systems

Online Computer Systems

20251 Century Blvd.
Germantown, MD 20874
(301) 428-3700
Opti-Net Software

Saber Software Corporation

P.O. Box 9088
Dallas, TX 75209
(800) 338-8754
Network menu software

SilverPlatter

1 Newtown Executive Park
Newtown Lower Falls, MA 02162
CD-ROM Databases, MultiPlatter System

Western Digital Corporation

2445 McCabe Way
Irvine, CA 92714
(800) 227-4637
Ethernet Interface Cards

About the Author

John Rutherford is director of the Faculty Computing Center, a library-based computing facility serving academic and library automation from Central Connecticut State University's Elihu Burritt Library. Prior to assuming his current position, he was assistant director of information services at the University of Petroleum & Minerals, Dhahran, Saudia Arabia. He received his M.L.S. from the University of Michigan, Ann Arbor in 1980.

19

Communication Is the Key:
Interconnected Multiuse Novell LANs

T. Scott Plutchak
Medical Center Library, St. Louis University

ABSTRACT

In 1989, the St. Louis University Medical Center Library installed a Novell local area network which connected three distinct physical locations. The Library's network is connected to approximately twenty other Novell networks in the Medical Center. The wide area network also provides access to the University's DECnet system and to BITNET electronic mail. Networking has had a dramatic and positive impact on the ways in which the library serves its clientele.

Introduction

In the best of all possible organizational worlds, the implementation of something as significant as a Local Area Network (LAN) is a careful process of reasoned examination, consideration of all possibilities, data gathering, evaluation, planning, budgeting, and carefully staged implementation. In the real world, it may be more a case of seizing opportunities as they arise. The St. Louis University Medical Center Library is firmly operating in the real world.

The Library first considered installing a LAN in 1988. At that time, there were several automated systems in the Library, but no integrated library system, per se (as of this writing in the spring of 1991, this is still the case). Circulation transactions were manual, cataloging was done through OCLC, the PHILSOM network (Periodical Holdings in Libraries of Schools of Medicine) was used for serials control, and a variety of online networks (DOCLINE, PHILNET, OCLC) were used for interlibrary loan. We were also implementing Library Corporation's Intelligent Catalog, a CD-ROM based, stand-alone catalog station.

Organizational Background

The University supports four major libraries: Pius XII Memorial Library on the main campus, Omer Poos Law Library, the Library at Parks College, and the Medical Center Library. The director of each library reports to a separate administrator, but all four sit on a Council of Library Directors which coordinates cooperative ventures.

In 1988, the Council began to plan for a University-wide Integrated Library System. This process was expected to take several years before a system would be implemented, however, so local area networking was investigated as a vehicle for improving existing services and as a platform for developing new services for our primary clientele at the Medical Center.

Our planning efforts have been guided by the Library's Strategic Plan, which was developed during an intensive two-year period, beginning in 1987. The Plan states: "The Mission of the Medical Center Library is to assure access to information and to assure the development of lifelong learners for the improvement of health." The first goal under that mission is "to play a pivotal role in developing information management policies and systems at the Medical Center." While planning for an integrated library system moved forward, we felt that a strong commitment to local area networking within the Medical Center would play a crucial part in meeting this goal.

Goals

Our primary reason for networking was to establish the Library's LAN as a significant piece of the "information infrastructure" at the Medical Center. Being one of the first departments in the Medical Center to network, we would place the Library in a strategic position to provide services as networks expanded and to influence information management policy.

Alongside this broad outlook, we were also interested in achieving some of the other efficiencies for which departments look into networking: the ability to share files and printers and to save expenses by using network software rather than single workstation software. However, throughout the planning and implementation of the network our primary focus was to establish communication links rather than to concentrate on any particular library system or subsystem.

Selection and Implementation

About the same time that the Library began to look into possible LAN implementation, Medical Center Computer Services (MCCS) was beginning a similar investigation. The MCCS investigation was constrained by their organizational situation. They operate strictly on a cost recovery basis providing VAX services and microcomputer support throughout the Medical Center. However, there is no central information authority at the Medical Center and MCCS has no mandate to determine policy or establish directions for the Medical Center as a whole. The University's main campus has an Office of Computing and Information Systems (C&IS) which, on paper, has responsibility for computing throughout the entire University; in practice, MCCS operates autonomously in cooperation with C&IS.

Given this structure, the strategy that MCCS adopted in order to establish networking standards was to become an authorized Novell dealer. This enabled them to provide equipment and software as well as onsite service and support at a lower cost than Medical Center departments could achieve outside of the University. They have marketed their products effectively and while departments still have complete freedom to utilize MCCS or to go outside the University, cost and connectivity considerations have generally led to the selection of MCCS as the vendor of choice. In effect, the MCCS strategy enabled them to implement *de facto* standards which could not be implemented by administrative fiat.

The Library was very eager to get involved on the ground floor of these developments and both the Library and MCCS came to the conclusion simultaneously that Novell was the vendor to use. Both departments were concerned with long term developments and were looking for a company that was financially stable, that was continuing to develop new products, and that was fairly well positioned to become a *de facto* standard. Novell met all of these requirements.

The fact that MCCS had elected Novell as the network of choice was in itself an important reason for the Library to be interested in Novell. Since the overriding goal of network development was to increase communications throughout the Medical Center we felt that it was essential to do everything possible to establish standards. The Library became the first department to contract with MCCS for network installation and until very recently, was the largest network on campus. Installation began in the fall of 1989 and was performed by MCCS staff.

The process was as follows: the file server was loaded with the Novell network software and the WordPerfect Office (WPO) shells and run through diagnostic tests in MCCS. The Library sent a preliminary list of users names and passwords to MCCS and shells for these users were configured. Simultaneously, an active hub was installed in the ceiling in the center of the main floor of the Library and coaxial cables were run through the ceiling and walls from the hub to each location that would have a networked computer. Once the cable was run, the file server was moved to its permanent location and connected. MCCS staff then went around the library to each computer and installed the network interface card and the batch files that were necessary for connecting to the network.

The installation proceeded virtually problem-free and was completed within about a week. Except for the brief period when a card was being installed, every computer was fully functional during the entire installation period.

Continuing implementation has been complicated by the fact that during the last year the Library has undergone significant renovation. Offices have changed location and the reference and circulation/interlibrary loan areas have been renovated on a grand scale. This has involved moving computers which had been connected to the network as well as adding additional computers. However, by working closely with MCCS we have been able to deal with the cabling problems very effectively. Where it was possible to anticipate the need for new cabling, we ran it in advance so that we were able to hook up computers as soon as they were moved. In some cases, however, it was not practical to move cabling in advance of moving computers. Fortunately, MCCS staff have always been available to recable and move systems in very short order.

As each workstation was attached and configured, users were given one-on-one instructions on how to connect. Classes on basic network operations were given by MCCS staff as each library department was brought on to the network.

Initially, each person's computer was configured so that work continued as usual, with login to the network as an option. As people became more comfortable with the network environment, AUTOEXEC.BAT files were changed so that the workstation would login to the network immediately upon being turned on. At present, all workstations connected to the network are configured this way. When a workstation is turned on, it prompts for a username and password which immediately brings up that user's WPO shell.

For the first year, the Library's network functioned in isolation from the rest of the Medical Center. Electronic mail was very heavily used within the Library, but there was virtually no connection to any other networks. In the summer of 1990, MCCS hired a network manager whose first task was to examine all the existing networks, resolving any lingering inconsistencies and then to implement WordPerfect Office Connections providing electronic mail between networks. The interface is set up in such a way that there is no difference from the user's standpoint in sending a mail message to someone on the same file server or someone on a different file server. This capability came up in the fall of 1990 and has begun to have a radical effect on the flow of information throughout the Medical Center.

In addition to the WordPerfect Office Connections software, each shell now also contains a menu selection "SLUNET." When this is selected, a terminal emulator program (EM320) is loaded, allowing the workstation to emulate a DEC terminal and connect to the Medical Center's VAX computer. From here one can log into the main campus VAX cluster which provides access to BITNET electronic mail. Although there is no automatic way to pass messages from one mail system to the other, this set of connections does enable every individual with access to a networked computer to also access the VAX computer resources.

The final piece worth mentioning is that it is also possible to dial-in to the network. MCCS has loaded a program called CO/Support onto a computer connected to the MCCS file server. This computer is called the "chatterbox" and contains two high-speed modems. If one has another copy of Co/Support on a remote computer, it is possible to dial-in to the chatterbox and connect to any file server on the network. At 2400 baud, the connection is too slow to do effective word processing, but there is a good file transfer capability that allows one to move files easily back and forth between a file server and a home computer. Several Library staff members have home computers and make extensive use of this.

Overall Configuration

The Library's network uses Novell NetWare software (Version 2.15), running on Arcnet cards over coaxial cable. Arcnet was selected by MCCS rather than Ethernet for several reasons. Although it runs considerably slower than Ethernet, it has certain advantages in being more fault-tolerant during installation and it is also much cheaper. Since MCCS had no previous experience with installing networks and funding would come from limited individual department budgets, Arcnet provided an attractive solution.

At the present time there is one library file server, an Everex 386. On the Library's main floor (second floor of the Learning Resources Center), fourteen IBM compatible systems are connected by coaxial cable to an active hub located in the ceiling near the center of the main floor. This hub is then connected to the file server.

In the basement of the Learning Resources Center, two IBM compatible systems, located in the Library's Video Production Services/Audio Visual Services office are connected to a separate active hub which is connected to the active hub in the library ceiling.

The connection of the systems in the Library's Educational Media Department, which is located in the School of Nursing Building across the street from the Learning Resources Center, is more complicated. Five IBM compatible systems are connected to an active hub located in the EMD area. This hub is connected to a second active hub in the School of Nursing Building which serves as a connection to the wide area backbone. A coaxial cable connects this hub to the MCCS file server, which passes the signal through another hub to the library file server. From the user's standpoint there is no difference in using a workstation in the Educational Media Department or one on the second floor of the Learning Resources Center.

As the accompanying diagram shows, signals originating on the library's file server can be routed to any of the twenty other file servers currently on the network. These other networks include several clinical departments, Medical Center Administration, the School of Nursing, Cardinal Glennon Children's Hospital, and the University Hospital, among others. Each network is separately password protected so that only individuals with an actual need can gain access to any particular file server.

Finally, the Novell campus-wide network is connected to the VAX computer maintained by Medical Center Computer Services over an Ethernet connection. This enables linkage to the VAX cluster at the main university campus one mile north. It is through the VAX cluster that one can obtain access to BITNET and thus, to international networking. As mentioned above, most connections to the VAX simply use an EM320 emulator. MCCS has also loaded Novell NetWare for VMS, letting the VAX act as another file server. Although limited use has been made of this capability to date, MCCS anticipates demand will grow.

Overall support and coordination of the network is provided by MCCS staff. In the spring of 1991, the Library hired a systems librarian, among whose principal responsibilities is to manage the Library's network. The systems librarian works closely with MCCS staff to insure coordination of efforts. This arrangement is extremely beneficial for us.

By the beginning of 1992, we anticipate connecting an additional three Macintosh SE computers to the network as well. Thomas Conrad Company (which supplies all the Medical Center's Arcnet equipment) manufactures Arcnet boards for the Macs. Novell provides a Value Added Product that will translate the Macintosh protocols to enable data to pass through the file server. The Macs will run the Macintosh versions of WordPerfect and WordPerfect Office.

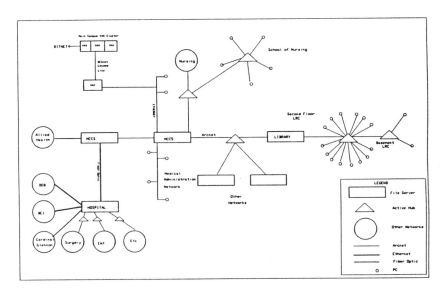

Figure 19.1
Diagram of St. Louis University Medical Center Networks

Users

At the present time, all Library staff have user rights on the Library's network and login at least once a day. Use of the network is dramatically tied to access to a workstation. While many of the staff (e.g., all of the reference librarians) have computers on their desks which are primary tools for their particular job, many others share terminals (e.g., the circulation staff). They use them almost exclusively for electronic mail and word processing. As might be expected, those individuals who work frequently at the computer have made more extensive use of all network features and are much more frequent and freewheeling users of electronic mail.

Beginning in the summer of 1991, we began prividing additional services across the Medical Center's campus-wide network including CD-ROM products such as Current Contents and the PC Physician. This may necessitate providing public access terminals so that students can gain access to some of those services. In addition, faculty and staff of the Medical Center who have access to other networks will also have selective access to certain library services. Because of the interconnection of the networks, it does not really matter which file server a desired program is on. Batch files can be created and accessed through the WPO shell to automatically log the user in to the appropriate file server.

System Use

All of the networks in the larger network system use WPO as a menu shell. This is a powerfully efficient system and we are extremely pleased with it.

WPO provides all of the standard "desktop" functions including personal calendar, calculator, database, scheduler, and such, as well as electronic mail. It can also be customized to provide menu guided access to software loaded on the file server or on an individual hard disk. This provides a great deal of flexibility. Some examples of this follow:

Everyone uses WordPerfect 5.1 for word processing. The WordPerfect 5.1 software resides on the file server and is configured in such a way that each individual's files are saved into their own secure subdirectory on the file server. Lotus 1-2-3 and FilePro are also on the file server. For network software, we purchase licenses based on the anticipated number of users. For WordPerfect, we use an educational site license. For Lotus 1-2-3 and FilePro, we obtained a limited number of simultaneous users based on our estimates of the likely use. If our network tracking indicates that we frequently run into the limit of allowable simultaneous users, we have the option of paying to extend the license.

Prior to establishment of the network, each of the three reference librarians used SmartCom II to access online databases. Each of their workstations is set up with a modem and separate Southwestern Bell data line that is separate from the Medical Center's telephone system. Rather than purchase a LAN version of the SmartCom software, we wanted to continue using the individual workstation copies already loaded on those hard disks. The WPO menu allows for this very simply. When a reference librarian logs in with her username and password, one of the selections on her menu will be SmartCom. When she selects that, the software is loaded from her hard disk. From her standpoint as a user, there is no difference between selecting Smartcom and selecting WordPerfect 5.1, which resides on the file server.

The only time this may create a problem is when logging into a different computer from the system one normally uses. The WPO menus are keyed to the username, not to the specific machine. If a reference librarian logs in on a workstation in technical services under her own username, SmartCom will still appear as a menu choice, but if she attempts to select that choice, WPO will return an error message saying, "program not found." She will still, of course, be able to use any programs that are loaded on the file server itself. While this is a potential problem, the actual number of instances in which this is likely to occur is so small that it has never resulted in any actual problems.

The WordPerfect Office menus can also be used to attach to a different file server altogether. This will become of increasing importance as more services on a variety of file servers become available.

Budget

Because we relied so heavily on MCCS for implementation of the network, costs have been extremely reasonable. As part of our cooperative arrangement, MCCS initially waived some of the labor costs since they were in essence using the Library as a beta-site for their own training. Our major costs were hardware (the file server and network cards) and the network software (Novell, WordPerfect Office)

The initial equipment setup which included the Everex 386 file server, one active hub, 12 Arcnet cards and associated connectors and cable came to $8,189. Labor for installation was set at a flat $1,000. The Novell NetWare software itself (for the 80 user version) was $2,500 and the WordPerfect Office software was purchased through a site license which enabled us to connect up to 40 users for $375.

The hardware connections to add the Video Production Unit and the Educational Media Department came to approximately $1,200. No additional network software was required since these areas were running off the Library file server.

In all cases, MCCS did the original negotiations and procurement. The Library simply paid MCCS through an interdepartmental order.

Budgeting for future costs has been somewhat problematic since MCCS has been moving gradually toward establishing fees for the provision of network management services. The Library pays on a time and materials basis for these services and during the two years that the network has been up we have paid MCCS approximately $5,400. This covers everything from adding new users to resolving network problems to running additional cable. With the hiring of the Library's systems librarian, we expect those costs to decrease in the coming year.

There is no separate special funding provided for network development at the Medical Center. The Library has certain discretionary funds available to it alongside the hard dollar University budget, so costs for the network were paid for by these funds and the regular operating budget.

Evaluation and Plans For the Future

There is no question that the implementation of the network has had a dramatic and far-reaching impact on the operation of the Medical Center Library. It has already provided us with benefits far beyond what we could initially see and we are very excited about the prospects it brings for the future. It has affected virtually every staff member and has consequently made us very dependent on the network.

The impact of electronic mail simply cannot be understated. It can have a tremendously liberating effect upon the entire organization. Although we anticipated that it would help us reduce some of our meeting time and would enhance communication among members of the Library staff, we could not have predicted some of the results that we have seen.

One particularly striking example was in the reference department. Prior to the Library's renovation, there were four staff members located in one not terribly large office with their work areas separated by six-foot partitions. We would not have expected there to be much need for electronic mail among members of the reference staff. However, in a busy reference department, when one needs to pass information along to a colleague, it frequently will require interrupting that colleague from her work with a client. If the information is important enough that it must be passed along then the interruption occurs. On the other hand, if the information is deemed not so important, it may be set aside for a time and all too often "slips through the cracks." With the availability of electronic mail, the reference librarians found that they could prevent either of these things from happening. They quickly became some of the heaviest users of electronic mail, sending messages to one another throughout the course of the day, greatly enhancing their ability to communicate with each other without jeopardizing their interactions with their clients.

The other fundamental benefit of electronic mail is somewhat more predictable and that has been dealing with library departments that are physically separated. As indicated above in the section on configuration, the Library is physically separated into three distinct locations. The LAN has enabled us to keep in close contact with each other in a way that was simply not possible before.

Now that the Library is network literate, we have a number of enhancements planned for the next year. They include: mounting the network version of Current Contents. This will be a cooperative venture with MCCS. The Library will fund the subscription and the Library's Systems Librarian will maintain the software but it will be loaded on the MCCS file server running under NetWare386. The MCCS help desk will provide triage for users, sending questions that are network oriented to MCCS staff and questions that are searching/information oriented to the Library.

The protocols established for providing access to Current Contents will be used to provide other sorts of services. Products currently being evaluated include the PC-SIG CD-ROM disk of shareware and the Physicians Medical Information Resource Guide.

We expect to implement a stand-alone CD-ROM network in the Library during the coming fiscal year. Once that network is operational it will also be linked to the campus network.

We have begun to receive requests for reference service, online searches, interlibrary loans, and document delivery over electronic mail. At present, these come in as regular electronic mail messages. We plan to create forms that individuals can pull up and fill in to more easily make such requests.

As we look down the road toward a University Integrated Library System it will be essential that any such ILS be accessible through the local area network.

Networking has literally changed the face of information use and management at the St. Louis University Medical Center. By adopting a proactive, cooperative policy that seeks to take advantages of opportunities as they arise, the Library has been able to position itself to effectively take on a central role in that development. From the standpoint of researchers, faculty, and students at the Medical Center, the very concepts of "Library" and "Computer Center" are changing. Our goal is that when a researcher turns on the computer and begins to select services from the menu it should be of no concern whether the particular package resides on the local file server, on the Library's, on MCCS's, or on any other server accessible through the network. We are beginning to see that vision coming to pass. The challenge for us is to continue to come up with innovative solutions for providing more services and more effective mechanisms of support to an audience that is becoming increasingly sophisticated and aware of the vast opportunities now before us.

List of Vendors

Digital Equipment Corporation
Digital Drive
Westminster, MA 01473
617-874-0111

Diversified Computer Systems
3775 Iris Avenue, Suite 1B
Boulder, CO 80301
(EM320)

Epson America, Inc.
P.O. Box 2854
Torrance, CA 90509

Everex Computer System Division
48431 Milmont Drive
Fremont, CA 94538
415-683-2247

Hewlett-Packard Company
18110 S.E. 34th Street
Camas WA 98607
1-800-752-0900

IBM Corporation
1133 Westchester Ave
White Plains, NY 10604
1-800-426-2468

Novell, Inc
122 E. 1700 S.
PROVO, UT 84601
1-800-453-1267

Lotus Development Corporation
55 Cambridge Parkway
Cambridge, MA 02142

Thomas Conrad Corporation
1908-R Kramer Lane
Austin, TX 78758
1-800-332-8683

WordPerfect Corporation
1555 N. Technology Way
Orem, UT 84057
1-800-541-5096

Zenith Data Systems
Hilltop Road
Saint Joseph, MI 49085
1-800-877-7704

About the Author

T. Scott Plutchak has been Director of the Medical Center Library at St. Louis University since 1989. He had previously served two years there as Associate Director. Prior to that he was at the National Library of Medicine, first as an NLM Library Associate and then as a Technical Information Specialist. He received a B.A. in Philosophy from the University of Wisconsin-Milwaukee, and an M.A. in Library Science from the University of Wisconsin-Oshkosh.

Acknowledgements

The author wishes to gratefully acknowledge the invaluable assistance of Suzy Conway, Assistant Director for Information Services, and George Booth, Systems Librarian, as well as the staff of Medical Center Computer Services, in the preparation of this article.

20

CD-ROM and Beyond: Networking in the Library with Novell NetWare

Maria R. Sugranes and Jonothon Cone
University Library, California State University, Long Beach

ABSTRACT

This chapter describes interconnected Token Ring and Ethernet networks using Novell NetWare, Opti-Net and Meridian Data components to provide access to CD-ROM products. The Novell network also provides shared access to software applications for selected library workstations. This chapter discusses problems of hybridization, wiring, making do with what you've got on hand, and potential for other network applications.

Introduction and Goals

CD-ROM networks at California State University, Long Beach Library have developed from fairly basic student needs, general strategic goals, and from the convolutions of a dynamic technology constrained by a limited budget. What follows is a description of a hybrid network created with a patchwork quilt methodology. The metaphor is not used idly. Ours is a frugal effort born out of necessity and some degree of ingenuity.

Our principal goal has been to deliver CD-ROM based bibliographic data to as many students as possible. The addition of a second library facility created a communications and delivery goal, namely to provide access to products at the two libraries. The second library was designed as an electronic library with universal or scholar workstations. This added the new objective of mounting PC software on the network. Since systems personnel would not be assigned to the new facility, remote management of the network also became important. Recognition that we were creating a powerful desktop system also implied that we could work toward the development of the universal workstation which would access CD-ROM products, online databases, our online catalog, local mini-computers and mainframes, PC-based products, and other sources on the Internet. All our work ultimately revolved around that possibility. Lastly, although the network was designed for student use, we wanted to ensure a capability for future expansion to library personnel in terms of access to the CD-ROM products, access to shared files and devices, and access to campus mainframes, including the Library's which hosts our online catalog.

Background

CSULB has an enrollment of approximately 32,000 students and is primarily a commuter campus, typical of Southern California. Computers are available throughout the campus, mainly in departmental computer laboratories. All the computer labs, including a general lab housed in the Main Library, are linked by a campus backbone through which students and faculty access various campus minicomputers, the Library's NOTIS online catalog, and computer systems on CSUNET, which provides gateways to BITNET and Internet.

Prior to 1989, the Main Library, which contains over one million volumes, had a total of four stand-alone CD-ROM workstations. The most popular products were ERIC, PsycLIT, MEDLINE, and CD Corporate. The workstations were also used for end-user online database searching, which created much congestion on these few units. As soon as CD-ROM networking technology became available, a library committee investigated possibilities and selected CD Net from Meridian, Inc. This configuration was outgrown almost before installation. Because of budgetary limitations, networking was not planned for the second facility, the North Campus Library. Immediately prior to installation there were personnel changes in the Systems department: a manager was hired as well as additional technical staff. Currently, the Systems department consists of eight technical professionals: PC/network programmer, PC support assistant, systems programmer (for NOTIS), mainframe computer operator, data entry clerk, two instructional computing coordinators involved in a separate non-library application computer laboratory, and a manager.

Users

The networks were designed primarily for student use. Although all librarians either have a computer or share one with another person, the emphasis has always been student and curricular support. Our first objective was to provide networked student workstations that would access CD-ROM products previously available on stand-alone workstations. Our next objective became to provide similar access from the instructional classrooms located in the Main Library and from the Reference Desk. The Library has an extensive bibliographic instruction program in which librarians demonstrate and instruct students in the use of our online catalog, COAST, a NOTIS system, and in various sources, particularly online or CD-ROM based services. It was imperative that the classrooms have access to the network since librarians could not check out a particular CD-ROM disk and use it even for a half hour without disturbing network use. Reference Desk access was also needed to provide ready reference support and to troubleshoot users' questions.

These access points are all in place at present and users seem quite satisfied with the system.

Still another objective is to address the needs of users who are asking for remote access to our CD-ROM products: faculty from their offices, students in departmental computer laboratories, students and faculty from their homes. Our online catalog is available remotely, why not the CD-ROM databases?

Although student use of bibliographic databases is the network's primary mission, now that the structure is in place, it is realistic to plan enhancements to meet other users' needs, namely, administrative, librarian and staff personnel desires to put "sneaker net" to rest. We could also provide, of course, CD-ROM access from librarians' offices. This idea is not being fully pursued at this time since there will be significant remodeling and construction in the Main Library. As funds become available and plans for the building remodelling settle, the network should grow to address these users' needs.

Computer Systems

The network started with a Meridian CD Net 100 optical server that housed five Toshiba SCSI drives. A 386 25MHz clone with 4MB of RAM and two 85MB hard disks was used as the Novell NetWare 286 v2.15 file server. The servers were attached via Token Ring to four Zenith AT class 640K computers. A second system was soon needed to service the recently completed North Campus Library. Given our limited budgetary base, we opted for an ALR 25MHz 386 with 4MB RAM and a Storage Dimensions 320MB SCSI hard drive for the file server, which would run Novell NetWare 386; a 25MHz 386 clone with 4MB RAM, and a small (40MB) hard drive for the optical server running Opti-Net CD-ROM networking software. These were in lieu of a second Meridian CD Net system, which would have proved costly. This equipment, along with NE2000 16-bit Ethernet cards and cabling and existing Hitachi CD-ROM drives, made up the new system. The workstations were again Zenith ATs, which were at that time obtainable from a campus contract. The two networks existed independently until the completion of a backbone drop to the new North Campus Library building. In order to connect the two networks using the campus backbone we acquired a Data Link Bridge, an intelligent broadband to baseband router, for the North Campus facility. A similar configuration was in place at the Main Library by virtue of the existing Computer Lab. The Computer Lab is heavily used by students, primarily for non-library applications such as access to mainframe or minicomputer datasets, computer programming, statistical packages and PC-based software. Upon installation of the connectivity equipment, the CD-ROM networks actually became one system with products being used by students in both facilities. Our latest additions have been upgrading of the first file server, centralizing the optical servers, and creating an IP Router using PC Route, a public domain software package.

System Use

People primarily use our system to access CD-ROM databases. We currently have ERIC, PsycLIT, Compendex, and MEDLINE mounted on the network. These products were selected by the Reference department and reflect student interest. There was much interest in Lotus's CD Corporate, but the network licensing costs were prohibitive. The products are accessible from seventeen student workstations, two classrooms, the Reference Desk, and the Systems department offices.

Novell NetWare can provide use statistics. After experimenting, we decided on a model and have been keeping accurate counts since the beginning of the spring 1991 semester. Breakdown of utilization is shown in Table 20.1 and is defined as any log on by a user to a particular product, not by the number of searches.

	MAIN	NORTH
COMPENDEX		
1990	562	852
1989	17	66
1988	18	59
1987	19	35
1986	24	25
1985	16	31
TOTAL	656	1068
ERIC 1980 +	562	334
ERIC 1966-1980	84 140	
TOTAL	646	474
MEDLINE		
7/90-12/90	166	134
1/90-6/90	60	48
7/89-12/89	37	37
1/89-6/89	33	38
TOTAL	296	257
PsycLIT		
1983 +	1211	479
1974-1982	124	107
TOTAL	1335	586
dBase	158	
Lotus 1-2-3	690	
WordPerfect	3177	

Table 20.1
Network Use Statistics
February - March 1991

An additional use of the network is access by selected workstations in the North Campus facility to a limited number of PC packages: WordPerfect 5.1, Lotus 1-2-3, and dBase III+. Although all the workstations could have such access, the interest in these programs is so overwhelming that the Library decided to limit access to six workstations rather than risk being inundated with PC users as opposed to library database searchers.

Access to these same programs by library personnel is under current consideration and in test. This article was composed in a Main Library office PC attached to the North Library file server that houses WordPerfect, and revised from another office in the Main Library. File sharing is economical and efficient. Administrative use of the network will undoubtedly occur, budget providing. Other contemplated uses are internal electronic mail and Internet access. Although both are available via campus mini-mainframe hosts, there are advantages to local connectivity: more direct and faster FTP and Telnet access are possible, as are simpler user interfaces and multiple sessions.

Selection/Evaluation

Meridian's CD Net 100 was purchased as soon as the technology was available. A library committee decided to acquire it after visiting an existing site. IBM Token Ring technology was chosen because of its established support. A small Banyan/VINES server was given to the Library by the campus Information Technology Services (ITS) department since the campus had standardized on Banyan/VINES previously and ITS was upgrading servers. When Systems personnel began the installation Banyan and Meridian were found to be incompatible. Banyan does not use IPX/SPX protocol required by Meridian, and would not be supporting it in the near future. The selection of new network operating system software clearly rested on Meridian compatibility. Novell NetWare was selected because it met that criterion. Other benefits included Novell's position as a market leader, its strong technical support, its reasonable price, and its potential expandability. A major consideration in Novell's favor was its ability to centrally control the network. Our license supports up to 100 concurrent users with expansion possible at a greater cost.

Our second installation allowed us to build on experience. Novell's performance in terms of installation, support, and user satisfaction was excellent. The Meridian CD Net was acceptable, but given in-house technical skills, we decided to look for a more open and flexible system that would allow us to upgrade easily with minimum expense. The objectives were still central control of the network, strong support, and reasonable costs. Consultation with other sites and conference attendance led us to select Opti-Net optical networking software from Online, Inc. Opti-Net allows for up to nine optical servers and thirty products per server. Each product can consist of a maximum of sixty-four physical drives. Eventually we reconstructed the Meridian unit to run the Opti-Net software. Budgetary constraints were the principal reason for the selection of Ethernet cards and thin-net (10Base2) cabling. Additionally, Systems personnel were familiar with Ethernet and Ethernet was the campus networking standard.

Installation

Installation of the networks was implemented in three stages: installation of the Main Library in late 1989, of North Campus Library in the summer of 1990, and connection of the two facilities by late fall of 1990. Continuing enhancements to both sites characterize the last stage.

The Meridian CD Net 100 on Token Ring was the first installation. Our programmer had networking experience with Novell so the actual work was not troublesome for him. The main problem was cabling. Having been on site for a short time, we did not feel confident working in the physical plant. It was difficult to find a company that would do a small cabling job in a state facility, and it was even more difficult to coordinate the efforts of that company and the local Plant Operations staff in coming to an understanding of our project. The only requirements were to string Type 1 cable around a room's perimeter and to extend it to the adjacent room where the servers were situated. Our plans had been to extend the network to the classrooms located on other floors. Given the bureaucratic difficulties, however, we opted to contract for wiring the one room and the nearby Reference Desk but to wait for classroom access.

The North Campus Library opened in February 1990, with six stand-alone CD-ROM workstations; funds were not then available for networking. Later on that spring, we were able to divert funds for the project and connect thirteen workstations to the network. We were now very familiar with Novell NetWare and found that the Opti-Net software was easily installed. Since our programmer had experience with Ethernet and student help was available to us, we decided that we could cable the site ourselves. The new facility had been designed with electronics in mind. A grid of conduit lay beneath the cement flooring and was accessible via communication closets. Although it was messy and arduous work, the cabling was completed quickly. It has yet to give us any problems.

As previously noted, the campus is connected by a broadband cable TV backbone with Ethernet support. Broadband Ethernet differs from baseband Ethernet in that it uses RF signalling; baseband uses varying positive and negative voltages. The Broadband Ethernet sends data over the campus cable TV network on two unused channels (one for transmit, one for receive). It requires a head-end unit that retransmits incoming data to outbound channels, amplifiers, splitters, and taps. The DLB bridges between broadband and baseband Ethernet. It has three component parts: a broadband RF modem, a baseband Ethernet card, and a data filter that route packets intelligently.

Administration of the backbone is managed by the campus Information Technology Services. A tap to the North Campus Library was finally installed in September 1990, practically the first day of the term. Although it might have been wiser to work during the next student break, we had a few duplicate CD-ROM products whose subscriptions were due; we therefore had to proceed quickly with the connectivity portion of the project.

The Ungermann-Bass Data Link Bridge (DLB) had been received. Installing it at North Campus Library was a matter of connecting a coaxial cable from the broadband tap to the DLB, connecting a cable from the back of the DLB to the existing baseband cable with an Ethernet transceiver, and plugging it in.

Installing the connection to the Main Library was more complicated. The plan was to tap into the existing DLB in the Library Computer Lab. Due to the distance constraints of thin-net cable (600 ft.), we had to move the file server from the second floor Reference area to the Library computer room, which is closer to the DLB. This would limit the total length of the Ethernet cable. In moving the file server we wanted to minimize any disruption of services. To avoid this, the CD-ROM search software was temporarily installed on workstations' local drives.

After moving the file server, the next step was connecting the Ethernet to our existing Token Ring. This could be accomplished by installing both Token Ring and Ethernet NICs in the same file server because Novell NetWare internally routes between different network media. Two Ethernet network interface cards were installed in the file server to complement the existing Token Ring card. Our student assistant made moving the file server possible by running Type 1 cable from the second floor MAU to the basement computer room and an Ethernet cable from the DLB in the Computer Lab, also in the basement, to the computer room. He ran another Ethernet cable from the computer room to the fourth floor Systems offices via the building's telephone wiring closets. This was needed to access network resources, manage the network remotely, and allow future connections to the network, but it also created a problem: the finished cable was almost a thousand feet long. Placing the two Ethernet cards in the file server allowed us to divide this segment, thereby overcoming the distance problem and speeding network response by separating library traffic from Computer Lab traffic. Using the Ethernet cards as a bridge saved us the cost of a dedicated bridge. We terminated the cables and connected the first of the two new Ethernet cards in the file server to the cable from the DLB without any interruption to the Computer Lab service. Next we connected the new Token Ring cable from the second floor to the existing Token Ring card in the file server. We then connected the new Ethernet cable from the fourth floor to the second of the new Ethernet cards in the file server. After rebooting the file server, and making some configuration changes to the software, everything functioned perfectly.

Although the two networks were now connected and the workstations could connect to both file servers, they still could not see each others' CD-ROM (optical) servers because one was running Opti-Net and the other was the Meridian system. At first we installed both the Opti-Net and Meridian software drivers in the workstations. It worked, but left much to be desired: local memory overhead was high because two different sets of drivers had to be loaded; drive mapping was not consistent; and access speed was different and somewhat perceivable. It seemed that managing the two programs would have been difficult over time. At this point we decided to explore the possibility of converting the Meridian unit to Opti-Net. Although the Meridian unit in whole is a proprietary software and hardware system, most of the hardware is generic: a clone 286 10MHz motherboard with 1MB RAM, 5 Toshiba XM-3201B SCSI CD-ROM drives, a monochrome video card, a floppy drive and controller, and an Emulex SCSI controller with a custom EPROM from Meridian. We contacted

Emulex to check if their card might work with Opti-Net. Unfortunately, Emulex didn't support CD-ROM drives and could be of no help. Meridian was undoubtedly not going to be helpful. The next best thing seemed to be to replace the SCSI card with an inexpensive one that worked with Opti-Net. After removing the Meridian workstation drivers and rebooting the "reincarnated" optical server, users had virtually transparent access to the entire network.

Hovever, there was a problem: when workstations at both the Main and North Campus Libraries tried to access the rebuilt optical server simultaneously, it crashed. To correct this we temporarily put a 386SX clone (the programmer's personal system) with more memory next to the optical server and transferred the Token Ring card and the SCSI card and cable to the clone. The SCSI cable was then connected to the CD-ROM drives in the former Meridian machine. This solved our problems. We concluded that the increase in speed and memory for cache was preventing overload. Since the "loaner" had to be returned, we decided to upgrade the file server's motherboard to a caching 33MHz 386 with the intent of using the original to upgrade the hybrid optical server. The displaced 10MHz 286 motherboard was saved for the next project.

With the network operational, we focussed our attention to further connectivity possibilities. Novell NetWare did not support TCP/IP on the file server or the workstations. As a workaround we decided to build an IP router that would be separate from the NetWare file server. We began by downloading public domain software packages from the Internet: NCSA Telnet, FTP, and Clarkson packet drivers. These programs were installed onto the programmer's office computer. The next step was to build the router itself. We downloaded another public domain package: PC Route, a PC-based IP routing software; took an old, broken XT clone, and installed the 10MHz 286 motherboard we had liberated from the Meridian optical server, and added two Western Digital WD8003e's; loaded and configured the software; and hooked it up in parallel with the file server to the DLB and the thin-net main trunk line to the fourth floor. All this now allowed individual workstations to access Internet hosts. This brought us closer to one of our underlying objectives, the creation of a true universal workstation that can access networked CD-ROMs, PC software, our online catalog, and other online catalogs simultaneously.

The next project was to add classrooms in the Main Library to the network. Again, departmental staff were responsible for the wiring. The classrooms were relatively distant from each other and from the file server. Given this distance Token Ring had to be used to connect the classrooms. Since we could not afford to buy new Token Ring equipment, we changed some of the workstations that were closest together to Ethernet, forming a small loop that would tap into the main Ethernet cable in the wiring closet on the second floor. We then installed the Token Ring cards in the classroom workstations and were going to run Type 1 cable from the MAU to the classrooms. Unfortunately, we only had enough Type 1 cable to connect one classroom. However, with a little ingenuity and some solder we connected to the other classroom using twisted-pair wire left over from another job. Although we were somewhat apprehensive about this arrangement, it has worked flawlessly.

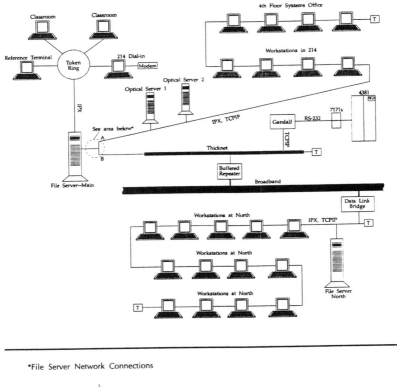

Figure 20.1
University of California, San Diego Library Computer Networks

The last enhancement was to relocate the optical servers to the computer room in the Main Library. One was at the North Campus Library hosting six Compendex CD-ROM disks; the other one was in the Main Library in the Reference department and thus accessible to many people. The reasons for the relocation were threefold. First, we had experienced problems due to dust particles getting into the CD-ROM drives and inhibiting their function. Second, we needed to manage Opti-Net from a central location since unlike Novell it cannot be remotely managed. Lastly, we needed convenient access to the optical servers in order to update or replace CD-ROM disks. The only change made was to replace the Token Ring card in the Main Library optical server with an Ethernet one.

At the moment, we are planning to add more workstations in the Main Library Reference area, but do not envision cabling any new locations. Remodeling plans are underway, and until those plans are solidified installation of new locations are on hold.

Costs

The Systems department is not allocated a definite budget every year. Although this can be obviously problematic, there is at least one positive consequence: if there is firm commitment to a project from all levels and confidence in the implementing personnel, the funds will be found. Hence, our planning and selection necessitated the utmost frugality with the allocations for the network being at best episodic.

CD Net	
Meridian server/software	7,481
Novell software and file server	8,554
Token Ring cards and MAU	5,595
Token Ring cable	2,598
North Library	
Novell NetWare (2nd copy)	2,000
ALR file server	6,792
Opti-net software	1,280
Clone optical server	2,027
Ethernet cards (25)	4,500
Ethernet cabling	851
Novell NetWare upgrade	3,500
Connecting the two libraries	
Data Link Bridge for North	8,542
ThinEthernet transceiver	280
Upgrades &installations to new locations	
File server motherboard	1,056
SCSI controller for Meridian server	359
WD8003e cards for IP router	333
CD-ROM drives (4)	2,942
Cabling and parts	603
TOTAL	59,293

Table 20.2
Network Costs

The initial installation was originally estimated at approximately $13,000. Funds had not been allocated for cabling or for the Novell file server and software since the available Banyan software/hardware was assumed to be compatible.

The funds for networking the North Campus Library were obtained by taking advantage of an opportunity. A California state lottery grant of approximately $56,000 had been awarded previously for the purpose of providing NOTIS access to North Library and other sites via the campus backbone. The equipment selected would indeed have allowed us to meet those objectives. However, a different, less expensive solution was devised resulting in a surplus of $25,000. In effect, we then had $25,000 for other connectivity support. Networking the CD-ROMs was the ideal project. We worked with that figure, making such decisions as buying Ethernet instead of Token Ring; slower servers that were reasonably priced; and cabling on our own, knowing that once the network was up, we would likely get further funds for needed enhancements. This indeed has occurred. Future costs will entail approximately $800 per CD-ROM drive and $180 for network adaptation of existing workstations. Ongoing costs are the subscriptions to the various CD-ROM services, some of which are higher for network use, and the annual Novell maintenance fee, $1,137 per copy for 100 users. Table 20.2 is a detailed listing of our expenditures broken down by installation episodes.

Evaluation

The CD-ROM network in place is used successfully by students, faculty, and librarians. Users cannot tell that there are two physical networks since access is transparent. Response time is perceived as equal regardless of the database being accessed. The network seldom fails, although this was not always the case.

Initially, users, particularly librarians, complained about the response time. This was particularly true of the Meridian CD Net configuration in the Main Library. The problem was solved by reconstructing the Meridian optical server, upgrading the motherboard, and adding more memory. We could have upgraded the Meridian system, but given the lack of funds, our own workaround solution was thriftier and very flexible. Thus it can no longer be said that we have a Meridian product since we adapted the server and are running Opti-Net software. (Meridian, Inc. recently announced that they will market a version of the CD Net software which doesn't require their proprietary hardware.) We also removed the local CD-ROM drives from the workstations that had them because some of the CD-ROM search software, like PsycLIT, would try to look at both CD-ROM drives—the networked one and the empty local drive. The time that it took for the software to determine there was no CD-ROM in the local drive was about a minute and a half, so users would have to wait patiently during this time while the program initialized. The drives we removed had been used to run CD-ROM products that are not licensed for network use. They will now be mounted on new non-networked dedicated CD-ROM workstations.

The Opti-Net software is able to host most CD-ROM products. The products that cannot be mounted on the network are ones whose workstation memory requirements exceed certain limits: 503K after Novell and Opti-Net drivers are loaded on an AT, 573K on a 386 machine with QEMM 5.11 (which are now only available in non-student locations), or, which bypass the Microsoft Extensions and access the CD-ROM directly. The products we now have use Dialog OnDisc and SilverPlatter software and work very well.

Performance of the Ethernet media has proven to be indistinguishable from that of the Token Ring. Up to this time the network's failures have been traced to insufficient memory or speed on the various servers. The network cards we purchased were not the most expensive available. So far none have failed.

Cost effectiveness is essential to further implementation of technology advances. Unfortunately, it is probably the weakest link in the evaluation process, particularly in non-commercial settings that are not dependent on quantifying their productivity. Without rigorously maintained use statistics it is almost impossible to quantify success or its counterpart. Nevertheless, cost reductions are now being realized by the need to acquire CD-ROM drives and network cards—not entire workstations--when the Library adds a major new CD-ROM title. Maintenance costs on the drives and the disks are being reduced since students no longer handle the equipment and disks. Although we may not have had equipment or software vandalism or theft because we had student assistants stationed in the area, we now know that disks cannot be stolen or drives damaged (someone did try to play an audio cd a few years ago). Indeed, student assistants need not be hired for security functions and can be wholly attentive to troubleshooting and otherwise helping users. Finally, the most obvious cost benefit for us has been the ability to subscribe to only one set of products and be able to serve fully two physical facilities on our campus. Installation of the connected networks saves us over $3,000 in annual subscription costs.

There are cost related benefits to networking that are not quantifiable. A stand-alone workstation serves one student. If another student needs to use the product, someone waits. What is a student's time worth? What does the Library loose by his or her inconvenience? How do you quantify user dissatisfaction fiscally? Conversely, having the product available to simultaneous users yields the potential of larger user satisfaction. Again, this is not quantifiable in dollars and cents.

A LAN management system yields excellent statistics. Thus, an additional benefit of our network is the ability to generate useful data for the librarian subject specialists who now can better decide what products to select, include on the network, or publicize.

Although not yet in place, there is a further benefit that is even more difficult to measure. When the products on the CD-ROM network become accessible to the various computer laboratories on campus we will be reaching a remote audience we may never have met. Strange as it may seem, some students never darken our doors. These students will now have research sources at their fingertips on their own turf. Undoubtedly we will gain many new users via this remote functionality.

Given our budget situation, it would probably have been impossible to install a LAN for librarian and administrative file sharing. The costs could not be justified. Had it not been for the need for the instructional application, the "administrative" functionality could not have been implemented. Thus, an added cost benefit of the

LAN has been the generation of a new application—one that would not have been developed on its own.

If we could redo the networking project what would we do differently? Hindsight is a great instructor. We all learned enormously from this project, but given the time and resource constraint we would probably not change much of our strategy.

Had present personnel been in place the Meridian technology might not have been purchased as quickly. At the time of selection, it was about the only thing available. Given a later time frame a more careful evaluation would have taken place, since there are now more options to choose from: LANtastic, CBIS, SilverPlatter, Ebsco. Nevertheless, clouded by the fact that Opti-Net and Novell work diligently, it is hard to fathom selecting anything else. Given our current staffing, we would again opt for an open system rather than a proprietary one. On the other hand, if technical personnel were not available a turnkey system would be the only viable option. Given our two locations, we would still opt for central control and for the client-server relationship rather than a peer-to-peer model. With more funds we would have purchased faster drives and bigger, faster servers at the outset. Given more funds we might have opted for twisted-pair Ethernet (10BaseT) over thin-wire Ethernet (10Base2).

Planning for future growth is the best part of our job. Planning with the knowledge that funds are not likely to be available forces creative impulses to the forefront. At present we are testing Pegasus E-mail, a public domain electronic mail package along with Charon SMTP mail gateway. The combination of Charon running on a dedicated old IBM XT with a network interface card in the computer room, and Pegasus installed on the file servers will allow library personnel to send and receive Internet mail without having to log on to one of the campus host computers.

We would like to offer off-site access to the CD-ROM products. We are experimenting with old IBM PCs which will be used as dial-in stations to provide remote access to the network via the campus port selector. Licensing concerns may not allow for this project to be fully implemented. We do, however, have agreements tied to the number of concurrent users which may make the user's point of origin irrelevant.

Given our remodeling situation, it would be unwise to add many locations in the Main Library building at this time. Since construction will span eighteen months to two years, however, we may proceed to wire a few administrative workstations and enable that staff to share Lotus 1-2-3 files and WordPerfect documents. We have cable and the workstations in place; the additional costs would be network cards.

Some of our plans will unavoidably have fiscal impact. We would like to make the CD-ROM products available to the departmental labs connected to the backbone. This would require adding a bridge in parallel with the Banyan/VINES servers since they do not route IPX packets. We would also like to add Macintosh support to our network. We could do this by adding a LocalTalk card to the file server or connecting a LocalTalk card to an EtherTalk box such as Kinetics FastPath

Product Description	Vendor/Source
Software	
CD Net	Meridian
Opti-Net	Online Systems
NetWare	Novell
WordPerfect	WordPerfect
dBase III+	Ashton-Tate
Lotus 1-2-3	Lotus
MS DOS Extensions	Microsoft
Packet Driver	splicer.cba.hawaii.edu:/ncsa
PCRoute	splicer.cba.hawaii.edu:/pcroute
NCSA Telnet	splicer.cba.hawaii.edu:/ncsa
Pegasus Mail	splicer.cba.hawaii.edu:/pegasus
Charon	splicer.cba.hawaii.edu:/pegasus
Hardware	
ALR file server 386/25;4MB;300MB Storage Dimensions; 64K cashe	ALR distributed by OverByte
Optical Server: Clone 386/20; 4MB;40MB disk	Micro Telesis
CD Net Model 100 286/10; 1MB; 5 CD-ROM drives	Meridian Data
File Server: Clone 386/25; 4MB; 64Kcache 2-80MB disk	Intl. Data Systems
Data Link Bridge	Ungermann Bass
Router	Old Meridian motherboard and PC case
WD8003e cards for IP router	Alliance/Infonet/Valcom
ThinEthernet transceiver	Ungermann Bass
File server : 386/33; 4MB; 64k cache	K-Tronics
AT-Bus SCSI controller	Online
Hitachi CDR 1700	Hitachi distributed by Laser Resources
Token Ring MAU 8228-001	IBM
Token Ring NICs 3391	IBM
Token Ring cables, adapters	IBM
Ethernet cards WD8003E NE2000	Alliance Infonet/Valcom
Cable	
Type 1 plenum cable	IBM
ThinNet cable, plenum	Anixter
BNC connectors (male)	Anixter
BNC Ethernet terminator (50 ohms)	Anixter
BNC Inline Coupler (female)	Anixter

Table 20.3
Products and Vendors

and enhancing the Novell software. Another idea is to create an outbound modem
pool to connect to commercial online services. Attaching a dedicated PC with a string
of modems to the network would accomplish this and take us to the creation of the
ideal universal workstation

All these projects are within our reach. Given some funding support we will be able to accomplish them and thus better serve users at CSULB.

Vendor Addresses

Alliance/Infonet
3505 Cadillac, Bldg. D
Costa Mesa, CA 92626
(714) 966-2500

ALR: Overbyte Computers
21502 South Main St.
Carson, CA 90747
(213) 518-3002

Anixter
4905 E. Hunter,
Anaheim, CA 92807
(213) 585-3217

K-Tronics
14388 Hoover St., Suite A9
Westminster, CA 92683
(714) 897-3234

Laser Resources
6285 E. Spring St., Suite 103
Long Beach, CA 90808
(213) 521-9071

Meridian Data Inc.
4450 Capitola Rd, Suite 101
Capitola, CA 95010
(408) 476-5858

Novell
610 Berryessa Road
San Jose, CA 95133
(408) 729-6700

Online
20251 Century Blvd.
Germantown, MD 20874
(301) 428-3700

Ungermann-Bass
4675 Macarthur Court, Suite 470
Newport Beach, CA
(714) 955-1414

Public Domain Software

Splicer.cba.hawaii.edu is an excellent source for anonymous FTPable netware: patches, utilities, upgrades, applications. Another source is sun.soe.clarkson.edu.

About the Authors

Maria R. Sugranes has been Manager for Automated Systems at the University Library and Learning Resources, California State University, Long Beach since June 1989. Previously she was Manager of Northrop Corporation's corporate office Library in Los Angeles and Systems Librarian working on various databases for the corporation. Other experience was Coordinator of Bibliographic Instruction at Cal State Long Beach and Coordinator of Media Services for the Huntington Beach Union High School District in Huntington Beach, California. Ms. Sugranes has an M.L.S. from the University of Southern California and an M.A. in Instructional Media from California State University, Long Beach.

Jonothon Cone joined California State University Library and Learning Resources in November 1989 as Assistant Systems Software Specialist. His previous jobs include work for various consulting firms specializing in networked-multiuser systems. Mr. Cone has his B.S. in Computer Science from the University of California, Riverside.

21

The Davis Reference Information Network: The Development and Management of a Multiple Function LAN in an Academic Library Environment

Tim Bucknall, Rikki Mangrum, and Will Owen
Davis Library, University of North Carolina, Chapel Hill

ABSTRACT

Davis Library, the main research library at the University of North Carolina at Chapel Hill, implemented a local area network in 1989. The LAN utilizes an Ethernet bus topology to link fifteen MS-DOS microcomputers to a Novell 386 file server running NetWare 286. The Davis Reference Information Network performs a wide variety of functions, of which the most heavily used is the U-Search CD-ROM service. This service provides eight public search terminals with access to both a local CD-ROM drive and the fourteen networked drives of a Meridian CD Net. The entire network is developed and maintained in-house and is constantly evolving to meet the growing and changing needs of the Library's clientele.

Introduction

Late in 1988, staff in Davis Library at the University of North Carolina at Chapel Hill began to plan the implementation of its first local area network. The primary goals of this project were to explore the networking of CD-ROM products, to investigate the impact of LANs on reference services to the university community, and to begin cooperation with other units on campus in the shared provision of information resources and services.

Davis Library is the central research facility in a multi-library system which also includes the R. B. House Undergraduate Library, Wilson Library (special collections), and ten departmental libraries. (Separately administered Health Sciences and Law Libraries are also present on campus.) Within the main library, the Humanities Reference Department and the Business Administration/Social Science Reference Department have coexisted since the 1950's. Over the years, the two departments had each evolved independent policies and procedures designed to serve the differing needs of their respective clienteles. Since Davis Library opened in 1984 with the two reference desks located, face to face, within one hundred feet of each other, the spirit of independence has been replaced by a growing desire for cooperation and the joint provision of services. The implementation of a local area network provided an important opportunity for the two departments to work together toward that goal.

At the same time, a "federal" model of computing and information services was emerging on campus. In this model, the Library, the academic and administrative Computing Centers, various independent research units such as the Institute for Research in Social Science, and other distributed centers of computing and information services maintain their traditionally autonomous modes of operation. While remaining independent, these units cooperate to plan and implement solutions to the information needs of the entire university community. Access to electronic databases is a fundamental part of this service, and the installation of a local area network within the library, connected to the broader campus network, was seen as a key area for exploring the integrated development and management of these services. With these goals in mind, and at the invitation of Novell, Inc., Davis Library forwarded a proposal for the funding of a campus-wide program of information resource management.

Hardware Configuration and Network Implementation

In 1989, a grant from Novell, Inc. to the University of North Carolina provided the Library with a LAN file server, twelve network interface cards, and network software. The Academic Affairs Library provided the network stations and cabling. The Library also funds the licensing and administrative costs of all bibliographic databases, machine readable data files, and software made available on the LAN.

The LAN hardware centers on a Novell 386 file server equipped with a 150MB hard drive running NetWare 286 Advanced v. 2.15 Rev. C., and a Meridian Data CD Net optical server housing fourteen CD-ROM drives. The file server is perhaps the weakest link in the network; the one time that the server suffered a sudden power loss, the hard disk was irreparably damaged and had to be replaced. We have since installed an uninterruptible power supply to ward off a recurrence of that disaster, which brought the network down for nearly two weeks. Luckily, at that time we were still in the early stages of implementing and testing the network, and service to the public was not seriously disrupted.

NetWare 286 is an excellent network operating system. Installation is menu-driven, and extremely intelligent. If a series of operations is required during installation, likely default choices are highlighted as you move through the menus. The network supervisor must supply information about the type of hardware present in the file server and in the stations on the network. Once all configuration information is complete, the installation routine optimally configures the operating system to the installed hardware. Thus, the software operates at maximal efficiency; however, any change in the hardware platform will require a regeneration of the operating system. Given the ease of system generation, however, this is not a serious problem.

A broadband network connects most of the buildings on the UNC campus. This backbone provides the basic connectivity for all computer systems on campus, and has many different "channels" (much like cable-TV channels) in operation. One of these channels is devoted to interconnecting Novell networks via an interface card made by Allen-Bradley. We have installed this Allen-Bradley card in our file server, and thus have access to any other Novell network so attached to the campus broadband.

Within the Library, fifteen MS-DOS microcomputers are connected to the network via an Ethernet bus topology. Four of these are for staff use, and support routine office automation activities such as word processing and database management in addition to providing access to the CD-ROMs for reference purposes. Of the public-access stations, eight are used exclusively for searching bibliographic and full-text databases on CD-ROM, one is dedicated to running an automated reservation system for the public-access terminals, and two primarily provide access to government information now being released on optical discs. All of these public stations have local printers attached, and all have local CD-ROM drives as well as access to the networked drives in the Meridian CD Net.

Much of the workstation equipment now connected to the network was already owned by the library, rather than selected specifically for the CD-ROM network. A mixture of IBM, Zenith, and generic clones in PC, XT, and AT classes are utilized. As a result of the lack of standardization, subtle and not-so-subtle differences in equipment required time-consuming adjustment before all terminals were working smoothly and dependably. At present, the LAN uses four different types of network cards with a total of six different jumper settings, and a variety of different software utilities and environment settings at each terminal.

The networking software used at every workstation consists of a network shell composed of two parts: IPX, which directs messages to the file server or to other parts of the network, and NET3, which directs workstation activities either to DOS or to NetWare. The 3 in NET3 indicates that it operates with DOS version numbers starting with 3; other versions of NET are available to operate with earlier or later versions of DOS. The shell must be correctly configured for each type of Novell or Novell-compatible network card used. The Novell operating system provides a program (SHGEN) which generates IPX for each type of network card. SHGEN can be run from a floppy disk, a hard disk, or a file server. In addition to taking into account the type of network card used, the SHGEN program configures IPX to allow for the interrupt and I/O base channels used by the card. Different computer models may require different settings in order to avoid conflicts with other hardware devices such as hard disk controller cards, CD-ROM driver cards, and video display cards. In our case, we had not kept records of the interrupt and I/O base channels used by such devices and had to experiment with different jumper settings at each terminal until we found a configuration that would work. Each new setting required reconfiguring the network shell. In addition to using SHGEN, a utility program called DCONFIG can be used to configure the IPX program for a different jumper setting. Needless to say, we now keep records for all settings on all devices attached to each terminal.

Each workstation requires a copy of Microsoft Extensions for CD-ROM program (MSCDEX.EXE) to allow access to CD-ROM drives. MSCDEX works in tandem with device drivers for each type of CD-ROM player used by the station; device driver software is loaded at each workstation by the CONFIG.SYS file. Most workstations on the Davis Reference Information Network require two device drivers, one for the local CD-ROM player and one for the Meridian Data CD Net. MSCDEX and the device drivers indicate to the system how many CD-ROM servers and CD-ROM drives of each type to expect and assigns each drive a drive letter. MSCDEX can be run either from the file server or from the workstation and must in either case be loaded after all networking software has been loaded. Currently, MSCDEX resides on the hard disk of each workstation, allowing us to continue operation of the local CD-ROM player even if the file server is down.

The Meridian Data CD Server can be operated using IPX alone, or can be operated using NetBIOS in addition to the other parts of the network shell. NetBIOS is an emulator program that allows NetWare to handle applications that were written for IBM networks. The Davis Reference Information Network operates using NetBIOS. Using NetBIOS in addition to IPX and NET3 allows us to preserve local RAM by configuring workstations to access only a specified number of CD-ROM drives in the Meridian unit. Running under IPX/NET3 alone, each workstation would have to load all fourteen drives. Because each drive occupies 8K of RAM, using only IPX/NET3 would leave very little memory for search software. Currently, most workstations use NetBIOS to load MSCDEX for four CD-ROM drives in the Meridian unit. A set of programs provided by Meridian Data allows us to select which four of the fourteen CD-ROM drives are assigned to an available MSCDEX logical drive. MOUNT allows interactive selection and deselection of available discs. CMOUNT allows command driven operations. We typically use CMOUNT commands included in a batch file to mount the correct disc(s) for each database. MOUNT can be used to bypass batch files when necessary. The CMOUNT command instructs the system to load each disc by name into a specific MSCDEX drive. The disc's volume label displayed by MOUNT or on the CD Net status screen is the disc name used in these commands. MOUNT references MSCDEX drives by letter, as does DOS, but CMOUNT uses numbers. MOUNT and CMOUNT cannot manipulate a workstation's own CD-ROM player and the drive letter assigned to the local drive by MSCDEX cannot be reassigned to any other physical or logical drive.

All facets of hardware and software installation and maintenance of the Davis Reference Information Network have been managed in-house. This includes planning of the LAN layout, cabling, installing network cards, installing software, and designing and implementing the end-user interfaces for each type of terminal. Since the proposal submitted to Novell included the general purpose of the public services LAN, we were able to complete much planning for the network's configuration and function in advance. A great deal, however, was worked out by tackling projects one at a time and balancing the planned development with what would actually work. At the time the project was first conceived in 1988, we were aware of no similar network which had been successfully completed, so all those involved in planning and implementing the system were working in unknown territory. Cooperation with staff working on somewhat similar projects at the UNC Health Sciences Library and at the School of Information and Library Science, as well as with the University's Networking Systems office, was vital in many cases.

The physical structure of the reference room, in which the LAN is located, did not easily accommodate networking. The desirability of a location close to the reference service desks and removed from quiet study areas, as well as the need for adequate electrical outlets and false ceilings or conduits through which to run the Ethernet cable, restricted the number of choices for a physical location. As a result of these requirements, we selected an area between the two reference desks. Although this has contributed to congestion in the area and to a rather high level of noise at the reference desks, it represented the best compromise of service and technical requirements.

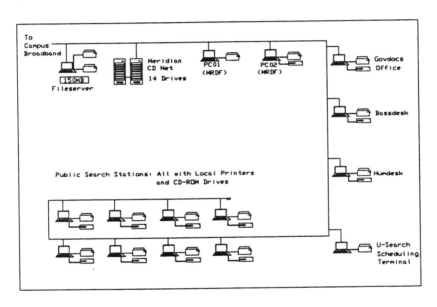

Figure 21.1
Davis Reference Information Network Diagram

Costs

Funding for the LAN project has come from several different sources. The workstations already owned by the Library and used for CD-ROM searching before the LAN implementation were purchased using equipment funds from the Library's operating budget, supplemented by trust funds. We estimate that we paid approximately $4,000 per workstation to acquire them four to five years ago; they would probably cost little more than half that today. The file server, network operating system software, and network interface cards which we received from the Novell grant would have been valued at approximately $10,600. Those elements of the network were in place at the end of the 1988-89 fiscal year. In the following year we budgeted $20,000 for the purchase of the Meridian CD Net, which was our major acquisition for the year. In fiscal 1990-91 we budgeted $23,000 for the acquisition of four additional workstations, network interface cards to attach other PC's in the two reference departments to the network, spare parts to provide the basis for an inventory against emergencies, security devices and new furniture for the workstations, and replacements for two of the older Zenith XT's. We will also upgrade some of the older equipment to insure that every machine on the network has a hard disk and that most are equipped with color monitors. As we continue to expand the LAN, we expect to continue to fund new hardware acquisitions. To date, capital expenditures for the LAN's physical plant total about $85,000, including the value of the Novell grant.

A major component of ongoing costs is supplies, including printer ribbons, paper, toner cartridges, and diskette and tape backup media. These costs vary over time, but between $3,000 and $5,000 a year must be allocated to cover operating expenses. We should note that we request patrons to limit their printing to fifteen pages per appointment, and that we encourage them to download citations to floppy disks rather than printing them and consuming library supplies.

Database license fees and the acquisition of non-bibliographic data files are the other major category of expenses related to the LAN. Database license fees, including multi-user access fees, for the Davis Reference Information Network amount to approximately $28,000 per year. Another $2,000 to $3,000 a year is typically spent for the non-bibliographic data files housed in the Library's Machine Readable Data Files Center, but accessible via the LAN.

Personnel costs are much harder to assess. Two reference librarians and one systems librarian are responsible for the planning and implementation of the LAN, in addition to their other duties. Another reference staff member performs many of the routine chores of supply management, backup, and local database maintenance. All staff in both reference departments handle patron inquiries about the service, assist users at the terminals, and respond to the mundane problems of paper jams and worn-out ribbons.

Apart from the personnel costs, we therefore estimate approximately $30,000 a year in software and data charges, $5,000 for consumable supplies, and $15,000 for hardware, maintenance, and physical plant expenses, for an average annual cost of $50,000. It should be noted that these costs are for the Davis Reference Information Network alone and do not reflect additional expenditures of approximately $20,000 a year for InfoTrac (located in the R. B. House Undergraduate Library) and several CD-ROM databases which reside in other departmental libraries.

The U-Search CD-ROM Service

The Davis Reference Information Network performs a wide range of functions. The network is used to share word processing, spreadsheet, and database programs among the staff, to facilitate interdepartmental communication, and to enhance access to the library's machine readable data files collection. The primary and most developed function of the Davis Library LAN is to provide multiple-user access to data and bibliographic databases on CD-ROM. The bulk of this access is through a service called "U-Search," which consists of eight public terminals accessing up to fifteen CD-ROM products on a combination of local and networked CD-ROM drives. The service has proven to be immensely popular, with up to 4,000 uses in a single month.

The U-Search Service originally began in 1987 with each of the two reference departments offering its own independently administered and physically separated CD-ROM service. Neither department opted to dedicate one terminal for each database. Instead, each department installed search software for all of their databases on each of their search terminals; users would then check out the CD-ROM disk from the appropriate reference desk and search from that department's search stations. Demand grew quickly and soon sign-up sheets became necessary to cope with the growing number of users. As the library added more databases, providing the service became increasingly problematic. Maintaining separate terminals and databases, handling a sign-up sheet on which the most heavily used databases were often booked for days in advance, and trying to explain differences in departmental policies all became a burden on the reference staff. In addition, the system restricted access by limiting all databases to a single user. The opportunity to network, while presenting some short-term problems, provided a long-term solution.

Our decision to combine networked and local CD-ROM drives was largely dictated by the fact that we had twenty-six CD-ROM discs and only fourteen drives in the Meridian CD Net server. Rather than dedicating some stations to network access and others to stand-alone products, we opted to increase flexibility by providing both options at each station whenever possible. Because we could not network all databases, we decided to network those which had proven to be the most popular with our users. Thus, ERIC, MLA Bibliography, ABI/Inform, PsycLIT, and Compact Disclosure discs were placed in the Meridian Server. GPO was also added because of its value to the documents staff. We continue to circulate the remaining products— Newspaper Abstracts, Periodical Abstracts, Dissertation Abstracts, Electronic Encyclopedia, Books in Print Plus, PAIS, Sociofile, Religion Index, and the Oxford English Dictionary—from the reference desks for use in the local CD-ROM drives.

The U-Search Service is available to a diverse clientele, including graduate and undergraduate students, faculty, staff, and local residents. We provide two levels of user support. Each search station has a notebook containing one page of locally developed basic instructions and documentation for each database. Additional assistance for more complex problems is available from either reference desk.

The automated scheduling system for the U-Search Service is perhaps a feature unique among CD-ROM LANs. Although the LAN development staff and both reference departments would have preferred a non-scheduled "first-come first-served" operation, we felt that this would prove inordinately complex for patrons because of the wide range of factors which must be taken into account before it can be determined if a given database will run on a given terminal at a given time. To deal with the complexity of reserving time for patrons on fifteen databases used on eight terminals for varying lengths of time, while accommodating user preferences for floppy diskette size and keeping track of incompatibilities between terminals and databases, an electronic scheduling program was designed and programmed in-house. The scheduling interface of this Clipper-compiled dBase program is available directly to users, who book their own reservations on a dedicated scheduling terminal. Additional features available to staff include the ability to review and print the day's calendar of appointments, to cancel reservations, and to search the calendar by patron name. Lists can be searched by database or by terminal, so that patrons can be notified in case unexpected problems occur. Like all parts of the network, the scheduler is subject to revision and improvement.

Functionality of Specific CD-ROMs on the Network

The fifteen CD-ROM databases currently accessible through the U-Search service are produced by seven different vendors. The oft-lamented and well documented lack of standardization among vendors has had many implications for the development and implementation of the Davis LAN. Memory requirements vary among vendors, which affects our ability to run certain databases on machines with less available RAM. Differences in video display requirements also create incompatibilities. One vendor no longer supports PC-DOS machines, but requires XT or higher to function properly. While some products are easily installed and work well in a networked environment, other products have labyrinthine installation procedures, provide slow access, and perform poorly when networked.

Davis Library currently subscribes to two Wilson CD-ROMs, the MLA Bibliography, which is networked, and the Religion Index, which is not networked. Wilson is perhaps the most idiosyncratic of the vendors. Contrary to the current trend, they do not provide a fully networkable product, nor do they charge extra for simultaneous disc access. Although Wilson's CD-ROMs may be read by several users concurrently, their search software may not; search directories installed on the server may only be used by one person at a time. Therefore, we run the Wilson software from a local hard drive wherever possible. We have, however, been forced to create a search directory on the server to support access from one staff terminal which does not have a hard disc.

The installation of search software directly to the server is not supported by Wilson version 2.2 and must be accomplished by installation to local disc and subsequent transfer of the files to the server. Several attempts and calls to Wilson technical support revealed that, for search software run from a server, the CD-ROM drive type must be installed as "magnetic" regardless of the type of drive the server actually supports.

Regardless of whether the Wilson software is installed on the server or locally, it still requires more RAM to run than is available after attaching to the network. Because we could not afford memory upgrades for all of our machines, we instead purchased Quarterdeck's Vidram program, which releases graphics memory on EGA and VGA cards to increase total usable RAM to 736K. We have found that although Wilson's products are somewhat difficult to install and that they require extra RAM to run on our network, these faults are balanced by the lack of network licensing fees and by the relative stability of their software in our network environment.

UMI is the vendor for four of the CD-ROM subscriptions which we currently receive. ABI/Inform runs from the CD Net (although limited to a single user at a time), but Periodical Abstracts, Dissertation Abstracts, and Newspaper Abstracts are run only on local CD-ROM drives. In our original network configuration, all of our UMI products except Periodical Abstracts were networked using UMI search software version 1.5 and were accessible from several terminals simultaneously. Unfortunately, the network became afflicted with a mysterious malady which caused it to lose track of the Meridian unit containing the fourteen networked CD-ROM drives. This, of course, brought all searching to a screeching halt. The problem was resolved when the UMI discs were removed from the network. Apparently, the network was unable to keep track of the large number of temporary files which were being created by the UMI software, especially when a single product was being searched by several patrons simultaneously. We now avoid this problem by allowing only one user at a time to search ABI/Inform, the only UMI product which is now in the Meridian CD Server. We plan further tests of network compatibility with later releases of the UMI software.

Another serious problem with the UMI software is the length of time it takes to load products mounted in the Meridian CD Server. In our network environment, the single ABI/Inform disc takes about one minute and forty seconds to load on a Zenith XT, while Dissertation Abstracts, spread across four discs, takes almost three minutes to load.

UMI's CD-ROMs, whether networked or not, have been the least stable of the products on the Davis Reference Information Network. They have been the most prone to crash inexplicably in the middle of a search, and are the only multi-disc sets that require the user to go through a special routine to change discs. For these reasons, UMI products have thus far proven to be the least satisfactory of our major products. We hope that these problems will be resolved by the version 2.3 UMI software which we have recently received but not yet tested.

The product which functions most capably on our network is Compact Disclosure. It has rarely crashed, even when the network itself has been unstable. Its software can be run successfully from either the local drive or from the server. As an added bonus, the search software can be installed from the CD-ROM disc itself. On the down side, the Compact Disclosure software always looks for the disc in the first logical CD-ROM drive. Because we have chosen to mount Compact Disclosure on the Meridian server, we are required to mount a server drive, rather than the locally attached drive, as the first logical drive. If the local drive is defined as the first logical drive, the search software searches the empty local drive and aborts without checking network drives. While this quirk poses no logistical problems at present, we have learned that any lack of flexibility in the networked environment is the harbinger of trouble.

From SilverPlatter we receive GPO, PsycLIT, and ERIC, all of which are networked, and Sociofile, which is not networked. The search software is run from the server. Generally, these products run smoothly and reliably. However, we have discovered and overcome two quirks in the SilverPlatter software version 1.6 to make their products run more quickly and effectively. The first trick is to include in the batch file which calls the search software a "dir d:" command, where d: is the CD drive you wish to search. This command should be placed after the discs are mounted but before the search software is loaded and will improve response time significantly. The second quirk in the software is its requirement that the first drive in the CD Net contain a SilverPlatter product, even when the local CD-ROM drive is being searched. Therefore, the batch file which runs Sociofile on the local drive "h:" also loads GPO on network drive "d:" and executes a "dir d:" before calling the search software. Since these two anomalies in the software were discovered and their solutions implemented in the batch files, SilverPlatter products have been relatively stable on our network, although they do occasionally lock up in the middle of a search.

We have no plans to network the CD-ROMs produced by our remaining three vendors, Tristar Publishers (Oxford English Dictionary), Grolier (Electronic Encyclopedia), and Bowker (PAIS and Books in Print), primarily because of their relatively low use. There are, however, implications for running these discs on a local CD-ROM drive attached to a networked station. The batch file which calls the Electronic Encyclopedia must also switch Vidram off because Grolier makes use of the graphics display. Books in Print Plus has great difficulty in running, even with Vidram on, since it requires 539K of free RAM in order to load the search software. Largely as a consequence of its gluttonous memory requirements, we have decided not to renew our subscription to BIP.

Selected Problems and Their Solutions

The implementation of a local area network to support simultaneous multi-user access of CD-ROM databases has eased many of the problems caused by our former departmentally divided, single-user configuration. Policies have been examined for fairness and consistency. Waiting times for access to the most popular databases have been greatly reduced. As a result, overall use statistics have skyrocketed, with patrons having nearly twice the access to databases as they had prior to networking. However, the network has introduced certain new complications which require attention and consideration.

Although scheduling CD-ROM appointments solves some of the problems of licensing restrictions and of terminal/database incompatibility, it also presents problems of its own. By assigning searchers to half hour or full hour slots, scheduling creates an intrinsic inefficiency. When patrons use less than their allotted time, their search station is likely to stand idle until the next person arrives. Although we do allow drop-in use of partially unused and forfeited appointments, patrons are often reluctant to use the system without an appointment.

Sometimes patrons attempt to use more than their allotted time. Although this has proved to be only an occasional problem, it is one which usually necessitates intervention by the reference staff. It requires both diplomacy and a firm hand to remove a patron who, oblivious to the fact that he is inconveniencing the next appointment, has literally waited until the last minute to begin printing the fifteen pages of search results he has obtained over the past hour of searching.

Overall, neither patrons nor staff feel that the problems caused by scheduling appointments have significantly degraded the U-Search system. Staff are seldom required to police what has turned out to be an essentially self-regulating appointment system, and patrons seem happy to trade optimal usage of search terminals for guaranteed search times.

To maintain compliance with license agreements which allow fewer than eight simultaneous users, we acquired the Saber Menu system along with Saber Meter. The metering program allows the menu system to track the number of simultaneous users of a database and to prevent use which exceeds that allowed by the license agreement. This allows us to purchase, for instance, a four user license for a database, even though we have eight public access terminals. The scheduler will only book four appointments for that database at any given time, and the meter program will prevent a fifth user from accessing the database.

The Saber Menu system allows a programmer to declare certain menu choices to be contingent upon factors such as the type of hardware present, the user's login profile, etc. This means that a single menu program will appear slightly different on each terminal. For example, the ability to run Wilson software is dependent on the presence of an EGA or VGA video adapter (which we use Vidram to borrow memory from), so Saber Menu displays the Wilson databases menu item only on terminals equipped with such hardware. The flexibility of Saber Menu is also important for presenting appropriate options for formatting floppy disks, depending on the type of installed drive. It saves a great deal of staff time if users are presented with only the formatting option that applies to their particular terminal.

Probably the most serious problem with the networked U-Search system is one which we have yet to find a way to effectively overcome. By allowing self-scheduling and direct patron access to CD-ROMs, the librarians have essentially removed themselves from the search process and are no longer able to determine if patrons are using effective search strategies or even searching an appropriate database. When cleaning up the search terminals' hard disks we routinely find downloaded files with names like "ABI" or "PSYCLIT" saved in the MLA directory. The problem of patrons using the wrong database is exacerbated by users who do not exit the search software at the end of their search. When this occurs, the next person often erroneously assumes that the database on the screen is the one that they wish to search. This is particularly true when the database on the screen is produced by the same vendor as the database that they want to use. For example, an experienced ERIC user seeing the introductory PsycLIT screen might assume it was ERIC, not realizing that both products use the same basic SilverPlatter software. Although in some instances this problem can be avoided by shortening the time-out option which returns the system to the main menu, this solution is not viable in our situation because we generally have a large turnover in a very short amount of time when appointment periods end.

One problem which is of concern to every network supervisor is security. Our first level of defense against abuse of the U-Search system is the Novell security software, which has proven both effective and easy to use. The Novell package provides a wide range of security options which can limit access to the system or to selected directories by time or by station. This versatility has come in handy on a number of occasions. Recently, for example, a user has repeatedly accessed our network from another location on campus, logged in as "supervisor", and attempted to guess the password. Although the chances of anyone successfully deducing the password are quite remote, we deemed it prudent to enable "supervisor" login only from terminals within the Davis Library building.

Prior to network implementation we discovered that students had installed personal software on our CD-ROM search terminals. This type of misuse of the local hard drive is now precluded by Saber Menu, which presents each user with a list of databases which may be accessed from that terminal, but does not allow the user to exit to DOS. Instead we have provided a menu choice which enables the patron to select and run frequently used DOS commands, including formatting and displaying a directory of a floppy disk. A final security precaution which we have been forced to take (because of a past incident of theft) is the removal of all keyboards during times when the library is open but the reference departments and U-Search service are not (chiefly the hours of 10 PM to midnight).

A final drawback to the Davis local area network is the substantial amount of staff time which is required to keep it operational. Although system maintenance and troubleshooting have decreased dramatically since the initial period after network implementation, the complexity of the configuration and the age and diversity of the public search terminals necessitate significant staff involvement. One of the most frustrating maintenance problems is the "ripple effect" which occurs when one change results in a host of new problems. For example, because we did not have enough RAM left after loading network software to run some packages, we decided to run Vidram in the AUTOEXEC.BAT. Some terminals could not run Vidram, however, because they do not have EGA/VGA monitors, so those packages which require extensive RAM must be removed from the menus of these terminals. In addition, the scheduling program must be configured so that it will not assign those memory intensive packages to the terminals which do not run them. Meanwhile, for the machines with EGA/VGA monitors, Vidram must be turned back off in the batch files which run programs requiring graphics capability (e.g. Grolier's Electronic Encyclopedia). Between these types of changes and normal maintenance, it seems rare that a week goes by without the service demanding some sort of attention from the system supervisors.

Impact of the LAN on CD-ROM Use

Two interesting observations can be made from the usage patterns of the CD-ROMs accessible through the U-Search Service. First, the amount of use varies greatly from package to package (see Table 21.1). The top three products account for almost 50 percent of public searches, while the three least used products make up less than 2.5 percent. Second, most searches are relatively brief in duration. Over 50 percent of searches take less than twenty minutes, while searches over seventy minutes comprise less than 4 percent of the total.

DataBase	Networked Use?	# of Network users	Use 7/90 to 3/31	% of use
ABI/Inform	Y	1	3835	18.3
Books In Print	N	1	372	1.8
Compact Disclosure	Y	1	1313	6.3
Dissertation Ab.	N	1	1343	6.4
Electronic Ency.	N	1	189	0.9
ERIC	Y	No Limit	2586	12.4
GPO	Y	No Limit	682	3.3
MLA Bibliography	Y	No Limit	2023	9.7
Newspaper Ab.	N	1	895	4.3
Oxford Eng. Dict.	N	1	113	0.5
PAIS	N	1	1360	6.5
Periodical Ab.	N	1	1059	5.1
PsycLIT	Y	8	3587	17.1
Religion Index	N	1	183	0.9
Sociofile	N	1	1378	6.6

Table 21.1
CD-ROMs Available on U-SEARCH

The conversion of the U-Search service from stand-alone to network access has greatly changed the number of CD-ROM uses at Davis Library. During the fiscal year beginning July 1989 and ending June 1990 we had 14,673 total uses of the two Humanities Reference and four Business Administration and Social Science Reference CD-ROM stations. After the two search areas were consolidated to form the current U-Search service and the network was implemented in September 1990, the number of searches has increased dramatically. The number of searches from July 1990 to February 1991 has reached 18,109, as compared to 9,417 uses over the same period last year. Even given that the number of search terminals was increased by two (or 33%) for most of the current fiscal year, this accounts for only a portion of the almost 100 percent increase in CD-ROM use.

In fact, there are a number of reasons for the recent surge in CD-ROM usage in Davis Library. Two of the reasons are directly related to networking the service. Obviously, the ability of the LAN to allow multiple simultaneous access to some of the most heavily used products has decreased waiting times and limited the number of vacant machines. Perhaps a more interesting reason, and one which we had not anticipated, has its basis in human psychology. As numerous studies have shown (and as any reference librarian can tell you), many patrons are loath to ask for assistance. By implementing electronic self-scheduling, by networking the most heavily used discs, and by moving the stations further away from the reference desks, we have inadvertently increased usage by allowing U-Search patrons to utilize the service without having to "bother" the reference staff.

Other Uses of the LAN

Although the primary function of the Davis Reference Information Network is to provide public access to CD-ROMs through the U-Search Service, the LAN also performs many other valuable functions. The LAN has greatly expedited staff work by allowing the sharing of office software across the two reference departments at a lower overall cost than purchasing individual software copies. It also allows for the sharing of files, simplifying group project work. Statistics on the use of software and CD-ROM databases are cooperatively collected and processed on the network, greatly simplifying this monthly task. A single staff member can handle tasks such as routine backups, maintaining the scheduling program, and routine disk maintenance for both departments. This not only results in a more efficient use of staff time, but ensures that regular backups of critical files are made and that stray and temporary files are taken care of quickly.

Broadband connections to other UNC file servers allow staff to experiment with new or upgraded software purchased by other departments, while broadband connections to mainframe services facilitate the use of electronic mail and access to specialized databases located elsewhere on campus. For example, reference staff in Davis Library can search the Louis Harris Poll data, administered at another site by the Institute for Research in Social Science. Use of the electronic mail services has also increased dramatically in both departments, since staff no longer have to compete for the terminal equipped with a modem.

Staff on duty at each reference desk can use the desk terminals to access CD-ROM databases for ready reference as well as internal files and programs used routinely in assisting library users. Commonly used staff applications include a catalog of locally held machine readable data files; a special scheduling program interface which allows cancellation of CD-ROM reservations and viewing of the day's U-Search appointments; a utility which sends closing messages to all terminals fifteen minutes prior to termination of service; an easy way to send messages between desks without tying up phone lines; and ready access to networked CD-ROMs, including GPO, which has proved invaluable to the documents staff. During quiet periods at the desk, staff can use the terminal to work on projects or read electronic mail if they choose.

For the end-user of the Library's Machine Readable Data Files Center (a separate collection of primarily statistical information in both magnetic and optical formats), the LAN enhances and simplifies access and use. Commercial software such as dBase is available for manipulating data extracted from these files, even on workstations which lack hard disks. If the user wants to manipulate the data with software the Library does not own he or she may be able to use software residing on another server on the campus networks. Similarly, users logged in to other servers can also apply for a guest account on the Library's server, and request that specific data files be loaded for their use from the remote location. This is particularly useful to individuals extracting large amounts of data from federal data sets, such as the Economic Censuses.

Evaluation

Despite a few initial (and perhaps inevitable) problems when the LAN was first implemented, the Davis Reference Information Network has proven to be an enormous success. The network has enabled us to provide more people with greater access to more information. In fact, the service is now so popular that it has become a major problem to schedule downtime to experiment with the system or to make major changes.

The overall functionality of the Novell network and Meridian CD Net server has been good. Search response times have been relatively quick, system failure has been rare, and no significant hardware problems have been recently encountered.

The Davis Reference Information Network has also proven to be cost-effective. For the 1990-91 fiscal year we project that more than 25,000 CD-ROM searches will be conducted, for a cost to the Library of $50,000. Thus, each search costs less than $2, a fee which seems very reasonable when compared to the price of equivalent online searches.

Perhaps the most significant step in the evolution of our network was the decision to develop the system in-house rather than to pay a vendor to supply a turnkey system. Although this decision saved money by allowing us to use the wide variety of search terminals already owned by the library, it also forced us to implement complicated policies, procedures, and technical solutions in order to accommodate the diversity of terminal types. More importantly, however, by opting for an in-house development we were able to custom design a system which meets our specific needs.

In-house development has necessitated a great deal of staff involvement, not only in establishing the system, but also in its daily maintenance. This high degree of involvement has made staff familiar with numerous aspects of the Davis Reference Information Network. Thus, technical problems can be handled internally without having to rely upon the vagaries of a vendor supplied support staff. In addition, overall knowledge of the network has made reference staff aware of system limitations and potentials and has allowed them to develop new applications to run on the system. Finally, general awareness of electronic sources has been raised and there has been a significant increase in staff planning for automation. Overall, we are happy with our decision to develop the LAN in-house. The advantages of the increase in staff involvement and expertise, of the ability to reuse old equipment, and of the opportunity to develop a system suited for our individual needs, outweigh the disadvantage of extensive staff time commitment, and have made in-house development both attractive and affordable.

Future Plans

The great success of the U-Search service has prompted us to look for new ways to augment access to the Davis LAN. The first priority is to extend the service within the library. This phase will be implemented in the summer of 1991, when all reference staff microcomputers will be linked to the network and an additional public terminal will be added. The next priority is making our CD-ROMs available over the campus broadband to other UNC Novell networks. Currently, site license restrictions preclude this option with all of our packages except GPO and ERIC. We will probably make these available soon, once we have resolved the thorny issue of remote user support. A final goal, and one which we have sought to work towards for some time, is the opening of the network to dial-in access. At the time of this writing, however, dial-in access is neither technically feasible on this campus nor legally permissible for most products.

While we continue to work on the development of the Davis LAN, the future directions of its *raison d'etre*, the U-Search service, are uncertain. The recent decision of UNC to adopt a new online catalog (probably from DRA) opens for the first time the possibility of tape loading as an alternative electronic access mode. It is increasingly likely that the most heavily used bibliographic databases currently available through U-Search will be made accessible through other electronic media. Should this occur, the U-Search Service would continue to provide access to CD-ROMs, but the focus would be on less heavily used products. One possible scenario entails the dedication of the service to the government produced CD-ROMs which are now being produced in increasing numbers. In this period of increasing technological change, however, it is difficult to foresee the future. As with other library services, we will continue to adapt our network to best meet the evolving needs of our community.

About the Authors

Tim Bucknall is the Coordinator for Electronic Information Services in the Humanities Reference Department at Davis Library at UNC-Chapel Hill. He received his M.L.S. from UNC in 1989 and is currently pursuing graduate studies in art history.

Rikki Mangrum is the Microcomputer Services Librarian for Business Administration/Social Sciences Reference in Davis Library, where she provides support for the Library's Machine Readable Data Files Center. She was previously employed as a reference librarian at the University of Georgia at Athens. She received her M.L.S. from UNC in 1988.

Will Owen is Systems Librarian in the Academic Affairs Library at UNC-Chapel Hill, where he has provided microcomputer support since 1985. Prior to that he worked for the Library's Collection Development Department. He has an M.L.S. from North Carolina Central University and an M.A. in Comparative Literature from SUNY Albany.

22

Integrating Library Computing with a Banyan/VINES OPTI-NET LAN

Barbara Burke
Colorado State University Libraries

ABSTRACT

In 1990, Colorado State University Libraries installed a one-server, fifty workstation Banyan/VINES local area network (LAN), with connectivity to CSUNET, the campus network, and beyond to regional, national, and international networks. This LAN, LIBLAN, is both for staff communications and resource sharing, and to provide a foundation for a public-access CD-ROM LAN, to maximize patron accessibility to CD-ROM databases and information services. LIBLAN is a major implementation project, combining old and new equipment, software, and skills to transform a substantial stand-alone microcomputing environment to a powerful network, providing unprecedented opportunities for not only computing, but communications and sharing of files and equipment.

Background Information

Colorado State University was founded in 1870 as Agricultural College of Colorado. Designated as Colorado's land-grant college in 1879, the emphasis then, as now, was on the land-grant concept of a balanced program of teaching, research, extension, and public service. While a full-range university, Colorado State has notable programs in agriculture, engineering, forestry, veterinary science, and other traditional land-grant curricula. Now the second largest university in the state, the annual student enrollment is 20,795, supported by a faculty of 1,625 and a staff of 3,337.

Colorado State University Libraries consist of Morgan Library on the main campus, and several small branch libraries at research locations supporting the engineering, atmospheric sciences and veterinary programs. The Libraries have a faculty of 41, a full-time staff of 78 classified employees, and employs over 145 students each year (for a total of 24 FTE). The staff is organized into three divisions, and eleven departments or units. The collection includes 1,221,000 volumes of books and periodicals, 205,810 microforms, 11,720 serial subscriptions, and 1,931,000 government documents (in paper or microform). The reference service is divided into three areas: Social Science, Humanities and Business; Sciences and Technology; and Government Documents. Each reference area provides CD-ROM products and workstations in the appropriate subjects for that reference service.

Status of Computing

The primary computing support for Colorado State University has historically been mainframe centralized processing. As PCs have evolved, they have been incorporated into the computing environment, first as stand-alone workstations for small-scale applications; but as they became smaller, more powerful and less expensive, they have taken on many of the applications formerly requiring mainframe computing capacity. An aggressive campus "Computing Initiative" of the past few years has promoted PC computing access campus-wide, with the introduction of a number of student microcomputer laboratories and college/department networks. Part of the initiative was to install a fibre-optic campus "backbone," to which local area networks could be connected, and thus have access to campus, regional, national, and world networks through gateways on the backbone. No one LAN standard has emerged campus wide; the campus network includes some Novell systems, PC-NET, UNIX-based LANs and a growing number of VINES systems. Banyan had offered a university grant program which essentially provided the initial software free. Subsequent support and upgrades would be at normal university rates. Many departments and administrative units have taken advantage of the grant program, and there are forty-two VINES servers already in place or in the installation process.

Computing in the CSU Libraries has also historically been mainframe-based until recently. The Libraries have used several integrated library automation systems, including OCLC, RLIN, NOTIS, and currently CARL. A number of local applications were developed for the university mainframe—such as batch systems to produce serials catalogs, or storage inventories. In 1985 only two PCs were in the libraries, to support accounting activities and Fee-Based Online Searching Services (FBOS). In the succeeding five years, approximately thirty-eight staff PCs and eight public (CD-ROM) PCs were acquired, and a MicroVAX II system for the administrative offices. All of the PCs were stand-alone workstations, requiring multiple copies of software (WordPerfect, Lotus, and such) and an active "Sneaker-net" for sharing—carrying files back and forth between machines and users on floppy disks. The only sharing was with the MicroVAX and even Sneaker-Net could not provide communication between PC and MicroVAX users, as their operating systems and software were completely different.

The CD-ROM stations were also stand-alone, one user/one disk. Located in three reference areas, each one had to have the appropriate CD-ROM drivers and software loaded, and allowed only one user to use one CD-ROM disk at a time. Patrons were signing up for half-hour blocks; reference staff were spending a higher percentage of their time swapping out disks and assisting patrons with dealing with disparate searching interfaces. Several different brands of CD-ROM drives were owned, often using different caddies, which complicated the situation further.

All automation operations in the Libraries are overseen by an administrative unit, Library Technology Services (LTS). Staff include the Coordinator of Library Technology Services, a Senior Systems Analyst, and the Microcomputer Services Librarian, who is also the LAN Manager. With the installation of the LAN, LTS was authorized to hire student laboratory assistants to help with LAN troubleshooting and support, as well as troubleshooting our CARL (Colorado Alliance of Research Libraries) OPAC terminals. In the first year, students worked between 24 and 30 hours/week.

By early 1990, it was obvious that further proliferation of stand-alone workstations in the Libraries, both for staff and patron use, didn't make sense, especially in the light of the opportunity for communication with the campus, regional, and national communities through networking. The Libraries needed a LAN for staff communication and file and computing resource sharing. Another critical need was for a patron-accessed CD-ROM service which allowed multiple simultaneous users of each product, and simplified the installation and maintenance requirements of staff. In both situations, the two keywords were "connectivity" and "sharing."

Analysis of LAN Requirements: Uses and Users

It may seem obvious why an institution needs a LAN; however, an important initial exercise is to brainstorm and carefully consider what the LAN will be expected to accomplish immediately and in the future for the institution. We learned this the hard way. An early decision for an MS-DOS VINES Ethernet LAN was challenged when we became aware that many of the colleges to whom we needed to communicate were developing UNIX systems. Working with the networking consultant from Colorado State's Academic Computing and Networking Services (ACNS), we articulated a very complete set of requirements, covering both current and future needs, and received their recommendations. The final choice was VINES, after all; however, it was a decision reached with confidence after a careful identification of our needs.

The Process

Preliminary Identification of Needs. The obvious uses and needs for a local area network present themselves easily: electronic mail, productivity software (word processing, spreadsheet, database, etc.), sharing data, and sharing equipment. These formed the basis of our list of requirements.

Clarification of Technical Questions/Feasibility. As we brainstormed, we identified uses or issues for which we needed more information: What does this mean? Is this technically feasible? If technically feasible, is it financially practical (cost-effective)? These questions were listed and sent to the ACNS staff, who met with library staff to review the needed information.

Articulation of Final List of Requirements. A document was prepared incorporating all of the requirements identified, and sent to the ACNS networking consultant for review and response. In summary, the requirements specified that existing PCs and peripherals be used; that the first configuration could support fifty workstations, with potential for growth; that hardware and software support would be available on campus; that both hardware and software could be shared across the system, yet workstations could function in stand-alone mode when desired; that the system would provide security both at the physical level and for confidentiality of users' files; and that equipment be compatible with other customized workstations used in the Libraries, such as for RLG or OCLC. Capability of handling electronic mail locally, on campus, and across the nation and world using various networks was required, including the ability to attach and send files. The workstations also needed to be able to function as terminals to access online catalogs, commercial databases and services, the proposed CD-ROM LAN, and other specialty files and applications. Also desired was the ability to switch easily from LAN to CD-LAN, OPAC, terminal mode, and stand-alone mode. We also eventually needed to develop applications where library patrons could complete book order, ILL, Fax, and document delivery requests, as well as ask reference questions, all online.

The document was submitted with an understanding that a system which meets all of the requirements may not exist. However, desirable was a system which met as many of the requirements as possible, and was "mainstream" enough to likely be compatible with emerging technologies and future developments.

While the analysis of requirements for a libraries LAN was being developed, the ACNS networking consultant was investigating CD-ROM networks. Those requirements were identified, several products were considered and one extensively site-tested, and the final recommendations for the LAN included recommendations for a compatible CD-ROM network. The major requirements were the ability to use existing equipment and CD-ROM drives, provision of multiple access to multiple disks, acceptable response time even with heavy traffic, and elimination of multiple installations of products and drivers, all at an acceptable per workstation cost.

CD-ROM networking systems investigated were: Artisoft, Meridian Data, and Online (Opti-Net). Artisoft and Meridian were eliminated early, as being incompatible with the IP protocol of the CSU backbone network, or not compatible with VINES. Opti-Net was acquired for testing within a VINES environment. CD-ROM products from DIALOG, Cambridge, PAIS, and OCLC were tested. All products worked, although some required minor adjustments to the software. A few specialized products, such as HYDRODATA, did not work on the LAN. However, these products require more mediation from librarians in their use, and are not good candidates for a CD-ROM LAN anyway.

Selection of the System

The networking consultant responded with detailed proposals for both the Libraries' LAN and the CD-ROM LAN, addressing our requirements documents. Banyan Systems' VINES for the LAN was recommended, with the following justifications: existing equipment would be used; the MS-DOS environment, familiar to staff, would be maintained (although VINES is based on the UNIX system, the

LIBRARY COMPUTING WITH A BANYAN/VINES LAN 307

user interface is a DOS shell); connectivity with the campus "backbone" and subsequently other wider ranging networks would be possible, although varying levels of compatibility would depend upon the disparity of the communicating systems; Banyan/VINES was emerging as a prevailing standard on the CSU campus, with an accompanying support structure; and the Banyan university grant program, which provided the first set of software free, would release monies for additional workstation or server equipment purchases. Opti-Net met all the requirements for the CD-ROM LAN, was compatible with VINES, and more cost-effective than other products tested for our configuration.

Banyan/VINES—The System

Banyan Systems, Incorporated, first released its networking software, VINES, in 1984. The company is named after the banyan tree, a tropical species which has branches which reach to the ground, digging in to form new roots; from these roots new trunks grow, resulting in a "networked" tree—many trunks and branches and roots interrelated. The acronym VINES stands for VIrtual NEtworking System. An understanding of the concepts of "virtual" and "transparent" are necessary to comprehend how VINES works, not only as a single-site LAN, but in joining multiple LANs into a wide area network (WAN). In computing, virtual means "conceptual or appearing to be, rather than actually being." The flip side of virtual is transparent, or "exists but does not appear to." In a VINES network the services, devices, and storage exist, but in many different actual physical locations; however, this is transparent to the user who through the DOS interface has access to resources in much the same way as with a stand-alone workstation. While the VINES server actually runs the UNIX system, the LAN manager and PC clients use the familiar DOS (Disk Operating System) and do not need to know UNIX. An example of "virtual storage" would be a large hard drive on the network server which can be used by many users, each assigned a directory on a "virtual" drive. In our library, a virtual "drive" has been designated as "H" (mnemonic for "Home"), with user subdirectories given the address H:\USERNAME. There is no actual piece of equipment equivalent to an "H" drive, as with a "C" hard drive or an "A" floppy drive; each directory is just part of the storage of the larger hard drive in the server, but the user uses and manages it as if it were on a local hard drive designated "H". Another virtual drive (on the server hard drive) is designated "E" (for "Executables"), where our application software resides. Printers and other peripherals can be used as if attached to the local workstation, although they may be several offices, or even floors or buildings, away from the user. This virtual concept is the foundation and strength of VINES, allowing multiple servers, devices, services and users to interact as one system, accessed with familiar DOS commands and practices. VINES supports not only single-site LANs, but also wide area networks with the combining of more servers and users. In a campus environment such as ours, with many other VINES installations, the VINES' WAN capability makes it desirable over single-site LAN systems, such as Novell or IBM.

This interconnectivity is accomplished through a global-naming system, called StreetTalk. All users, services and servers in the network are given StreetTalk names, which are used as the basis of communication between them. StreetTalk is designed to handle from one server and a few users and services to unlimited servers, services, and workstations. At least, there is no software limitation on numbers of servers, services, and workstation nodes; the only practical limitation would be having adequate hardware support. StreetTalk names consist of three elements: item@group@organization. A single-site LAN will usually have only one organization, with several groups, and many items (users, services, lists, etc.) When a number of single-site LANs are connected into a WAN, as with our campus, the organizations usually identify the actual site of the user or service.

In LIBLAN, the organization is "Libraries," we have eleven groups, nine of which represent our departments, and over 200 items, including users. Some examples of our StreetTalk names are:

```
Barbara Burke@Admin@Libraries
CATLaser@Printers@Libraries
UserList@Acquis@Libraries
Student@Catalog@Libraries
```

Other VINES installations on campus also have StreetTalk names, with different organizations and groups, such as JSmith@Engr@ACNS.

Profiles are created for each user which specify which services and drives the user has access to. This profile is used each time the user logs on, placing them in their H:\Username directory, and identifying the file, print, and mail services they may use. The profiles reside on the server, which is why users can log in on any VINES workstation, even in other locations, and still have access to their home LAN and services.

VINES has a nickname capability which can save many keystrokes. The full StreetTalk name (item@group@organization) can be represented by a brief nickname. For example, the nickname BBurke represents the full name Barbara Burke@Admin@Libraries. Lists can also be created, so that electronic mail can be sent to a list name, or nickname, and actually be sent to a number of users who have been included in the list. We have established lists for the members of Administrative Council, Libraries Faculty Council, Libraries Staff Association, and such. The Administrative Council list has the nickname AC; mail can be sent to over fifteen users by simply addressing it to AC.

Users, services, profiles, and lists are created, modified and deleted by the LAN Manager and cannot be changed by regular users. However, users do have their own private Address Book (AddrBook) where they can create nicknames and lists exclusively for their own use. Nicknames in the AddrBook can represent a StreetTalk name, or any electronic mail address that can be communicated to through VINES. This is handy for storing electronic mail addresses for colleagues in other departments or institutions that you communicate with regularly.

VINES networks have four types of services: File services, Print services, Communications Services and System services. Services are given three-part StreetTalk names just like user names. The virtual drives assigned to users are examples of file services. Print services establish selected printers as "network" printers, allowing users to queue print jobs to a printer physically removed from their workstation. In LIBLAN, most of the print services are laser printers, while most workstations also have a draft quality local printer.

The VINES security features control access to services and virtual drives through Access Rights Lists (ARL); for example, although many users can get to virtual drives such as H:, they will only be able to get into those subdirectories for which they have been included on the Access Rights Lists. They will have access to print services if the print service is identified in their profile, and their StreetTalk address, or user identification, is included on the user list for the print service. Access to all network services throughout VINES is controlled by the single user identification. The login procedure includes use of a secret user-defined password, which the user can change at any time. Security of users' files is better on the network than it was on the stand-alone PCs.

VINES also allows regular backup of the server, either a full backup or incremental (all changes since the last full backup). We started with a 150MB tape backup system, but since our backup now takes two or three 150MB tapes, we have recently purchased a 1.3GB tape backup system. Our entire system will be backed up on one 2"x 3" 1.3GB tape.

Installation and Implementation

Once the decision was made for an Ethernet VINES LAN with connection to our campus backbone, many planning issues had to be addressed. We were not just networking a few PCs together. We were going from no network at all to a large scale, fifty workstation, server-based LAN, complete with software, hardware, and training issues inherent in bringing a large staff into a new system. Our users ranged from experienced MS-DOS practitioners, to those with only MicroVAX experience, to those with no computer experience at all—and within these categories, they ranged from micromaniacs to microphobics.

Equipment

One reason for choosing VINES was that all of our existing equipment (PCs, printers, modems, mice, etc.) could be used. This included one Macintosh on board, and the potential for others later. (The Macintosh connectivity was to be included in the "next version" of VINES; we still haven't seen it but are regularly assured it is in development).

We owned thirty-eight PCs, which included eight dedicated to CD-ROM services. They ranged from ancient slow IBM XTs with monochrome or fuzzy CGA monitors, to a few 80286s with EGA video. Some had hard drives, most either 10 or

20MB. We also had a variety of single workstation licensed software products: WordPerfect, Lotus 1-2-3, PC-FILE, and so on. A new 80386/25MHz PC was recommended as a server, and sixteen additional PCs were required to provide workstations for the MicroVAX users (the MicroVAX would be phased out) and for each department head. The server was ordered and equipped with a 337MB hard drive, 8MB RAM, a 150MB tape back-up system, and an UPS (uninterruptible power source). The additional workstations ordered were 80386SX with dual floppy drives, VGA monitors and no hard drives. VINES workstations can be anything from an 8088 processor and up; however, as application software is downloaded from the server to the workstation PC, where it is processed, faster workstations are an advantage in heavy-duty word processing, merging, spreadsheet, and database applications. 80386 PCs also offer greater memory management and utilization. As prices for 80386SX were becoming lower, we took advantage of the opportunity to upgrade our workstation levels.

We owned three Hewlett-Packard LaserJet Series II printers, and many dot-matrix or ink-jet printers. Two more laser printers were ordered to make a total of five for use as network printers. The dot-matrix and ink-jet printers were to be used as local printers.

Planning

It was soon obvious that the LAN installation would require some careful logistical choreography. The PCs, including the server, could not be installed until the cabling and "drops" (outlets) were in; the software installation depended upon the server, and so forth. A detailed planning document was developed, actually made up of several individual plans, with an accompanying timeline reflecting the interdependent relationships between the activities.

The Ethernet Foundation

Underlying the whole project was the cabling of the building—a thicknet building "spine" with a connection to the campus backbone; repeaters and thinnet "legs" which brought cabling to all of the areas in the building needing immediate or planned drops. The first phase included the installation of drops to network the fifty-four PCs already on hand or to be ordered; the legs, however, would be placed in a pattern that would allow additional drops to be added as needed. We worked with cabling specialists from ACNS, using maps of the floors of the library with drop locations marked—both those to be immediately installed, and those planned for future installation. ACNS responded with recommendations for the location of the spine, the backbone connection, three repeaters (Digital Ethernet Multi-port Repeater, or DEMPR) and fifteen legs. The architecture of an Ethernet network is driven by known limitations of Ethernet cable: the cable from the telecommunications center to a repeater has a limit of 165 feet; each of the legs from a repeater has a maximum length of 600 feet.

Although this may sound like a long distance, each wire must, for example, travel through the false ceiling, down the wall of an office to a drop, from the drop to the PC, from the PC back to the drop, back up the wall to the ceiling, on through the ceiling to the next office, down the wall to the drop, and so on. Morgan Library has 120,108 square feet on five floors, and LAN cabling and drops were needed extensively throughout three floors. There were a few locations without false ceilings, which influenced the number of repeaters, and presented a challenge in providing secure wiring aesthetically acceptable. Once the cabling plan was approved, that work was ordered, as well as the new equipment. We had the inevitable wait for both, which provided time for planning the actual implementation: the deployment of equipment, the organization of the LAN, establishment of an implementation group, identification of naming and storage conventions, training, and the transition from the MicroVAX to the LAN. This was accompanied by an estimate of costs, technical support needs, and a timeline which covered cabling to training.

Equipment Deployment

Sixteen new PCs were ordered to enable us to bring sixteen more staff into the network than we could have with the existing equipment. However, we faced a common dilemma: the new machines were faster and more powerful, where the new users were not necessarily the power users who could take advantage of that additional speed and power. Those power users were already working with the slower, older equipment. It was decided to do a "Microcomputer Use Assessment," designed to identify the uses and needs and match them to the available equipment. The assessment consisted of three steps: presentations to department meetings which included all departments in the libraries; interviews with each department head to complete a survey form addressing hardware and software needs of their department; and evaluation of the surveys with subsequent deployment recommendations, including cost estimates, to be submitted to the Libraries' administration for approval. The recommendations not only included what PC, monitor, or printer was to go where, but also the shifting of CD-ROM and/or hard drives from older equipment into new, and the transfer of files from hard drives to server, for example. Literally every piece of equipment had to be opened and retrofitted in some way—from simply the addition of an Ethernet interface card, to transfer of one or more cards or drives to other equipment. One of the recommendations was to replace eight 8088 or 80286 CD-ROM workstations with the new 80386 SX PCs. This usually involved moving a hard drive, CD-ROM drive, all the CD-ROM interface software, and often a modem, a math coprocessor, a mouse and more. Another equipment decision to be made was the location of the servers and tape backup system. Several considerations influenced the server location: relationship to building spine, repeaters, and legs; proximity to LAN management personnel; and security from inadvertent or deliberate interference. We put our server equipment in the same office as the LAN Manager, which is not a staff or public use area, and is locked when no one is there.

The server equipment was delivered directly to our network consultant, who completed the server configuration and installed the VINES software, as well as WordPerfect 5.1 and WordPerfect Office. The server was then delivered to us and connected to the Ethernet. The consultant showed us what to do to bring each workstation into the network. Two students with microcomputer experience with both hardware and software were hired to help with the deployment. A space in the library, temporarily vacant and with a LAN drop, was used for configuring the hardware and installing and testing the network software. The first PCs to be set up were CD-ROM workstations. We took this opportunity to upgrade several 8088 or 80286 CD-ROM PCs with new 80386SX PCs. This involved moving hard drives, CD-ROM drives, math coprocessors, modems, special video cards, and more from the old PCs into the new, and transferring the CD-ROM software and drivers. We did call upon ACNS technical staff to help with these configurations. When the CD-ROM stations were completed, we were left with a mix of new PCs, the superseded CD-ROM PCs, and other stand-alone PCs, mostly of XT vintage, to reallocate as recommended from the Microcomputer Use Assessment. Some simply required the addition of an Ethernet adaptor card and network software; others needed hard drives moved, monitors changed, modems and other peripherals moved, and user files on local hard drives saved to the server and restored to the appropriate reallocated machine. In retrospect, I would not recommend buying new PCs without hard drives and then moving older hard drives from older PCs into them. We used SpinRite on each hard drive to low-level format and clean the drive up for the new user. This was time consuming, and some of the older drives proved to be difficult to reformat. Installing the Ethernet cards was also tricky, since you must configure each card for unused addresses and interrupts. The software programs "Checkit," from Touchstone Software Corporation, and Manifest from Quarterdeck, were invaluable in identifying used addresses and interrupts so that unused ones could be selected for the network card. Even so, occasionally a persistent interrupt or address collision took hours or even days to track down and correct. In some instances we had to disable COM2 in order to gain an interrupt for the network card. Since some of our machines have no hard drive, two sets of the network DOS.BAT files for the workstation were developed—one for booting from C:> and one for booting from a floppy in A:>. After the PCs were physically configured and the software installed, they were moved to work locations and users given a brief introduction to logging in and out and using electronic mail and getting to WordPerfect. More in depth training was also provided, as described later in this article.

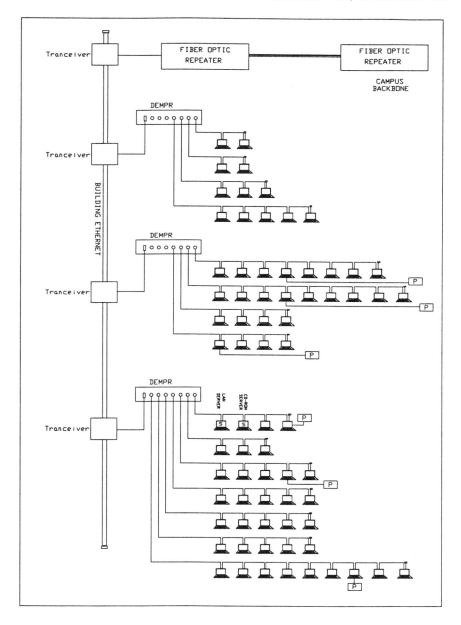

Figure 22.1
Colorado State University Network Organization

LAN Organization

While plans for deployment of hardware were underway, decisions regarding the organization of the network were needed. VINES structure, as previously mentioned, is based on a three-part naming system: item@group@organization. We knew the organization would be "Libraries" but needed to decide first on what groups to be created within the organization "Libraries" then on what users and lists to establish within the groups. We decided to use eleven groups, roughly analogous with the department structure of the libraries. This three-part naming system is the basis of the electronic mail service, and needed to be consistent with campus use and compatible with Internet and other networks.

Support

Early in the planning process we identified several kinds of support we would need: short-term technical assistance with the installation and modification of hardware; ongoing troubleshooting support for both hardware and software problems; departmental operations support and liaison with Library Technology Services; and a policy-making group for establishing policies of practice and to influence long-range planning. Proposals were developed for two levels of short-term technical support: ACNS engineering support for the more complex installations or modifications; and student technical support for installing Ethernet cards, network software, and straightforward printer, card, or peripheral connections. A separate proposal was prepared for ongoing troubleshooting support at the student level, with more technical ACNS support built in to the budget. A LAN Operations Group (LOG) was established to address first-line troubleshooting and liaison with LTS during the installation/implementation process as well as for ongoing support. Members of LOG are representatives of the departments of the libraries, with those departments geographically separated within the building having more than one representative. Information about the LAN is channelled through the LOG representatives; they in turn communicate with LTS regarding new users, changes in users status (resignations and transfers), problems encountered in their departments, training needs and more. LOG has been meeting once a month, very informally addressing issues which have come up at the user level. LOG is developing a series of LAN tip sheets, simple one-page instruction sheets addressing small aspects of LAN use. Examples of tip sheets are: "Moving Your LAN Workstation Equipment," "Login and Logout," "Passwords," and "Guidelines for Troubleshooting your LAN PC." LOG representatives have shared the task of developing the tip sheets. Using the short, modular format, revisions can be easily made without having to reprint a large document, and new tip sheets can be added as needed. A notebook containing tip sheets will be available in each department; the tip sheets are also available online in a directory accessible by all staff. Policy decisions are reviewed by an already existing forum, the Administrative Council, which is made up of Director, Associate and Assistant Directors, Department Heads and Unit Heads, with final decision-making the responsibility of the Director of Libraries.

Data Storage and Naming Conventions

With over fifty PCs in the network, some with and some without local hard drives, guidelines were developed regarding the use of local or network storage. These are not hard-and-fast rules, but suggested uses based on the nature of the files (department specific or of interest library-wide?), the size of files, needed security of data, and such. Since the network files are backed up regularly, large files which would be tedious to back up with floppies may reside on the network. On the other hand, a database which would only be used by one department and can be backed up on a few floppies might be maintained on a local hard drive. The option is always there to transfer a file from a local hard drive to the network or vice versa. Guidelines were also developed for naming files, although these are suggestions only and staff may still use their own naming systems. The intent was to encourage staff to use descriptive, unique names, especially if files are to be shared across departments.

Training

Several kinds of training needs were identified. The LTS staff, and in particular the LAN Manager, received in-depth training on the management and features of the VINES network software. We expected as many as seventy or eighty of our staff to be initial users of the LAN; staff that ranged from micromaniac to microphobic in their experience, aptitude, and attitude about microcomputing. Some would need minimal training in the mechanics of the LAN; others would need everything from basic "Introduction to the Micro and MS-DOS," to use of the LAN, and to use of applications software, especially WordPerfect 5.1, our network word processor. We knew that a successful transition from stand-alone computing (or no computing) to using the network largely depended upon the coordination of training with the placement of equipment and the expectation that the network would be used. A training program was planned, utilizing campus training resources and developing appropriate in-house training. Over a several week period, training sessions were offered in MS-DOS, Managing Your Hard Drive, using VINES and electronic mail, and WordPerfect 5.1 (upgrade sessions for experienced users and introductory training for new users). Finally, so that LOG representatives could handle first-line troubleshooting, they needed a little more training on the features of VINES and the electronic mail system.

MicroVAX II Support

We also had to plan for the transition of our administrative staff from the MicroVAX II system, which used the DEC's All-in-One software (electronic mail, word processing, scheduling, etc.) to an MS-DOS interfaced VINES system. Each MicroVAX user reviewed and weeded their files, and identified those to be converted to WordPerfect 5.1. Our Systems Analyst prepared the files on floppies which were sent to an outside vendor, who returned them in WordPerfect format. The MicroVAX was left in operation for about two months overlapping with the LAN to allow users to make the shift with a minimum loss of productivity.

CD-ROM LAN

The server and software for an Opti-Net CD-ROM LAN were ordered, but the actual implementation was deferred until after the base LAN was in place. This time was used to address such questions as: What CD-ROM products were to be networked?; What are the network license costs?; Would the networked products be available on all or selected CD-ROM workstations?; What handout and training needs would result from broader access through networking?; and more. These issues have been addressed, culminating with the implementation of a four-workstation CD-ROM LAN in summer 1991. This implementation schedule was chosen because it gave staff time to become familiar with the system and to develop handouts and training plans before students and faculty returned in the fall and it presents patrons with a new system at the beginning of a semester rather than after they are in the middle of the term and their projects.

Topology

LIBLAN has an Ethernet bus topology, with one server, one connection to the campus backbone, three repeaters (repeaters), fifteen legs, seventy-two drops, and the potential for expansion through the addition of server(s), repeaters, legs, and drops as needed. In the bus topology each leg is functionally independent from the others; limited to a total of 600 feet, PCs are daisy-chained together, with terminators at each end of the leg. If one PC goes down, or the Ethernet connection is incorrectly broken, the whole leg goes down; however, the rest of the LAN is not affected. Signal lights on the repeater indicate when a leg is down. Our ringing telephone usually tells us before the repeater light is noted. A quick manual check of each workstation on the leg will usually reveal the problem—more often than not an individual disconnected their PC incorrectly, or their connection was jiggled loose.

Costs

There were three categories of costs to be considered: start-up, ongoing maintenance, and expansion. Start-up costs are one-time expenditures to get the system established and running. They include the building spine, backbone connection(s), cabling, drops, system hardware (server, tape backup system, uninterruptible power source, repeaters, transceivers) and additional workstation equipment needed for the initial installation. Included in start-up costs are labor or support costs for installation of both hardware and software. Ongoing maintenance costs were budgeted to include: VINES software support, ACNS software and hardware support, student assistant technical support, consumable supplies (such as paper, toner cartridges for system printers), software upgrades, and equipment replacement. A dynamic organization is never "finished" with its LAN installation. Part of each year's budget is support for expansion: more drops, PCs, printers, upgrades to or replacement for server(s), additional storage capacity, additional application software packages, and more. Our initial installation provided microcomputing capacity to all of our departments, and electronic mail connectivity between all administrators. Our immediate expansion plans, currently underway, include PCs for each librarian's office, and additional PCs for the CD-ROM service. We have recently purchased fifteen additional PCs for staff use, and eight for our CD-ROM service. Future expansion will include additional staff and CD-ROM PCs as needs justify. Costs for all of the above are constantly changing, with a trend towards "more bang for the buck." We estimate a drop at $100 or less (Ethernet connection to building spine, including outlet and Ethernet cables to PC); Ethernet cards are under $200. We have purchased locally made IBM clone PCs at very competitive prices. Since the company is local, service and guarantee work is done almost immediately. Our warranty on equipment from this company is one year's parts and labor, and two years' labor. This has been a necessity given our volume of purchase. Most hardware failures occur within the first few months of purchase, but we have had monitors, drives, and such. replaced just under the one year. Another cost, time, is substantial for the computing support staff, as well as staff users who must learn new hardware and software procedures. Depending on the complexity of the software and the aptitude of the user, the learning curve can affect productivity and must be recognized and accommodated.

Evaluation

Jim Seymour, in his January 30, 1990 column, reveals:

> LAN administration is the worst job in America. I manage only a small network. Two file servers, 40 workstations, 30 printers, all good equipment—Compaq, IBM, Hewlett-Packard, Epson. Just a few, simple (ha!) applications. I used to be mentally and physically healthy, a marathon runner, a well-balanced social individual, a kind person. Now it's a pack a day, regular therapy sessions, and when I'm able to sleep, I curl up in a corner behind the refrigerator where it's warm.
>
> —*Bob Kulpa Miami, Florida*[1]

I laughed when I read Bob Kulpa's plaintive letter in PC Magazine. In April 1990 we were in the first stages of planning a LAN for the Colorado State University Libraries. It was so wonderful to anticipate: we could communicate through electronic mail, not only in the library, but campus-, nation-, and world-wide; we could share files; we could share laser printers and other equipment. We could network CD-ROM products, allowing multiple users of the same file, and requiring only one installation of often contrary CD-ROM access software. Our lives would be different, and so much better. A year later, I can sympathize with Mr. Kulpa. At times the warm corner behind my refrigerator has looked like a tempting hide-away. However, our lives are different, and better. But the transition to a LAN was/is a complicated, demanding, often frustrating project. There is much more to it than "hooking a few PCs together." It requires careful planning, continuous communication, coordinated training, constant troubleshooting, continuous review, and regular upgrading. We now have the basic LAN implemented and are working on the implementation of the CD-ROM LAN and a new phase of the regular LAN—fifteen new staff PCs and eight new CD-ROM workstations. By way of evaluation, I would make the following observations:

Hardware: The choice of an IBM PC-based system was the only cost-effective way for us to go, since we already owned so much equipment. Experienced PC users did not have to adjust to a new platform, and new users had a ready-made support system of colleagues, LTS and ACNS staff.

Software: VINES is based on a UNIX system, with a DOS shell for the user. Again, experienced users could use their expertise, and new users had an excellent support system for DOS. Banyan has since announced that it will allow third parties to develop compatible applications, and allow access to the UNIX structure. Our campus is divided between three platforms: MS-DOS, Macintosh, and UNIX. Banyan has been a good choice because it is addressing compatibility issues between the three.

Speed/Performance: LIBLAN is used primarily for word processing and electronic mail, with a few users developing large spreadsheet or database files. Our one 80386 25MHz server handled the traffic well, with the only objectionable slowdowns occurring during tape backup, or when we put too many drops on a leg. We have recently upgraded the server to 33MHz and have hard drive and tape backup upgrades planned for summer 1991.

Storage: Our original 337MB hard drive has been sufficient for the first year. However, since we are soon going to add the CD-ROM LAN and fifteen new staff workstations, we have acquired a second, 660MB, hard drive. We will leave all applications software on the 337MB hard drive, and use the larger 660MB drive for user files.

Tape Backup: Soon after the LAN became operational, our weekly full backup procedure required two tapes. Scheduled to occur at 4:00AM, the first tape would fill, and then the backup process would halt until someone came in at 8:00AM and changed the tape. It would take another 30 to 60 minutes to finish backing up, during which time the entire system would be extremely slow. We have recently purchased a 1.3GB tape backup system which we will install this summer. Our entire LAN will be backed up on one tape, at 4:00 AM, with no slowdown occurring for users.

Training/Ease of Use: LAN Management: The LAN manager and backup staff attended a concentrated three-day introductory training session provided by vendor staff in August 1990, and an advanced session in January 1991. Since the interface is

DOS, learning management techniques was like learning another MS-DOS application. The VINES software is fairly easy to learn, and voluminously documented. One weakness, however, is the lack of inclusion of management functions to track down and diagnose system problems. For users, the DOS shell facilitated training for experienced staff and provided normal DOS frustrations for new users. The rank beginner was provided with DOS, LAN, electronic mail, and WordPerfect training, often in such a close sequence that there was some confusion between products and functions. In implementing our current expansion, new users are being given LAN and electronic mail instruction first; then later in the summer DOS and WordPerfect will be offered. We have a variety of disk-based tutorials and videotapes for those who want information before the training. Learning to use LIBLAN is no harder than learning any other relatively simple DOS application.

Troubleshooting/Support: Despite such a large initial installation, and both LAN management staff and users learning about the system simultaneously, troubleshooting has not been a large problem. The hardware and software are stable, with most of the problems attributable to user ignorance—the inevitable learning curve—or frustration by more experienced users that information about advanced use and features wasn't being disseminated more quickly. We have had no serious "crashes"; the worst downtime was three hours, when a short in a cable on the leg the server was on was discovered and the cable replaced. Short, planned downtime has occurred a few times, to stop and restart services and to replace the 80386 25MHz server with an 80386 33MHz main board. Given sufficient notice and consideration of the time chosen, staff are quite patient with short planned downtimes. We also have a source of support which hasn't been mentioned yet. With so many VINES installations on campus, a VINES Managers Group has been meeting monthly since fall 1990. This forum is used to disseminate information, share in problem-solving, compare notes on performance of services and equipment, and recently several ad hoc groups organized to address common issues: naming conventions, electronic mail address compatibility, campus trading and selling of equipment, preparation of outside vendor support RFP, and more. With this group identified, there are many people to call when troubleshooting a new problem; managers frequently use electronic mail to ask for information from their colleagues.

In summary, we have been satisfied with our VINES LAN, and have discovered no area in our requirements (or expectations) where it has not provided what we need. VINES has become a *de facto* campus LAN standard, which has resulted in greater and smoother connectivity with other campus units, and support from both the ACNS and other campus VINES users.

What Next?

The year 1990 was "The year of the hardware." The sheer logistics of networking over fifty PCs and attendant peripherals dominated the activities of LTS staff. For users, learning the keyboard, basic MS-DOS, communicating electronically, and word processing were their challenge. The years 1991 and beyond will be the "Year(s) of Refinement and Expansion." LTS, while always having an active hardware support role, will spend more time on training, getting the most out of software, developing or helping staff develop applications, taking advantage of campus and national connectivity to enhance library services, and incorporating new technology into a sound LAN base.

Notes

1. Letters. *PC Magazine* 9(8): 21, April 24, 1990.

Additional Reading

Laubach, Edwin G. 1991. *Networking with Banyan/VINES*. Pa., Windcrest Books.
Schlack, Mark. May 15, 1991. Can Banyan Grow VINES? *Datamation* 37(10): 26-32.

Products and Vendors

The following products were selected by Colorado State University for their LIBLAN, running the VINES and OPTI-NET software. Products were purchased either directly from the manufacturer, or through state bid-selected vendors, or local vendors identified by the manufacturer.

Software

LAN: VINES - Version 4.10, Banyan Systems Inc., 115 Flanders Road, Westboro, MA 01581. Includes Network Mail, Network Management, PC Network Printing, TCP/IP Routing, TCP/IP Server-to-Server, LAN Server-to-Server, MacVINES Mail Gateway

WordPerfect 5.1, network licenses, WordPerfect Corporation, 1555 North Technology Way, Orem, UT 84057.

WordPerfect Office, network licenses, see address above.

VIRUSCAN, CLEAN-UP, workstation licenses, McAfee Associates, 4423 Cheeney Street, Santa Clara, CA 95054-0253

Lotus 1-2-3 Release 2.2, server and workstation nodes, Lotus, 55 Cambridge Parkway, Cambridge, MA 02142.

Opti-Net: Opti-Net CD-ROM/LAN Management Program, 9-100 users, OPC-OPTN-002, Online Products Corporation, 20251 Century Boulevard, Germantown, MD 20874.

Hardware

Servers and workstations: VINES LAN Server - IBM compatible 80386 33MHz PC, 80387 math coprocessor, 16MB RAM, two serial/1 parallel ports, high density 5 1/4" floppy drive, monochrome monitor and card, 101 enhanced keyboard; Opti-Net CD-ROM LAN server–IBM compatible 80386 25MHz PC, 4MB RAM, two serial/parallel ports, high density 5 1/4" floppy drive, monochrome monitor and card, 101 enhanced keyboard; Workstations: A variety of IBM compatible PCs, from 8088 to 80386, with or without hard drives, one or more floppy drives, monochrome or color monitors. (VINES server must run UNIX and VINES, so motherboard of prospective server PC must be a Banyan "certified" brand/model, or tested thoroughly for compatibility).

Hard drives: (1) Micropolis 338MB hard disk drive, model 1558-16, with Western Digital WD1007N hard drive controller card; (2) Fujitsu M2263 - High Capacity Hard drive (660MB), used with same Western Digital controller card.

Tape backup system: WANGTEK 6130 HS 1.3GB tape backup system, with Adaptec 1542B controller card, and 36 ISSI 1.3GB computer backup cartridges. (Original backup system was 150MB system provided through Banyan vendor).

Network interface cards: For LAN server–Western Digital 8013E Ethernet card; for OPTI-NET server and all workstations–Racal Interlan NI5210-16 Ethernet cards.

UPS: APC Uninterruptible power supply, APC 520ES.

Optical Storage Units: Five Optical Storage Units (OSU), Model OSU-202, each with 4 half-height SONY CD-ROM drives, with 1 controller card for two OSUs, for use with Opti-Net CD-ROM/LAN Management Software, Online Products Corporation, 20251 Century Boulevard, Germantown, MD 20874.

CD-ROM Caddies: Item no. 1321, for SONY CD-ROM drives, from Educorp, 7434 Trade St., San Diego, CA 92121

About the Author

Barbara L. Burke has been with the Colorado State University Libraries since 1974. She has been Assistant Engineering Sciences Librarian, Assistant Collection Services Librarian, and currently is Microcomputer Services Librarian and manager of the libraries' local area network, LIBLAN. She has extensive experience in online searching, CD-ROM installation and troubleshooting, and microcomputer applications in university libraries.

23

Networking a Library with 3+Open

Susan G. Bateman and Sanjay R. Chadha
Houston Academy of Medicine—Texas Medical Center Library

ABSTRACT

Houston Academy of Medicine—Texas Medical Center Library has a large 3Com 3+Open local area network (LAN) based on Microsoft's LAN Manager. At present the LAN provides office automation, internetworking, management information and decision support. The original intent of the Library's LAN was to share resources and provide office automation tools for the staff. Most of the original LAN workstations were double disk drive models without hard disks. The network server provided a convenient and secure place to store documents. Sharing resources across the LAN provided automated tools to support the administrative functions of the Library.

As the Library's end-users became more sophisticated, the purpose of the LAN evolved. End- users were becoming increasingly aware of services and data available on various external networks. And, end-users started demanding technological solutions to access systems and services outside of the Library. On the other hand, the Library also realized the managerial potential of the LAN and started building management information systems that take advantage of the sharing concept of the LAN in ways that go beyond simple sharing of physical resources.

Background of the Library

Houston Academy of Medicine–Texas Medical Center Library is the principal cooperative medical information resource and service for Houston and surrounding areas. Begun in 1949 with the merging of the libraries of the Houston Academy of Medicine and Baylor College of Medicine, the Library is unique among medical libraries in the United States due to it's consortium status. It serves not only the faculty, students, and practicing physicians from the two original institutions, but also all twenty-two institutions of the Texas Medical Center. A board of directors comprised of representatives from the participating institutions govern the Library.

The Library has more than 16,000 card holders, and also is a member of Houston Area Research Library Consortium (HARLiC) which provides reciprocal library privileges to card holders of Rice University, University of Houston, and Texas A&M University. The Library is also the home for Harris County Medical Society Archives and Historical Research Center. The Library has consistently ranked amongst the top medical libraries in the United States and Canada. In May of 1991, the National Library of Medicine awarded the Library the Regional Medical Library (RML) contract.

To meet the needs of such diverse and demanding roles, the Library has assembled a team of very high quality professionals and systems. This complex arrangement of sophisticated clients, proficient staff, and multiple institutions with multiple standards form the backdrop against which systems staff of the Library rise to the challenge of providing solutions that work.

History of the Library's LAN

The Library's first LAN was a sixteen-node Televideo system operating under the CP/M operating system. All the terminals were Televideo systems. Word processing and flat file databases were the primary functions. CP/M did not catch on, so when IBM's personal computers started gaining in popularity, the Library abandoned the Televideo network for an IBM-compatible network.

In 1985 the Library purchased 3Com's DOS-based EtherSeries network operating system. The primary uses of the network were electronic mail and word processing. EtherSeries ran under IBM DOS, on an IBM 8088 XT which had 640 KB of RAM and a 20MB hard disk. The Library attached a Hewlett-Packard LaserJet and an Epson MX100 to the file server. There were also two IBM 8088 XT print servers on the network. These print servers had Epson dot matrix printers connected to them. The workstations were mostly IBM 8088 personal computers (PCs) with two double density floppy drives and 256KB of RAM. The network media consisted of thick and thin Ethernet cable segments. The Library installed a single port Ethernet repeater after another expansion of the network exceeded the stated Ethernet length limitation. The repeater connected two segments into a bus topology.

The Library quickly outgrew the 20MB capacity of the IBM XT file server as more users were added to the network. In 1988, the Library upgraded the network operating system to 3Com's 3+Share and purchased a dedicated 3Com 3S/401 3Server. This server had an 80386 microprocessor, 150MB of disk storage with a 150MB tape backup, 2MB of RAM, one parallel port, one asynchronous port, and two synchronous RS232 ports. The Library replaced the Epson printers with two Hewlett-Packard LaserJet Series II printers connected to the print servers. The operating system required 384KB on the workstations, so the Library upgraded the end-users' workstations to 640KB by adding memory expansion boards. A monetary gift from a Friend of the Library enabled the Library to reconfigure and recable all three floors of the Library using RG-58 thin coaxial cabling and a 3Com multiport repeater.

In 1990 the Library upgraded to 3Com's OS/2 based 3+Open operating system. At this time, the Library upgraded the 3S/401 server to a total of 8MB of RAM and the OS/2 version 1.1 operating system.

Current LAN Environment—3+Open

Hardware

The Library has one file server located in the Systems Department running 3Com's 3+Open Network Operating System. The file server is 3Com's 3S/401

3Server. The 3S/401 is a 16MHz 80386 dedicated server. The server has 150MB of hard disk storage partitioned into two physical partitions. The network operating system resides on the 32MB "C" partition. The remaining 120MB "D" partition is for programs and file storage. Users with hard disks in their network workstations use them for storing personal data files because the server's storage space is approaching ninety percent. The server also has an internal tape backup unit with 150MB capacity. The Library added an AST Multiport serial board to accommodate additional shared printers connected by four low impedance serial cables from the server to four departments (Administration, Information Services, Technical Services, and Interlibrary Loan). These cables connect Hewlett-Packard LaserJet Series II printers to the network. An additional Hewlett-Packard LaserJet III with 3MB of RAM connects to the server's parallel port in the Systems Department.

There are sixty-eight network drops throughout the Library with sixty-seven percent of the workstations being 286 or 386 IBM compatible PCs. These 286 and 386 PCs have hard disk capacities ranging from 20 to 40MB with 1 to 2MB of RAM. Thirty-two percent of the workstations are 640KB IBM 8088 PCs and XTs. Most of the 286 and 386 systems have EGA or VGA color monitors while the 8088s have monochrome monitors. Each network workstation has either a 3Com 3C501, 3C503 or 3C505 Etherlink board. Approximately forty-seven percent of the network workstations also have stand-alone dot matrix printers, mostly Epson's.

Eventually, expansions and recabling of the network exceeded the length limitation of thin coaxial Ethernet segments. The limits of .2 inch diameter thin Ethernet, or thinnet, is 1,000 feet (305 meters). The Library chose to use thinnet over standard .4 inch diameter Ethernet because thinnet is less expensive and easier to install, even though standard thick Ethernet has a length capacity of 3,280 feet (1,000 meters). The Library hired contractors to perform the recabling and they installed a 3Com Multiconnect Modular Multiport Repeater. This repeater reconfigures the topology into a six segment star. Topology is a term referring to the network's physical or logical layout. The repeater was placed on the first floor of the Library. Two segments run down into the basement offices, one segment runs up to the second floor, and three segments run throughout the first floor. The Library chose 3Com's Multiconnect Repeater because it provides the flexibility of adding any combination of up to fifteen thick coaxial, thin coaxial, twisted-pair or fiber-optic segments. Moreover, a fully loaded Multiconnect with fifteen RG-58 Thinnet modules supports up to 1,024 network devices. Lastly, for maintenance purposes, the Library can shut down network segments without affecting other segments.

The Library's computer room houses a variety of internetworking equipment which connect the LAN to other systems. One segment from the repeater goes to a Proteon IP (internet protocol) router. A router is a device that passes same or interoperable protocol packets between physically separate networks. Routable protocols include, among others, TCP/IP (transmission control protocol/internet protocol), IPX/SPX (InterNet packet exchange/sequenced packet exchange), and DECnet. The router connects the Library's LAN to the TCP/IP Baylor Information

Network (BIN), our connection to the Internet. The router also connects to a Compaq Systempro running SCO Unix. This machine will eventually be our MIS/DSS database server. The router also connects to a DELNI (Digital Equipment Local Network Interconnect) which provides multiple Ethernet-compatible connections. Four DECserver 200/MC (modem control) terminal servers connect to the DELNI. Terminal servers provide an interface between asynchronous serial devices and remote hosts on DEC LAT (Digital Equipment Corporation Local Area Transport) or non-LAT networks. LAT is a non-routable protocol so the Library added a bridge to pass the LAT packets. A bridge is a protocol-independent device that can pass packets across networks using compatible addressing schemes. A Chipcom Ethermodem III Bridge interconnects the University of Texas Health Science Center (UTHSC) broadband LAT network with the Library's Ethernet LAN. This configuration also serves to connect BIN with UTHSC.

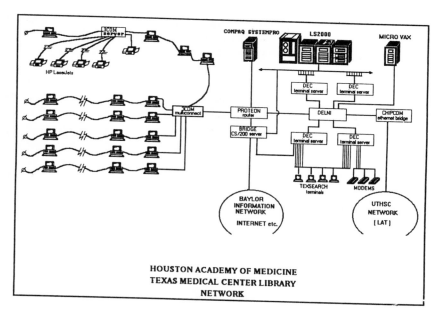

Figure 23.1

Houston Academy of Medicine–Texas Medical Center Network

LS2000

The Library has an Online Public Access Catalog (OPAC) from Ameritech Information Systems referred to in the Library as LIO. AVATAR Systems originally developed the LS2000 system, then sold it to OCLC Local Systems Division. OCLC eventually sold LS2000 to Ameritech Information Systems. The system runs on a

Data General MV8000 Series II computer and provides access to all the Library's collections including serials. The OPAC was one of the first to accommodate a consortium of libraries, and is searchable by individual libraries or as a combined collection. There are five libraries in the consortium:

1. HAM-TMC Library
2. UT M.D. Anderson Library
3. UT Dental Branch Library
4. UT School of Public Health Library
5. UT Mental Sciences Institute Library

The consortium share all the bibliographic records and the client data. Each library maintains their item records in the system. The libraries also have varying privileges and circulation policies for their respective clients. The system hardware consists of the DG MV8000 computer, three 500 MB Winchester drives, one Data General 6250 bpi Model 6300 tape drive, four Micom Statistical Multiplexors, a variety of 1200 and 2400 baud modems, and a subsystem for serials called SC350. The multiplexors provide OPAC access to the other libraries through dedicated phone lines. The SC350 Serials subsystem runs on a separate IBM token ring network. Each library establishes a periodic link between SC350 and LS2000 during which the systems exchange and update each other's data. The system is written in MIIS which is a combined operating system and programming language. It supports standard MARC format, multiple languages, diacritics and offers physical and logical levels of security.

The heavily used LS2000 system has a total of ninety-six ports. Even though LS2000 itself does not support networking, the Library provides network access by assigning several ports for network use through DEC and Bridge Communications terminal servers. The DEC terminal servers provide access to LS2000 on the UTHSC LAT network, and the Bridge terminal server provides access to LS2000 on the TCP/IP network. The OPAC is thus available on the Internet through the Bridge Communication Server. The Library has a comprehensive hardware and software maintenance contract with Ameritech to support LS2000 and its subsystems.

Software

The Library's PC network operating system is 3Com's 3+Open LAN Manager version 1.1. The server operates under OS/2 version 1.1 while all of the workstations are running versions of DOS with the network administrator's 386 OS/2 workstation as the only exception. The 3+Open operating system allows us the flexibility of connecting OS/2, DOS or Macintosh computers onto the same network, although the Library does not have any Macintosh systems on the network at this time.

3+Open offers helpful network administration and security advantages. The network administrator can schedule backups at any time even when the network is up. In our case, the network administrator schedules backups to start at 3:00 in the morning. 3+Open backups degrade server response time so early morning backups after the Library closes will not effect end-users. Resource auditing assists in optimizing available network hard disk space, programs, files, and printers. The network administrator audits software license use to assist in determining when to purchase additional licenses. The network administrator assigns read, write, create, delete, execute only, and/or modify attributes access rights to the shared resources. Each end-user has exclusive rights to his/her own personal subdirectory and access to a shared data directory. End-users also have rights to send print jobs to any of the networked laser printers.

When a user logs in, he/she is automatically linked to the nearest networked printer, the logical drive E: data subdirectory, and the logical drive F: program directory. These logical drives are physically on the D: network partition. Login starts the 3+Menus program. 3+Menus provides a user-friendly interface between the network end-users and programs. The network administrator can make revisions at any time to the main menus because it is stored on a shared area.

The Library has added several of 3Com's value added software packages to the LAN. The most popular 3Com software is the electronic mail system, 3+Mail. LAN users in the Library have become very accustomed to communicating with others via electronic mail. Mail problems provoke more end-user irritation than any other network service! 3+Mail allows end-users to create, reply to, and forward electronic mail messages to other end-users or distribution groups on the network. End-users can also attach up to twenty-five separate files with each message. The network administrator maintains the electronic mail group names. Currently, there are twenty-two electronic mail group names.

With more and more libraries connected to the Internet, the Library felt a need to be connected in order to participate in professional forums and exchange electronic mail with colleagues. The Library found a solution to electronic mail connectivity by installing MSD, Inc.'s Promulgate Electronic Mail Gateway software. Promulgate allows us to send and receive messages across the Internet. Promulgate translates outbound 3+Mail messages into the RFC 822 message format, while it translates incoming Internet messages into 3Com mail format. The Promulgate software resides on a dedicated 8088 networked PC XT. The SCO Unix component of the gateway resides on a Compaq Systempro. The key selling point of an electronic mail gateway product was not having to purchase and learn a Unix based electronic mail package for Internet electronic mail. The end-users can continue to use the familiar 3+Mail with all of its functionality intact. The network administrator can add shortened alias names for the sometimes long Internet addresses. For example, an end-user can send a message to the alias SusanB which actually points to the Internet address SusanB@tmcpcnet.library.tmc.edu. The Library also purchased 3+Internet. This software provides electronic mail and file transfer connectivity to other 3+Open networks via modems. Our 3Com support contract vendor, Hilton-Pieper & Associates, Inc., can dial-in remotely to diagnose a variety of network problems or transfer files. The Library does not often communicate with any other 3Com networks, and our vendor rarely uses the remote diagnostic capabilities, so the Library has not justified the 3+Internet purchase.

One of the more significant strategic advantages that the Library contemplated when deciding on the 3+Open system was its Demand Protocol Architecture (DPA). DPA gives us the option of selecting the most efficient protocol as our base network protocol and then loading other protocols as needed. End-users can load or unload protocols to more efficiently utilize conventional memory available for DOS applications. End-users load NBP (NetBIOS Protocol) as the base network protocol, then demand load XNS (Xerox Network Systems) protocol to run 3+Open Mail. As the ability of the Library to connect with the plethora of networks in the Texas Medical Center was becoming increasingly important, demand loading internetworking protocols was of extreme value.

The Library added 3+Open TCP (transmission control protocol) with DPA to enable connections to TCP/IP networks. TCP provides FTP (File Transfer Protocol) and DEC VT 100/52 emulation capabilities. A 3+Menus option loads the TCP, then the 3VT emulation software package. The end-user can then type in the host name or host IP address. The network administrator periodically downloads various Internet resource guides for host address reference. Upon logging off the remote host, the TCP protocol stack unloads from the workstation's RAM. TCP has proven to be a good purchase decision because it allows us access to the Internet with its abundance of resources. The Library is one of the few libraries where end-users can access the Internet from their LAN workstations without first having to log into a local host.

Our office automation software includes WordPerfect 5.1, Microrim's R:Base for DOS, Computer Associates' SuperCalc 5, Lotus 1-2-3 release 3.1, and Borland's Paradox 3.5. The end-users have been pleased with the functionality of WordPerfect 5.1. The Library uses custom macros to print envelopes and letters on letterhead to the laser printers. End-users also create merge files for efficient mass mailing of form letters. The Library just recently purchased Lotus 1-2-3 to fulfill some compatibility requirements. It is uncertain whether Lotus will become the Library's standard spreadsheet. Supercalc was chosen several years ago because it was more cost effective and ran on all classes of PCs. Lotus 1-2-3 release 3.1 only runs on 286 and above classes of PCs. The Library is in the process of converting R:Base databases into Paradox. The main reason for this database standardization is that a Library Management Information System (MIS) is being written in Paradox.

MIS/DSS Project

The Library has aggressively pursued technology to provide better client services. The most common use of computers in libraries has been for online catalogs. In general, most libraries have automated or computerized technical services. However, libraries are not automating public services as readily due to the complexities of process, lack of a standardized approach to these services across libraries, and other such factors. Libraries in general are using personal computers for support in most function areas; however, these computers are not necessarily a part of any unified system within the library. Thus there is a need for a system to automate the remaining functional areas (primarily public services) of the library, provide the kind of reporting and analysis facilities not provided by the present systems, assimilate information from all the diverse library systems, and compile the information from the management perspective. The basic components required for such a system in the Library were in place. But, the Library lacked a scheme to tie them all together into an overall system with strategic, planning, and control objectives. This is where the MIS/DSS project came in.

The MIS/DSS project attempts to answer such descriptive information questions as:

o What materials are our clients using (collection usage)?
o What areas of client interest are not adequately covered by our collection (through analysis of Interlibrary Loan activities)?
o Who are the clients using our resources most frequently?
o Which Institution is using our services most?
o What are the peak times for questions?

And, the MIS/DSS addresses analytical informational questions such as:

o Why are no fellows using a service?
o Why are only students using a service?
o Why has the gate count gone up without a corresponding rise in the Library's activities?

Some of the answers are indicative in nature. For example, they may foretell a trend that the Library must adjust to. Similarly, the Library may obtain answers using the MIS/DSS that identify unresolved issues and problems. The DSS modules are the highlight of the system, providing the managers with tools and data to analyze and assist in making operational, managerial, and strategic decisions.

The Library provides a variety of client services such as computer and clinical searching, photocopying by staff, and interlibrary loan. The Library records a wealth of data in providing services which relate directly to the questions listed above. A client services function of the MIS/DSS is to provide transaction processing over the LAN. The Library developed several modules to automate key public service activities, collect data for management reports, and provide decision support. These modules, among other things, allow Library staff to receive and record requests from clients directly into the computer system. The Library is working on providing remote access and self-service access to these services over a WAN (wide area network). The system has significant resource requirements. The Library expects to generate approximately fifty megabytes of data every year and store at least three years' data online for analysis. The Library will archive the prior two years' data, providing full five years' data upon which to base projections on. The system has seven main modules.

1. Information Services module
2. Circulation module
3. Technical Services module
4. Photocopy/Interlibrary Loan module
5. Accounting module
6. Administrative module
7. Decision Support modules

The Information Services, Circulation, and Photocopy/Interlibrary loan modules are collections of submodules that provide for automation of most tasks conducted by these departments. Specifically, the module allows for recording of desk statistics, computer, clinical and rerun requests, photocopy requests, interlibrary loan requests, new card requests, processing of the recorded requests, their tracking and analysis. Additionally, the modules allow for generation of management information reports and invoicing of the services provided in an easy and straightforward manner. One significant difference between current procedures and those incorporated in the modules for providing services is that the Library has built many policies and department rules into the module. These policies and rules are thus invoked uniformly for all transactions. Further, as circulation is the only place in the Library with a cash register, the Circulation module also assumes the role of cashier to receive payments and deposits. The module allows circulation to fulfill these roles within the MIS domain.

The Accounting module interacts with all the public services modules, automatically generates invoices, and maintains the accounts receivable for the Library. It also maintains and posts the status of each invoice to the original transactions. The Library developed the Technical services module to assist Collection Development in the analysis of serial subscriptions of the Library as well as to allow serials to record and track invoices for serial subscriptions.

The MIS/DSS system is written entirely in Paradox, a PC relational database package from Borland International. At this time, there are approximately eighty tables in the system. The modules share all data and the system fully supports multiple end-users for all resources. The Library expects the databases to outgrow the capabilities of traditional file servers. The system is currently occupying about 45MB of server disk space. Eventually, the Library intends to replace the current server with a separate database server to meet the needs of MIS/DSS. However, the Library will continue using the Paradox programs as the front end to the future database server through a product called Paradox SQL Link.

End-Users

Although the original intent of the LAN was to provide general office automation support for in-house staff, the Library foresees the LAN serving library clients with eventual self-service/remote access modules for the MIS/DSS. The Library hopes to accommodate this through another dedicated server, possibly the dedicated database server itself.

Personnel

The Library's Systems Department employs one part-time staff and five full-time staff members. The full-time employees consist of a Systems Director, Systems Analyst, two Systems Specialist, and a Systems Technician. The Systems Analyst is mainly responsible for the MIS/DSS project. One Systems Specialist maintains the Library's online catalog system. The other Systems Specialist functions as the LAN Administrator and maintains the WAN connections. The Systems Technician maintains all of the hardware in the Library including the installation of network interface cards. The part-time Computer Operator performs the nightly backups and reports for the online LS2000 catalog system.

Evaluation

Actual costs for the LAN were difficult to obtain because the Library has continually enhanced the network. Additionally, costs related to PC hardware and software have steadily decreased making some of these costs seem excessive in relation to the current market. Our current LAN has evolved over the past seven years. The Library has attuned LAN growth to its needs while trying to keep costs within certain budgetary constraints. An evaluation of the approximate costs can be broken down into the following components of the LAN :

- o Transmission medium, or cabling
- o Network repeater
- o Shared resources : server, printers, software
- o End-user workstations
- o Maintenance and support contracts

The Library budgets one hundred dollars per network drop when considering expansions to the coaxial cabling. This figure includes labor and all the necessary hardware such as connectors, wall plates, terminators, and RG-58 cable. So, with sixty-eight networks drops throughout the building, the Library has invested approximately $6,800 in network cabling.

The Library purchased the original single port Ethernet repeater for $2,300. Three years later, the fifteen segment capacity 3Com Multiconnect Repeater cost $1,295 plus $295 per segment module. Comparing these two items on per segment costs, the multiport repeater was very cost-effective. Hardware prices continue to drop rapidly while functionality rises as quickly.

In 1985 the Library purchased the 3Com 3S/401 3Server for $14,000. The 3Server was a state-of-the-art piece of equipment. The price included the 3+Share network operating system. The Library purchased the 3+Mail electronic mail software separately for $2,000. Later, to satisfy the 3+Open network operating requirements, the Library purchased a 6MB server memory board for $2,500. The upgrade increased the server's total memory to 8MB. The 3+Open and 3+Open Mail software upgrades cost $2,000 and $750; respectively. To eliminate the print servers, the Library added an AST Multiport serial board for $500. Four low impedance serial printer cables cost approximately $200 each for installation and materials. The five shared laser printers cost approximately $1,700 each. The Library has invested approximately $43,000 in the above LAN hardware and software. This cost does not include the end-user workstations.

For the end-user workstations, the Library has set 386 IBM compatibles as the unwritten standard. The Library configures the 386 workstations with a 3Com Ethernet board, 2MB of RAM, 40MB hard disk, one 1.2MB floppy and a VGA interface card and monitor. The Library pays approximately $2000 for workstations with these specifications. The maintenance costs include all repairs to network workstations and peripherals. If the Systems Technician is unable to repair the equipment, it is sent out for repair. Hourly labor for repairing equipment is about $75 per hour with a minimum of one hour per order. Onsite repair costs soar up to $150 per hour with a two hour minimum. The Library rarely uses onsite repair services.

The Library has a hardware/software support contract with a 3Com network vendor. The contract costs $5,000 per year which includes unlimited telephone support and sixteen hours of on-site support. The Library negotiated overnight replacement of our 3Com server into the support contract in the event of a catastrophic hardware failure.

Salaries of systems personnel would be another direct cost of maintaining the LAN. For reasons of privacy, this information was not available. Certain computer journals list current salary information for computer professionals.

Each year the Library assigns separate budgets for computer supplies, network maintenance, software, and hardware. For the 1990-91 fiscal year the budget for maintenance, supplies, software, and hardware was $7,000, $5,400, $5,000, and $30,000; respectively. The Library has typically had a difficult time staying within the budget while satisfying the growing technological needs of the end-users.

Benefits gained from implementing a LAN are very difficult to measure due to the intangible value of those benefits. The Library can say intuitively that the LAN implementation has improved the efficiency and effectiveness of the staff, but how does the Library place a quantitative value on that improvement? There exist perceived benefits by the end-users. These perceived benefits may be encompassed in the singular phrase "connectivity." Connectivity facilitates the sharing of resources, documents, and ideas. The Library's end-users certainly notice the value of these perceived benefits when the network is down!

List of Vendors

3Com
3165 Kifer Road
Santa Clara, CA 95052-8145
(800) NET-3COM

Ameritech Information Systems
4950 Blazer Memorial Parkway
Dublin, OH 43017-3384
(800) 292-2244

AST Research, Inc.
2121 Alton Avenue
Irvine, CA 92714-4992
(714) 863-1333

Borland International, Inc.
1800 Green Hills Road
P. O. Box 660001
Scotts Valley, CA 95067-0001
(408) 438-5300

Compaq Computer Corporation
P. O. Box 692000
Houston, TX 77269-9976
(713) 374-2726

Computer Associates
(Supercalc 5)
1240 McKay Drive
San Jose, CA 95131
(800) 531-5236

Data General Corporation
4400 Computer Drive
Westboro, MA 01581
(800) 344-3577

Digital Equipment Corporation
146 Main Street
Maynard, MA 01754-2571
(508) 493-5111

Epson America
2780 Lomita Blvd.
Torrance, CA 90505
(213) 539-9140

Hewlett-Packard
16399 W. Bernardo Drive
San Diego, CA 92127-1899
(800) 752-0900

Hilton-Pieper & Assoc, Inc.
6001 Savoy, Suite 207
Houston, TX 77036
(713) 782-6665

Lotus Development
55 Cambridge Parkway
Cambridge, MA 02142
(800) 345-1043

Micom Systems, Inc.
4100 Los Angeles Avenue
Simi Valley, CA 93062-8100
(805) 583-8600

Microrim (R:Base)
3925 159th Avenue N.E.
Redmond, WA 98052
(800) 248-2001

Microsoft Corporation
One Microsoft Way
Redmond, WA 98052-639
(800) 227-6444

MSD, Inc.
131 Park Street, N.E.
Vienna, VA 22180
(703) 281-7440

Proteon, Inc.
Two Technology Drive
Westborough, MA 01581
(508) 898-2800

SCO
400 Encinal Street
Santa Cruz, CA 95061
(800) 347-4381

WordPerfect Corporation
1555 N. Technology Way
Orem, UT 84057
(801) 225-5000

About the Authors

Susan G. Bateman has been a Systems Specialist at the Houston Academy of Medicine–Texas Medical Center Library in Houston, Texas since 1987. She is responsible for LAN planning, implementation, and training at the Library. She has a B.S. from Louisiana State University in Environmental Health and a M.S. from Houston Baptist University in Management, Computing and Systems. She has seven years of combined computer and networking experience.

Sanjay R. Chadha is a Systems Analyst at the Houston Academy of Medicine–Texas Medical Center Library in Houston, Texas. He has a B.S. in Engineering and a M.B.A. in Information Systems and Marketing. He has four years of combined experience in computers, expert systems, database design, and programming. He has taught graduate and undergraduate courses in Data Processing. His primary responsibility at the HAM-TMC Library is planning, designing, and implementing the Management Information/Decision Support System.

24

Internetworking a Library within an Enterprise Network

Ellen Moy Chu

Division of Computer Research & Technology Library, National Institutes of Health

ABSTRACT

In January 1985 the Division of Computer Research and Technology Library at the National Institutes of Health began as users on the Division 3Com EtherSeries local area network. This chapter reviews the evolution of library networking activities which includes server administration, installation and implementation of an independent 3Com EtherSeries network, upgrade to the 3Com 3+ Series, and collaboration in a 3Com 3+ public network to provide information services campus-wide. Library applications described encompass library office automation and shared files, software, and peripherals; networking of the circulation system for library staff; communications with users via broadcast messages, newsboards, and electronic mail; networking and internetworking of the library online catalog, information files, and CD-ROMs. These experiences are related within the context of the complex multiplatform and multinetwork environment of the larger organization or enterprise, the National Institutes of Health.

Introduction

Today, organizations are connecting employees throughout the enterprise by linking local area networks and computer systems at distant geographic locations and with a variety of platforms, operating systems, and protocols. Emerging standards and the convergence of technologies for connectivity and interoperability are creating new communications and information infrastructures. Not only do these changes transform how people get their work done, they also create new functions and roles for employees. Within the organization, new groupings and alliances develop, both formally and informally, introducing new relationships among components. This case study describes our library's networking experience within the context of the larger organization, as part of our Division local area network (LAN) and as part of networking and internetworking at the National Institutes of Health (NIH).

One day in 1984, workers appeared in our library to pull coaxial cable through the ceiling spaces. We were warned repeatedly not to step on these orange cables or dire consequences would transpire. There was talk of an "Ethernet" during the days of installation throughout our building. Then, in January 1985, two members of technical staff scheduled appointments to install network adapter cards and software in our personal computers for a "project." Thus, began our odyssey into networking.

We grabbed the coattails of the project to carve out new roles and functions for staff and the library. The experience has provided significant growth opportunities in network learning, in new relationships with other employees throughout the organization, and in staff development. Library staff became active members of the project, then contributed with independent developmental work. I will describe Division networking activities to provide the environmental context within which we operated. This will illuminate our library's integration within the organization-wide networking infrastructure.

Background

The National Institutes of Health, a national biomedical research center, has a major campus installation in Bethesda, Maryland, with offices and facilities nearby, as well as in Frederick, Maryland, Montana, North Carolina, and Arizona. NIH has over 14,000 employees, including 310 within the Division of Computer Research and Technology (DCRT). DCRT has three main functions: conducting research, developing computer systems, and providing computer facilities. These activities support biomedical research and administration at NIH. Our library's clientele includes Division and NIH staff interested in computer science, mathematics, and statistics, along with computer applications in biomedical sciences, engineering, and information science. Over 57 percent of registered borrowers are from other parts of NIH, which has over fifty buildings in or near the Bethesda campus. Library staff include two librarians, a library technician, and a part-time student clerk.

In the early 1980's, various Division components began projects to network different user communities for distributed processing. DCRT's conceptual plan for future computing architecture at NIH was to provide for the diversity of computing approaches. Exploration of a broadband network at NIH and developing telephone technology would support the linking of workstations, local networks, and the NIH Computer Center both locally and to collaborators worldwide. So began a multifaceted effort bringing Division components into close cooperation to support the institutional needs of scientific research and administrative activities at NIH. Since the Division mission includes computing support to NIH components, DCRT is a microcosm of NIH, with staff using all of the major platforms at NIH.

This case study starts with library participation in Division efforts to network IBM and Apple personal computers and workstations. The project brought together three DCRT components in a collaborative effort. These were the Computer Systems Laboratory, the Data Management Branch, and the Personal Computing Branch (at that time known as the Personal Workstation Office). The Computer Systems Laboratory supervised and developed cabling and connections of the DCRT Ethernet. The Data Management Branch addressed personal computing approaches to interface local and network facilities to the mainframe for database management systems. The Personal Computer Branch's participation would form the basis for providing guidance to other NIH organizations interested in interfacing personal workstations via LANs.

At first, the Division Ethernet connected these computers: The NIH Computer Utility serving 17,000 registered users with IBM 370 and DECsystem-10 operated by the Computer Center Branch; over 50 personal computers (IBM XTs and ATs); PDP11/23, 11/24, 11/34, and 11/70; MASSCOMP68000; Silicon Graphics workstation; Symbolics Lisp Engine; Apollo; and Apple SE. The cabling in the Division buildings support Transmission Control Protocol/Internet Protocol (TCP/IP), DECnet and Xerox Network Systems (XNS) protocols.

Our networking experiences began first as users, exploring network technology, followed by development and implementation of applications for library staff and services. During the course of the second stage, library staff installed a server, an independent network, and is now engaged in a collaborative effort to provide campus-wide information services on a public network.

Exploring the Division Network

In January of 1985, both of the library's IBM XTs and one AT were connected to the Division Ethernet for the pilot project.

Originally, project staff managed two 3Com 3Servers and one IBM XT for file server functions. Computer Systems Laboratory staff installed transceivers in the ceiling cabling to which thick Ethernet cable was attached and dropped for connection to our workstations. Personal Computer Branch staff installed 3Com Etherlink network interface cards and workstation software on our computers and connected these nodes to the thick Ethernet cables. They also gave a brief training course and provided assistance as needed.

Our role was to use the LAN in this pilot project; we were part of their test population representing nontechnical users. We were to experiment with the DCRT 3Com LAN facilities, providing input about positive and negative features. For our part, we wanted to investigate incorporation of this technology to improve library operations and services. Our use of personal workstations since 1983 had introduced many positive innovations in our library, and we were curious what future benefits might accrue from networking.

Selection of coaxial cable as the transmission medium throughout the building provided the nominal data transmission rate of 10 megabits per second. The Ethernet cable was pulled in a bus (continuous, linear) topology. Technical staff selected 3Com Ethernet EtherSeries which used the IEEE 802.3 network standard based on the XNS protocol. This bus standard uses Carrier-Sense Multiple Access with Collision Detection (CSMA/CD) which defines ways to avoid data collisions when workstations compete for the right to send a message in this contention scheme. When a user sends a message, the workstation sends a signal and if no carrier signal is detected, the message is sent. If a data collision is detected, a jam signal stops workstation transmissions and the workstations retransmit after individual random wait periods.

The 3Com EtherSeries network software, based on DOS 2.X, provided for user sharing of server disk and volumes, print spooling for shared printers, electronic mail, and security for private and public shared volumes. Network operating system commands included login and logout of the server; create, modify, and delete volumes; link to and unlink from volumes; create, modify, and delete users by the network administrator; and list a directory of users or volumes. The command syntax was so esoteric that, by April, a technical staff member created a "DOware" shell to reduce confusion and to simplify navigation to network functions and applications. The shell provides help messages which explain what the DOware command will execute and how to set parameters to individual needs. We mastered the concept of logical, versus physical, drives. In order to link to and unlink from network software and volumes, the user must specify logical drives in the command.

This early period was noteworthy for LAN crashes, with a frequency which tempered our initial enthusiasm. Downtimes occurred with cabling and transceiver problems, as well as resulting from developmental testing by technical staff. Also, the technology was so new that problems arose due to bringing together hardware and software designed without networking considerations. We had been forewarned that our personal computer software packages had not been designed for network use and we might destroy data if we tried multiuser access to these software applications. We tried single user access to dBase III and Lotus 1-2-3. This was quickly abandoned because data was lost if the network crashed during a work session. Consequently, we continued to use these and other software applications in stand-alone mode on the workstation, followed by file transfer to the server volumes in order to share information among staff. These included monthly statistical spreadsheets and dBase acquisitions and interlibrary loan transaction files. Library staff created shared volumes with passwords and read-write privileges for these files stored on the server disk. We discovered that the first one to link to such volumes had read-write privileges, but others who linked later could read only. EtherSeries did not have record locking. Instead, 3Com used semaphores to set a flag making the file local for the first user and to prevent data destruction by simultaneous writes by users who linked to the volume after the first user. Project network administrators installed a Hewlett-Packard LaserJet printer for network users.

We experimented with electronic mail. Among its many convenient features, the mail system allowed attachment of files to messages and creation of mail groups for mass mailings. For library staff we discovered this was a convenient way to transmit messages about daily minutiae, as well as to exchange files or other data. We began sending our monthly bulletin to users by the network electronic mail system. Having created the bulletin on local workstations, the file was uploaded to our Computer Center DEC10 for distribution to users on that computer; followed by export to the IBM 370 mainframe for users there. This was the first clue that we would confront connectivity and interoperability issues in delivering information services to our users' diverse computing platforms and protocols.

In August we set up a library newsboard. The newsboard contained current news items and announcements, the recent issues of our monthly bulletins, and information about a special personal computing book collection. Division network users could either set up their login script for immediate display of this newsboard, or, they could type "do news lib" to read our newsboard when desired.

The DOware creator also programmed the capability to flash news announcements at login. This was very effective in reminding people about scheduled events and deadlines. We simply sent a message to the network administrator requesting a news flash, specifying how many days to display the message.

In 1986 we began creating public volumes for remote user read-only access to information files. These included our journal holdings list, brief descriptions of the online databases which we accessed for demand and periodic searches, and listings of books ordered on approval.

Library Networking Applications

Having surveyed LAN capabilities, we saw opportunities to upgrade library services in a major way. Our networking goals were to:

1. Install or use LAN applications to streamline library operations with: shared disk storage space, shared software and printers, and backup of library files.
2. Develop and/or install LAN applications to enhance library services, such as an online catalog and CD-ROM publications for staff and users.
3. To promote proactive library role and staff image as information professionals in the "computer division."
4. Explore access to information on other systems or available on Internet.

Library Operations

We had already begun sharing library files among staff. Backups of our server files were performed by project leaders. We began sharing printers and performing our own backups when we acquired a server and backup unit. Library uses include office automation functions using dBase III+ 1.1 and WordPerfect 5.1, ASSISTANT 4.35 online catalog and circulation system, Kermit 2.31+NIH1 communications software for 3Station user, and electronic mail. A mail gateway has expedited distribution of our monthly bulletin and other mass mailings to library users on various computer systems and LANs. A Fax gateway allows convenient file transfers. We plan to access the NIH Administrative Database on the IBM mainframe to check status of procurements with a newly developed PC interface.

New Applications

Online Catalog

We had already completed a retrospective conversion in anticipation of an online catalog and had begun investigating DOS systems. LAN access to an online catalog, as well as other information systems, would provide a means to enhance accessibility to our services. Specifically, this technology would provide remote access to users in outlying buildings who had problems with limited parking on campus. Our Division staff, in three other buildings would also be able to use our information systems from their offices. The LAN would provide access after 5:00PM and on weekends when the library was closed.

In the spring of 1987, having surveyed the DOS network market, we tested BibSearch, Data Trek, and the ASSISTANT turnkey library systems. We selected ASSISTANT, an integrated network system with online catalog, circulation, acquisitions, and serials modules. The catalog and circulation modules were initialized in January 1988. Remote access to the catalog module for DCRT staff began in April. During this period we were the most active users of the LAN, and library applications provided a testbed for developmental investigations.

The ASSISTANT, programmed in C, uses the Btrieve network file management system. Division staff in four buildings on the NIH campus can search by call number, title, author, subject, and keywords. Boolean searches are available in menu and command line modes. The system indicates item availability. User response has been very positive, prompting other NIH staff to request internetworking access from their 3Com networks or dial access. Users can write search list output to file or to the printer. Currently, the system allows only one printer definition which is a problem for remote users who do not use Hewlett-Packard printers. The vendor is aware of this shortcoming and we look forward to enhancement in this area. With remote access, we are unable to track any difficulties unless the user contacts us. We plan to migrate to new releases of the serials and acquisitions modules.

CD-ROMs

Our independent project was networking of CD-ROM publications. When searching for a networking solution for CD-ROMs in late 1988 through the beginning of 1989, the only systems available for 3Com networks were AGAnet and Opti-Net. We were able to arrange for a test of Opti-Net in April 1989, with five concurrent users searching on one disk. The encouraging results led to our purchase of this software solution the following month.

Licensing for networking of CD-ROMs began in May 1990. At that time, it was impossible to negotiate site licensing, and licenses per node was unrealistic economically, particularly since we could not predict which users would access the systems. We obtained a six user and a single workstation license for Computer Select, and three user licenses for both Microsoft Programmer's Library and Lotus Prompt. The latter was a special arrangement since a staff member works with Lotus in testing new releases. The licensed users provide telephone consultative services to NIH staff and/or work on developmental projects. The workstation license was for the library public workstation which also had access to the Microsoft Programmer's Library. We have a number of CD-ROM publications which are accessed in stand-alone mode in the library. There was less demand for LAN access or no network versions to these publications: *Microsoft Bookshelf, Books in Print Plus with Reviews, CD-ROM Sourcedisk, CDMARC Subjects, Oxford English Dictionary* and *Science Citation Index.*

PUBnet

At this time, primary users of the Library networked information are on the DCRT 3Com LAN. This network has over 250 nodes in four buildings on the campus. Users include a cross section of administrative, scientific, and technical staff using primarily IBM PS/2s and Apple Macintoshes. A larger audience has opened up with implementation of a 3Com campus public network described below.

During this past year, we began collaborating with Personal Computer Branch staff on the implementation of The Public Network (PUBnet), the Campus Users Research Exchange (CURE, the 3Com users group) network to provide campus-wide access to information and services.

A copy of the online catalog and information files were installed on a PUBnet server in February. In March, we sent over our optical server with Opti-Net 1.20 software and an Online CD reader with three CD-ROMs (Computer Select, ICP Software Directory, and Microsoft Programmer's Library). We upgraded to a two concurrent user license for Computer Select and a fifteen-user license for Microsoft Programmer's Library. The Computer Select is operational. We are in the process of installing an upgrade of our DNET menu system to provide metering and password protected access to CD-ROMs. Installation of PUBnet dial access with PC Anywhere communications software now enables Macintosh users with PC MacTerm and terminal emulation by users with non-DOS operating systems to access our information systems. PUBnet uses the NIH RESnet data highway for improved performance.

Library information on PUBnet includes: the online catalog, contents of the library brochure, listings of books on approval available for user review and comment in the library, and CD-ROMs. We also provide journals holdings information and the most recent copy of our monthly bulletin.

Implementation

3Com 3Server

Project staff recommended we install and operate our own server to address our storage needs which would not be met on their server. We installed a library 3Com 3Server in September 1986.

This file server, and other 3Com file servers, do not have a monitor, floppy disk drives, or keyboard. Communications with the file server, to install or reconfigure network software and services, required a remote console connection from a workstation on the network with special network software. The server had a thumbwheel, toggle switch, and pushbuttons to boot the server in DOS mode, network operational mode, and to run diagnostics. Installation and configuration involved booting the server in DOS mode. The server administrator then accessed the server from a workstation using a diskette with software for a 3Console connection. One then followed system documentation instructions and the installation script to format the disk and set system and service parameters. Technical staff advised us on the answers to provide when we did not accept default settings. EtherShare, EtherPrint, and EtherMail services were installed by inserting and removing diskettes as directed.

Library staff network files and contents of home directories had to be moved to temporary server locations so that the DCRT network name service could be edited to point to the new server and new user locations on the library's server. After name service changes, data was moved into the appropriate library server user locations. Data migration procedures are carefully planned and supervised to avoid inadvertent data loss.

Upgrade to 3+Series

Data migration was required again when we used 3+Path to upgrade from EtherSeries to the 3+Series, version 1.2.1. The upgrade required reformatting the server disk and installing new software. Once again, remote console connections provided communications with the server in DOS mode and we were advised on what answers to provide in the installation script. After all installations and reconfigurations of services, Personal Computer Branch technical staff perform the 3Opt system tuning to optimize our server performance These staff are certified 3Wizards, having taken required courses and passed an examination.

The 3+Series written for DOS 3.1 provides record and file locking capabilities for multiuser application software. New network services included: 3+Route to internetwork, 3+Remote for dial access, 3+Menus, and 3+Start. Sharenames could now be created by users and servers for shared multiuser applications and files with options for passwords and access for public read-only, private read-write, and shared read-write capabilities. 3+Route and 3+Remote introduced the capability to internetwork with other 3Com LANs by dial access or on the NIHnet. 3+Menus which include network administration selections can be customized with additional selections for local needs. We use this menus system for library staff. Many administrative procedures were simplified with menus. 3+Start provides software to create and to administer 3Station volumes on the server. We used 3+Start for 3Stations described below.

Additional Hardware

Originally each library workstation and the 3Server were individually connected to the Ethernet with thick Ethernet cable. As we added 3Com 3Stations, we needed more cabling to accommodate an island configuration. The 3Stations are driveless and diskless, depending upon server disk space to operate. The Ethernet network adapter is built in and no fan is required. One creates a Start (boot) volume in 3+Start and sets system configuration on the 3Station, including the name of the Start volume name. The Start volume contains the AUTOEXEC.BAT, CONFIG.SYS, network drivers, and any other drivers or executables needed for that workstation. We borrowed a DEC DELNI multiport transceiver to cable several nodes to one thick Ethernet cable. We also borrowed a 3Com server backup unit.

This unit was cabled into our server and we set 3+Backup for automatic and unattended nightly backups.

Independent Network

In late 1988, to operate an independent library LAN, we installed a 3Com 3S/401 server, another DEC DELNI multiport transceiver, 3Com 3+ Version 1.3.1 network software, and 3Com Netconnect.

The server vendor sent a 3Wizard to design our network design for cabling and distribution of services between the two servers. This was reviewed by Division technical staff. We used a star topology to cable nodes and servers into a DELNI. Finally, the 3S/401 server was configured with an Etherlink card and connected to the DCRT Ethernet cable. This time installation procedures of network software had been simplified by 3Com. The 3S/401 model has an internal backup unit. A tape cartridge from 3Com allowed a quick installation option copying software directly from the tape. It was not necessary to install with a large number of diskettes. Figure 24.1 shows the configuration during spring 1990 when we operated as an independent network. Netconnect is the 3Com bridge-router software which handled the internetworking of the library's network with the DCRT LAN, and through this LAN to other NIH 3Com LANs.

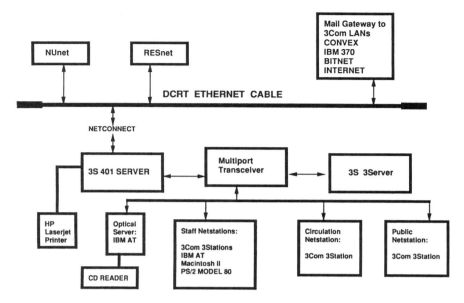

Figure 24.1
NIH Division of Computer Research and Technology Library 3Com LAN

We now had to install and enable services previously managed by the DCRT LAN administrator. These were the Name Service and Locator on the 3Server and 3+Start on the 3S/401 server. We continued, as before, with File, Print, and Mail services. The Name Service uses the 3N program to manage a database of account names and aliases, server names, and domain names for local and remote domains. The three part format is user name:domain:organization. Our domain name, "dcrt-lib," was defined as a network name by the DCRT LAN name service. The organization name is "nih" throughout the organization. User names must conform to the naming convention established by the Division Connectivity Group to minimize name duplication and to facilitate mail addressing when the sendee does not know the exact form of the user name entered on the network. In the 3Com version of NetBIOS, Locator centralizes NetBIOS-defined names in its dynamic name table. In August 1990 we upgraded to 3+Version 1.6 and replaced our original 3Server with a Model 3S/531 server in October.

Return to DCRT LAN

This past fall, we returned to the DCRT LAN as a local domain. This involved deinstalling Netconnect, and disabling the Name, Locator, and Start services. We disconnected the cable connection from the 3S/401 server Etherlink card and now cable the server with the thin Ethernet T-Connector in the back panel BNC connector. At that time, library cabling was converted to thin Ethernet to simplify reconfigurations of nodes. Previously, all Etherlink cards had a jumper set for a DIX (thick Ethernet cable) connection. Now, we can take the default for BNC (thin Ethernet cable) connection.

CD-ROM

The Opti-Net 1.20 software solution for networking CD-ROMs consists of: (1) the optical server, a workstation configured for full NetBIOS network access, with Microsoft Extensions for CD-ROM (MSCDEX.EXE) and with Opti-Net server software and cabled to the CD reader(s); and, (2) installation of Opti-Net user software on user workstations. User stations must also use MSCDEX.EXE, as well as an Opti-Net driver and program.

We installed an Etherlink Plus board on an IBM AT. The workstation was configured to boot with network drivers and with 3Com full NetBIOS and MINSES12 which are required for Opti-Net operations. Most workstations boot with partial NetBIOS to save memory. 3Com Link Plus Optimizer allowed downloading 3Com's MINDS drivers and NetBIOS onto the board to free up memory. The Online 4-drive CD reader was attached to this optical server and appropriate device driver statements were added to config.sys. Installation of Opti-Net is menu-driven. For the optical server, one follows the script for the server. Then each CD-ROM is installed on Opti-Net, given a name and is "mounted." The "optinet" command then operates the dedicated optical server.

We changed user access procedures. The user workstation is configured with the Opti-Net driver and must also boot with full NetBIOS and MINSES12. It then uses a batch file or menu selection to call a batch program on the server which temporarily loads MSCDEX.EXE, initiates a session, opens and closes a database, and exits. In this way, we could change procedures centrally, minimize user installations, and memory load.

Networking CD-ROMs to remote users has been extremely complex. A patch developed in-house was required to edit our NetBIOS name table entries in order to internetwork from our LAN to users on the DCRT LAN. Within a library network, one can control the user workstation configurations. In the course of visiting our Division staff users experiencing problems, the extraordinary range and complexity of their installations led to our advice to boot computers to login, free of any of their applications. Many of these users have loaded up their computers with hardware and software for testing and evaluation, as well as for very sophisticated applications. The RAM crunch is particularly felt by this type of user. MSCDEX.EXE takes 28K, the user workstation driver takes 4K, and NetBIOS takes 23K of memory. We use the Blue Max memory management system on our PS/2 Model 80s. A memory management system is usually necessary to assure full operation of many CD-ROM retrieval systems. With installation on PUBnet, we have discovered that PS/2 Model 80s which have disks partitioned through the high alphabets cannot use server batch files linking to drive letters existing on their computers. It has been an administrative chore to control distribution of the Opti-Net driver for our 100 user license. Online has announced a new release of Opti-Net which will eliminate loading the user station with a driver.

Current Hardware

Current library staff and public user network hardware comprise:

File Servers

3Com 3Server Model 3S/401, 2MB memory, 150MB HD, 80386 with 600MB internal backup unit

3Com 3Server Model 3S/531 8MB memory, 630MB HD, 80386 with 2.3GB internal back-up unit

Workstations

3Com 3Stations (80286 drive-less, disk-less workstations)

4 3Com 3Stations with 1MB RAM (2 at PUBnet)

2 Model 2E 3Com 3Station with 4MB RAM

IBM AT 20MB HD with 3Com EtherLink 3C500 adapter

IBM PS/2 Model 80 #858011, 8MB, 110MB HD, 3COM Etherlink/MC adapter

IBM PS/2 MODEL 80 #8580-A31, 8MB memory, SCSI 320 MB HD 3Com Etherlink/MC adapter

Macintosh II 80MB hard disk with EtherTalk

Printers

HP LaserJet Series II
LaserWriter II NT

Other

ELGAR IPS400 +600 (2) intelligent power supplies

Cabletron MR-9000C multiport repeater

Optical Server (Now at PUBnet)

IBM AT—Network Optical Server Dedicated Mode 20MB hard disk with: 3 Com Link Plus Optimizer, Etherlink Plus adapter, 1-Online 4-drive half ht. CD-ROM unit Model CDI100S

Staff

Installing and administering a server and a network required acquisition of technical knowledge and skills. In 1987, a 3Com network administrator training course supported server operations. Staff helped review pilot sessions of courses developed by the NIH Training Unit for both users and administrators. In 1990, 3Com training for the backup network administrator also supported our daily operations. Before installation of the 3+Menus, new employees needed extensive training to navigate through the LAN. Frequent reconfigurations to accommodate upgrades, or to work around system problems or limitations raises the stress level for all. Many adjustments are done on the fly or for temporary holding actions which impact normal operating procedures. Staff flexibility is required. Furthermore, it was and is essential to have procedures developed for other staff to handle routine network tasks when administrators are absent, as well as for disaster situations.

Technical Support

Library staff have installed and maintained networking hardware and software. We have also performed preliminary troubleshooting and attempts to resolve problems. When it gets too technical, we have relied on support from the three Personal Computer Branch 3 Wizards.

Our Guardian hardware server maintenance contract with 3Com entitles us to use Ask3Com bulletin board on CompuServe and direct telephone assistance. We do not use it because it is easier and faster to consult the local experts and, if necessary, have them use Ask3Com. We also do not want to wade through technical documentation. Their workload in assisting users and operating the DCRT LAN has led them to negotiate for contractor services in these areas. A contract may be in place within six months.

Vendor selection is subject to procurement at NIH. Although the Division had developed an excellent working relationship with one vendor who provided responsive and solid support, our purchase requests were assigned to the lowest bidder. Our preferred vendor would provide advisory services to assure we were ordering the right version or model of network software and hardware, and that we had not omitted some essential item. In some of our procurements, although we requested their General Services Administration contracts, purchases were directed elsewhere. Procurement frowns upon ordering from the same vendor frequently. With this background, we are frequently hamstrung by the situation.

Network Maintenance

Every morning, backup status files are checked to assure successful backup, prior to changing the tape cassette for the next run. Backups have saved us many times. Problems with the 3S/401 server required restoring the ASSISTANT application to the other server while repairs were underway. On several occasions, files have become corrupted and restoration from tape backups cleared up the problems. We also archive tapes and take them home to avoid a complete disaster at the library. Frequent checks are made to verify sufficient file server disk space and to monitor for computer virus infections. Periodically, we run software to check for computer viruses.

From the earliest days, we had learned troubleshooting workstation issues required determination if the problem was a network or local problem. Prior to memory management systems, we had to introduce procedures for rebooting workstations without network drivers to have enough memory to run certain applications.

Documentation

Our documentation includes: (1) blueprint of LAN cabling and file server hardware and applications; (2) file server configuration reports; (3) periodic backup tape logs; (4) workstation hardware description including DOS version and hard copies of the CONFIG.SYS and AUTOEXEC.BAT files; and (5) purchase, upgrade, warranty, service contract, and repair records. We try to document unusual messages or incidents for each workstation and server. These are the details technical staff and repair services request to diagnose problems. Our backup log also alerts us if there are large increases in server storage use.

Library Network Costs

As we planned for a server followed by a network, Division staff advised us on what hardware components and software costs to anticipate in our budget. Many of the overhead costs, such as cabling and 3Com software upgrades were funded by other Division laboratories and branches. In addition, as part of Division LAN activities, we often are able to get loaners or surplus from other parts of the organization. These may be permanently transferred to us, or paid back with items we order. In return, we provide whatever we can if there is need elsewhere. This trading around has netted us with one IBM AT, two 3Com 3Stations, and three IBM 8513 monitors. We transferred our original 3Server to the Network Task Group.

Our LAN costs are summarized in Table 24.1. Supplies includes backup tapes and printer supplies excluding paper.

Description	1986	1987	1988	1989	1990
Hardware	$8,841	$1,936	$20,704	$16,622	$18,217
Software	899	967	1,275	1,278	1,124
Service/Warranties	75	260	260	2,950	
Supplies	160	662	641	307	697
ASSISTANT	5,000				
ASSISTANT Maintenance	800	800	800		
CD-ROM Subscriptions/Licenses		1,958	4,663		
Training	587	965	1,196		
TOTALS	$9,815	$3,910	$28,441	$22,524	$29,647

Table 24.1
DCRT Library Network Costs

Current Environment

DCRT LAN

There are currently eleven servers on the DCRT 3Com LAN, two servers in the library's local domain on the DCRT LAN, two servers in the domain for staff in Building 31, two servers on the DCRT Token Ring, and one server in Philadelphia for a software development contractor. Servers include an IBM XT print server, a Compaq DeskPro 386, several PS/2 Model 80, 3Com 4XX and 5XX servers. Figure 24.2 displays the LAN configuration.

Applications vary from server to server. Some servers provide menus; others provide DOware. If a user has a license to use a specific application, and there is a network version, one may access the application on one's local server, or arrange to access another server with the application. Some of the applications include:

Database management system	Shared files
DOware shell	software upgrades
Electronic mail	documentation
FAX gateway	working groups
Group calendar	Shared printers
Library information dissemination	Shareware for IBMs and MACs
CD-ROM publications	Test or evaluation copies
information files	software
online catalog	training courses
Mail gateway interface	new releases
Presentation graphics	Word processing

Networking at NIH

DCRT recommended and supports 3Com Ethernet and Token Ring LANs for the estimated 7,000 IBM PCs and clones and 4,000 Macintoshes at NIH. There are over 100 3Com LANs at NIH, several operating 3+Open. The largest is a wide area network at the National Institute of Allergy and Infectious Diseases which interconnects eleven 3Com LANS in ten buildings at NIH, serving over 1000 users including some at remote sites 2000 miles away. With the departure of 3Com from the network management business, investigations are underway for migration paths to other systems. The original plan had envisioned migration to 3+Open, with an eventual path to LAN Manager codeveloped by 3Com and Microsoft. The announcement that Microsoft will be the sole supporter and developer of LAN Manager poses many questions. 3Com had supported both the hardware and software in networking. There are some misgivings about support and development for LAN Manager based on OS/2. The Division also supports DECnet among VAX users, is installing the Andrew File System (AFS) for Advanced Laboratory Workstations (ALW), and is networking Silicon Graphics workstations at NIH.

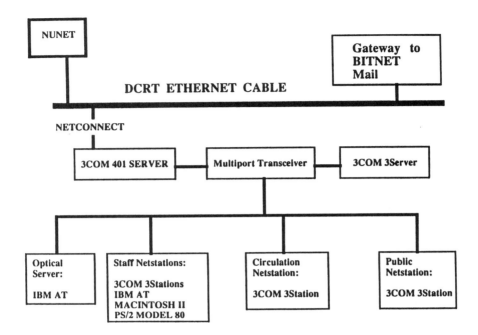

Figure 24.2
DCRT Library Network

Library users have extended computing platforms to include: Cray supercomputer at Frederick Cancer Research Facility; CONVEX mini-supercomputer replacement of DECsystem-10; iPSC-860 Scalable Highly Parallel Computer (Touchstone); and additional Apple workstations. Connectivity to some of these and other users is possible through a mail gateway. The Personal Computer Branch 3Com mail hub concept was adopted and developed by Computer Center Branch staff to provide a mainframe electronic mail gateway. Two high-speed central Ethernet networks connect to all remote NIH LANs and furnish connections to BITNET and Internet. One handles TCP/IP and DECnet; the other handles 3Com XNS. The mail gateway processes and reformats messages to pass mail from one protocol to another.

The original plan for a broadband campus backbone was replaced by a two-pronged approach. The NIH Computer Utility Integrated LAN and Workstation Support Network (NUnet) and the Research Oriented Network (RESnet) provide the two data highways to interconnect LANs in an NIHnet. T-1 and T-3 leased lines from the telephone company provide high-speed data transmission. NUnet operates at T-1 level, providing 1.5 megabits per second. This will be upgraded to T-3 service at 45 megabits per second. By the end of February, 78 LANs in 30 buildings have been connected, the most distant being at Research Triangle Park in North Carolina. A T-1 line also links the Frederick Cray. RESnet furnishes high-speed connectivity for scientific applications with fiber optic cabling, at 10 megabits per second, with one segment at 100 megabits per second. NUnet and RESnet Cisco routers support 3Com XNS, DECnet, and TCP/IP protocols.

New working groups formed in the course of networking NIH have brought together employees from many different parts of the Division and at NIH. These include the Division Connectivity Group, the 3Com CURE users group, the Division Server Administrator Group, and the Technical Lan Coordinators. The Connectivity Group, drawing members from all parts of DCRT, meets biweekly to identify and work together on NIH connectivity issues. Accomplishments include recommendations for a naming convention to standardize and minimize duplication of NIH user names across the various networks.

This group determines protocols supported, with recent debates about AppleTalk. The CURE users group meets monthly for question and answer sessions, announcements, and presentations. The DCRT Server Administrator Group now meets twice a month to evaluate and determine a migration path from 3Com. NIH 3Com networks have Technical LAN Coordinators who meet with Computer Center Branch staff for training and consultations for 3Com-NUnet related topics.

The NIH Training Unit has worked with the Personal Computer Branch to develop in-house training for network users and administrators.

Evaluation

How Well Has the Network Lived Up to Planned Goals?

For the Library we hoped to streamline operations and to share peripherals. This goal has been met with convenient shared access to files including acquisitions, interlibrary loan, cataloging work files, spreadsheets, and procedures. This has eliminated sneaker power to use another workstation or to transport information on diskettes. Two printers are shared among five employees. We have restored files and partitions from daily backups on numerous occasions which underscores the importance of this function.

Our second goal, to develop and/or install LAN applications to enhance library services has been achieved in the main. We had originally planned for Division-wide access. With installation of the online catalog, we immediately drew user requests for internetworking or dial access. Networking CD-ROMs has enhanced Division staff advisory or developmental activities in their own offices. With the installation of PUBnet, we are reaching users campus-wide. Some PUBnet users have never visited our library. Perhaps, PUBnet access may encourage them to drop by. Many may not. For these NIHers, PUBnet represents an electronic outreach program to previous non-users. The current information provided represents a starting point of basic information systems. We anticipate other information systems will be considered for our evaluation and possible implementation.

The third goal, to promote a proactive library role and staff image as information professionals in the "computer division" has met with great success. In presenting our interface of DCRT with NIH users, we hoped to showcase Division projects in practice. Our activities with CD-ROMs, including their networking and internetworking, allowed us to share our knowledge with other NIH staff. We presented seminars for the Office Technology Coordinators and the CURE users group, in addition to advising people who were starting up their local systems. Our deep involvement with the technical side of implementing a server, a network, and applications fostered credibility and respect with our Division collaborators. We also kept abreast of technologies they investigated which enhanced our reference services.

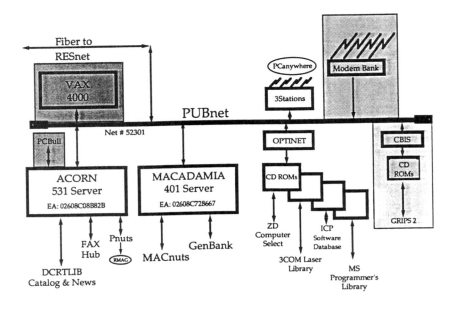

Figure 24.3
The Public Network at NIH

The goal to access information on other systems and Internet continues on an exploratory footing.

Questions about cost-effectiveness are difficult to deal with, given our Division developmental environment. We are part of a Division effort, providing a testbed to evaluate emerging technologies which are immature. As noted in the costs section, our library does not pay for the centralized cabling program within DCRT or throughout NIH, or for the network software site upgrade license. We paid for upgrades to new versions, but not upgrades within versions. In addition, many pieces of hardware are loaned to us, as needed and when available, by other DCRT components. Examples include two DEC DELNI multiport transceivers, the 3Server backup unit, numerous cables and Ethernet boards. By monitoring local activities, we also request transfer of hardware to us when others upgrade equipment.

Unforeseen aspects relate to the time crunch and the technostress. Progress has been slower than we would like for lack of additional staff or dedicated support for these new activities. Our local support is based on our 3Wizards' availability, often involving joint overtime. In addition, the continuous stream of upgrades and new releases constantly requires new installations which start a new cascade of troubleshooting. Library staff have discussed the burnout issue.

Decisions

There were very few areas of choice for us in this networking experience. Since we were riding a project administered by others in the Division, we had no say in the choice of the network type or brand. Their selection of 3Com Ethernet in 1984 was based, in part, by the fact that 3Com at that time had an open architecture. Their recommendations to NIH represent an effort to standardize across the organization. We would have chosen Novell NetWare, which due to its market share drives software developers to address their system first. With the departure of 3Com from the network management business, we are participating in the decision making to determine whether to migrate to Lan Manager, NetWare, or other possible alternatives. We expect to follow the organizational lead to remain compatible and to have a broad range of staff support on technical questions.

When we articulated our anticipated storage requirements for our library projects, project leaders recommended that we operate our own server and migrate from the server they were administering. At that time, a 3Server provided 70MB hard disk storage. Perhaps we might have objected to this suggestion and lobbied higher management to have them acquire and administer another server. By becoming a server administrator, we took on the installation and daily maintenance work, as well as version upgrade efforts which necessitated data migrations and significant staff time. However, server management has provided autonomy for numerous local adjustments when we wanted to make them.

We are still undecided about whether we made the right decision to leave the DCRT LAN to set up our own network. In 1988, our catalog, circulation, and other library network applications were buffeted by downtimes. With many different project groups using our Division Ethernet cable, an experiment with hardware or software installation by one of the project groups would bring the network down. Failures on individual taps also had adverse effects. It was highly unsatisfactory to have our production mode applications unavailable. Manual operations during downtime had to be entered whenever the network returned to operational status. There was no way to access information during downtime. The clincher was a two-day down period when a group experimented with a laser link to another building.

We announced our unhappiness with the fact that, although termed a production LAN, our Division LAN was still in developmental mode. The library appeared to be the only user operating a production mode application. Our efforts to go independent were rewarded as we were unaffected by ensuing downtimes on the DCRT LAN. However, we then had to survive two months of troubleshooting the 3S/401 server internal backup unit which was finally replaced. This was followed by other problems which were resolved by replacement of the system board three months later. Our exit did reform DCRT LAN management in reaction to our drastic action. By setting up an independent network, our CD-ROM networking application for DCRT staff remote access was delayed until we could resolve the NetBIOS internetworking solution.

Our decision to return to the DCRT LAN this past fall was based on repeated assurances by technical staff that the DCRT LAN was stabilized thanks to the efforts of the Black Hole Gang. The Gang is charged with bringing stability to our Ethernet by providing clearance procedures for attachments and installations on the Ethernet cable. We returned on a trial basis, retaining our domain. At our request, our cabling is set up so that with one swap in cable connections, we can pull the plug and run independently after reinstalling some network services. Our local domain name would then become an independent network name. Our library system vendor has indicated that it would be acceptable to keep a backup copy of our system on one of the Model 80s. This will provide a viable way to stay on the DCRT LAN. We would prefer this solution, as it would free staff from a variety of network administrative tasks to set up temporarily as an independent network to ride out possible crashes.

Our decision to buy a 3Com 3S/531 server last fiscal year was to lay the groundwork in preparation for migration to 3+Open. With the announcement of 3Com's cessation of server manufacture, we now have an expensive piece of hardware with an uncertain future. We thought this 3S/531 server would provide high performance and high capacity for the future network environment. We had a two-year budget plan to purchase this server one year and upgrade memory the second year. Our Division Token Ring uses IBM PS/2 Model 80s for server functions. If we had seen into the crystal ball, we would have gone this route.

Another unexpected hardware outcome was the use of our 3Com 3Stations. We purchased four 3Com 3Stations which are user-proof when set up with a menu and appropriate 3Start boot volume settings. 3Stations were economical solutions to providing circulation, staff, and public workstations. In fact, they turned out to be unpopular for public workstations, with many users wanting to write to file and depart with information on diskettes. We now need to purchase public workstations with diskette drives to meet public preferences. They are satisfactory as communications servers and some have been sent to PUBnet. Again, this is another piece of hardware discontinued by 3Com.

Our decision to acquire service contracts should have been an immediate course of action. Having lived through the delays of getting service combined with procurement actions, we now have in place on-site service contracts for our servers and our CD-ROM readers. 3Com announced these service contracts will continue to be available. However, price increases for next year are stunning. We plan to configure our second PS/2 Model 80 as a backup server which may alter the contract terms we select.

There is more to networking than cabling. Looking back, with six years of experience behind us, we pause often to reflect on what happened to and for us, how we personally have changed in how we react to the changing technological environment, and how our relationships with other Division staff and components have evolved. For the Division, the profound change in how we work together and what we are doing is the most impressive part of the networking experience. Many new formal groups and informal collaborations for training or cooperative ventures have brought together Division staff who used to have very little personal contact. Technical staff are now involved in training and support functions. The library staff got involved in the technical functions. These changes are forcing us all to examine the consequences of the new role boundaries.

Having largely completed development and implementation phases, we are consolidating and evaluating this first cycle. With a migration to another networking solution looming, it appears we may be into the new cycle before completion of these consolidation and evaluation efforts.

About the Author

Ellen Moy Chu started at the Division of Computer Research and Technology Library in 1974, finding a MEDLINE account, a dumb terminal, and a mainframe batch circulation system. Since then, the library has added access to OCLC, DIALOG, LEXIS/NEXIS, and STN. A new batch circulation system was designed in-house and inaugurated in 1979, followed by a mainframe document indexing system. In 1986, she served as Lead User in the Office of the Director, DCRT. With Lead User training, she provided installation, assistance, and troubleshooting for PCs and conducted OD staff training. NIH training activities include Associate Instructor for classes in PC-DOS, Advanced PC-DOS, Kermit, and dBase.

She has been the DCRT Library network administrator from 1988 to 1990, the server administrator from 1986-88 and 1990 to date. She shared her networking experiences in 1990 at the Fedlink Automation Conference and the SLA Annual Meeting. A graduate of Wellesley College, with an M.L.S. from the Catholic University of America, she has networked with librarians as a member of the OCLC Users Council Executive Committee (1981-82), the FEDLINK Executive Advisory Committee (1977-80), the President of the DC Chapter of SLA (1984-85), and the cofounder of Washington, D.C. ASSISTANT Users Group 1988.

25

The Evolving Local Area Network:
A Multi-Purpose, Multi-Protocol LAN

Michael Ridley and Paul Lavell
Health Sciences Library, McMaster University

ABSTRACT

The Health Sciences Library at McMaster University installed its first local area network in 1986. This tiny network which linked only three computers and ran only one software package has grown substantially over the years. Currently, the Library is a participant in a campus-wide LAN which offers a vast array of resources and provides a vehicle for a large number of library services. As the Library moved from being a manager of its own independent microcomputer LAN to being a participant in a campus-wide network it has had to react to changing technical environments, new applications, and differing modes of network administration and control.

As the LAN has evolved and been extended the Library has increased its understanding of the technology and the services it can support. During the past five years the network has become an essential resource forming the backbone of the growing number of computer-based activities.

Overview of the Health Sciences Library

The primary mandate of the Health Sciences Library is to support the educational, research, and clinical programs conducted by and for the faculty, students, and staff of the McMaster University Faculty of Health Sciences. The Library is also a resource for the McMaster Division of the Chedoke-McMaster Hospital, other McMaster University Faculties, the Hamilton-Wentworth District Health Library Network, the Northwestern Ontario Medical Programme (NOMP), and the McMaster Health Region. The Library's mandate outlines a wide range of responsibilities involving many groups at remote locations. Like many libraries in academic health centres, it has clinical as well as academic responsibilities.

The Health Sciences Library is located in the McMaster University Medical Centre (MUMC), a building which houses both the Faculty of Health Sciences and the McMaster Division of the Chedoke-McMaster Hospital.[1] The Library has a staff of thirty-five with nine librarians, a collection of 43,000 monographs and 1,800 current serials titles. The Faculty supports programmes in medicine, nursing, occupational therapy, and physiotherapy. It offers extensive graduate, post-graduate, and continuing education programmes. From its inception in 1965 the medical programme has been based on an innovative educational philosophy of problem-based, self-directed learning in a small group setting.[2] There are six teaching hospitals located in Hamilton and McMaster is responsible for the NOMP programme (based in Thunder Bay, 1000 km from Hamilton) which seeks to train physicians who will work in remote parts of the province.

The Library is administratively separate from the other campus libraries although it maintains many cooperative agreements and ventures with the University libraries. The director of the Library reports to the Vice President, Health Sciences.

Short History of the Network

In 1986 the Acquisitions and Serials Department of the Library wanted to acquire an acquisitions system. For reasons of cost and functionality there were two specific technical requirements: it must be microcomputer-based and it must allow multiuser access. At the time there were few true multiuser microcomputer systems and two were identified: the Sydney Micro Library System, now marketed by International Library Systems, and Data Trek from Data Trek Inc.

After deciding to purchase the Sydney system, it was necessary to install a network. Because the campus computer centre, Computing and Information Services (CIS), had been using 3Com's EtherSeries LAN software in a number of their student PC labs, the Library decided to adopt it. Our initial thin-wire Ethernet LAN was only 10-feet long and interconnected with only three PCs (two user workstations and the PC file server which ran the Sydney system). The "world's shortest Ethernet," as it was referred to locally, operated until the Faculty installed a full coaxial Ethernet system into the entire building in 1987.

While the Faculty of Health Sciences' computer centre, the Computation Services Unit (CSU), had a wide array of computers, access to these resources was primarily via modem or directly connected terminal. The proliferation of personal computers indicated that alternative, high speed and high capability access methods were needed. In addition, many groups within the Faculty were developing independent databases and computer-based services which were not easily accessible by others within the building. Connectivity and access became key issues. During 1986 the Faculty of Health Sciences undertook a large review to define its computer needs and investigate the introduction of a large-scale Ethernet system into the building.[3] The Library was a key participant in the needs assessment and implementation of the network.

The Faculty of Health Sciences was in many ways slow to catch on to the benefits of networking. By the time the Faculty installed its Ethernet the University had already established a large network. In 1985 CIS began installing an Ethernet system in a number of the main University buildings (Engineering and Science) and has continued to develop a well-defined network which displayed considerable forethought regarding widespread access to campus resources.[4] Since the campus Ethernet LAN preceded the Faculty installation certain technical choices were pre-determined.[5] The central concern about networking was to ensure a single, virtual network without isolation either by way of network hardware or software. Since network independence but also network integration were goals it was important to adopt certain accepted standards. The campus computing centre had explored a variety of microcomputer LANs and had already selected and implemented 3Com's 3+ LAN software. After the Faculty installed its network, the Library migrated from EtherSeries to 3+. In addition to the 3+ LAN protocols the staff also began using TCP/IP for connections to campus mainframe computers and services.

Initially, in order to maintain more local control over the network, a protocol filter was established on the bridge between the Ethernet in MUMC and the campus trunk. The filter prevented 3+ XNS packets from passing to the campus network from the Faculty of Health Sciences. As a result, the Faculty was able to maintain its own 3+ name server and independently control its 3+ networking activities. While the filter prevented the Faculty from utilizing the microcomputer-based 3+ resources on the backbone (i.e., the independent 3+ networks could not talk to each other), it did not affect TCP/IP access to any campus mainframe or minicomputer resource. This separation of the 3+ networks ended in 1989 and the fully integrated network began.

The Library has moved from a small, self-contained network running a single application involving a hand full of staff to a campus communications system with global linkages and running dozens of services and involving virtually all the Library's staff. The LAN has quickly changed the nature of library operations and services.

Current Status of the Network

The current Ethernet LAN at McMaster University is an extensive installation involving nearly all the major buildings on campus. Within the Faculty of Health Sciences alone there are over 350 PCs, terminals, or workstations connected to the network.

The actual physical network involves a series of backbones linked to the campus trunk (see Figure 25.1). The backbones contain legs and twigs which extend around the specific buildings. Links to the trunk are made by a variety of bridges and fibre connections. The Chedoke Division of the Chedoke-McMaster Hospital, located 5 miles from MUMC, is connected to the network via a T1 microwave link. The Occupational Therapy and Physiotherapy Department, located in another building on the Chedoke Division grounds, are linked via a 19.2KB leased line (See Figure 25.2). And, the Health Sciences Library has implemented a series of departmental computing resources on the network (See Figure 25.3).

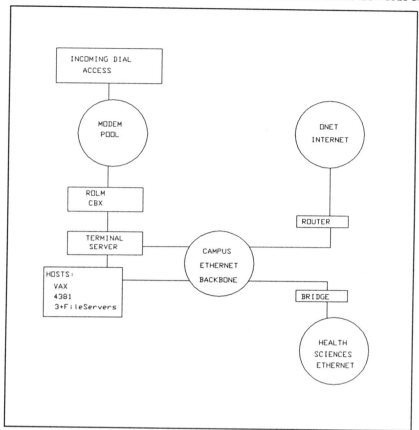

Figure 25.1
Organization of McMaster University Networks

The single Ethernet has multiple network protocols existing simultaneously on the same physical cable. The three principle protocols are XNS, LAT, and TCP/IP. Recently, the campus computer centre, Computing and Information Services (CIS), began implementing a microcomputer implementation of the Sun Network File System (NFS) produced by Beame and Whiteside Inc. NFS, and a small Novell network are able to coexist with 3+ and TCP/IP and share the same network. Utilizing the various protocols requires the workstation to have the specific network drivers loaded. It is possible to have simultaneously loaded both the 3+ and the TCP/IP drivers.

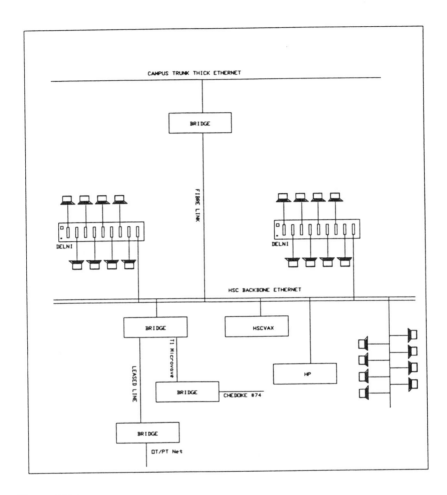

Figure 25.2
Diagram of McMaster Health Science Centre Network

User workstations on the network are primarily IBM compatible personal computers although it is possible to connect Macintoshes, Sun workstations, and terminals (via terminal servers). The PCs are generally connected by individual cables and transceivers and use either a 3Com or a Western Digital Ethernet card. It is possible to use a DELNI to connect eight PCs through a single transceiver connection. It is also possible to use "thin wire" Ethernet to connect as many as 27 PCs if the thin wire can be attached to an Ethernet leg or backbone and not a twig (using DEMPR or DESPR devices). The TCP/IP user workstation software is BWKTEL, a

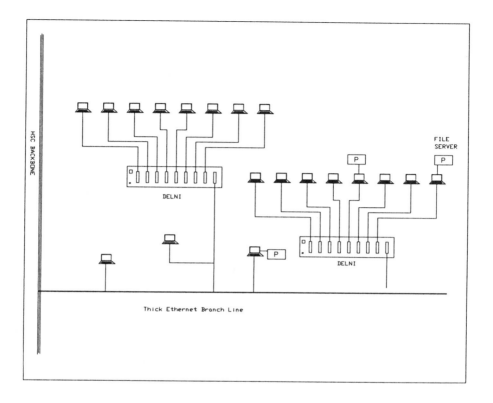

Figure 25.3
Diagram of McMaster Health Science Library Network

product of Beame and Whiteside Associates. The University maintains a site license to BWKTEL and BWKERM (its modem-based counterpart). The Macintoshes on the network are connected via the 3+ NuBus card or the Connectics card and use NCSA's Telnet software. Since the Telnet software supports only TCP/IP access, the Macintoshes are currently used exclusively for terminal emulation access to mainframe or minicomputer hosts. In the future, Macintosh-based file and print servers will be established.

Nearly all of McMaster's major computing resources are available via the network. This includes such resources as a DEC VAX 8530, a DEC VAX 6420, two IBM 4381s, an X.25 PAD, and a variety of Unix-based computers. A number of 3+ file servers have been implemented on PCs to provide a variety of services discussed later.

Within the Faculty of Health Sciences branch, the typical network usage during office hours varies from 10 percent to 35 percent of capacity, peaking at nearly 40 percent. During off peak hours usage falls to under 5 percent. Since Ethernet usage of 45 percent can represent a saturated network, the Faculty is exploring means of redistributing the network traffic. The campus backbone has experienced extremely high loads and CIS is currently planning to reconfigure the backbone to increase network throughput.

The administration and management of the network is a complex web of overlapping committees and areas of jurisdiction. Within the Library, network decisions are made by the Head of Systems and the Computer Systems Specialist in consultation with the Library's Management Committee. The Faculty maintains a number of groups overseeing network issues. The Administrative and Academic Computing Advisory Committees recommend computing directions to the Dean and Vice President, Health Sciences. Both the Head of Systems and Technical Services and the Director serve on these groups. In addition, a Health Sciences Center Network Implementation Subcommittee (HSCNISC) was established to focus on network issues and concerns. The 3+ User Group was established to increase Faculty awareness of 3+ resources and to monitor the expansion of the network. The Head of Systems and Technical Services sits on both groups. At the University level there are two important groups: the Operations Planning Committee on which the Faculty has a representative, and the network coordinating group which includes the Faculty's Network Analyst, the chair of the NISC. The former group explores overall campus computing directions while the latter group is concerned with the technical operation of the network, its growth, and its expansion.

Network Applications Used by the Library: 3Com 3+

The 3Com 3+ LAN applications are primarily those which utilize shared microcomputer resources such as multiuser databases, networked software, disk space, and printer access. There are dozens of 3+ file servers connected to the network. Most are private servers used by specific departments for local data and local resource sharing. 3+ has the following hardware and software requirements:[6]

Hardware Requirements

Workstation. The workstation must be an IBM or IBM compatible, with 384k of memory available (recommended) after loading the network drivers and a network adaptor card.

File Server. The file server must be an IBM or IBM compatible, with 384k of memory available (recommended) after loading the network drivers, hard drive and a network adaptor card.

Software Requirements

DOS 3.1 or higher is needed and the 3Com installation diskettes. A workstation can have a higher version of DOS on it than the file server but it is recommended that they have the same version.

3+ allows for three types of users on the system: network user, server user, and administrator. As a member of the network, the network user has access to the file server, programs, disk space, and printers. The user rights are limited by the Administrator—the Administrator may allow the user access to certain programs but the user cannot delete program files, change default settings permanently and can dictate where files may be saved. The server user is a user who signs on using the file server name. The server user can preform some of the Administrator duties like: installing programs on the network, allowing access to programs to the users and deleting software on the file server. The server user cannot add new users to the file server nor can he/she delete users on the file server. The Administrator has full access to the file server and has full privileges to 3+Share commands. The Administrator controls sharenames, applications, users, the rights that users have, and devices on the file server.

While 3+ has a number of options available (as shown below) when the software is installed, only two are required: 3+Name and 3+Share.

3+Share: consists of the file and print services. File and Print manages the sharing of disks, directories, files and output devices.

3+Name: manages the names of users and server on the network.

3+Mail: allows network users to exchange messages and files on their network, and, using the 3+Route or 3+ Net Connect on other networks.

3+Remote: provides dial-in network access for stand-alone personal computers.

3+Route: provides network-to-network communication and resource sharing among 3+ networks.

3+Net Connect: supports network bridges between networks (Ethernet-Token Ring)

3+Start: allows workstations with EtherStart PROMs to boot up directly from the network, with out using a floppy diskette or a hard drive.

3+Backup: copies network files from any 3+Share 3Server on the network to a cartridge in the 3Server Tape Backup unit.

3+Turbo Share: allows 3+Share to use the Expanded Memory.

The Library has a small PC file server with a 90MB hard disk which is used for a number of activities: the Sydney system, networked copies of communications software (BWKTEL), shared disk space, and locally developed programmes. A draft quality printer is attached to the server and is available as a shared printer.

Providing shared disk space via the network allowed the Library to extend the life of a number of its aging PCs equipped with only two floppy disk drives. With an Ethernet card these users now had access to the file servers with its large, fast disk drive and a printer they could use as if it were directly connected to their own machine. A number of commonly used programmes or data files are mounted on the server to ensure wider access. For example, in-house programmes to manage a small archival collection and history of medicine backlog were placed on the server so that the archivist, the acquisitions staff, and the reference staff had access to the database.

The network was originally installed to permit us to use the Sydney Micro Library System to run a multiuser version of their acquisitions module. That module, still in operation, is used by a group of three or four staff to order material, check financial information or monitor data. The system occupies approximately 20MBs of space on the server.

There are a number of public file servers on campus which the Library accesses. The Computation Services Unit maintains a server on which is mounted a number of resources for staff and students. CSU maintains network versions of a number of key resources such as WordPerfect, Quattro, Minitab, and BWKTEL. In addition, CSU regularly mounts interesting freeware packages and utilities which network users can access. Students are encouraged to use this software via the networked computers in the Library and other student areas in the Faculty. Computing and Information Services also maintains a public 3+ server. Like the CSU server, this maintains networked software for student use (WordPerfect, VP Planner, BWKTEL). New releases of BWKTEL and related software are available via this server.

A recent development in file server applications in the Library has been the utilization of CSU's VAX as a 3+ server. The Library has been acquiring computer-assisted instructional (CAI) software since 1985. Seven PCs in the audio-visual area are available for students to use the packages. The software itself is held at the AV circulation desk and charged out to users much like reserve material. After years of physical damage to the CAI disks, combating viruses, and planning to make the CAI more widely available, it was decided that the software should be moved to a 3+ file server.

The Computation Services Unit's VAX 8530 is used for a variety of research and administration computing. When the Library considered placing its approximately 100 CAI packages on the network it was suggested that the VAX might be a better server than a PC. Using the SMB 3+ Server software from Syntax, subdirectories on the VAX can operate like sharenames (or subdirectories) on a 3+ file server. Since the VAX was already operational and had lots of potential disk space it was an obvious decision to use this facility.

The CAI programmes themselves are expected to require approximately 100MBs of disk. However, in order to combat infections which may be introduced or to eliminate temporary files which may be added by users, it was decided that a complete backup of the software would refresh the CAI directories each night. As a result, a "clean" version is made available at the beginning of each day. This method of reducing the impact of infection would require twice as much disk space.

Three disadvantages of this service have arisen. Because of the substantial memory overhead of the network software, some programmes cannot run. These will still need to be circulated via our Audio-Visual desk in the Library. Some programmes require specific configurations (e.g., VGA colour, a mouse, etc.). Since the type of PC which can access the CAI is virtually unrestricted, the system must try as much as possible to adjust to the target machine or warn users about possible problems. Lastly, the software which allows the VAX to operate like a PC file server imposes a performance penalty. In particular, disk access is slow. However, this has not yet been a significant problem.

Linking the VAX to the 3+ network also gave connected PCs direct access to its high-speed draft quality printer. The availability of this printer (in conjunction with the laser printer connected to CSU's PC file server) has reduced the need for the Library to maintain its own set of public printing facilities. Library users can direct printing to the CSU printers which are conveniently located adjacent to the Library.

Network Applications Used by the Library: TCP/IP

In addition to applications using the 3+ LAN, the Library makes extensive use of the network services available via the TCP/IP protocols. These applications and resources are typically large-scale computers (minis and mainframes) which allow terminal access to their facilities.

McMaster provides an extensive electronic mail environment. The principal electronic mail systems in use are VMS Mail on a VAX 6420 and PROFS on an IBM 4381 (both are nodes on NetNorth/BITNET). The Vaxnotes conferencing system is also available on the VAX.

The Library is a heavy user of electronic mail and an active promoter of the technology with the Faculty and the University as a whole. Much Library, Faculty, and University communication is now done via electronic mail. The Library has actively participated in the Faculty's attempt to get all incoming medical and nursing students to use electronic mail and computer conferencing.

Most of the Library's managers consider electronic mail to be a vital tool. Since the VMS Mail system is linked to NetNorth/BITNET, the staff also uses the electronic mail system for external communications providing a valuable means of keeping in touch with colleagues and learning about new developments. In this context, staff members have become enthusiastic participants in the many library information science and health sciences lists being distributed over NetNorth/BITNET. Two lists originate at McMaster (SRCML-L@mcmvm1: a private list for directors of health sciences libraries in Canada, and INCLEN-L@mcmvm1: a list for the International Clinical Epidemiology Network).

The proliferation of lists on NetNorth/BITNET has resulted in a search for a more effective means of managing the list activity at McMaster. One partial solution implemented by CIS is the "Bulletin" facility. This application allows only one copy of list activity to be received and maintained on the campus node but anyone with access to the VAX can read the messages and respond to the list activity. The Bulletin facility allows users to manage high activity lists in a more useful manner.

Computer conferencing is another application which the Library has adopted extensively. The Library's interest in computer conferencing began in 1987 when it was a principal participant in the trial use of the CoSy conferencing system at McMaster. As a result of that experience the University decided to make conferencing a supported, campus application. The Library's experience with CoSy is documented in a number of publications.[7,8]

The Library has three primary uses of Vaxnotes: (1) administrative conferences; (2) library service conferences; and (3) conferences as information sources.

Since 1987 the Library has been using computer conferencing as a management information tool for the librarians and managers of the Library. A number of conferences were established to allow the management group to easily exchange ideas and information. The Director of the Library and the two senior managers use yet another conference to discuss relevant issues. The activity in these conferences varies but it has been considered a valuable means of information exchange. As the research points out, it is suitable for some but certainly not all management communications.[9,10]

The Library has also created a number of public conferences which allow the Library to provide information services in a conferencing context. Two of particular interest are: (1) MEDLINE: a conference to discuss various aspect of the database, the CD-ROM versions in the Library and utilization of Grateful MED, and (2) MORRIS: a conference to discuss the use of McMaster's NOTIS online catalogue which is called MORRIS (McMaster Online Resource Retrieval Information System). These conferences, while not busy, are a steady vehicle for the dissemination of information.

The Library makes heavy use of the Vaxnotes as an information resource, particularly in the area of computing and information technology. There are many conferences on such topics as electronic mail, communications, and microcomputer hardware and software to which library staff will post questions or participate in dialogues of interest. Many times the interactions in the Vaxnotes conferences have resulted in valuable information for staff or clients of the Library.

FTP (File Transfer Protocol) and Telnet capabilities are available from a number of the minis and mainframes on the campus network. By using these remote login and file transfer capabilities, the Library has been able to access the numerous online catalogues available on the Internet as well as take advantage of other computer-based resources such as the large software collections available from SIMTEL20, UWARCHIVE, and others. A locally implemented version of FTP allows staff to directly transfer PC files to and from the major VAX computers on campus. This file transfer protocol is significantly faster than the Kermit protocol and facilitates the transfer of large files (e.g., search output and large reports).

While the public terminals which access MORRIS within the Library are primarily IBM 3151 terminals hard linked to the system, staff access MORRIS via their networked PCs. The connection from the network to the IBM 4381 is made via a series of 7171 protocol converters. Since the network software (BWKTEL) permits simultaneous sessions, it is possible for a staff member to be logged on to MORRIS, electronic mail, and a number of other resources and simply toggle between applications. As more and more resources are dependent on network access and network resources, the ease of application switching is a crucial requirement.

The design of the network within the McMaster University Medical Centre established a parallel Ethernet configuration. The Faculty and the hospital had separate physical networks which were interconnected via a gateway. This separation was initiated because of the hospital's concern for confidentially of patient data. However, the gateway facility was implemented to permit controlled access to clinical data for teaching and research purposes. It also permitted hospital staff, many of whom are tutors in the Faculty's programmes, to access University resources. This design has only been partially implemented. While hospital staff are making use of University resources it has been very difficult to gain access to hospital resources for educational purposes. Concern over access and confidentiality has continued to restrict such usage.

From the network it is possible to directly access Datapac (one of Canada's national packet switched data networks) via an X.25 PAD. From Datapac the staff can access a wide variety of database services, electronic mail systems, and other computer-based resources. Having Datapac access via the high-speed network allows operating speeds higher than the 2400 baud maximum of the public Datapac ports. Within the Faculty, Datapac is used primarily to link to the MEDLARS system for access to MEDLINE. Easy access to data networks is one factor explaining the fact that the McMaster area has the highest number of MEDLINE users in Canada. CSU staff have been successful in making Grateful MED (version 4.0) operate over the Ethernet as opposed to the normal modem based access. While this implementation is still experimental it does point to improved user services by linking important user-friendly front-end programmes to high-speed data networks.

The Library's use of administrative computing services has also increased as a result of network access. The University's financial accounting system (FAS) runs on the IBM 4381 and is available from the network. Many staff use this system to monitor acquisitions budgets and operating budgets. CIS is progressively adding new campus information applications to their computing facilities. Campus-wide job postings are available via a public system as are the Material Safety Data Sheets (MSDS) which are made available to comply with health and safety legislation. Additional sources are anticipated.

Effects of the LAN on Library Operations and Services

Possibly the single most important development of the network has been the introduction of the personal workstation approach to computing. The Library's commitment to placing a computer on the desks of all appropriate staff has meant that this workstation must have access to all the resources (software, hardware, services) that a particular staff member might need.[11] The network is the final component. It is the vehicle which links people and resources and makes it cost-effective for the Library to provide a variety of expensive resources to all staff. Such a workstation could not be based on simple terminals or even on PCs with low-speed modem connections.

While many of the computer resources and services on campus were available previously via dial-up modems, they were not nearly as widely used. The problems of dial-up connections (low-speed, slow login process, busy lines, limited capabilities) served to inhibit the use of many computing resources. As more computer-based resources and services became available, fewer and fewer people wanted to tie up their phone line for connecting to these services. The introduction of the network permitted high-speed access with a guaranteed connection. The ease of connection coupled with the communication performance of the network caused staff to utilize new and different resources and services. Hence, while the applications remained somewhat the same, the access method radically changed causing staff attitudes and behaviour to change.

A simple example of this was the transfer of large data files. As a part of research project linking Canadian and Indonesian researchers via a computer conferencing system, the Library needed to upload search results into the conferencing system.[12] Even at 2400 baud these data transfers took a considerable length of time and tied up equipment during the process. The availability of high-speed transfers reduced a reluctance to supply extensive research results to the project participants.

The Faculty of Health Sciences supports faculty and students in widely distributed settings (MUMC and the regional teaching hospitals as well as NOMP programme). The microwave extension of the Ethernet which permits the interconnection of parts of the Chedoke Division has provided a link to faculty who often felt remote and uninvolved. The network is helping to alleviate problems traditionally associated with a decentralized organization.

The new residency programme in family medicine based in Northwestern Ontario requires library services. The network will facilitate access to the widely dispersed residents and their preceptors and allow them to tap into a variety of library services. In a similar vein, the library has been involved in a number of international projects which involve remote library services using telecommunications links.[13,14]

The proliferation of network resources resulted in the need to provide a simple menu interface for the users of the network. CSU developed a menuing system which would operate on all the publicly accessible computers (those in the Library and the student areas). The menu provided easy access to the various 3+ servers as well as the mainframe resources on campus. As new services become available, such as the CAI software, they can be quickly added to the menu. The provision of the menuing system should facilitate the use of the vast array of network resources.

Using a LAN: Problems and Issues

LANs are a complex technology. If the Library is maintaining its own independent LAN it will require considerable local expertise to attend to hardware and software problems. As the LAN becomes connected to a larger network, such as a building or campus network, the complexities of LAN management and control increase.

Large networks require dedicated network staff who understand the technical details of LAN construction and operation. Typically these would be provided by the campus computing centre. However, the library cannot absolve itself of responsibility for understanding network operations. The experience of the Health Sciences Library suggests that many network applications and uses are not well understood by computer centre staff and the library must be an active participant in the design and operation of the network. As has been suggested earlier, the LAN has become a fundamental component to library operations and services. For the library to ensure effective operations the LAN must perform in appropriate ways. This requires the library to have the technical expertise to understand network developments and work with network staff throughout the University to maintain and improve the LAN.

Reliance on the LAN for library operations and services results in the need for consistent, reliable LAN operation. From 1985 to 1990 the Health Sciences Library dramatically increased its acquisition and use of computer technology. The Library had three PCs in 1985, and forty PCs in 1990; it had two modems in 1985, and ten modems and twenty-three network connections in 1990. The financial implications of such a technology change are not insubstantial. The purchase of new equipment and the maintenance and upgrading of old equipment is a new expense for the Library and must be planned for and managed carefully.

Furthermore, other resource needs develop. For example, increased use of VMS Mail caused allocation problems. As the Library became a heavy user of electronic mail the staff required more disk space to receive and store messages. Limited disk space on the VAX for an individual's files and mail manage can reduce the effectiveness of the service. Overflowing an IDs disk allocation can result in electronic mail being disabled and messages refused.

By 1990 the one person systems department in the Library was unable to handle the hardware and software problems, training needs, and user consultations. The effectiveness of the network and the computing resources was being drastically undermined by the lack of local support. The Library was slow to recognize the source of staff discontentment with computers and computer-based resources. Part of the problem was the difficulty in obtaining a new position in the Library during a time in which budget cuts and austerity measures were forcing the Library and the University to reduce costs. However, by readjusting existing staff positions the Library was able to create the new position of Computer Systems Specialist. The Computer Systems Specialist allowed the Library to vastly improve support service to staff and users. Progress towards increased networked resources and services have accelerated.

Using a network involves a complex set of instructions and a new level of understanding on the part of the user. Incorporating network use into staff activities highlighted the central role of user training and support. It is possible, via menus and interface software, to hide the structure and operation of the network from the user. This approach which utilizes scripts, batch files, user "recipes" and other techniques tends to make the network a "black box" which the user does not understand. While users should be isolated from the technical complexities of the network, it is a mistake to isolate them from an operational and intellectual understanding, especially when adequate training and support would give them this understanding and probably increase their effectiveness. The "black box" approach falls apart quickly when the user experiences a network related problem. The user with no understanding of the network cannot perform even the simplest diagnosis nor can they be useful in trying to explain the problem to technical staff. While it is not essential for all users to know the full background of the network, all users should have a sufficient understanding of the network to be able to identify a network problem and provide an explanation of what occurred to the systems staff. Feedback to the user after the problem has been corrected is also important. Users should know what the problem was, how it was fixed or how the problem will be resolved and what should be done if the situation occurs again. An informed staff will greatly reduce concern about the network and facilitate the rapid identification and correction of problems.

Initial training and ongoing support is obviously central. However, libraries must be aware that even experienced users will need assistance migrating to new versions of the software or responding to changes in operation. Even the smallest change can cause trouble for new or inexperienced users and often changes happen without the libraries' prior knowledge. Library system staff need to be on top of modifications and new procedures. This is particularly true of computer resources managed by other departments. The library system staff must be conversant enough with the network and its applications to react to these changes and guide users through the new environment.

Complete user confidence in the network is an important prerequisite to expanded use. User confidence in the network must be earned, often slowly, and is very quickly lost as a result of problems or uncertainties. Because of the Sydney problems, discussed later, it took a long time for the Technical Services staff to accept the network. Demonstrated performance over a long period of time is essential. A corollary to this is if you accept the network and you depend on it then it must be available at all times.

The network has been very reliable and stable. This was a key concern if the Library were to use it for day-to-day operations (e.g., acquisitions, cataloguing, communications, etc.). The campus and the Faculty have made key commitments to providing a production network. The Faculty has a Network Analyst who works closely with the Library and other network users to ensure network operation and effectiveness. There are specific procedures for problem reporting and a mechanism for user notification of unanticipated interruptions in service. However, user perceptions change as they adopt the network as an important tool. Unexpected downtime causes considerable frustration.

Using microcomputer software in a networked environment raised problems which were largely unexpected. The current networked applications are certainly more stable than when the Library installed its first multiuser application. However, each new package presents its own difficulties and problems. Integrating new equipment and new software is a much more complex task in a network environment. A full testing and debugging period is mandatory in order to be aware of adverse effects on existing operations and services.

An example of the complexities which can arise can be illustrated by the problems encountered trying to run the Sydney Micro Library System on the 3+ LAN. While Sydney ran under 3Com's EtherSeries software the staff experienced no problems with the multiuser aspects of the system. Multiple users could access the system, updating records virtually simultaneously, and no problems were experienced with file or record locking.

As the Library moved to the full Faculty implementation of the Ethernet and migrated from EtherSeries to 3+, difficulties arose. Regularly the acquisition staff would lock up the system because of record contention. This often resulted in corrupted indexes and necessitated a full index rebuild which caused the system to be unavailable for a number of hours. Determining the problem involved a long process in which all parties denied responsibility. Sydney support worked at length with us on the problem. However, since they recommend the use of the Novell LAN software with their system they were unfamiliar with 3+ and could not replicate the problem at their Novell sites. The 3+ support people indicated that the application was at fault. Local network support people suggested hardware problems.

Eventually the Library systems staff discovered the problem. The Sydney system relies on a custom interpreter, PCBUS Language Interpreter written by Infopoint Systems, to run in an MS-DOS environment. In virtual desperation, the Library contacted this company and explained the problem. They too denied the problem was theirs. However, about six months later the company was involved in an install of the Sydney system in a 3+ environment for a client in Hong Kong. The same problem arose and a deficiency in the way the interpreter worked with the main Sydney code was discovered. A new version of the interpreter was eventually incorporated into the product and the problems the Library was experiencing disappeared. This process took nearly twelve months and caused considerable concern in the acquisitions area.

Another unexpected problem with 3+ was the high memory overhead required to run the software. A fully networked PC with DOS, the 3+ software, and the TCP/IP drivers have only 437K left for application software (see Table 25.1). In a number of cases this was insufficient to run specific programmes. With a 286 or 386 machine it is possible to use products such as Quarterdeck's QRAM to move software drivers into high memory or memory reserved for video. It was much more difficult with the basic PC machines.

The memory problems were one of the factors inhibiting the Library's implementation of networked CD-ROMs. Most CD-ROM applications require a full 512KB of available memory. Having tested the CD Net software in the 3+ environment the Library soon discovered that only specially equipped PCs would be able to access the CD-ROMs (e.g., 286 or 386 machines with sufficient free memory).

Since the object in networking the CD-ROMs was to make the service widely available the need to specifically modify machines undermined this goal.

Software	Version	Memory Used
DOS	3.30	61K
BWKTEL	4.6	35K
3Com	1.1	129K
Available		437K

Table 25.1
Memory Use in Network Workstations

Until the memory requirements for Sydney were reduced as a result of a new release, some workstations could not load both the TCP/IP and the 3+ drivers and still access Sydney. Until this problem was corrected by the new release, these staff members had to reboot with an alternate CONFIG.SYS and AUTOEXEC.BAT to load only the appropriate drivers.

Acquiring network versions of software can save money and time and facilitate increased staff productivity. However, problems can exist when you have a single-user software program with many users wanting access to it. This problem was resolved by the use of batch files. A user will start a batch file which will search to see if the "CHECK" file exists. If it does not it will create the "CHECK" file and allow the user access to the program. The next user trying to access the program will find that the "CHECK" file exists, will receive a message "Program in Use," and then will be returned to the menu. The "CHECK" file is deleted after the user has exited the application.

Some software are not network compatible and require a local hard drive or floppy drive. Check to ensure the files the program needs to open and write to are not in a read only location. Using the DOS assign command to tell the software that it is working on the "C" drive when in fact it is on drive "G" can often permit a non-network compatible programme to operate on the network.

The administration and control of a LAN is an important consideration. When the Library had its own self-contained "thin" Ethernet, it was in complete control of all aspects of the network and its operation. When the Library deinstalled this network and adopted the Faculty and campus-wide Ethernet it became merely a user, albeit a high-traffic user, in a large network. Decisions about network management and network resources became a campus-wide concern and the administrative complexities of running on the network increased. To a certain degree, the decision to integrate the networks resulted in a loss of local autonomy (both for the Library and CSU). Network management was a campus-wide issue and developments might not follow the path favoured by the Faculty. However, involvement in a large network gave Faculty users of the network vastly increased resources and access to technical and support services which were previously unavailable. The loss of autonomy was more than compensated by the improved services for students, faculty, and staff.

An example of the complexity of interconnected networks arose during discussions concerning the removal of the network filter that logically separates the various 3+ networks. A critical issue in linking the Faculty 3+ network with the campus 3+ network was the version of 3+ being run on the respective networks. Linking the networks required consolidation of the 3+ name server and would require the campus to upgrade its version of 3+. It was not obvious to CIS that this upgrade was necessary. However, the Faculty was already operating on the newer version and could not retrofit an older version. Eventually the campus upgrade was completed and the two networks joined.

Another example of this problem is the use of 3Com's 3+Start product. CIS uses 3+Start to boot up PC from a networked server. Hence, the PC requires no hard disk or floppy disk. A PROM on the 3+ Ethernet card directs the PC to a specific server where DOS and the network drivers are found and can be loaded into the PC. Unfortunately, the difficulties in using a 3+Start server which links to different resources has meant that the Library cannot incorporate 3+Start into the PCs in the Audio-Visual area. This has required the continued use of "start up" disks, available from the AV circulation desk, to boot up the PCs.

Security

The use of file servers to support the work of many users introduces a number of equipment and data security issues. A file server can simplify data security since it is possible to do regular backups for all users. Individuals are notorious for not protecting their own data. With a file server, the Library can operate a regular backup service to protect its staff. However, a file server is also a single point of failure which can have widespread effects. Equipment failure on the server might leave a large number of staff without the resources to do their jobs. As a result, disaster recovery procedures are vital.

Care should be placed on the location and access to the file server since it is the one piece of the network which should not fail. A problem experienced by the Health Sciences Library with it's file server has been with its location in the technical services area. The file server has been bumped by library and cleaning staff resulting in lost information. Because it is in an open area it attracts large amounts of dust which can effect server operation. An advantage of the open location is that staff can quickly check to see if the file server is frozen and inform the systems staff who can then easily access the machine. In addition, in the 3+ configuration the shared printer must be directly attached to a server. Since the printer must be in an area easily accessible by staff, the server was also positioned in a staff area. At the present time a new location is being sought with all the advantages of the old location but none of the disadvantages.

Future Developments

As connectivity and network capabilities increase it seems obvious that the potential of networks for library services have only been partially realized. Future developments in the Health Sciences Library involve adding applications and services to the existing network as well as expanding direct user access to network resources. Providing a seamless link between the computer-based resources of the Library, the Faculty, the University, and the academic and commercial networks is a key area of library development.

An expanded high-speed network would link all the regional hospital libraries and facilitate increased traffic and support the transfer of graphics and even video. CD-ROM networking is still a concern although the Library hopes to find a technical solution which involves a TCP/IP-based server rather than the limited PC servers of most existing implementations.

New applications need to be added to the Library's server for the benefit of the staff. This would include resources such as a Library-wide scheduling system (for people, resources, and room bookings) and a more sophisticated menuing system which will increase access to the available resources. As the University upgrades the backbone networks and introduces new networking capabilities the Library is in a position to rapidly exploit these services. The key to future developments is understanding the technology and its potential.

Conclusion

The Health Sciences Library at McMaster University has had an extensive involvement in all aspects of local area network installation, management and use. As a result of this involvement the LAN has become an essential resource.

However, the Library has had to meet new challenges because of the network and its overwhelming effects. Issues which require constant attention are user needs and expectations, the impact of increased hardware and software requirements on budgets, the need for informed library systems staff, and realization that new capabilities require careful attention to change within the workplace. The staff in the Health Sciences Library have always approached change and innovation with enthusiasm and an open mind. The willingness of the staff to adopt new technologies and work through the frustrations of new developments are the most important factors in the evolution of the LAN.

Notes

1.   Beatrix H. Robinow, October 1972, "New Medical Library Buildings IV: The Health Sciences Library, McMaster University, Hamilton, Ontario," *Bulletin of the Medical Library Association* 60(4): 559-565.

2.   J.F. Mustard, V.R. Nuefeld, W.J. Walsh and J. Cochran, *New Trends in Health Sciences Education, Research, and Services: The McMaster Experience*, 1982, New York: Praeger.

3.   Faculty of Health Sciences., Administrative Computing Advisory Committee. 1986, "Recommendations for a High Speed Local Area Network (LAN) in the Health Sciences Centre." Hamilton: McMaster University.

4.   Diana Van Hoesen, January 1988, "McMaster University," *Cause/Effect* 18-20.

5. Bob Shepard, January 1986, "Ethernet at McMaster," *Directions: Computing News* 86(1): 3-5.

6. 3Com.,1987, *3+ Installation and Configuration Guide*, Santa Clara, CA: 3Com.

7. Khursh Ahmed and Michael Ridley, 1988, "Computer Conferencing in Health Sciences–CoSy at McMaster," *Proceedings of the 12th Annual Symposium on Computer Applications in Medical Care*. Edited by Robert A. Greenes. New York: Institute of Electrical and Electronics Engineers, 556-561.

8. Dave Cook, and Michael Ridley, December 1990, "Computer-Mediated Communications Systems," *Canadian Library Journal* 47: 413-417.

9. Cook, 413-417.

10. Elaine B. Kerr, and Starr Roxanne Hiltz, 1982, *Computer-Mediated Communications Systems: Status and Evaluation*, Orlando: Academic Press.

11. Michael Ridley, June 1987, "Personal Workstations at the Health Sciences Library of McMaster University," *OCUL Applications* 1(2): 4-5.

12. Gabi Pal, Jim Brett, Tom Flemming, and Michael Ridley, November 1989, "Providing Electronic Library Reference Service: Experiences from the Indonesia-Canada Tele-Education Project," *Journal of Academic Librarianship* 15(5): 274-278.

13. Pal et al., 274-278.

14. Elizabeth Alger, Vic Neufeld, Michael Ridley, April Jones, and Peter MacDonald, 1990, "Computer Communications and Information Technology in Support of Community Oriented Medical Education," *Improving Community Health Through Applied Technology: Proceedings of the Third National and First International Conference on Information Technology and Community Health* (ITCH90), Victoria, B.C., Sept 30 - Oct 3, 1990, Victoria: University of Victoria, 29-33.

About the Authors

Michael Ridley is the Head of Systems and Technical Services at the Health Sciences Library, McMaster University (Hamilton, Ontario, Canada). He holds an M.L.S. from the University of Toronto and an M.A. from the University of New Brunswick.

Ridley is a past President of the Canadian Association for Information Science and is currently an Associate Editor for the Public Access Computer Systems Review. His research interests include computer mediated communications systems especially in conjunction with library services in the developing world. BITNET: mridley@mcmcaster Internet: mridley@sscvax.mcmaster.ca.

Paul Lavell is the Computer Systems Specialist at the Health Sciences Library, McMaster University (Hamilton, Ontario Canada). He holds a diploma in Marketing from Mohawk College and is currently enrolled in a B.A. programme at McMaster University.

Lavell's main responsibility is to ensure the smooth operation of the Library's diverse computing hardware and software. BITNET: lavell@mcmaster Internet: lavell@sscvax.cis.mcmaster.ca.

26

Library use of a Campus-Wide Asynchronous LAN

Pamela Snelson
Drew University

ABSTRACT

Drew University aggressively promotes the use of microcomputers throughout the campus, achieving the goal of providing one computer per person. A campus-wide voice/data network links these computers together into an asynchronous LAN. This chapter describes the Library's use of the LAN.

Introduction

Drew University is an independent University composed of a College of Liberal Arts, a Graduate School, and a Theological School. Committed to extending the use of technology in support of learning, Drew has sponsored a series of initiatives to advance this goal. The Computer Initiative was designed to take the first major step toward the integration of information technology into Drew's liberal arts program by giving every undergraduate student, every faculty member, and every staff office a personal computer. Begun in the fall of 1983, the Computer Initiative was fully implemented as of September 1987 when the total number of personal computers reached about 2,000 or a 1:1 ratio of PCs to people. The major result of a second program, the Knowledge Initiative, was the creation of a fully integrated technology system in 1988. Library use of this simultaneous voice/data network is the focus of this chapter. A broadband network connection was added in 1990.

The University Library collection, numbering close to 500,000 items is housed in three locations. The main library encompasses most of the collection. A separate Methodist Library was established in 1982 when the archives of the United Methodist Church were installed at the university. A small Science Building Library, consisting of reference material and bound journals, serves the needs of the Chemistry Department. The facilities are linked through the Libraries' Data Research Library System, OAK (Online Access to Knowledge). The system currently offers automated circulation, cataloging, Acquisitions, online catalog, and serials control.

Goals of the Network

The common technology infrastructure provided by the campus network and PCs is intended to create opportunities for use, initiative, and creativity which help meet individual and institutional goals and needs. The distinctive, and perhaps experimental, underlying concept of this plan is the notion of pervasiveness: the technologies which are of greatest interest are those which can be provided to everyone in his or her normal working environment and can be made part of every person's daily life. It is our belief that the long-term impact of technology within a liberal arts environment will not come from specialized high-tech labs but from the use of shared tools which facilitate information access, processing, and exchange among and for people. The campus network is primarily designed to accomplish this approach.

The network provides four functional components: (1) a data network linking the three campus computer centers (academic, administrative and technology systems), all PCs on campus and external networks; (2) an electronic mail facility allowing for the interchange of document oriented information through the data network; (3) a voice system which allows full and timely communication among all members of the campus community and with the external world; and (4) a voice processing facility including voice mail, voice menuing and delivery of standard information.

Users of the System

In principle the installed system provides every person at Drew with access to every other person, every database, every major computer resource, every external network connection, and every personal computer. In reality each member of the university community—student, faculty and staff—has a network account. No categories of people are excluded from the network. Use of system capabilities varies with the individual. Some university committees conduct much of their business on the network. Professors give class assignments and receive work electronically in disciplines that range from music to political science to biology.

Electronic mail services allow a wide range of transactions between the library and university community. One unique feature is the ability to send Library notices (recall, fine, overdue, and/or personal reserve) directly to student and faculty electronic mail boxes. Besides vastly reducing paper costs, the electronic sending of notices allows the receivers of notices to respond electronically to the Library. Library staff use the network daily since it provides access to the library automation program. Non-university people use the library catalog on the network through public terminals located in the library.

Network Connections and Equipment

Network services are provided through connection to a VAX 6310, a VAX 6330, a Digital ULTRIX system, and a Prime 4450. Faculty, students and staff access the network through a variety of IBM-compatible PCs and terminals. A common terminal emulation software (Kermit) is provided to all users. In the Library, for example, public connections to the network are via DEC VT-320 terminals and are directly wired to the VAX 6330. Library staff may connect via either terminals or

PCs. Each users equipment, whether it is a PC or a terminal, connects to the network using Intecom equipment consisting of a phone unit and an asynchronous data interface, a proprietary digital device not unlike a modem.

System Use

The Drew network offers services which can be grouped into four areas: Academic Computing, Administrative Computing, Network Services, and Voice Services. Academic Computing offers programming languages, statistical packages, and other applications running on a VAX 6310 with 32 megabytes main memory, 2.4 gigabytes storage and 72 ports. A networked Digital ULTRIX system including 5000, 3100, and 2100 series systems was recently added. Administrative Computing supports a single, comprehensive, relational administrative information system including all facets of university operations. The system runs on a Prime 4550 with 16 megabytes main memory, 2.5 gigabytes storage and 120 ports. Network Services include library automation, electronic mail with about 70,000 active messages at any one time, call accounting software handling 1.3 million calls per year, external network connections, and about 60 other applications. This operations runs on a VAX 6330 with 2,500 accounts, 64 megabytes main memory, 5 gigabytes storage, and 128 ports. A voice and data switching system with 2,500 voice and 2,500 data ports, Voice Services is actually a nearly one million dollar Drew telephone company. It handles about 2.5 million external calls per year running on a mixed fiber/copper switched network with 131 trunks and one T-1. Voice mail/voice processing handles about 5 million calls per year on an Octel system with 100 hours of storage and 48 ports.

The network benefits the Library in many ways. Most important, it allows the entire campus community easy access to the online catalog. Since "LIBRARY" is one of the options on the top-level network menu, the access is prominent and obvious. The Library submenu options include Grolier's American Academic Encyclopedia, user search guides, the online catalog, library hours, a book recommendation form, and a form for placing titles on course reserve. The online encyclopedia is a favorite item. When we needed to remove the encyclopedia for system maintenance for several days, the level of campus complaint was surprising.

The campus electronic mail system is Digital's All-in-1. Once the installation of the automated library system placed terminals or pcs at the desk of each staff member, serious intralibrary use of electronic mail became feasible. Minutes of meetings and the weekly in-house newsletter are routinely distributed through electronic mail.

Selection

Serious planning for the campus network began with a lengthy national search for telecommunications and networking consultant support. After careful evaluation we selected Telegistics, Inc. as having the best match of capabilities with our needs. Their services included system design, RFP preparation, and evaluation and contract negotiation. We now have a unique partnership with Bell Atlanticom (network integration), Digital Equipment Corporation (computer hardware), Intecom/Wang (voice-data switching capabilities), and Octel which created a fully integrated educational data and voice communications network. The University was careful not to let technical expertise steer network planning decisions. The system was to be designed for our use. We took the approach of looking at our use and asking "What is the appropriate technology?" One wants to avoid being excited by the technology itself and become very excited about what technology can do for education.

Installation and Implementation

The campus network was fully operational for one year before library automation was added. Although network connections were available in all staff offices, additional connections were needed for public terminals and terminals at the Circulation and Reference Counters. The wiring was installed by a local electrical company; connections and terminal setups were done by Drew telecommunications staff. Light pens and laser guns needed to read barcodes were easily hooked into the campus network by campus technicians.

Costs

It is very difficult to determine which network costs are library specific. Startup costs included the additional cabling needed to connect all library offices and public areas ($12,000), and various terminal ends and VAX connectors ($2,000). The Library does not pay for ongoing maintenance of the network, nor does the Library have a formal agreement with the Network Center for specified services. Costs for staff, maintenance contracts, and such, are part of the Network Center budget.

Evaluation

The Drew network does exactly what it should for the Library; it provides a transparent interface between library services and the campus community. In addition, the network is the backbone of our automated library system.

Since the campus network serves as the library network, there is shared downtime. For example, the entire campus network is disrupted if the library software requires a system reboot. Likewise, maintenance on network hardware or software may require that the library system be unavailable. Although inconvenient at times, this has not been a major impediment to service or functionality. Network staff now understand the effect of 3 hours downtime on 30+ staff and librarians that have come to depend on the automated system or daily functioning. Network and library personnel work together to schedule downtime at the most suitable time.

An unexpected disadvantage to running the library system as part of the campus network is in the area of software pricing. The cost of both the initial price and ongoing maintenance for third party software used with our automated library system was based on a VAX 6330 despite the fact of multiple uses of this computer and that library automation alone would need a much smaller device.

A campus network can provide a cohesive structure for all a university's myriad technology. At Drew University, rather than a collection of hardware and software, computer technology is the integrated use of all these components.

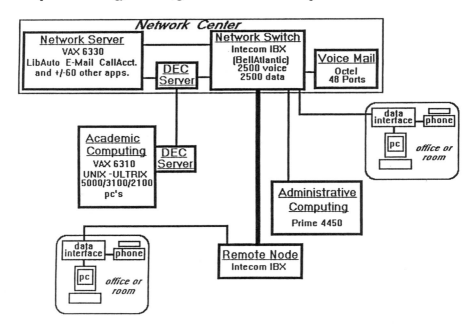

Figure 26.1
Drew University Campus Network Organization

About the Author

Pamela Snelson is Assistant Director for Automation and Public Services at Drew University Library. Her position is unusual in that it combines responsibility for overall library automation with public services rather than the more traditional route of technical services. While at Drew, Snelson also served as Coordinator of Access Services, Head of Periodicals Department and Reference Librarian.

Holding an M.L.S. and a M.A. in Political Science, Snelson is currently working toward her Ph.D. at Rutgers University's School of Communication, Information and Library Services. Her doctoral research is in the area of access to information and examines the effect that changes in modes of access have on the process of information seeking.

Appendix: Vendors and Products

3Com Corp.
3165 Kifer Road
Santa Clara, CA 95052-8145
(408)562-6400
(800)NET-3COM

Products Include:
3+Share network operating system
3+Open network operating system
EtherLink network interface cards

3M Data Storage Products Division
St. Paul MN 55144-1000
(800)328-9438

Products Include:
DC 2000 Mini Data Cartridge Tape

Above Software, Inc.
2698 White Rd.
Suite 200
Irvine, CA 92714
(800)344-0116

Alliance/Infonet
3505 Cadillac, Bldg. D
Costa Mesa, CA 92626
(714)966-2500

ALR: Overbyte Computers
21502 South Main St.
Carson, CA 90747
(213)518-3002

American Institute
55 Main St.
Madison, NJ 07940

Offers training in Networking Personal
Computers

Ameritech Information Systems
4950 Blazer Memorial Parkway
Dublin, OH 43017-3384
(800)292-2244

Products Include:
LS2000 library management system

Anixter:
4905 E. Hunter,
Anaheim, CA 92807
(213)585-3217

Distributor for DEC products

Apple Computer
20525 Mariani Ave
Cupertino, CA 95014
(408)996-1010

Products Include:
Macintosh computers
AppleShare file server software
HyperCard
AppleTalk Network System
EtherTalk Network Interface Card
LocalTalk Network Cabling System

Archive Corporation
1650 Sunflower Avenue
Costa Mesa, CA 92626
(714)641-0279

Products Include:
ARCHIVEXL Tape Drive
QICstream Backup Utility Software

Artisoft
Artisoft Plaza
575 E. River Road
Tucson, AS 85704
(602)293-6363
FAX: (602)293-8065

Products Include:
LANtastic network operating system

AST Research Inc.
2121 Alton Avenue
Irvine, CA 92714-4992
(714)863-1333

Products Include:
IBM-PC compatible microcomputer systems
SixPakPLUS Memory Expansion and I/O
Card

Banyan Systems Inc.,
115 Flanders Rd.
Westboro, MA 01581

Products Include:
Banyan/VINES

Borland International, Inc.
1800 Green Hills Road
P. O. Box 660001
Scotts Valley, CA 95067-0001
(408) 438-5300

Products include:
Programming Languages
Paradox
Quattro Pro

Cayman Systems
University Park at MIT
26 Landsdowne St.
Cambridge, MA 02139
(617)494-1999
FAX: (617)494-5167

Products Include:
Gatorbox LocalTalk
Ethernet AppleTalk
TCP/IP router.

CBIS
5875 Peachtree Industrial Blvd
Building 100, Suite 170
Norcross, GA 30092
(404)446-1332

Products Include:
CD Connection
CD Server
Network-OS network operating system

Cubix Corporation
2800 Lockheed Way
Carson City, NV 89706
(702) 883-7611

Claris Corporation
5201 Patrick Henry Dr.
Box 58168
Santa Clara, CA 95052-8168
(408)727-8227
FAX: (408)987-7447

Products Include:
FileMaker Pro

Club American Technologies, Inc.
3401 West Warren Ave.
Fremont, CA 94539
(415)683-6600

Colorado Memory Systems
800 S. Taft Ave.
Loveland, CO 80537
(303)669-8000

Products include:
Magnetic Tape Backup Systems

Compaq Computer Corporation
P. O. Box 692000
Houston, TX 77269-9976
(713)374-2726

Computer Associates
1240 McKay Dr.
San Jose, CA 95131
(800)531-5236

Products include:
Supercalc 5

Data General Corporation
4400 Computer Dr.
Westboro, MA 01581
(800)344-3577

Digital Communications Associates

1000 Alderman Dr.
Alpharetta, GA 30201-4199

Products include:
IRMA 3 Convertible3278 emulation board.

Digital Equipment Corporation

146 Main Street
Maynard, MA 01754-2571
(508)493-5111

Products include:
VAX minicomputer systems
VMS Mail
VAXnotes
Network equipment:

Diversified Computer Systems, Inc

3775 Iris Avenue, Suite 1B
Boulder, CO 80301

Products include:
EM320 terminal emulation software

Educorp

7434 Trade St.,
San Diego, CA 92121

Products Include :
CD-ROM Caddies for Sony CD-ROM drives

Epson America, Inc.

P.O. Boc 2854
Torrance, CA 90509

Products include:
Printers
IBM-PC compatible microcomputers

Everex Systems Inc.

48431 Milmont Drive
Fremont, CA 94538
(800)821-0806
(415)683-2247

Products Include:
Everex Mini Magic Memory Expansion Card
IBM-PC compatible microcomputers
Modems

Farallon Computing

2000 Powell St.
Suite 600
Emeryville, CA 94608
(415)596-9100
FAX: (415)556-9020

Products Include:
Star Controller LocalTalk networking hubs
LocalTalk network connectors PhoneNet and
Star Connectors
Star Controller EN Ethernet networking hubs
PhoneNet Ethernet boards
Liaison software router
Timbuktu software - for controlling other
computers via network

Fifth Generation Systems, Inc.

11200 Industriplex Bvd.
Baton Rouge, LA 70809-4112
(800)225-2775

Products include:
Fastback Plus1.5

Hewlett-Packard Company

18110 S.E. 34th Street
Camas WA 98607
(800)752-0900

Products include:
LaserJet printers
ThinkJet printers
DeskJet printers
DeskWriter printers

IBM Corporation

Old Orchard Road
Armonk, NY 10504
(800)426-2468

Products include:
IBM Token Ring LAN
PS/2 microcomputers
Mainframe computer systems
Token Ring network interface cards

LANSystems Inc.

300 Park Avenue South
New York, New York 10010
(800)628-5267

Products include:
LANSight

Library Technologies, Inc.

1142E Bradfield Rd.
Abington, PA 19001
(215)576-6983

Products Include:
Bib-Base

Lotus Development Corporation

55 Cambridge Parkway
Cambridge, MA 02142
(800)345-1043

Products include:
Lotus 1-2-3

McAfee Associates,

4423 Cheeney St.,
Santa Clara, CA 95054-0253

Products Include:
VirusScan, CleanUp

Maynard Electronics

460 E. Semoran Blvd.
Casselberry, FL 32707
(305)331-6402

Products Include:
MaynStream Tape Backup Systems

Meridian Data, Inc.

5615 Scotts Valley Dr.
Scotts Valley, CA 95066
(408)438-3100
(415)438-3100

4450 Capitola Rd, Suite 101
Capitola, CA 95010
(408)476-5858

Products include:
CD Net
CD Server

Micom Systems, Inc.

4100 Los Angeles Avenue
Simi Valley, CA 93062-8100
(805) 583-8600

Products include:
Protocol converters
Multiplexers
Network Equipment

Microrim

3925 159th Avenue N.E.
Redmond, WA 98052
(800)248-2001

Products include:
R:Base

Microsoft Corporation

One Microsoft Way
Redmond, WA 98052-639
(800)227-6444

Products include:
MS-DOS
Microsoft Extensions for CD-ROM
OS/2 operating system
OS/2 LAN Manager
Microsoft Bookshelf
Microsoft Windows
Microsoft Word

Missouri Library Network Corporation

10332 Old Olive Street Rd.
St. Louis, MO 63141
(800)444-8096
(314)567-3799
FAX: (314)567-3798

Reseller of CD-ROM and other Library products

Novell, Inc.

122 East 1700 South
Provo, UT 84606
(800)453-1267

Products include:
Novell NetWare

NuvoTech

2015 Bridgeway, Suite 204
Sausalito, CA 94965
(800)4nuvotech
(415)331-7815
FAX: (415)331-6445

Products Include:
TurboNet ST self-terminating LocalTalk connectors
SCSI Ethernet connectors
LocalTalk hubs
Ethernet hubs
Ethernet boards

Odesta Corp

4084 Commercial Ave.
Northbrook,IL 60062
(708)498-5615
FAX: (708)498-9917

Products Include
Double Helix

Online Computer Systems

20251 Century Blvd.
Germantown, MD 20874
(301)428-3700

Products include:
Opti-Net software for networking CD-ROM

Pioneer Communications of America

600 East Crescent Ave.
Upper Saddle River, NJ 07458-1827
(201) 327-6400

Products include:
CD-ROM drives

Proteon, Inc.

Two Technology Dr.
Westborough, MA 01581
(508) 898-2800

Products include:
network routers

Qualtec Data Products Inc.

47767 Warm Springs Blvd.
Fremont, CA 94539

Products include:
Qualtec Mac-Kit

Quarterdeck Office Systems

150 Pico Blvd.
Santa Monica, CA 90405
(213)392-9701
Fax: (213)399-3802

Products Include:
DESQview
Vidram
QRAM
QEMM
Manifest

Saber Software Corporation

P.O. Box 9088
Dallas, TX 75209
(214) 361-8086
(800) 338-8754

Products include:
Saber Menu
Saber Meter
Saber LAN Administration Pack

SCO

400 Encinal Street
Santa Cruz, CA 95061
(800)347-4381

Products include:
SCO UNIX operating system

SilverPlatter Information, Inc.

One Newton Executive Park
Newton Lower Falls, MA 02162-1449
(617)969-2332

Products include:
MultiPlatter CD-ROM Network system
Database products

Telesensory Systems, Inc.

455 North Bernardo Ave.
Mountain View, CA 94043-5274
(800)227-8418

Products include:
VERT Plus speech synthesizer

Thomas Conrad Corporation

1908-R Kramer Lane
Austin, TX 78758
(800)332-8683

Ungermann-Bass

4675 Macarthur Court, Suite 470
Newport Beach, CA
(714)955-1414

Products include:
Network interface cards
routers

VTLS, Inc.

1800 Kraft Dr.
Blacksburg, VA 24060
(703) 231-3605

Western Digital Corporation

2445 McCabe Way
Irvine, CA 92714
(800)847-6181
(714)863-0102

Products Include:
EtherCard network interface cards
Hard disk controller cards

Win Laboratories

11090 Industrial Rd.
Manassas, VA 22110
(703) 330-1426

WordPerfect Corporation

1555 N. Technology Way
Orem, UT 84057
(801) 225-5000

Products include:
WordPerfect
WordPerfect Office

Zenith Data Systems Corporation

Hilltop Road
Saint Joseph, MI 49085
(800)877-7704

Products include:
IBM-PC compatible microcomputer systems

Index

DEMCO